WordPress®
FOR
DUMMIES®
2ND EDITION

by Lisa Sabin-Wilson

Foreword by Matt Mullenweg
Cofounder of WordPress

WILEY

Wiley Publishing, Inc.

WordPress® For Dummies®, 2nd Edition

Published by
Wiley Publishing, Inc.
111 River Street
Hoboken, NJ 07030-5774

www.wiley.com

For general information on our other products and services, please contact our Customer Care Department within the U.S. at 877-762-2974, outside the U.S. at 317-572-3993, or fax 317-572-4002.

For technical support, please visit www.wiley.com/techsupport.

Wiley also publishes its books in a variety of electronic formats. Some content that appears in print may not be available in electronic books.

Library of Congress Control Number: 2008937854

ISBN: 978-0-470-40296-2

Manufactured in the United States of America

10 9 8 7 6 5

WILEY

About the Author

Lisa Sabin-Wilson has worked with the WordPress software since its inception in 2003 and has built her business around providing technical support, hosting, and design solutions for bloggers who use WordPress. She reaches thousands of people worldwide with her WordPress services, skills, and knowledge regarding the product.

Lisa operates a few blogs online, all of which are powered by WordPress. Her personal blog (justagirlintheworld.com) has been online since February of 2002; her design business at E.Webscapes (ewebscapes.com) has been online since 1999. She also provides a successful Web hosting service, Blogs About Hosting (blogs-about.com), which caters to blogs and bloggers on a global scale.

When she can be persuaded away from her computer, where she is usually hard at work providing design solutions for her WordPress clients, she sometimes emerges for public speaking appearances on the topics of design, blogging, and WordPress. She has appeared at national conferences such as the annual South By Southwest Interactive Conference, and meet ups local to her Southeastern Wisconsin area like Web414.

Lisa consults with bloggers both large and small. Bloggers come in thousands of different flavors, from business to personal, from creative to technical, and all points in between. Lisa is connected to thousands of them worldwide and appreciates the opportunity to share her knowledge through *WordPress For Dummies*. She hopes you find great value in it, as well!

When she's not designing or consulting with her clients, you can usually find her either at her favorite coffee shop sipping espresso, on a mountaintop somewhere hitting the slopes with her husband and kids, or 100 feet beneath the ocean waters, scuba diving with her husband and swimming with the fishes.

Dedication

My husband, Chris Wilson, is the single biggest source of encouragement and motivation I have in my life. In writing the first edition and this second edition of *WordPress For Dummies*, he had my back every step of the way. Always helping, always encouraging, always listening and sharing. He told me he's proud of me. I'm proud of you too, baby — for being the best husband in the world. I love you!

Author Acknowledgments

Many, many thanks and kudos to Matt Mullenweg, the core development team from Automattic, and every single person involved in making WordPress the best blogging platform available on the Internet today. To the volunteers and testers who destroy all those pesky prerelease bugs for every new version release, the WordPress community thanks you! And to each and every WordPress plugin developer and theme designer who donates his or her time, skills, and knowledge to provide the entire WordPress community of users with invaluable tools that help us create dynamic blogs, thank you a thousand times! Every person mentioned here is an invaluable asset to the overall WordPress experience; I wish I could name you all, individually, except that there are literally thousands of you out there!

Huge thanks to Melody Layne, Steve Hayes, Amy Fandrei, and Rebecca Senninger from Wiley Publishing for their support, assistance, and guidance during the course of this project. Just the mere fact they had to read every page of this book means that they deserve the Medal of Honor! Also, many thanks to technical editor Paul Chaney and other editors of the project who also worked hard to make sure that I look somewhat literate here.

To any family members and friends whom I have neglected during the process of writing this book, thank you for not abandoning me!

Finally, I thank my family — my husband, Chris; my children, Ben and Melissa; and my parents, Donald and Penny Sabin — for their unending support for this book, and in life.

Publisher's Acknowledgments

We're proud of this book; please send us your comments through our online registration form located at www.dummies.com/register/.

Some of the people who helped bring this book to market include the following:

Acquisitions and Editorial

Project Editor: Rebecca Senninger

   (Previous Edition: Susan Christophersen)

Acquisitions Editor: Amy Fandrei

Copy Editor: Kathy Simpson

Technical Editor: Paul Chaney

Editorial Manager: Leah Cameron

Editorial Assistant: Amanda Foxworth

Sr. Editorial Assistant: Cherie Case

Cartoons: Rich Tennant (www.the5thwave.com)

Composition Services

Project Coordinator: Katie Key

Layout and Graphics: Reuben W. Davis, Sarah Philippart, Christin Swinford, Ronald Terry, Christine Williams

Proofreaders: John Greenough, Dwight Ramsey, Penny L. Stuart

Indexer: WordCo Indexing Services

Publishing and Editorial for Technology Dummies

   Richard Swadley, Vice President and Executive Group Publisher

   Andy Cummings, Vice President and Publisher

   Mary Bednarek, Executive Acquisitions Director

   Mary C. Corder, Editorial Director

Publishing for Consumer Dummies

   Diane Graves Steele, Vice President and Publisher

Composition Services

   Gerry Fahey, Vice President of Production Services

   Debbie Stailey, Director of Composition Services

Table of Contents

Foreword

*T*here used to be a program from Microsoft called FrontPage that was the first visual interface for creating Web sites that I saw. It worked like Word or Publisher, so with very little knowledge, I was able to hack together the world's worst Web site in just a few hours without worrying about what was going on under the hood.

Years later when I look back at that Web site, I cringe, but at the time it was incredibly empowering. The software, though crude, helped me publish something anybody in the entire world could see. It opened up a world I had never imagined before.

Now, using software like WordPress, you can have a blog or Web site light-years beyond my first one in both functionality and aesthetics. However, just as my first Web experience whetted my appetite for more, I hope that your experience entices you to explore the thousands of free plugins, themes, and customizations possible with WordPress, many of which are explained in this book.

WordPress is more than just software; it is a community, a rapidly evolving ecosystem, and a set of philosophies and opinions about how to create the best Web experience. When you embrace it, you'll be in good company. WordPress users include old media organizations such as CNN, *The New York Times,* and *The Wall Street Journal,* along with millions of personal bloggers like myself for whom a WordPress blog is a means of expression.

Matt Mullenweg

Cofounder of WordPress

Introduction

• •

*L*et's see . . . it was 2003 when I discovered the wonders of WordPress. Way back then (and in Internet years, that's actually a lot of time), I was using Movable Type as my blogging platform. My friend Chelle introduced me to the WordPress software. "Try it," she said. "You'll really like it."

As somewhat a creature of habit, I felt reluctant to make the change. The growing buzz around the WordPress software made me curious, however. Shortly thereafter, Six Apart, the maker of Movable Type, made a drastic change in the licensing requirements. All of a sudden, software that used to be free cost money. As soon as Six Apart made that move, a mass exodus from Movable Type to WordPress seemed to occur. All the cool kids were doing it, so I decided to give it a shot.

I haven't looked back. I've been with WordPress ever since.

The next year, 2004, blogging was being touted as the latest Internet trend. Representatives of the mainstream media looked on — openmouthed — as bloggers attained press credentials to major events; bloggers got book deals and press attention; bloggers earned five-figure monthly incomes from in-blog advertising; blogs were recognized and read by the general public; and blogs became accessories as ubiquitous for the young as the latest cell phone.

In 2005, businesses caught on to the phenomenon and began to embrace it. Major public-relations companies launched campaigns that included, or focused on, blogs. Chief executive officers and Fortune 500 companies joined the fray.

In 2006, blogs went from trend to mainstay. No longer novelties, blogs became natural extensions of daily communication, frequently replacing e-mail newsletters.

Blogs are here to stay. Authors, students, parents, business owners, academics, hobbyists — you name it — use blogs as a matter of course.

Technorati.com has been tracking the growth of the number of blogs for four years. As of April 2007, Technorati was tracking over 70 million blogs and seeing a growth of approximately 120,000 creates each day. Technorati's David Sifry estimates that approximately 1.4 blogs are created every second of every day (see www.sifry.com/alerts/archives/000493.html).

WordPress has been a huge part of the blogging boom. Today, it's the most popular blogging platform for personal, business, and corporate bloggers alike.

To a brand-new user, some aspects of WordPress can seem a little bit intimidating. After you take a look under the hood, however, you begin to realize how intuitive, friendly, and extensible the software is.

This book presents an in-depth look at two popular versions of WordPress:

- ✔ The hosted version available at WordPress.com
- ✔ The self-hosted version available at WordPress.org

The book also covers managing and maintaining your WordPress blog through the use of WordPress plugins and themes.

If you're interested in taking a detailed look at the blogging and Web site services provided by WordPress, you happen to have just the right book in your hands.

About This Book

This book covers all the important aspects of WordPress that new users need to know to begin using the software for their own blog (or blogs). I cover the two most popular versions of WordPress, highlighting all the important topics, such as these:

- ✔ Setting up and using a hosted blog at WordPress.com
- ✔ Locating good hosting services for the self-hosted version of the software (available at WordPress.org)
- ✔ Installing and setting up the WordPress.org software
- ✔ Navigating the Administration panels of both the hosted and self-hosted versions of WordPress
- ✔ Adding media files to your blog
- ✔ Finding and installing free themes to use in your WordPress blog
- ✔ Using basic coding to design your own WordPress theme or modify the one you're using

✔ Using templates and tags in WordPress

✔ Installing, activating, and managing WordPress plugins

✔ Discovering the potential pitfalls associated with each version

✔ Understanding the challenges you face when running a WordPress–powered site, such as dodging comment and trackback spam

✔ Exploring RSS feed syndication

✔ Migrating your existing blog to WordPress (if you are using a different blogging platform, such as Blogspot, Movable Type, or TypePad)

✔ Discovering the power of WordPress as a Content Management System (CMS) to create a full Web site, not just a blog

✔ Finding support, tips, and resources for using the WordPress software

With WordPress, you can truly tailor a blog to your own tastes and needs. All the tools are out there. Some of them are packaged with the WordPress software; others are third-party plugins and add-ons created by members of the WordPress user community. It takes a little research, knowledge, and time on your part to put together a blog that suits your needs and gives your readers an exciting experience that keeps them coming back for more.

Conventions Used in This Book

Throughout the book, I apply the following typography conventions to guide you through some of the information I present:

✔ When I ask you to type something, the text that you're supposed to type is in **bold.**

✔ When I suggest a keyword that you may want to enter in a search engine, that term appears in *italics*.

✔ Text that appears in this `special font` is certain to be a URL (Web address), e-mail address, filename, folder name, or code.

✔ When I use a term that I think you may not be familiar with, I apply *italics* to that term to let you know that I'm defining it.

✔ In some instances, I give you a basic idea of what a Web address or block of code looks like. When the text that you see may be different, depending on your settings and preferences, I apply *italics* to that text.

What You Are Not to Read

Don't read supermarket tabloids. They're certain to rot your brain.

This book covers the details of how to set up, use, and maintain the software for WordPress.com and WordPress.org. I don't intend for you to read this book from cover to cover (unless you're my mother — then I won't forgive you if you don't). Rather, hit the Table of Contents and the Index of this book to find the information you need.

If you never intend to run a hosted WordPress blog on your own Web server, you can skip Chapters 6, 7, and 8.

If you have no interest in setting up a hosted blog at WordPress.com, skip Chapters 3, 4, and 5.

If you aren't interested in digging into the code of a WordPress template, and don't want to find out how to apply CSS or HTML to enhance your design, you can skip Part V of this book, which contains Chapters 12, 13, 14, and 15.

Long story short: Take what you need, and leave the rest.

Foolish Assumptions

I'll never know what assumptions you've made about me at this point, but I can tell you a few things that I already assume about you:

- You know what a computer is. You can turn it on, and you understand that if you spill coffee on your keyboard, you'll have to run out and get a replacement.

- You understand how to hook yourself into the Internet and know the basics of using a Web browser to surf Web sites and blogs.

- You have a basic understanding of what blogs are, and you're interested in using WordPress to start your own blog. Or you already have a blog, are already using WordPress, and want to understand the program better so that you can do more cool stuff and stop bugging your geeky best friend whenever you have a question about something. Or, even better, you already have a blog on another blogging platform and want to move your blog to WordPress.

- You know what e-mail is. You know what an e-mail address is. You actually have an e-mail address, and you send and receive e-mail on a semi-regular basis.

If, when you approach your computer, you break out into a cold sweat, looking similar to a deer caught in headlights, and say to yourself, "Here goes nothing!" before you even sit down in front of your monitor, you may want to brush up on your basic computer skills before you begin this book.

How This Book Is Organized

This book is made up of six parts that introduce you to the WordPress platform, including detailed information on two very popular versions of WordPress: the hosted version of WordPress.com and the self-hosted version of WordPress.org. Also included is detailed information on WordPress themes and templates.

Part 1: Introducing WordPress

The first part gives you an overview of WordPress and the advantages of making it your blogging platform. You might think of WordPress as coming in three "flavors": vanilla (WordPress.com hosted solution), chocolate (WordPress.org self-hosted solution), and Neapolitan (WordPress MU, the multiuser solution). In this part, you also discover some of the fun aspects of blogging, such as RSS feed syndication and reader interaction through comments.

Part II: Using the WordPress Hosted Service

Part II takes you through signing up with the hosted service for a blog. You tour the Administration panel, explore writing and managing your blog, find out how to change the various themes available in this version, and discover how to enhance your blog and widgets.

Part III: Self-Hosting with WordPress.org

Part III explores the single-user version of the WordPress software available at WordPress.org. You install this software on your own hosted Web server, so I give you valuable information about domain registration, Web hosting providers, and a few of the basic tools (such as FTP) that you need to install to set up a WordPress blog. I also familiarize you with the Administration panel, where you personalize your blog and explore many of the settings that you need to manage and maintain your WordPress–powered blog.

Part IV: Flexing and Extending WordPress

This part shows you how to add images to your pages, including how to create a photo gallery on your site.

This part also reveals how to find, install, and use various WordPress plug-ins to extend the functionality of your blog. It also steps into the world of WordPress themes, showing you where to find free themes, install them, and use them.

Part V: Customizing WordPress

Part V takes an in-depth look at the structure of a WordPress theme by taking you through each of the templates and explaining the template tags each step of the way. You find information on basic CSS and HTML that helps you tweak the free theme that you are using or even create your own theme.

This part also looks at the use of WordPress as a Content Management System (CMS) to power a full-blown Web site as well as a blog.

If the topics covered in this part of the book aren't ones you're interested in getting involved with yourself, the last chapter of this part talks about bringing in the professionals — the consultants who can help you achieve a custom-designed blog, as well as assist you with search engine optimization.

Part VI: The Part of Tens

The Part of Tens is in every *For Dummies* book that you will ever pick up. This part introduces ten Web sites that have really stretched the functionality of WordPress through plugins and themes. This part also shows you ten popular free WordPress themes that you can use to create a nice, clean look for your blog. Further, in this part you discover ten great WordPress plugins that you can use to provide your visitors (and yourself) some great functionality.

Icons Used in This Book

Icons are those little pictures in the margins of the book that emphasize a point to remember, a danger to be aware of, or information that I think you may find helpful. Those points are illustrated as such:

Tips are little bits of information that you may find useful — procedures that aren't necessarily obvious to the casual user or beginner.

When your mother warned you, "Don't touch that pan — it's hot!" but you touched it anyway, you discovered the meaning of "Ouch!" I use this icon for situations like that. Out of curiosity, you may very well touch the hot pan, but you can't say that I didn't warn you!

All geeky stuff goes here. Even though an aura of geekiness surrounds the use of the WordPress software, I surprised myself by not using this icon very much in this book. But I do use it in certain places, and when I do, it probably has to do with technical mumbo-jumbo that would have made your eyes glaze over had I elaborated. Luckily for you, these items are short and sweet, but I don't promise that they won't bore you to death. Good thing I use them sparingly, hey?

When you see this icon, read the text next to it two or three times to brand it into your brain so that you remember whatever it was that I thought you needed to remember.

Where to Go from Here

As I mention in the "What You Are Not to Read" section of this introduction, take what you need, and leave the rest. This book is a veritable smorgasbord of WordPress information, ideas, concepts, tools, resources, and instruction. Some of it will apply directly to what you want to do with your WordPress blog. Other parts deal with topics that you're only mildly curious about, so you may want to skim those pages.

Part I

Introducing WordPress

The 5th Wave   By Rich Tennant

"Hi, all. Turns out that the rash I posted about last night is contagious..."

In this part . . .

Ready to get started? I know I am! This part of the book provides a brief introduction to WordPress and blogging. WordPress is unique in offering three versions of its software, and I tell you about each version so that you can choose the one that's right for you.

Chapter 1

What WordPress Can Do for You

. . . .

In This Chapter

▶ Seeing how WordPress can benefit you

▶ Participating in the WordPress community

▶ Understanding the different versions of WordPress

. . . .

*I*n a world in which technology advances faster than a speeding locomotive, WordPress is blogging made easy — and free! How else can you get your message out to a potential audience of millions worldwide and spend exactly nothing? There may be no such thing as a free lunch in this world, but you can bet your bottom dollar that there are free blogs to be had. WordPress serves them all up in one nifty package.

The software's free price tag, its ease of use, and the speed at which you can get your blog up and running are great reasons to use WordPress to power your personal or business blog. An even greater reason is the incredibly supportive and passionate WordPress community. In this chapter, I introduce you to the WordPress software so that you can begin to discover how effective it is as a tool for creating your blog or Web site.

Discovering the Benefits of WordPress

I work with first-time bloggers all the time — folks who are new to the idea of publishing on the Internet. One of the questions I'm most frequently asked is "How can I run a blog? I don't even know how to code or create Web sites."

Enter WordPress. You no longer need to worry about knowing the code, because the WordPress blogging software does the code part for you. When you log in to your blog, you have to do only two simple things to publish your thoughts and ideas:

1. Write your post.

2. Click a button to publish your post.

That's it!

WordPress offers the following competitive advantages as the most popular blogging tool on the market:

- ✔ **Diversity:** Three versions of WordPress are available to suit nearly every type of blogger: a hosted turnkey solution, a version to install on the Web server of your choice, and a multiuser version that lets you offer blogs across a group or organization. I go into detail about each of these versions later in this chapter, in the "Choosing a WordPress Platform" section.

- ✔ **Ease of use:** WordPress setup is quick, and the software is easy to use.

- ✔ **Extensibility:** WordPress is extremely extensible, meaning that you can easily obtain plugins and tools that let you customize it to suit your purposes.

- ✔ **Community of users:** WordPress has a large and loyal members-helping-members community via public support forums, mailing lists, and blogs geared to the use of WordPress.

The following sections fill in a few details about these features and point you to places in the book where you can find out more about them.

Easy to set up and use

WordPress is one of the only blog platforms that can brag about a five-minute installation — and stand behind it! Signing up for the hosted version of WordPress takes approximately the same amount of time.

Mind you, five minutes is an *approximate* installation time. It doesn't include the time required to obtain domain registration and Web hosting services or to set up the options in the Administration panel.

When you complete the installation, however, the world of WordPress awaits you. The Administration panel is intuitive, well organized, and easy on the eyes. Everything is clear and logical, making it easy for even a first-time user to see where to go to manage settings and options.

The WordPress software surely has enough meat on it to keep the most experienced developer busy and happy. At the same time, however, it's intuitive and friendly enough to make a novice user giddy about how easy getting started is. Each time you use WordPress, you can find out something exciting and new.

Extend WordPress's capabilities

I've found that the most exciting and fun part of running a WordPress blog is exploring the flexibility of the software. Hundreds of plugins and themes are available to let you create a blog that functions the way *you* need it to.

If you think of your blog as a vacuum cleaner, plugins are the attachments. The attachments don't function alone. When you add them to your vacuum cleaner, however, you add to the functionality of your vacuum, possibly improving its performance.

All WordPress blogs are pretty much the same at their core, so by using plugins, you can truly individualize your blog by providing additional features and tools to benefit yourself and your readers. When you come upon a WordPress blog that has some really different and cool functions, 98 percent of the time, you can include that function in your own blog by using a WordPress plugin. If you don't know what plugin that blog is using, feel free to drop the blog owner an e-mail or leave a comment. WordPress blog owners usually are eager to share the great tools they discover.

Most plugins are available at no charge. You can find out more about WordPress plugins and where to get them in Chapter 10. Chapter 17 lists my choice of ten popular WordPress plugins available for download.

In addition to using plugins, you can embellish your WordPress blog with templates and themes. WordPress comes prepackaged with two themes to get you started. Figure 1-1 shows the famous Kubrick theme, created by Michael Heilemann from `http://binarybonsai.com`, which is displayed by default after you install and set up your blog.

The theme's default form is blue and white, but a handy application built into the preferences lets you change the color of the top header.

This theme includes all the basic elements that you need when starting a new WordPress blog. You can extend your WordPress blog in a hundred ways with the use of plugins and themes that have been released by members of the WordPress community, but the Kubrick theme is a nice place to start.

Take part in the community

Allow me to introduce you to the fiercely loyal folks who make up the user base, better known as the vast WordPress community. This band of merry ladies and gentlemen comes from all around the globe, from California to Cairo, Florida to Florence, and all points in between and beyond.

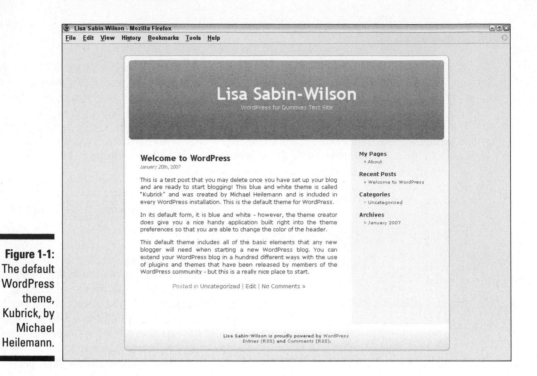

Lisa Sabin-Wilson - Mozilla Firefox

File   Edit   View   History   Bookmarks   Tools   Help

Lisa Sabin-Wilson

WordPress for Dummies Test Site

Welcome to WordPress
January 20th, 2007

This is a test post that you may delete once you have set up your blog
and are ready to start blogging! This blue and white theme is called
"Kubrick" and was created by Michael Heilemann and is included in
every WordPress installation. This is the default theme for WordPress.

In its default form, it is blue and white - however, the theme creator
does give you a nice handy application built right into the theme
preferences so that you are able to change the color of the header.

This default theme includes all of the basic elements that any new
blogger will need when starting a new WordPress blog. You can
extend your WordPress blog in a hundred different ways with the use
of plugins and themes that have been released by members of the
WordPress community - but this is a really nice place to start.

Posted in Uncategorized | Edit | No Comments »

My Pages
» About

Recent Posts
» Welcome to WordPress

Categories
» Uncategorized

Archives
» January 2007

Lisa Sabin-Wilson is proudly powered by WordPress
Entries (RSS) and Comments (RSS).

Figure 1-1:
The default
WordPress
theme,
Kubrick, by
Michael
Heilemann.

In March 2005, Matt Mullenweg of WordPress proudly proclaimed that the
number of WordPress downloads had reached 900,000 — an amazing land-
mark in the history of the software. But the real excitement occurred in
August 2006, when WordPress logged more than 1 million downloads, and in
2007, when the software had more than 3 million downloads.

Don't let the sheer volume of users fool you: WordPress has bragging rights
to the most helpful blogging community on the Web today. You can find
users helping other users in the support forums at http://wordpress.
org/support. You can also find users contributing to the very helpful
WordPress Codex (a collection of how-to documents) at http://codex.
wordpress.org. Finally, across the blogosphere, you can find multiple
blogs about WordPress itself, with users sharing their experiences and war
stories in the hope of helping the next person who comes along.

You can subscribe to various mailing lists, too. These lists offer you the
opportunity to become involved in various aspects of the WordPress community, as well as in the future development of the software.

The origins of WordPress

Once upon a time, there was a simple, PHP-based blogging platform called b2. This software, developed in 2001, slowly gained a bit of popularity among geek types as a way to publish content on the Internet. Its developer, Michel Valdrighi, kept development active until early 2003, when users of the software noticed that Valdrighi seemed to have disappeared. They became a little concerned about b2's future.

Somewhere deep in the heart of Texas, one young man in particular was very concerned, because b2 was his software of choice for publishing his own content on the World Wide Web. He didn't want to see his favorite publishing tool go to waste or to face a tough decision about moving on to something new and unknown. You can view the original post to his own blog in which he wondered what to do (`http://ma.tt/2003/01/the-blogging-software-dilemma`).

In that post, he talked briefly about some of the other software that was available at the time, and he tossed around the idea of using the b2 software to "to create a fork, integrating all the cool stuff that Michel would be working on right now if only he was around."

Create a fork, he did. In the absence of b2's developer, this young man developed from the original b2 code base a brand-new blogging application called WordPress.

That blog post was made on January 24, 2003, and the young man's name was (and is) Matt Mullenweg. On December 26, 2003, with the assistance of a few other developers, Mullenweg announced the arrival of the first official version of the WordPress software. The rest, as they say, is history. The history of this particular piece of software surely is one for the books, as it is the most popular blogging platform available today.

Don't worry if you're not a member of the WordPress community. Joining is easy: Simply start your own blog by using one of the three WordPress software options. If you're already blogging on a different platform, such as Blogspot or Movable Type, WordPress makes it simple for you to migrate your current data from that platform to a new WordPress setup. (See the appendix for information about moving your existing blog to WordPress.)

Choosing a WordPress Platform

Among the realities of running a blog today is choosing among the veritable feast of software platforms to find the one that will perform the way you need it to. You want to be sure that the platform you choose has all the options you're looking for. WordPress is unique in that it offers three versions of its software. Each version is designed to meet the various needs of bloggers. The three different versions of WordPress are the following:

- ✔ The hosted version at WordPress.com. (Part II of this book focuses on this version.)
- ✔ The self-installed and self-hosted version available at WordPress.org. (Part III focuses on this version.)
- ✔ The multiuser version, WordPress MU, available at `http://mu.wordpress.org`.

Certain features are available to you in every WordPress blog setup, whether you're using the software from WordPress.org, the hosted version at WordPress.com, or the multiuser version of WordPress MU. These features include but aren't limited to the following:

- ✔ Quick-and-easy installation and setup
- ✔ Full-featured blogging capability, letting you publish content to the Web through an easy-to-use Web-based interface
- ✔ Topical archiving of your posts, using categories
- ✔ Monthly archiving of your posts, with the ability to provide a listing of those archives for easy navigation through your site.
- ✔ Comment and trackback tools
- ✔ Automatic spam protection through Akismet
- ✔ Built-in gallery integration for photos and images
- ✔ Media Manager for video and audio files
- ✔ Great community support
- ✔ Unlimited number of static pages, letting you step out of the blog box and into the sphere of running a fully functional Web site
- ✔ RSS capability with RSS 2.0, RSS 1.0, and Atom support
- ✔ Tools for importing content from different blogging systems (such as Blogger, Movable Type, and LiveJournal)

Table 1-1 compares the three WordPress versions.

Table 1-1	Exploring the Differences among the Three Versions of WordPress		
Feature	**WordPress.org**	**WordPress.com**	**WordPress MU**
Cost	Free	Free	Free
Software download	Yes	No	Yes
Software installation	Yes	No	Yes
Web hosting required	Yes	No	Yes
Custom CSS control	Yes	$15/year	Yes — for the MU administrator, not for the end user
Template access	Yes	No	Yes — for the MU administrator, not for the end user
Sidebar widgets	Yes	Yes	Yes
RSS syndication	Yes	Yes	Yes
Access to core code	Yes	No	Yes — for the MU administrator, not for the end user
Ability to install plugins	Yes	No	Yes
WP themes installation	Yes	No	Yes
Multiauthor support	Yes	Yes	Yes
Unlimited number of blog setups with one account	No	Yes	Yes
Community-based support forums	Yes	Yes	Yes

Choosing the hosted version from WordPress.com

WordPress.com is a free service. If downloading, installing, and using software on a Web server sound like Greek to you — and are things you'd rather avoid — the WordPress folks provide a solution for you at WordPress.com.

WordPress.com is a *hosted solution,* which means it has no software requirement, no downloads, and no installation or server configurations. Everything's done for you on the back end, behind the scenes. You don't even have to worry about how the process happens; it happens quickly, and before you know it, you're making your first blog post using a WordPress. com blog solution.

WordPress.com has some limitations. You can't install plugins or custom themes, for example, and you can't customize the base code files. But even with its limitations, WordPress.com is an excellent starting point if you're brand new to blogging and a little intimidated by the configuration requirements of the self-installed WordPress.org software.

The good news is this: If you outgrow your WordPress.com hosted blog in the future and want to make a move to the self-hosted WordPress.org software, you can. You can even take all the content from your WordPress.com-hosted blog with you and easily import it into your new setup with the WordPress. org software.

So in the grand scheme of things, you're really not that limited.

Self-hosting with WordPress.org

The self-installed version from WordPress.org (covered in Part III) requires you to download the software from the WordPress Web site and install it on a Web server. Unless you own your own Web server, you need to lease one — or lease space on one.

Using a Web server is typically referred to as *Web hosting,* and unless you know someone who knows someone, hosting generally isn't free. That being said, Web hosting doesn't cost a whole lot, either. You can usually obtain a good Web hosting service for anywhere from $5 to $10 per month. (Chapter 6 gives you the important details you need to know about obtaining a Web host.) You need to make sure, however, that any Web host you choose to work with has the required software installed on the Web server. Currently, the minimum software requirements for WordPress include

- ✔ PHP version 4.3 or greater
- ✔ MySQL version 4.0 or greater

After you have WordPress installed on your Web server (see the installation instructions in Chapter 6), you can start using it to blog to your heart's content. With the WordPress software, you can install several plugins that extend the functionality of the blogging system, as I describe in Chapter 10. You also have full control of the core files and code that WordPress is built on. So if you have a knack for PHP and knowledge of MySQL, you can work within the code to make changes that you think would be good for you and your blog.

You don't need design ability to make your blog look great. Members of the WordPress community have created more than 1,600 WordPress themes (designs), and you can download them for free and install them on your WordPress blog (see Chapter 11). Additionally, if you're creatively inclined, like to create designs on your own, and know Cascading Style Sheets (CSS), you have full access to the template system within WordPress and can create your own custom themes (see Chapters 12 and 13).

Running a network of blogs with WordPress MU

Although the WordPress.com hosted service runs on the WordPress MU software, and the end-user configuration settings are very similar, setting up, administering, and managing this version of WordPress differ a great deal from the same processes in the WordPress.com or WordPress.org versions.

WordPress MU lets you run thousands of blogs on one installation of its software platform, on one domain. Its biggest claim to fame, of course, is the hosted version of WordPress.com, which uses the MU platform to run more than 1 million blogs and climbing.

When you install and use WordPress MU, you become administrator of a network of blogs. The administration interface for WordPress MU differs from WordPress.com and the software from WordPress.org, in that you're configuring options and settings for your blog as well as for multiple blogs across your network.

WordPress MU does everything the original software from WordPress.org does, so you can provide bloggers all the functionality that WordPress users have come to expect and enjoy.

WordPress MU isn't meant for the casual user or beginner. It's also not meant for bloggers who want to run five to ten of their own blogs on one domain. Who is it meant for, then?

- Blog networks (such as Edublogs.org) that currently have more than 150 blogs.

- Newspapers and magazines, such as *The New York Times,* and universities such as Harvard Law School that currently use WordPress MU to manage the blog sections of their Web sites.

- Niche-specific blog networks, such as Edublogs.org, that use WordPress MU to manage their full networks of free blogs for teachers, educators, lecturers, librarians, and other education professionals.

If you're interested in that software, check out more details at the WordPress MU Web site at `http://mu.wordpress.org`.

Chapter 2

WordPress Blogging Basics

In This Chapter

▶ Considering blog types

▶ Finding out what blog technology can do for you

▶ Outlining your initial blog plan

A lot happens behind the scenes to make your WordPress blog or Web site function. The beauty of it is this: You don't have to worry about what's happening on the back end in order to manage and maintain a WordPress site — unless you really want to. In this chapter, I delve a little bit into the technology behind the WordPress platform, including a brief look at PHP and MySQL, two software components required to run WordPress.

This chapter also covers some of the various blogging technologies that help you on your way to running a successful blog, such as the use of comments and RSS feed technology, as well as information about combating spam.

This Crazy Little Thing Called Blog

Blogging is an evolutionary process, and I have a strong feeling that blogs have evolved beyond personal journals to become tools for real journalism, business, and authorship.

A blog is a fabulous tool to use to publish your personal diary of thoughts and ideas; however, blogs also serve as excellent tools for business, editorial journalism, news, and entertainment. Here are some ways that people use blogs:

✔ **Personal:** This type of blogger creates a blog as a personal journal or diary. You're considered to be a personal blogger if you use your blog mainly to discuss topics that are personal to you or your life — your family, your cats, your children, or your interests (for example, technology, politics, sports, art, or photography). My own blog, which you'll find at `http://justagirlintheworld.com`, is an example of a personal blog.

✔ **Business:** This type of blogger uses the power of blogs to promote her company's business services and/or products on the Internet. Blogs are very effective tools for promotion and marketing, and these blogs usually offer helpful information to readers and consumers, such as ad tips and product reviews. Business blogs also let readers provide feedback and ideas, which can help a company improve its services. Search engines (such as Google, Yahoo!, and MSN) really like Web sites that are updated on a regular basis, and using a blog for your business lets you update your Web site regularly with content and information that your readers and consumers may find helpful. At the same time, you can increase your company's exposure in the search engines by giving the search engines a lot of content to sift through and include in the search results. A good example of this is a company called ServerBeach — it keeps a blog on the hosted WordPress.com service at `http://serverbeach.wordpress.com`.

✔ **Media/journalism:** More and more popular news outlets such as Fox News, MSNBC, and CNN are adding blogs to their Web sites to provide information on current events, politics, and news on a regional, national, and international level. These news organizations often have editorial bloggers as well. Editorial cartoonist Daryl Cagle, for example, maintains a blog on MSNBC's Web site at `http://cagle.msnbc.com/news/blog`, where he discusses his cartoons and the feedback he receives from readers.

✔ **Citizen journalism:** At one time, I might have put these bloggers in the Personal category, but blogs have really opened opportunities for average citizens to have a great effect on the analysis and dissemination of news and information on a national and international level. The emergence of citizen journalism coincided with the swing from old media to new media. In old media, the journalists and news organizations direct the conversation about news topics.

With the popularity of blogs and the millions of bloggers who exploded onto the Internet, old media felt a change in the wind. Average citizens, using the power of their voices on blogs, changed the direction of the conversation, with many of these bloggers fact-checking news stories and exposing inconsistencies, with the intention of keeping the media or local politicians in check. Many of these bloggers are interviewed on major cable news programs as the mainstream media recognize the

> importance of the emergence of the citizen voice through blogging.
> An example of citizen journalism is the Power Line Blog at `http://
> powerlineblog.com`.
>
> ✔ **Professional:** This category of blogger is growing every day. Professional
> bloggers are paid to blog for individual companies or Web sites. Blog net-
> works, such as WeblogsInc.com, hire bloggers to write on certain topics
> of interest. Also, several services match advertisers with bloggers, so that
> the advertisers pay bloggers to make blog posts about their products. Is it
> possible to make money as a blogger? Yes, and making money is becom-
> ing common these days. If you're interested in this type of blogging,
> check out Darren Rowse's ProBlogger blog at `http://problogger.net`.
> Darren is considered to be the grandfather of all professional bloggers.

Dipping Into Blog Technologies

The WordPress software is a personal publishing system that uses a PHP-
and-MySQL platform, which provides you everything you need to create your
own blog and publish your own content dynamically, without having to know
how to program those pages yourself. In short, all your content is stored in a
MySQL database in your hosting account.

PHP (which stands for *PHP Hypertext Preprocessor*) is a server-side scripting
language for creating dynamic Web pages. When a visitor opens a page built
in PHP, the server processes the PHP commands and then sends the results
to the visitor's browser. MySQL is an open source relational database management system (RDBMS) that uses Structured Query Language (SQL), the most
popular language for adding, accessing, and processing data in a database. If
that all sounds Greek to you, just think of MySQL as a big filing cabinet where
all the content on your blog is stored.

Every time a visitor goes to your blog to read your content, he makes a request
that's sent to your server. The PHP programming language receives that
request, obtains the requested information from the MySQL database, and then
presents the requested information to your visitor through his Web browser.

In using the term *content* as it applies to the data that's stored in the MySQL
database, I'm referring to your blog posts, comments, and options that you
set up in the WordPress Administration panel. The theme (design) you
choose to use for your blog — whether it's the default theme, one you create
for yourself, or one that you have custom-designed for you — isn't part of
the content in this case. Those files are part of the file system and aren't
stored in the database. So it's a good idea to create and keep a backup of any
theme files that you're currently using. See Part IV for further information on
WordPress theme management.

When you look for a hosting service, keep an eye out for the hosts that provide daily backups of your site, so that your content/data won't be lost in case something happens. Web hosting providers that offer daily backups as part of their services can save the day by restoring your site to its original form.

Archiving your publishing history

Packaged within the WordPress software is the capability to maintain chronological and categorized archives of your publishing history, automatically. WordPress uses PHP and MySQL technology to sort and organize everything you publish in an order that you, and your readers, can access by date and category. This archiving process is done automatically with every post you publish to your blog.

When you create a post on your WordPress blog, you can file that post under a category that you specify. This feature makes for a very nifty archiving system in which you and your readers can find articles/posts that you've placed within a specific category. The archives page on my personal blog (see it at `http://justagirlintheworld.com/archives`) contains a Topical Archive Pages section, where you find a list of categories I've created for my blog posts. Clicking the Blog Design link below the Topical archive pages heading takes you to a listing of posts that I wrote on that topic (see Figure 2-1 and Figure 2-2).

WordPress lets you create as many categories as you want for filing your blog posts by topic. I've seen blogs that have just one category and blogs that have up to 1,800 categories — WordPress is all about personal preference and how you want to organize your content. On the other hand, using WordPress categories is your choice. You don't have to use the category feature if you'd rather not.

Interacting with your readers through comments

One of the most exciting and fun aspects of blogging with WordPress is getting feedback from your readers the moment you make a post to your blog. Feedback, referred to as *blog comments,* is akin to having a guestbook on your blog. People can leave notes for you that are published to your site, and you can respond and engage your readers in conversation about the topic at hand (see Figure 2-3 and Figure 2-4). Having this function in your blog creates the opportunity to expand the thoughts and ideas that you presented in your blog post by giving your readers the opportunity to add their two cents' worth.

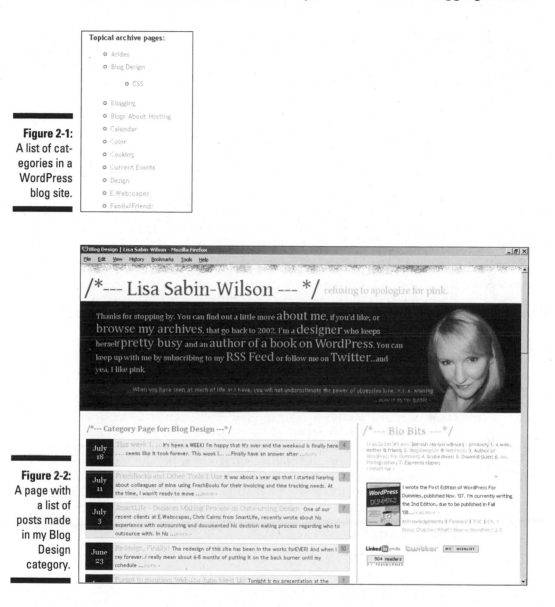

Figure 2-1:
A list of categories in a WordPress blog site.

Figure 2-2:
A page with a list of posts made in my Blog Design category.

In the WordPress Administration panel, you have full administrative control over who can and can't leave comments. In addition, if someone leaves a comment with questionable content, you can edit the comment or delete it. You're also free to choose not to allow any comments on your blog.

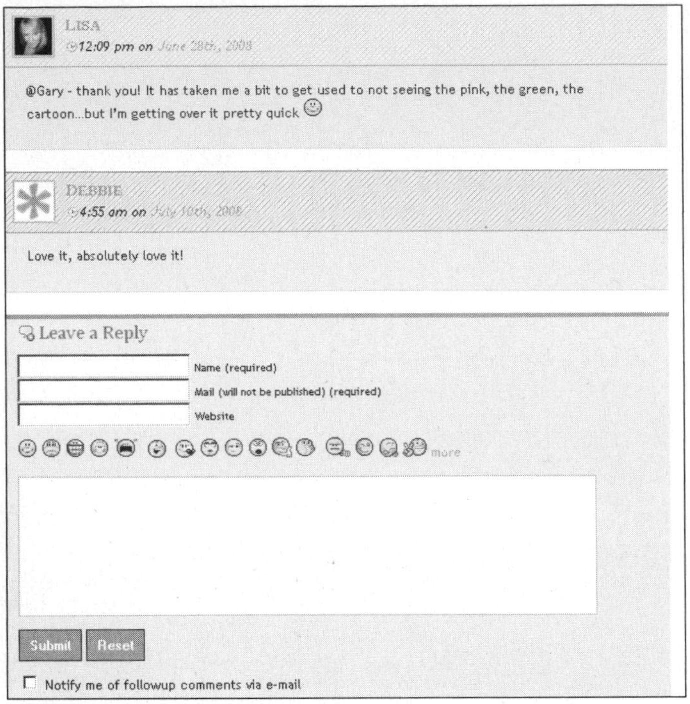

LISA
⏱12:09 pm on June 28th, 2008

@Gary - thank you! It has taken me a bit to get used to not seeing the pink, the green, the cartoon...but I'm getting over it pretty quick ☺

DEBBIE
⏱4:55 am on July 10th, 2008

Love it, absolutely love it!

⮂ Leave a Reply

Name (required)

Mail (will not be published) (required)

Website

😊😠😀😑😫 ☺ 😕😬😮😯😲😎 😋😖 😊😜😝 more

Submit   Reset

☐ Notify me of followup comments via e-mail

Figure 2-3: Readers use the form to leave their comments.

Some blog users say that a blog without comments isn't a blog at all. This belief is common in the blogging community, because experiencing visitor feedback through the use of comments is part of what has made blogging so popular. It's a personal choice. Publishing a blog without comments lets your readers partake of your published words passively. Allowing comments on your blog invites your audience members to actively involve themselves in your blog by creating a discussion and dialogue about your content. By and large, readers find commenting to be a satisfying experience when they visit blogs, because comments make them part of the discussion.

Feeding your readers

RSS stands for *Really Simple Syndication*. An *RSS feed* is a standard feature that blog readers have come to expect. So what is it, really?

The Introduction to RSS page on the resource site WebReference.com (`www.webreference.com/authoring/languages/xml/rss/intro/`) defines RSS as "a lightweight XML format designed for sharing headlines and other Web content. Think of it as a distributable 'What's New' for your site."

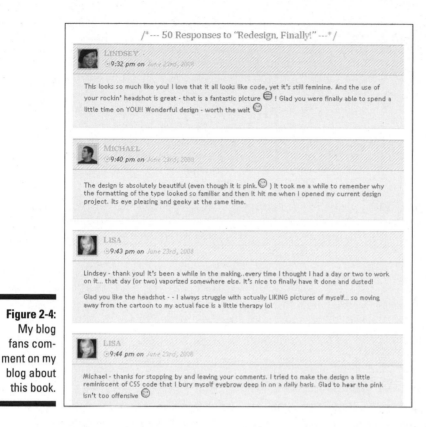

Figure 2-4:
My blog
fans com-
ment on my
blog about
this book.

Readers can use tools called *feed readers* to download your feed — that is, their feed readers are set up to automatically discover new content (such as posts and comments) from your blog and download that content for their consumption. Table 2-1 lists some of the most popular feed readers on the market today.

Table 2-1	Popular RSS Feed Readers	
Reader	**Source**	**Description**
Bloglines	`http://blog lines.com`	Bloglines is a free online service for searching, subscribing to, and sharing RSS feeds. You have no software to download or install; Bloglines is all Web based. You need to sign up for an account to use this service.

(continued)

Table 2-1 *(continued)*

Reader	Source	Description
Google Reader	`http://google.com/reader`	This free online service is provided by Internet search giant Google. With Google Reader, you can keep up with your favorite blogs and Web sites that have syndicated (RSS) content. You have no software to download or install to use this service, but you need to sign up for an account with Google.
FeedDemon	`http://feeddemon.com`	This is a free service that requires you to download the RSS reader application to your own computer.

For your blog readers to stay updated with the latest and greatest content you post to your site, they need to subscribe to your RSS feed. Most blogging platforms allow the RSS feeds to be *autodiscovered* by the various feed readers — meaning that the reader needs only to enter your site's URL, and the program will automatically find your RSS feed.

Most browser systems today alert visitors to the RSS feed on your site by displaying the universally recognized orange RSS feed icon, shown in the margin.

WordPress has built-in RSS feeds in several formats. Because the feeds are built into the software platform, you don't need to do anything to provide your readers an RSS feed of your content. Check out Chapter 8 to find out more about using RSS feeds within the WordPress program.

Tracking back

The best way to understand trackbacks is to think of them as comments, except for one thing: Trackbacks are comments that are left on your blog by other blogs, not by actual people. Sounds perfectly reasonable, doesn't it?

Actually, it does.

A trackback happens when you make a post on your blog, and within that post, you provide a link to a post made by another blogger in a different blog. When you publish that post, your blog sends a sort of electronic memo to the blog you've linked to. That blog receives the memo and posts an acknowledgment of receipt in a comment to the post that you linked to.

That memo is sent via a *network ping* (a tool used to test, or verify, whether a link is reachable across the Internet) from your site to the site you link to. This process works as long as both blogs support trackback protocol. WordPress does, and so do almost all the other major blogging platforms except Blogspot. (Blogspot users need to sign up for a third-party program called HaloScan to have trackback functionality in their blogs.)

Sending a trackback to a blog is a nice way of telling the blogger that you like the information she presented in her blog post. Every blogger appreciates the receipt of trackbacks to their posts from other bloggers.

Dealing with comment and trackback spam

Ugh. The absolute bane of every blogger's existence is comment and trackback spam. When blogs became the "It" things on the Internet, spammers saw an opportunity. If you've ever received spam in your e-mail program, the concept is similar and just as frustrating.

Before blogs came onto the scene, you often saw spammers filling Internet guestbooks with their links but not leaving any relevant comments. The reason is simple: Web sites receive higher rankings in the major search engines if they have multiple links coming in from other sites. Enter blog software, with comment and trackback technologies — prime breeding ground for millions of spammers.

Because comments and trackbacks are published to your site publicly — and usually with a link to the commenters' Web sites — spammers got their site links posted on millions of blogs by creating programs that automatically seek Web sites with commenting systems and then hammer those systems with tons of comments that contain links back to their own sites.

No blogger likes spam. As a matter of fact, blogging services such as WordPress have spent untold hours in the name of stopping these spammers in their tracks, and for the most part, they've been successful. Every once in a while, however, spammers sneak through. Many spammers are offensive, and all of them are frustrating because they don't contribute to the ongoing conversations that occur in blogs.

All WordPress systems have one very major, very excellent thing in common: Akismet, which kills spam dead. Chapter 10 tells you more about Akismet, which is brought to you by Automattic, the maker of WordPress.com.

Moving On to the Business of Blogging

Before getting started with blogging, you need to take a long look at your big plans for your Web site. A word of advice: Organize your plan of attack before you start. Have a good idea of what types of information you want to publish, how you want to present and organize that information, and what types of services and interaction you want to provide your audience.

It doesn't matter whether you're planning to start a personal blog as a diary of your daily life or a business blog to provide useful information to readers who are interested in your area of expertise. All potential bloggers have ideas about what type of information they want to present, and you wouldn't be considering starting a new blog if you didn't want to share that information (no matter what it is) with the rest of the world via the Internet. So having a plan of attack is helpful when you're starting out.

Ask this question out loud: "What am I going to blog about?" Go ahead — ask it. Do you have an answer? Maybe you do, and maybe not — either way, it's all right. There's no clear set of ground rules you must follow. Having an idea of what you're planning to write about in your blog makes planning your attack a little easier. You may want to write about your personal life. Maybe you plan to share only some of your photography and provide very little commentary to go along with it. Or maybe you're a business owner, and you want to blog about your services and current news within your industry.

Having an idea of your subject matter will help you determine how you want to deliver that information. My design blog, for example, is where I write about Web design projects, client case studies, and news related to design and blogging. You won't find pictures of my cats there, but you will find those pictures on my personal blog. I keep the two blogs separate, much in the same way that most of us like to keep a distinct line of separation between our personal and professional lives, no matter what industry we work in.

With your topic in mind, ask yourself these questions:

- ✔ How often will I update my blog with new posts? Daily? Weekly?
- ✔ Do I want to encourage discussion by letting my readers comment on my blog posts?
- ✔ Do I want to make every post available for public display? Am I okay with my boss or my family finding and reading my blog posts?
- ✔ How will I categorize my posts?
- ✔ Do I want to publish the full content of my posts in my RSS feed, or just excerpts?
- ✔ Do I want my blog posts to be easy for search engines to find?

When you have your topic and plan of delivery in mind, you can move forward and adjust your blog settings to work with your plan.

Part II
Using the WordPress Hosted Service

The 5th Wave   By Rich Tennant

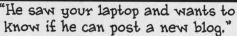

"He saw your laptop and wants to know if he can post a new blog."

In this part . . .

1f installing software on a Web server and hosting your own blog sound like things you'd like to avoid, WordPress.com may be your answer. In this section, you find out how to get — and use — a free hosted blog from WordPress.com.

Chapter 3

Getting Started with WordPress.com

. . . .

. . . .

*I*f installing software on a Web server sounds like something you'd rather avoid at all costs, WordPress.com has an alternative for you.

This part takes a complete look at the hosted service offered at WordPress. com, and in this chapter, you discover how to obtain a free blog through this service. You also find out how to get your hosted blog up and running.

Don't confuse WordPress.com with the blogging software available for download at WordPress.org! The two were created and developed by the same folks, and they do have the same name; however, they are different varieties of WordPress. (See Part III for information on installing and using the self-hosted version of WordPress.org.)

Creating a WordPress.com Account

To create your WordPress.com user account, follow these steps:

1. **In your browser, enter the URL** `http://wordpress.com`.

2. **On the page that appears, click the big Sign Up Now! button (shown in Figure 3-1).**

   You're taken to the WordPress.com signup page at `http://word press.com/signup`.

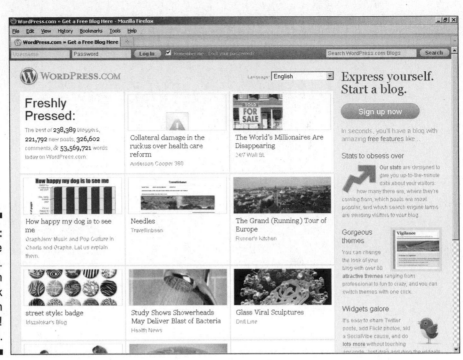

Figure 3-1:
On the
WordPress.
com main
page, click
the Sign
Up Now!
button.

3. **In the Username text box, enter the name you want to use to log in to your blog from now until forever.**

   This username must be at least four characters in length with letters and numbers only. This username cannot be changed for the blog you are creating right now. In the future, you can sign up for a new WordPress. com account with a new username; you also start over with a new blog.

4. **Enter a password of your choice first in the Password box and then in the Confirm box.**

   You use this password to log in to your new WordPress.com account. Choose, and then type, a password that you will remember, but not one that would be easy for any outside users to guess.

5. **Enter your e-mail address in the Email Address box.**

   This address is not made public on your blog; rather, it's used for communication between you and WordPress.com. You can change this address later, in the Options section in your WordPress.com Administration panel.

6. **Select the check box in the Legal Flotsam section.**

   Selecting the Legal Flotsam box lets the WordPress.com folks know that you've read its terms of service.

7. **Select either Gimme a Blog! or Just a Username, Please.**

   The Gimme a Blog! option signs you up with a WordPress.com account and sets you up with a new WordPress.com blog. The Just a Username, Please option just signs you up with a new WordPress.com account, without the blog-setup part. You may want only to reserve a username in WordPress.com for now, which is why you might choose the second option.

8. **Click the Next button.**

9. **In the Blog Domain text box, enter what you choose as your blog domain name.**

   Whatever you enter here becomes the URL address of your blog. It must be at least four characters (letters and numbers only), and you can't change it later, so choose carefully! (The domain name of your blog does not have to be the same as your username, although WordPress.com already fills in this text box for you, with your username. You can choose any domain name you want; WordPress.com lets you know whether that domain name is available within its network.)

10. **In the Blog Title text box, enter the name you've chosen for your blog.**

    Your blog title doesn't have to be the same as your username, and you can change it later in the Options section in your Administration panel.

11. **Choose your language preference from the Language drop-down menu.**

    Choose the primary language that you will be blogging in.

12. **Select the Privacy check box if you want your blog to be public. Deselect this box if you want your blog to be private and not show up in search engines. (By default, this box is checked for you.)**

    Some bloggers actually do not want their blogs to be indexed by search engines, amazingly enough. Like them, you may want to run a private blog for which you decide who can, and cannot, view the contents of your blog.

13. **Click the Sign-Up button, and you're done!**

    A new page opens with a message telling you that WordPress.com has sent you an e-mail containing a link to activate your account.

14. **Check your e-mail and click the link contained within it to activate your new WordPress.com blog.**

    A page loads with a message that your blog is now active. That page also displays your username and password. You receive another e-mail from WordPress.com that contains your username and password, as well as some useful links for navigating around WordPress.com — for example, the sign-in page, the Write Post page, and so on.

Your new blog is yours to use for the life of your blogging career at WordPress.com. You can log in to your blog any time by going to `http://wordpress.com` and filling in the login form shown at the top-left corner of the WordPress.com Web site, which you can see in Figure 3-1.

Have you ever signed up for a service on the Web, only to forget your user-name and/or password for that service mere weeks after the fact? Yep, me, too. It is a *very* good idea to file that e-mail from WordPress.com in a safe place for future reference. Just make sure that you remember where you put it. Or you can tell WordPress.com to remember you each time you enter the site. To do so, select the Remember Me check box; WordPress.com places a cookie in your browser files that tells it to remember your login credentials the next time you visit the site. (You need to have cookies enabled in your browser configurations for this feature to work.)

If you delete your cookies in your browser and then visit WordPress.com again, you won't see the WordPress.com menu bar and have to log in again. Likewise, after you delete the cookies in your browser, when you visit your new blog, it appears to you as though you are a visitor (that is, you see no menu bar with quick links for logging in to your Administration panel). In this case, you have to revisit the WordPress.com main site to log in again.

Navigating WordPress.com

When you've successfully logged in to your new account, WordPress returns you to the main WordPress.com Web site — only this time, you see some-thing slightly different at the top. The page now displays the WordPress.com menu bar, shown in Figure 3-2. The WordPress.com menu bar contains some shortcut links to some important areas of your Administration panel.

The WordPress.com menu bar also appears at the top of any WordPress.com blog you surf to, as long as you are logged in to your WordPress.com account. The WordPress.com menu bar consists of several helpful quick links for you to access your account, your Administration panel, and various options. From left to right, these quick links include

✔ **My Account:** Hover your mouse pointer over this link, and you see a drop-down menu that consists of the following:

   • *Global Dashboard:* Takes you to the Dashboard panel.

- *Stats:* Takes you to your statistics page in your WordPress.com Dashboard that displays information about your blog such as how many visitors you have on a daily basis, referrers, and keywords.

- *Tag Surfer:* Takes you to the Tag Surfer, where you can find out what people are talking about based on keywords.

- *My Comments:* Takes you to the My Comments section in the WordPress Administration panel, where you can view all comments you've left anywhere within the WordPress.com network of blogs.

- *Edit Profile:* Takes you to the Your Profile section in your Administration panel, where you can edit your own user profile.

- *Support:* Takes you to an area where you can get assistance from the folks who run WordPress.com (`http://support.word press.com`).

- *WordPress.com:* Takes you to the main WordPress.com Web site.

- *Logout:* Lets you log out.

✔ **My Dashboard:** Click this link to go to the Dashboard page. I discuss the Dashboard page in detail in the next section.

✔ **New Post:** Click this link to go to the Write Post page, where you can write and publish a new post to your blog. If you want to get started right away with a new post, see Chapter 4.

✔ **Blog Info:** Hover your mouse pointer over this link to see a drop-down menu with the following elements:

- *Random Post:* Loads, in the same window, a random post from the blog you are visiting.

- *Follow this Blog:* Loads the Blog Surfer page within your Administration panel, allowing you to subscribe to the blog you're visiting.

- *Add to Blogroll:* Automatically adds the blog you are visiting to your blogroll.

- *Get Shortlink:* Pops open a window on your computer with a short-ened version of the Web address (URL) of the page you are cur-rently visiting within the WordPress.com network.

- *Report as Spam:* Reports the blog to WordPress.com administra-tion as a spam blog.

- *Report as Mature:* Reports the blog to WordPress.com administra-tion as a blog containing mature content.

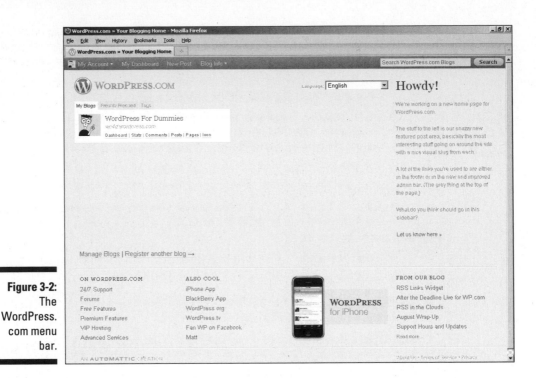

Figure 3-2:
The
WordPress.
com menu
bar.

Using the WordPress.com Dashboard

When you click the My Dashboard link in the WordPress.com menu bar (covered in the preceding section), you go directly to your WordPress.com Administration panel, starting at the Dashboard page (see Figure 3-3). Several modules within your Dashboard provide you with information about your blog, as well as actions you can take to navigate to other areas of the Administration panel, such as writing a new post, and adding a new link or blogroll.

The Dashboard modules are configurable; you can move them around on your Dashboard page and change the way the modules display. Hover your mouse over the title bar of the module you want to move, click once and drag it to the spot you'd like to display it, and then release your mouse button to drop it. This drag n' drop capability is available not only on the Dashboard page, but also on all the inner pages of the WordPress Administration panel so you can really configure it to suit your needs. You can also expand (open) and collapse (close) the individual modules by clicking your mouse anywhere within the grey title bar of the module. This is a really nice feature because it allows you to utilize the Dashboard for just those modules that you use regularly. The concept is easy: Keep the modules you use all the time open and close the ones that you only use occasionally — you can open those modules only when you really need them.

The navigation menu in the WordPress Dashboard appears on the left side of your browser window. When you need to get back to the WordPress Dashboard, click the Dashboard link that appears at the top of the navigation menu of any of the pages within your WordPress Administration panel. Each navigation item that appears in the menu has an arrow to the right of the header — clicking that arrow expands (open) the menu for that item. Likewise, clicking the arrow again collapses (close) the submenu.

Right Now

The Right Now module of the Dashboard gives you some stats on what is happening in your blog this very second. Figure 3-3 shows what was happening in my WordPress.com blog when I took a picture of it.

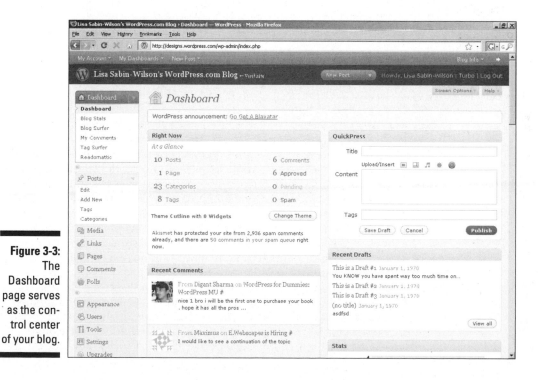

Figure 3-3:
The Dashboard page serves as the control center of your blog.

The Dashboard displays the following information under the At a Glance header:

- ✔ **The number of posts:** The number here always reflects the total number of posts you currently have in your WordPress blog. Figure 3-3 shows I currently have 10 posts on my blog. The number is blue; click the number and you go to the Edit Posts page, where you can edit the posts on your blog. I cover editing posts in Chapter 4.

- ✔ **The number of pages:** This is the current number of pages on your blog, which will change as you add or delete pages. (*Pages,* in this context, refer to the static pages you have created in your blog.) Figure 3-3 shows that my blog has 1 page.

  Clicking this link takes you to the Edit Pages page, where you can view, edit, and delete your current pages. (Find the difference between WordPress posts and pages in Chapter 4.)

- ✔ **The number of categories:** This is the current number of categories you have on your blog, which will change as you add and delete categories. Figure 3-3 shows that I currently have 23 categories for my blog.

  Clicking this link takes you to the Categories Page, where you can view, edit, and delete your current categories or add brand new ones. (For details about the management and creation of categories, see Chapter 4.)

- ✔ **The number of tags:** This is the current number of tags you have in your blog, which will change as you add and delete categories in the future. Figure 3-3 shows that I have 8 tags.

  Clicking this link takes you to the Tags page, where you can add new tags and view, edit, and delete your current tags. (You can find more information about Tags in Chapter 4.)

- ✔ **The number of comments:** This is the total number of the comments that are currently on your blog. Figure 3-3 shows that I have 6 Comments, 6 Approved, 0 Pending (waiting to be approved), and 0 Spam. Clicking any of these four links takes you to the Edit Comments page, where you can manage the comments on your blog. I cover the management of comments in Chapter 4.

The last section of the Dashboard's Right Now module in the Dashboard shows the following information:

- ✔ **Which WordPress theme you're using:** Figure 3-3 shows that I'm using the Cutline theme. The theme name is a link that, when clicked, takes you to the Manage Themes page where you can view and activate themes on your blog.

- ✔ **How many widgets you've added to your blog:** This is the number of WordPress widgets you're using in your blog. Figure 3-3 shows that I have 8 widgets. The number is a link that, when clicked, takes you to the Widgets page, where you can change your widget options by editing them, moving them, or removing them. (I cover widgets in detail in Chapter 5.)

✓ **Change Theme:** Clicking this button takes you to the Manage Themes page, which lists your currently active and all available themes for your WordPress blog.

✓ **Akismet Spam stats:** This is the last statement in the Right Now section and it gives you a quick look into how many spam comments and trackbacks the Akismet application has successfully blocked from your site. Figure 3-3 shows that Akismet has protected my blog from 2,936 spam comments. It's nice to know the spam protection is there, and working!

Recent Comments

The next module is Recent Comments. Within this module, you find

✓ **Most recent comments published to your blog:** WordPress displays a maximum of five comments in this area.

✓ **The author of each comment:** The name of the person who left the comment appears below it. This section also displays the author's picture (or avatar), if they have one.

✓ **A link to the post the comment was left on:** The post title appears to the right of the commenter's name. Click the link, and you go to that post in the Administration panel.

✓ **An excerpt of the comment:** This is a short snippet of the comment left on your blog.

✓ **Comment management links:** Hover your mouse over the comment, and five links appear that give you the opportunity to manage those comments right from your Dashboard (I discuss Comment management later in Chapter 4):

- *Unapprove:* This link only appears if you have comment moderation turned on.

- *Edit:* This link opens the Edit Comment page where you can edit the comment.

- *Reply:* This link displays a text box where you can quickly reply to the comment right from your Dashboard.

- *Spam:* Clicking this link marks that comment as spam.

- *Delete:* Clicking this link deletes the comment from your blog.

✔ **View All button:** This button invites you to see all the comments that have been left on your blog. Clicking the View All button takes you to the Edit Comments page, where you can view and edit, moderate, or delete any comments that have been left for your blog.

You'll find even more information on managing your comments in Chapter 4.

Incoming Links

Directly to the right of the Recent Comments section in the Dashboard is the Incoming Links section, which lists all the blog-savvy people who wrote blog posts that link to your blog. Figure 3-3, earlier in this chapter, shows that I don't have any incoming links to my blog. How sad is that? Because my blog is brand new, people haven't discovered it yet, but I'm sure as soon as they do, my Incoming Links list will start filling up in no time.

In the meantime, a message in the Incoming Links section says, "*This dashboard widget queries Google Blog Search so that when another blog links to your site it will show up here. It has found no incoming links. . . yet. It's okay — there is no rush.*" The phrase *Google Blog Search* is underlined because it's a link; when you click it, you go to the Google Blog Search page, which is a search engine for blogs only.

Your Stuff

In the Your Stuff section of the Dashboard, you see the following sections:

✔ **Today:** Click the links here to go to a page with options that let you manage today's posts. This page contains new or updated posts you've made during the current day.

✔ **A While Ago:** Click the links here to go to a page with options that let you manage posts and updates you made in past days.

What's Hot

Last but not least, the What's Hot section provides information about happenings in and around WordPress.com, including WordPress.com news, top blogs, top posts, fastest-growing blogs, and the latest posts made to blogs on WordPress.com. This section helps you stay in touch with the WordPress. com community as a whole.

QuickPress

The QuickPress module is a handy form that allows you to write, save, and publish a blog post right from your WordPress Dashboard. The options are very similar to the ones I cover in the section on writing posts in Chapter 4.

Recent Drafts

If you're using a brand new WordPress.com blog, the Recent Drafts module displays the message: *There are no drafts at the moment.* That is because you have not written any drafts. As time goes on, however, and you have written a few posts in your blog, you may save some of those posts as drafts to be edited and published at a later date. It is those drafts that will be shown in the Recent Drafts module. Figure 3-3 shows that I have 4 Recent Drafts showing in this box.

WordPress displays up to five drafts in this module and displays the title of the post, the date it was last saved, and a short excerpt. Click the View All button to go to the Manage Posts page where you can view, edit, and manage your blog posts. Check out Chapter 4 for more information on that.

Stats

The last module of the Dashboard page is Stats (see Figure 3-4). It includes a visual graph of your blog stats for the past several days. These stats represent how many visitors your blog received each day. The right side of the Stats module shows some specific information:

- **Top Posts:** This display lists the most popular posts in your blog, determined by the number of visits each post received. It also shows you exactly how many times each post has been viewed. Figure 3-4 shows that my post titled About Lisa Sabin-Wilson has been viewed 70 times. You can click the title of a post, and WordPress loads that post in your browser window.

- **Top Searches:** This area tells you the top keywords and search phrases people used to find your blog in search engines. Figure 3-4 shows that people used these search phrases to find my blog: *WordPress MU For Dummies* and *WordPress For Dummies*. It's nice to know how people are finding your site in the search engines!

- **Most Active:** This area tells you which posts in your blog are the most active, as determined by the number of comments left on each post. You can click the title of a post, and WordPress loads that post in your browser window.

TIP

If you find that you don't use a few modules on your Dashboard page, you can completely get rid of them altogether by following these few steps:

1. **Click the Screen Options button shown at the top of the Dashboard.**

   This button is located at the top of the Dashboard page, on the right side. Clicking this button drops down the Screen Options menu, displaying the title of each module with check boxes to the left of each title.

2. **Deselect the module you want to hide on your Dashboard.**

   The check mark is removed from the box and the module you deselected disappears from your Dashboard. If you have hidden one module and find later that you really miss having it on your Dashboard, you can simply enable that module again by selecting it from the Screen Options menu.

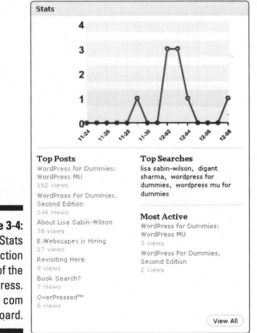

Figure 3-4:
The Stats
section
of the
WordPress.
com
Dashboard.

Setting Important Options Before You Blog

The options in this section help you get started and well on your way to managing your own WordPress.com blog. In this section, you discover how to set the primary options that personalize your blog, including creating your user profile, setting the date and time stamp (based on your own time-zone settings), and uploading a picture of yourself.

Setting your General options

To begin personalizing your WordPress.com blog by setting the General options, follow these steps:

1. **Click the Settings menu in the navigation menu.**

2. **Click the General link on the Settings menu.**

   The General Settings page opens (see Figure 3-5).

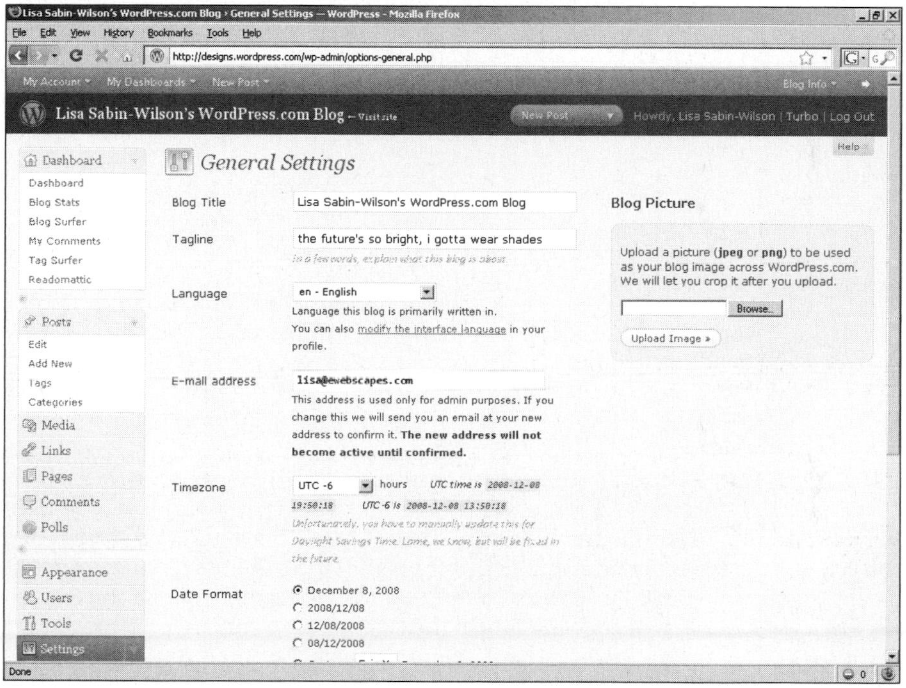

Figure 3-5:
The General Settings page in the WordPress Administration panel.

3. **Enter the name of your blog in the Blog Title text box.**

   You can revisit this page any time and change the blog name as often as you like.

4. **In the Tagline text box, enter a slogan or a motto that describes you or your blog.**

   The tagline should be a short (one line) phrase that sums up the tone and premise of your blog. Figure 3-5 shows I used a quote from a song by a group called Timbuk 3: "The future's so bright, I gotta wear shades." Although my tagline doesn't give you a description of my blog, it does give you an idea of my optimistic nature.

5. **From the drop-down Language menu, choose the language in which you want to publish your blog.**

Below the drop-down menu is a link that says *modify the interface language* — referring to the language in the WordPress Administration panel. So you can have your blog published in English but have the Administration panel displayed in Spanish, for example.

6. **Type your e-mail address in the E-Mail Address box.**

Enter the e-mail address that you used to sign up with WordPress.com. You can change this address, but be warned: If you change the e-mail address here, it won't become active until you confirm that you are in fact the owner of said e-mail address. This confirmation is accomplished through a simple process: WordPress.com sends an e-mail to that address, providing a link you can click to confirm that you are the owner. This e-mail address is used for administrative purposes only, which consists mainly of communication between you and WordPress.com.

Adjusting your Date and Time settings

After you configure the General options that I discuss in the preceding section, you can use the last section of the General Settings page to set your local time, so that your blog posts are published with a time stamp in your own time zone no matter where in the world you are. Use the following options to establish your settings in this area, as shown in Figure 3-6.

✔ **Timezone section:** Choose your UTC time from the drop-down menu. This setting refers to the number of hours that your local time differs from Coordinated Universal Time (UTC). This setting ensures that all your blog posts and comments left on your blog are time-stamped with the correct time. If you're lucky enough, like me, to live on the frozen tundra of Wisconsin, which is in the Central time zone (CST), you would choose –6 from the drop-down menu because that time zone is 6 hours off UTC.

If you're unsure what your UTC time is, you can find it at the Greenwich Mean Time (http://wwp.greenwichmeantime.com) Web site. GMT is essentially the same thing as UTC.

The Timezone option doesn't update automatically for daylight saving time (DST). If you live in an area of the world that practices DST, you have to update the Timezone option manually when it occurs.

✔ **Date Format:** Select how you want to display the date. The default format is F j, Y (F = the full month name; j = the two-digit day; Y = the four-digit year), which gives you the output of January 1, 2008. Select a different format by clicking the circle to the left of the option. You can also customize the date display by selecting the Custom option and entering your preferred format in the text box provided. You can found out how to customize the date format here: `http://codex.word press.org/Formatting_Date_and_Time`.

✔ **Time Format:** Select how you want to display the time. The default format is g:i a (g = the two-digit hour; i = the two-digit minute; a = lowercase ante meridiem and post meridiem, or a.m. or p.m.), which gives you the output of 12:00 a.m. Select a different format by clicking the circle to the left of the option. You can also customize the date display by selecting the Custom option and entering your preferred format in the text box provided; find out how at `http://codex.wordpress.org/ Formatting_Date_and_Time`.

You can format the time and date in several ways. Go to `http://us3. php.net/date` to find potential formats at the PHP Web site.

✔ **Week Starts On:** From the drop-down menu, choose the day the week starts in your calendar. The display of the calendar in the sidebar of your blog is optional. If you choose to display the calendar, you can select the day of the week you want your calendar to start with.

Timezone	UTC -6 ▾ hours *UTC time is 2008-12-08*
	19:50:18 *UTC -6 is 2008-12-08 13:50:18*
	Unfortunately, you have to manually update this for Daylight Savings Time. Lame, we know, but will be fixed in the future.
Date Format	⦿ December 8, 2008
	○ 2008/12/08
	○ 12/08/2008
	○ 08/12/2008
	○ Custom: F j, Y December 8, 2008
	Documentation on date formatting. Click "Save Changes" to update sample output.
Time Format	⦿ 1:50 pm
	○ 1:50 PM
	○ 13:50
	○ Custom: g:i a 1:50 pm
Week Starts On	Monday ▾

Figure 3-6: Date and time settings for your WordPress. com blog.

Click the Save Changes button at the bottom of any page where you set new options. If you don't click Save Changes, your settings aren't saved, and WordPress reverts to the previous options. Each time you click the Save Changes button, WordPress reloads the current page, displaying the new options that you just set.

Setting your profile: Tell us a little about yourself

The next set of options you need to update is your profile. This area lets you configure your personal settings to individualize your WordPress.com blog and tell the world a little more about yourself. This blog is, after all, about you, and this is your opportunity to brag and promote!

To get started telling the world about yourself, follow these steps:

1. **Click the Users menu in the navigation menu.**

2. **Click the Your Profile link on the Users menu.**

    The Profile page opens, as shown in Figure 3-7.

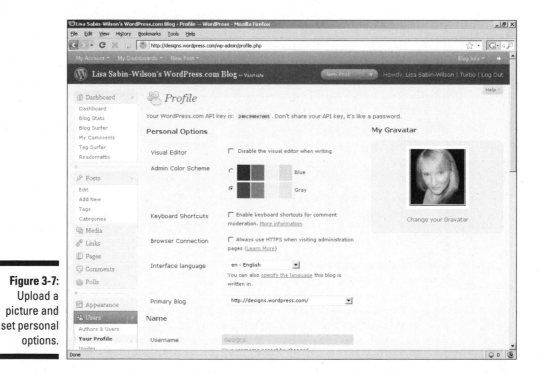

Figure 3-7:
Upload a picture and set personal options.

You can adjust all sorts of personal settings to let your visitors get to know you better. You can be liberal with the information you want to share or as stingy as you want. It's *your* blog, after all.

Choose carefully the information you share on your blog, especially if you have a public blog on WordPress.com — public blogs can (and are!) viewed by a worldwide audience! If you don't want people to know your real name, use a nickname. If you don't want to share a picture of yourself for fear of shattering computer monitors worldwide, you can choose not to upload any picture at all or to upload a picture of something that reflects the essence of you. (You can post a picture of a book if you're an avid reader, a picture of a camera if you're a photographer, and so on.) The options are endless, and no real rules apply to what type of personal information or how much of it you should (or should not) share with the rest of the Internet world.

Make your blog your own. Stake your claim and mark your territory in this section!

Personal options

In the first section of the Your Profile and Personal Options page, you can set four preferences for your blog:

- ✔ **Visual Editor:** Place a check in this box to indicate that you want to use the Visual Editor when writing your posts. Leave this box blank if you prefer not to use the Visual Editor. For information about the Visual Editor, including reasons why you would or would not want to use it, see Chapter 4.

- ✔ **Admin Color Scheme:** This option changes the colors in your WordPress Administration panel, which uses the Gray color scheme by default. The other option is Blue — the choice is yours!

- ✔ **Keyboard Shortcuts:** These shortcuts are designed to save you time navigating through the different areas of the Dashboard and Administration panel. Click the More Information link to read about how you can use keyboard shortcuts in your WordPress.com Administration panel.

- ✔ **Browser Connection:** You can select whether use the HTTPS connection when visiting your WordPress.com Administration panel. HTTPS refers to a secure browser connection called SSL-encrypt, which protects your Internet connection and keeps out potential hackers.

- ✔ **Interface Language:** The Interface Language option refers to the language that you want to set for the Administration panel only. Don't confuse this setting with the Language option on the General Settings page, which determines the language you publish your blog in. If you want to view the settings in your WordPress Administration panel in Italian but want your published blog to appear in English, you set the Interface Language option (shown in Figure 3-7) to Italian and the Language option (shown in Figure 3-5) to English. Capiche?

- ✔ **Primary Blog:** This option is the URL of your primary WordPress.com blog. Figure 3-7 shows that the URL of my primary WordPress.com blog is lswilson.wordpress.com. Because WordPress.com allows you to have several blogs under one account, if you have more than one blog, a drop-down menu appears here, and you can use it to choose the blog you want to set as your primary blog.

✔ **Proofreading:** WordPress.com gives you the ability to proofread the content that you write as blog posts or pages. This section gives you several different options to choose from that go beyond just the standard spell checker. The proofreader can check for things like clichés, duplicate words, double negatives, jargon, redundant phrases, and more. Click the link that says Learn More about These Options to read about how the proofreader can help you publish better content on your blog.

Name

The next section on this page is where you can input personal information such as your first and last names and your nickname, and choose how you want your name to be displayed publicly. Fill in the boxes with the information requested.

Contact Info

In this section, you provide your e-mail address and other contact information to tell your visitors who you are and where they may contact you.

Note that E-mail is the only required field here. This e-mail address is the one WordPress uses to notify you when you have new comments or new user registrations for your blog. The e-mail address that you signed up with is already listed here for you; if you'd like to change it, you need to do so on the General Settings page.

Aside from e-mail, you can provide your ID for various Internet chat programs such as Yahoo! IM, AIM (AOL Instant Messenger), and Jabber/Google Talk.

About Yourself

In this section, you can provide a little biography, as well as change the password for your blog. Figure 3-8 shows this section in detail.

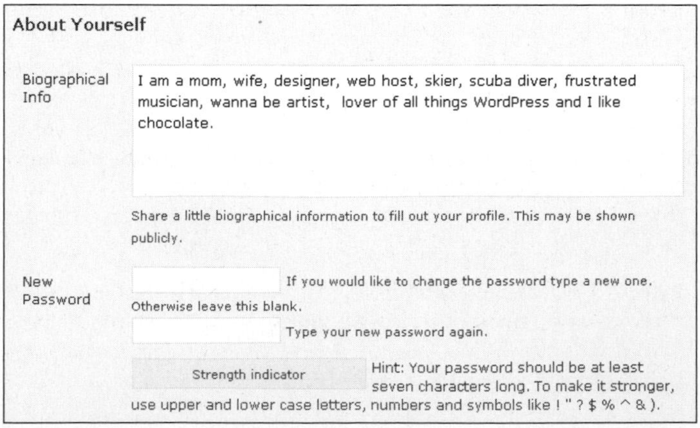

About Yourself	
Biographical Info	I am a mom, wife, designer, web host, skier, scuba diver, frustrated musician, wanna be artist, lover of all things WordPress and I like chocolate.
	Share a little biographical information to fill out your profile. This may be shown publicly.
New Password	If you would like to change the password type a new one. Otherwise leave this blank.
	Type your new password again.
	Strength indicator — Hint: Your password should be at least seven characters long. To make it stronger, use upper and lower case letters, numbers and symbols like ! " ? $ % ^ &).

Figure 3-8:
Provide an informative bio and set your blog password.

The two areas of this section are

- ✔ **Biographical Info:** Type your short bio in the text box provided here. Figure 3-8 shows that I provided a few details about myself and things I like to do (when I'm not blogging, that is). This information can be shown publicly if you are using a theme that displays your bio — so be creative!

- ✔ **New Password:** When you want to change the password for your blog, type your new password in the first text box (refer to Figure 3-8). To confirm your new password choice, type it again in the second text field.

    Directly below the two New Password text boxes is a little password helper. WordPress.com assists you in creating a secure password by giving you a tip about the password you have chosen. WordPress.com alerts you if the password is too short or not secure enough (by telling you that it's Bad).

When you create a new password, use a combination of letters, numbers, and symbols to make it hard for anyone to guess what it is (for example, aty89!#4j). When you have created a password that WordPress thinks is a good one, it says the password is Strong.

Change your password frequently. I can't recommend this practice strongly enough. Some people on the Internet make it their business to attempt to hijack blogs for their own malicious purposes. If you change your password monthly, you lower your risk by keeping the hackers guessing.

When you finish setting all the options on the left side of the Your Profile and Personal Options page, don't forget to click the Update Profile button to save your changes.

My Picture

Want to show the world your pretty picture? In the My Gravatar section of the Your Profile and Personal Options page, you can upload a picture (or a *gravatar*, which is a graphical image of you) of yourself or an image that represents you. This section is located on the right side of the Your Profile and Personal Options page (refer to Figure 3-7, earlier in this chapter).

The picture/avatar that you insert into your WordPress.com is used in several ways:

- ✔ **The WordPress.com Blog of the Day page at `http://botd.word press.com/top-posts`, which lists the top posts from the top blogs of the day:** If your blog is included in these lists, a smaller version of the picture you've uploaded to your profile appears next to the listing.

- ✔ **The WordPress.com Hawt Post (or "hot" post) on its main page at `http://wordpress.com`:** If the WordPress spotlight shines in your direction, your picture will be displayed here for your own 15 minutes of WordPress.com fame.

✔ **The WordPress.com directory (by topic) of its community blogs:** This directory is called the Tags page (http://wordpress.com/tags). Bloggers on WordPress.com can tag their posts with keywords that help define the topics of their posts; WordPress.com collects all those tagged posts and sorts them by name on the Tags page.

At the On the Tag: Blogging page (http://wordpress.com/tags/blogging), for example, you find the most recent posts that WordPress.com bloggers have made on the topic of blogging. If your blog appears in this directory, so does a thumbnail of your picture.

Follow these steps to insert a picture or avatar into your profile:

1. **Choose the image you want to attach to your profile, and save it to your computer.**

   To be safe in your image selection, be sure to upload an image that is at least 128 pixels wide and 128 pixels tall: 128 x 128. Later in these steps, you see how you can crop a larger image to the perfect size.

2. **In the My Gravatar section of the Profile page, click the Change Your Gravatar link.**

   The Gravatar.com window appears where you click the Upload a New Image from Your Computer link that opens the Select File from Your Computer window.

3. **Click the Browse button and select an image from your computer.**

4. **Click the Next button.**

   No matter what size image you chose, the Gravatar.com page allows you to crop your image to the correct size and lets you decide which part of your image to use for your picture display. When you click the Next button, the crop image page appears, and you can crop (cut) your chosen picture to the right size to be used as an avatar or icon (see Figure 3-9).

5. **Use the crop tool to highlight the area of the picture that you want to remain after cropping.**

   In Figure 3-9, the box with a dotted line (the crop tool) outlines the image I've chosen to use. This dotted outline indicates the size the picture will be when I'm done cropping it. You can move that dotted box around to choose the area of the image you want to use as your avatar. The Gravatar.com crop tool gives you two previews of your cropped image on the right side of the window: Small Preview and Large Preview.

6. **Click the Crop and Finish! button.**

   The Choose a Rating page opens, where you can choose a rating for your new Gravatar.

7. **Choose a rating.**

   The rating system works very much like the movie rating system we're all familiar with: G, PG, R, and X. A G rating means that your Gravatar is suitable for all ages, whereas an X rating means that your Gravatar contains some unmentionables that you would not want any kids to see. Use your absolute best judgment here!

8. **Choose an e-mail address.**

   You can assign your Gravatar to a particular e-mail address so that your Gravatar images appear on any blog you comment on, provided you use your assigned e-mail address to do so.

   When you're done, you get a message from Gravtar.com that says "Your new Gravatar is now being applied."

9. **Click the X in the upper right corner of the window to return to the Profile page in your WordPress.Com administration panel.**

   The Profile page now displays your newly uploaded Gravatar.

TIP

You can change your picture any time you want by revisiting the Profile page and following these steps to upload a new picture.

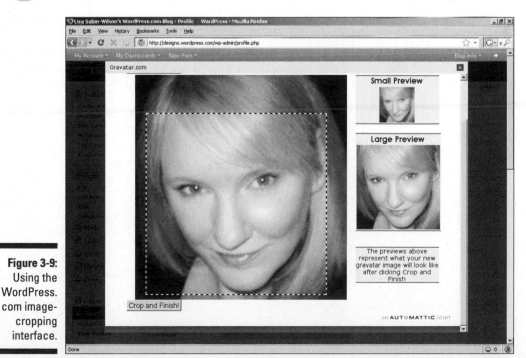

Figure 3-9:
Using the WordPress.com image-cropping interface.

Getting Help

I would be remiss if I didn't mention some of the places on the Internet you can visit to find more information on using WordPress.com (see Table 3-1) — beginning with the super bunch of users in the WordPress.com community.

Table 3-1	WordPress.com Resources Online	
Resource	*Description*	*Location*
WordPress.com Forums	These forums, provided to the community by WordPress.com, are populated by users who help users. Sometimes, WordPress.com developers and staff members also provide help through these forums.	`http://word press.com/ forums`
WordPress Codex	This comprehensive online document repository covers everything WordPress — not just WordPress.com. You have to search and dig a little to find what you need, but you can find some valuable nuggets of information here, especially for new users.	`http://codex. wordpress.org/ First_Steps_ With_WordPress`
Help	This little link appears in the top-right corner of every page in your WordPress.com Administration panel.	Click this link, and you are taken to the WordPress.com FAQ (Frequently Asked Questions) page at `http://faq. wordpress.com`.

Chapter 4

Writing and Managing Your Blog

....

....

The first chapter in this part covers the signup process and a few important settings and options that you configure when you first log in to your new WordPress.com blog. Now it's time to make a blogger out of you. In this chapter, I show you the tools you need to write your first post. When you understand that process, the blogging world is right at your fingertips.

This chapter also shows you the basics of categorizing your posts and links, uploading images to your blog posts, setting discussion and reading options for your blog, using static pages, and managing your users and authors. I don't have the space in this chapter to cover every option available, but I hit the high points of what you need to know.

Ready? Set? Blog!

In the Administration panel, click the Add New link on the Posts menu to display the Add New Post page, where you write, organize, and publish your first post. Start by thinking up a name for your post and entering it in the Title text box, shown in Figure 4-1. You can make the name snappy and fun if you want, but don't be cryptic. Use titles that give your readers a basic idea of what they're about to read in the posts. No set of hard-and-fast rules exists when it comes to creating titles for your blog posts, of course. Have fun with your title, and let it reflect your personality and style of writing. After giving your post a title, you can write the content of your post in the Post text box.

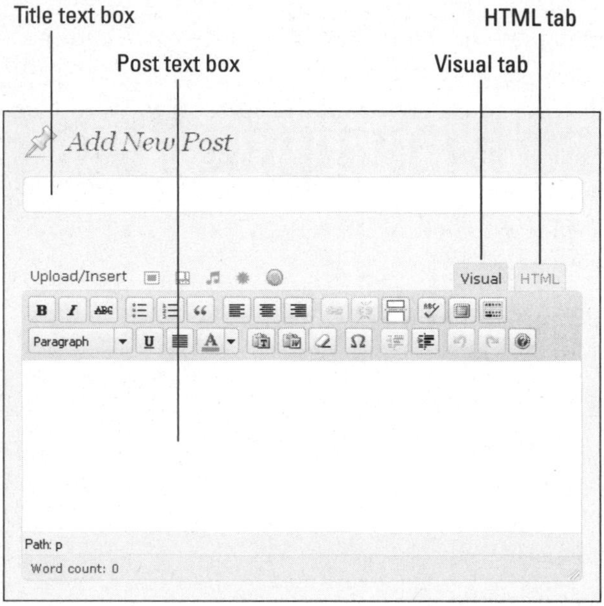

Title text box   HTML tab

     Post text box   Visual tab

Figure 4-1:
The area
in which
you write
your post.

The area in which you write your post is in Visual Editing mode, as indicated by the Visual tab that appears above the text. Visual Editing mode is how WordPress provides WYSIWYG (What You See Is What You Get) options for formatting. Rather than have to embed HTML code within your post, you can simply type your post, highlight the text you'd like to format, and click the buttons (shown in Figure 4-1) that appear above the box in which you type your post.

If you've ever used a word processing program such as Microsoft Word, you'll recognize many of these buttons:

- **Bold:** Embeds the `<strong> </strong>` tag to emphasize the text in bold (example: **bold text**).

- **Italics:** Embeds the `<em> </em>` tag to emphasize the text in italics (example: *italic text*).

- **Strikethrough:** Embeds the `<strike> </strike>` tag to put a line through your text (example: ~~strikethrough text~~).

- **Unordered List:** Embeds the `<ul><li> </li></ul>` tag to create an unordered, or bulleted, list.

- **Ordered List:** Embeds the `<ol><li> </li></ul>` tag that creates an ordered, or numbered, list.

- **Blockquote:** Inserts the `<blockquote> </blockquote>` tag to indent the selected paragraph or section of text.

- ✔ **Align Left:** Inserts the `<p align="left"> </p>` tag to align the selected paragraph or section of text against the left margin.

- ✔ **Align Center:** Inserts the `<p align="center"> </p>` tag to position the selected paragraph or section of text in the center of the page.

- ✔ **Align Right:** Inserts the `<p align="right"> </p>` tag to align the selected paragraph or section of text against the right margin.

- ✔ **Insert/Edit Link:** Applies the `<a href=" "> </a>` tag to the selected text to create a hyperlink.

- ✔ **Unlink:** Removes a hyperlink from selected text.

- ✔ **Insert More Tag:** Inserts the `<!--more-->` tag to split the display on your blog page. It publishes the text written above this tag with a Read More link, which takes the user to a page with the full post. This feature is good for really long posts.

- ✔ **Toggle Spellchecker:** This is a perfect tool for you, if you make spelling errors while you type. Use it to check your spelling before you post.

- ✔ **Toggle Full Screen Mode:** Expands the Post text box to occupy the full height and width of your browser screen. Use this to focus on writing without being distracted by all the other options on the page. To bring that Post text box back to its normal state, click the Toggle Full Screen Mode button again, and voilà — it's back to normal.

- ✔ **Show/Hide Kitchen Sink:** Displays a new formatting menu, providing options for underlining, font color, custom characters, undo and redo, and so on — a veritable kitchen sink full of options! I saw this option and thought, "Wow! WordPress does my dishes, too!" Unfortunately, the option's name is a metaphor to describe the advanced formatting options available with the Visual Editor.

If you'd rather embed your own HTML and skip the Visual Editor, click the HTML tab that appears to the right of the Visual tab above the Post text box. If you type HTML in your post — using a table or embedding video files, for example — you have to click the HTML tab before you insert that code. If you don't, the Visual Editor formats your code, and it most likely looks nothing like you intended it to.

At this point, you can skip to the "Publishing your post" section, later in this chapter, for information on publishing your post to your blog, or continue with the following sections to discover how to include images in your blog post and refine the options for your post.

WordPress.com has a nifty autosave feature that saves your work while you're typing and editing a new post. If your browser crashes, or you accidentally close your browser window before you've saved your post, the post is there for you when you get back. Those WordPress.com folks are so thoughtful!

Inserting media files into your post

Pictures, images, video, and audio files can greatly enhance the content of a post by adding visual and/or auditory effects to the words that you've written. Look right above the formatting buttons on the Write Post page (refer to Figure 4-1), and you see an Add Media toolbar. Have a look again; it's pretty small, but it's there! The Add Media toolbar has four small buttons:

- ✔ Add an Image
- ✔ Add Video
- ✔ Add Audio
- ✔ Add Media
- ✔ Add Poll

As of this writing, if you don't have any blog space upgrades purchased for your account, you can only upload images (jpg, jpeg, png, gif), documents (pdf, doc) and presentations (ppt) files. If you've purchased a space upgrade, you can upload other files — audio (mp3, mp4a, wav) and video (avi, mp4, mpg, mov, wmv) files. Chapter 5 has information on the upgrades that are available for your WordPress.com blog.

Adding an image

Adding an image or photo to your post is easy. Start by clicking the Add an Image button, which is the first button on the Add Media toolbar. The Add an Image window opens, letting you choose images from your hard drive or from the Web (see Figure 4-2).

To add an image from the Web after you click the Add an Image button, follow these steps:

1. **Click the From URL tab.**

2. **Type the URL (Internet address) of the image in the Image URL text box.**

   Type the full URL, including the http and www portion of the address. You can find the URL of any image on the Web by right-clicking it and selecting Properties.

3. **Type a title for the image in the Image Title box.**

   This gives the image a title so you can easily identify the image later when using the Media Library. A title also assists in search engine optimization because WordPress inserts a <title> tag in the HTML markup that looks like this: title="your image title here", which helps search engines identify the type of content on your page.

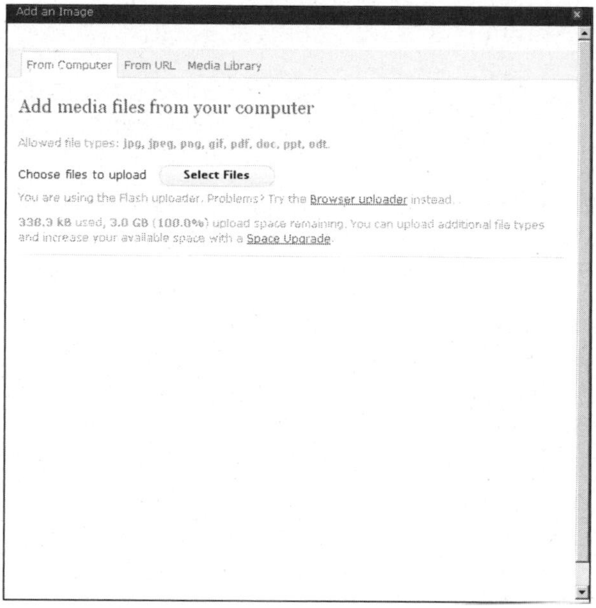

Figure 4-2:
The
WordPress.
com media
uploader.

4. **(Optional) Type a description of the image in the Image Caption box.**

   The description of the image provides image ALT tags, which help search engines find and list your site in their directories — so it's a good idea to provide a description if you can. Some WordPress themes also display the caption directly underneath your image on your blog.

5. **Choose your alignment option by selecting the None, Left, Center, or Right radio button.**

6. **Type a link or choose not to link the image:**

   • *None:* You don't want to link the image to anything.

   • *Link to Image:* You want to link the image to its individual URL or you can type any URL you like to link an image to another Web site or page.

7. **Click the Insert into Post button.**

To add an image from your hard drive after you click the Add an Image button, follow these steps

1. **Click the From Computer tab.**

2. **Click the Select Files button.**

   A dialog box opens, letting you choose an image from your hard drive.

3. **Choose an image or multiple images to upload.**

4. **Click Open.**

   The image is uploaded from your computer to your Web server. WordPress displays a progress bar on the upload and displays an image options box when the upload is finished.

5. **Edit the details for the image(s) by filling in the fields provided for you in the Add an Image box (shown in Figure 4-3).**

   • *Title:* Type a title for the image.

   • *Alternate Text:* Provides image ALT tags, which help search engines find and list your site in their directories.

   • *Caption:* Type a caption for the image (such as **This is a flower from my garden**).

   • *Description:* Type a description of the image.

   • *Link URL:* Type the URL you want the image linked to. Whatever option you choose determines where your readers go when they click the image you've uploaded:

   None: You don't want the image to be clickable.

   File URL: Readers can click through to the direct image itself.

   Post URL: Readers can click through to the post that the image appears in. You can type your own URL in the Link URL text box.

   • *Alignment:* Choose None, Left, Center, or Right. (See Table 9-1, in the following section, for styling information regarding image alignment.)

   • *Size:* Choose Thumbnail, Medium, Large or Full Size.

6. **Click the Edit Image button (shown in Figure 4-3) to edit the appearance of the image.**

   The image editor options include Crop, Rotate Counter-Clockwise, Rotate Clockwise, Flip Vertically, Flip Horizontally, Undo, Redo, and Scale Image.

7. **Click the Insert into Post button.**

   The HTML code needed to display the image within your published post is inserted automatically. The media uploader window closes and returns you to the Write Post page. (Alternatively, you can click the Save All Changes button to save the options you've set for the image(s) and then return at a later date to insert the image(s) in your post, without having to reset those options again.)

Along with inserting just one image into your post, you can use the media uploader to insert a full gallery of images. Go through the steps I outline in this section to upload images, but don't click the Insert into Post button.

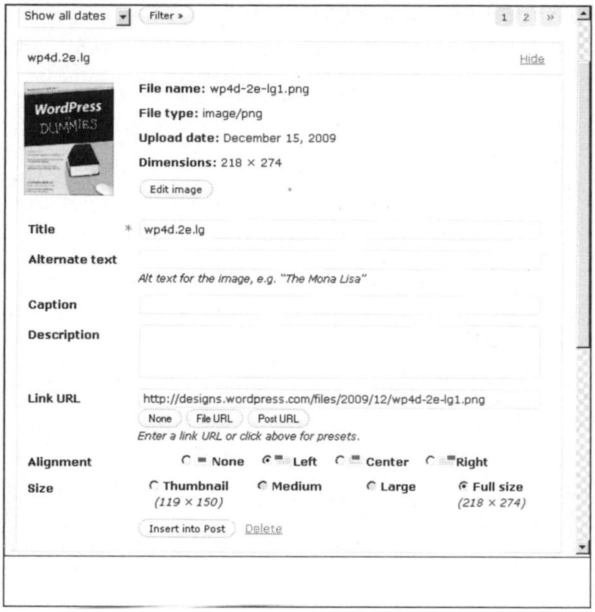

Figure 4-3:
Setting
options for
the image
after you
upload it.

Instead, click the Gallery link at the top of the media uploader window (refer to Figure 4-2).

You can configure the options for each image by clicking the Show link to the right of the image (as explained in Step 3 of the preceding steps). When you're done, click the Insert Gallery into Post button. A short piece of code is inserted that looks like this: [gallery]. That piece of code tells WordPress to display your gallery of images inside the post you are about to publish.

The interface that WordPress.com uses for file upload is Flash-based. Adobe Flash contains a specific set of multimedia technologies programmed to handle media files on the Web. Some browsers and operating systems aren't configured to handle Flash-based applications. If you experience difficulties with the media uploader, WordPress.com gives you a handy alternative method. In the media uploader (refer to Figure 4-2), click the Browser Uploader link to upload files in an interface that is not Flash-based.

Using audio, video, and other media files

The Add Media toolbar contains four other buttons:

✔ **Add Video:** Click this button and the media uploader box opens. In the URL box, type the URL for the video file you want to use in the URL field. WordPress.com also provides you instructions (and the correct code) for inserting a video from YouTube, Google Video, DailyMotion, and VodPod. Click the Insert into Post button to use that video in your blog post.

- ✔ **Add Audio:** Click the button and the media uploader box opens. In the URL box, type the URL for the audio file you want to use; then type the title of that file in the Title box. Click the Insert into Post button to insert a link to that audio file into your blog post.

- ✔ **Add Media:** Click the button and the media uploader box opens. In the URL box, type the URL for the media file you want to use; then type the title of that file in the Title box. Click the Insert into Post button to insert a link to that media file into your blog post.

- ✔ **Add Poll:** You can automatically set up an account with WordPress. com's sister company, Poll Daddy, to create and insert polls on your WordPress.com blog.

How do media files differ from image, video, and audio files? Media files include Microsoft PowerPoint presentation files (.ppt), Microsoft Word documents (.doc), and Adobe Portable Document Format (.pdf) files. While these types of files can also contain images, video, and audio files, you can use the media uploader to upload these files to your WordPress.com account so that you can display and link to them on your blog.

WordPress.com gives you 3GB of disk space for your free blog, and though it would take a lot of files to use up that amount of space, if you upload large image files, that space could go a lot quicker than you think. Keep the actual file size of the images you upload in mind when you use this feature; you can eat that disk space up before you know it.

Refining your post options

After you write the post, you can choose a few extra options before you publish it for the entire world to see. These settings are applied only to the post you're working on; they don't apply automatically to any future or past posts you make. You can find these options (see Figure 4-4) underneath and to the right of the Post text box.

Here are the options:

- ✔ **Excerpt:** Excerpts are short summaries of your posts. Many bloggers use snippets to show teasers of their blog posts, thereby encouraging the reader to click the Read More link to read posts in their entirety. Type your short summary in the Excerpt box. Excerpts have no word limit, but the idea is to keep them short and sweet.

- ✔ **Send Trackbacks:** I discuss trackbacks in Chapter 2, if you want to refresh your memory banks on what they are. If you want to send a trackback to another blog, enter that blog's Trackback URL in the Sent Trackbox To box. You can send trackbacks to more than one blog; just be sure to separate trackback URLs with spaces.

- ✔ **Discussion:** Decide whether to allow readers to submit feedback through the comment system and whether to allow pings and trackbacks (read more about pings and trackbacks in Chapter 2) by selecting the boxes here or leaving them blank.

- ✔ **Publish:** These are the publishing options for your blog post. I cover these options in detail in the "Publishing your post" section.

- ✔ **Tags:** Tags are a nice feature of WordPress.com; they let you add searchable and archived keywords for your posts in small subtopics. Type your chosen tags (or keywords) in the Tags box. Tags can be single words or several words; just make sure to separate tags with commas (for example: **books, movies, pop culture, and entertainment**).

- ✔ **Categories:** You can file your posts in different categories to organize them by subject. (See more about organizing your posts in the "Organizing Your Blog by Subject" section, later in this chapter.) Select the box to the left of the category name you want to use. Don't see the category you need listed here? Click the Add New Category link at the bottom of the Categories box, and you can add a new category.

- ✔ **Password Protect This Post:** You can password-protect a post by entering a password in this box. When you do, you can share the password with only the readers you want to let read that post. This feature is perfect for those times when you'd love to make a blog post about all the stupid things your boss did today but don't want your boss to see it. This feature also hides the post from search engines so that it doesn't show up in search results. If you don't want to password-protect the post, leave this box blank.

When you finish setting the options for your post, don't navigate away from this page, because your options have not yet been fully saved. You need to scroll all the way back up to the top and click the Save Draft button on the top right side of the page. Before you do that, however, you probably want to check out the next section, which discusses publishing options for your new blog post.

Publishing your post

You have given your new post a title and written the content of your new blog post. Maybe you've even added an image or other type of media file to your blog post and have configured the tags, categories, and other options for your post. Now the question is: Publish? Or not to publish (yet)?

WordPress.com gives you three options for saving or publishing your post when you are done writing it. Figure 4-5 shows the Publish Status section, which is located on the right side of the Write Post page.

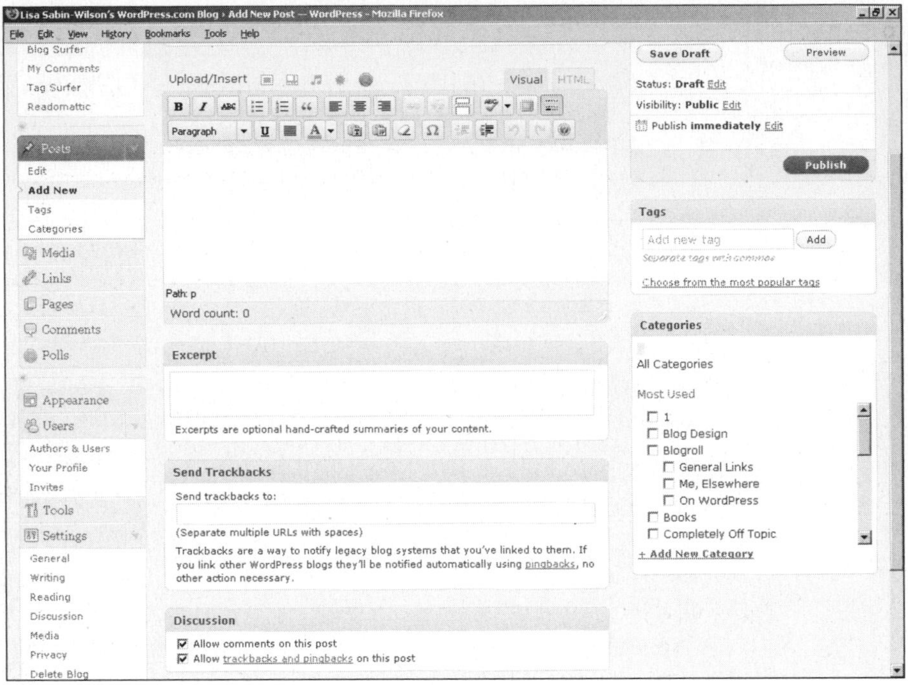

Figure 4-4:
Several
options
for your
blog post.

Figure 4-5:
WordPress.
com post
publishing
status
section.

The Publish Status drop-down menu offers three options:

✔ **Status:** Click the Edit link next to the Status option and a new menu
appears with the following options:

• *Pending Review:* Select this option to set the post status as Pending;
the post shows up in your list of drafts next to a Pending Review
header. This option lets the administrator of the blog know that
contributors have entered posts that are waiting for administrator
review and approval (helpful for blogs with multiple authors).

• *Draft:* Select this option to save the post, but not publish it to your
blog. Your post is saved in draft form, allowing you to return at a
later time.

Click OK when you're done to save your settings.

✔ **Visibility**: Click the Edit link next to the Visibility option and a new menu appears with the following options:

- *Public:* Choosing this option publishes your post to your blog for the entire world to see. Choose Stick This Post to Your Front Page if you want to publish this post to the very top of your blog, and keep it there until you come back and edit the status at a later date.

- *Password Protected:* This option allows you to password protect a post, which publishes it to your blog; however; for a reader to view the post, they have to know the password. When you select this option, a text box appears where you type the password for this post.

Click OK when you're done to save your settings.

✔ **Publish Immediately:** Click the Edit link next to the Publish Immediately option and a new menu appears where you can set the date (or time-stamp) of the post and publish the post right away. The date settings here allow you to set a date in the future for the post to publish, or you can back-date a post to publish on a date in the past.

Click OK when you are done to save your settings.

When you have chosen a publishing status, click the Publish button. WordPress saves your publishing-status option. Figure 4-6 shows my new blog post successfully posted to my blog.

Figure 4-6:
Successful blog posts make it to your front page.

If you want to publish your blog post right away, skip the drop-down menu options, and click the Publish button, which sends your new blog post to your blog in all its glory.

If you click Publish and for some reason don't see the post you just published to the front page of your blog, you probably left the Publish Status drop-down menu set to Unpublished. Look for your new post among the draft posts.

Organizing Your Blog by Subject

Categorizing your posts in WordPress provides an organizational structure for your blog. Each blog post that is assigned to a category is grouped with other posts in the same category. When your blog is a few months old, this structure creates a nice topical directory of posts for you and your readers.

Category lists generally appear in two places on your blog, letting your readers find all your posts by subject very easily. Almost all WordPress themes list categories within the blog post itself. Most themes also provide a list of your categories in the sidebar of your blog so that your readers can click a topic of interest.

Each category in a WordPress.com blog has its own RSS feed, making it easy for your readers to subscribe to a feed and keep updated on what you have to say in your blog about a certain topic.

Creating categories and subcategories

A brand-new WordPress.com blog has only one category to begin with: Uncategorized, as shown in Figure 4-7.

You can create new categories (and categories within those categories) by following these steps:

1. **Click the Categories link on the Posts menu.**

   The Categories page opens (refer to Figure 4-7).

2. **Under the Add Category heading, type the name of your category in the Category Name text box.**

3. **Leave the Category Parent drop-down menu set to the default option (None).**

The Category Parent drop-down menu lets you create subcategories. If you have a main category called Books, for example, Books appears in the Category Parent drop-down menu. To create a subcategory of the Books category, follow Steps 1 and 2 and then choose Books from the Category Parent drop-down menu.

4. **(Optional) Enter a description of the category in the Description text box.**

   Do this step now so that later, you'll know what you were thinking of when you created this category. A short summary will do. (Also, some WordPress themes are coded to display the category description in the sidebar of your blog.)

5. **Click the Add Category button.**

Categories you create now aren't set in stone. You can edit or delete them by revisiting the Categories page and clicking the name of the category you want to edit. The Edit Category page opens, and you can edit the category name, category parent, and description.

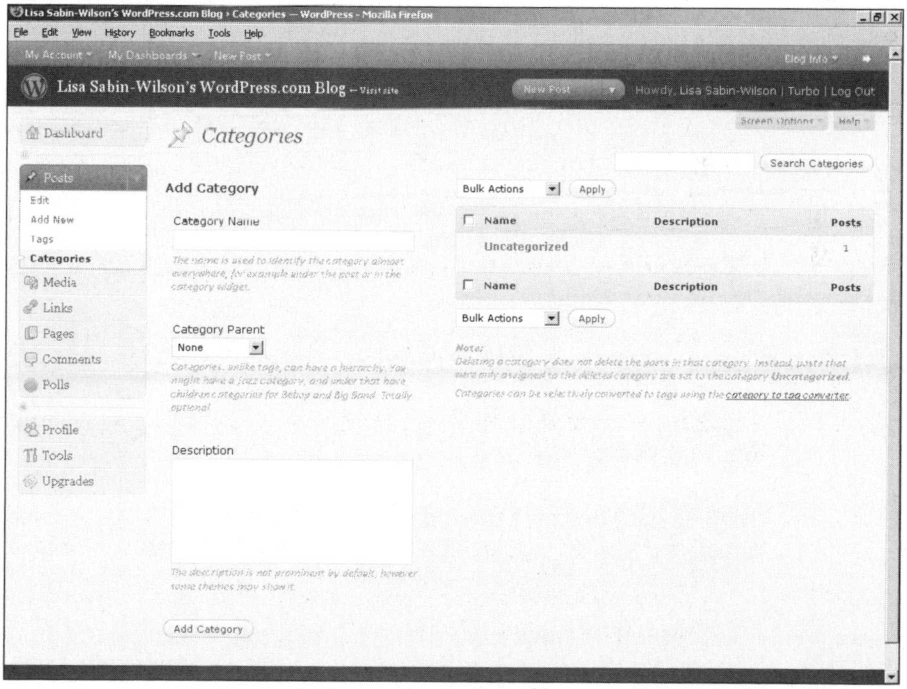

Figure 4-7:
The Categories page in the Administration panel.

Filing posts in categories and subcategories

The preceding section tells you how to create categories and subcategories. When you've created those categories and subcategories, you don't ever have to re-create them — they are always there for you to assign your blog posts to.

To assign existing posts to a category, follow these steps:

1. **Click the Edit link in the Posts menu.**

   The Edit Posts page appears, displaying a list of posts you've made.

2. **Click the name of the post you want to categorize.**

   The Edit Post page opens, displaying your post content and saved options.

3. **In the Categories section to the right of the Post text box, select the check box next to the category or subcategory (you can select more than one category and subcategory) that you want to assign to the post.**

   You can also use the Categories section before you publish a new post to assign it to the categories you'd like.

4. **Scroll up to the top of the Edit Post page, and click the Update Post button.**

   WordPress.com refreshes the Edit Post page, displaying the post you just edited; it reflects the changes you just made.

Creating and Categorizing Your Blogroll

A *blogroll* is a list of links that you display on your blog. In this section, I show you how to add and manage the links in your blogroll.

To view your default blogroll, click the Links menu. The Edit Links page opens and you see the default links that are already included in your WordPress.com blog. See Figure 4-8.

If you want to remove a link from your blogroll, select the box to the left of the link name; select Delete from the Bulk Actions drop-down menu at the top of the page, then click the Apply button (refer to Figure 4-8).

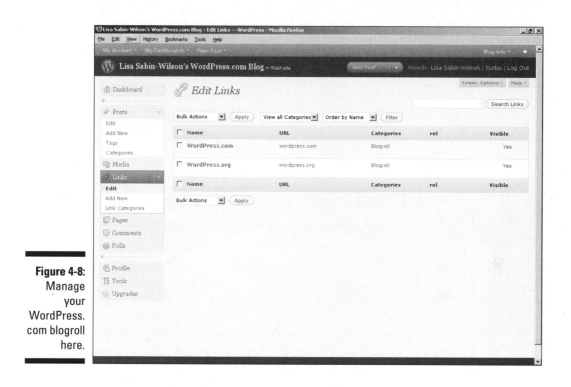

Figure 4-8:
Manage
your
WordPress.
com blogroll
here.

Creating link categories

WordPress.com lets you have an unlimited number of link categories on your blog. Link categories, much like the post categories discussed earlier in this chapter, provide you a way of separating your blogrolls (or list of links) into topical categories.

By default, WordPress.com sets up a link category for you called — by no coincidence — Blogroll. To add a new category, click the Link Categories link on the Links menu.

You add a new link category the same way you add new post categories (see the "Creating categories and subcategories" section, earlier in this chapter).

Adding new links to your blogroll

To add a new link to your blogroll, click the Links subtab and then click the Add New link. The Add New Link page opens, as shown in Figure 4-9.

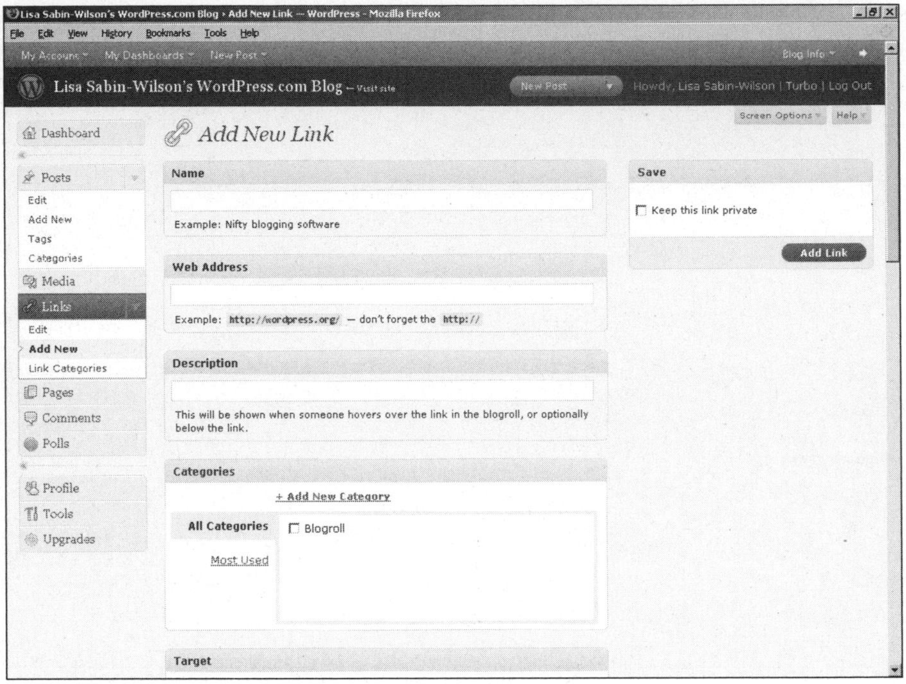

Figure 4-9:
Add a link to
your blogroll
by using
this tool
from Word
Press.com.

Follow these steps to add your new link:

1. **In the Name text box, type the name of the Web site you're adding.**

2. **In the Web Address text box, type the URL, making sure to include the** `http://` **part.**

3. **(Optional) In the Description text box, type a short description of the Web site.**

4. **In the Categories box, select the box to the left of the category you want this link to appear in.**

5. **(Optional) Select the target for your link in the Target box.**

   The target tells your browser how you want this link to load in your visitor's browser window after the visitor clicks it. You have three choices:

   • *_blank:* Loads the link in a new browser window.

   • *_top:* Loads the link in the top frame (if your site is designed with frames).

   • *None:* Loads the link in the same browser window (the default setting, should you choose to overlook the Target option).

The third option — None — is my personal preference and recommendation. I like to let my visitors decide whether they want a bunch of new browser windows to open every time they click a link on my site.

6. **(Optional) Select the Link Relationship (XFN) option, and define why you're providing this link.**

   XFN stands for XHTML Friends Network and allows you to indicate the relationship you have with the people you are linking to by defining how you know, or are associated with, them. Table 4-1 lists the different relationships you can assign to your links.

7. **(Optional) Select advanced options for your link in the Advanced box:**

   - *Image Address:* This option associates an image with the link, and some WordPress themes display the image on your site along with the link. Type the URL for the image in the Image Address box. For this purpose, you need to know the direct URL to the image (for example, `http://yourdomain.com/images/image.jpg`).

   - *RSS Address:* Type the RSS feed URL for the blog you are linking to. WordPress displays the link to the site's RSS feed alongside the link that appears on your site. Not all WordPress themes accommodate this feature.

   - *Notes:* Type your notes in the Notes box. These notes aren't displayed on your site, so feel free to leave whatever notes you need to further define the details of this link. A month from now, you may not remember who this person is or why you linked to her, so you can add notes to remind yourself.

   - *Rating:* Use the Rating drop-down menu to rate this link from 0 to 10, 0 being the worst and 10 being the best. Some WordPress themes display your blogroll in the order in which you've rated your links, from best to worst.

8. **Scroll to the top of the page, and click the Save button.**

   Your new link is saved, and a blank Add New Link page opens, ready for you to add another new link to your blogroll(s). Additionally, in the Save section at the top right, you can choose to keep this link private — this option, if checked, will not display the link publicly on your blog. It would be kept protected and for your eyes only.

Table 4-1	Link Relationships (XFN) Defined
Link Relationship	*Description*
Identity	Select this check box if the link is to a Web site you own.
Friendship	Select the option (Contact, Acquaintance, Friend, or None) that most closely identifies the relationship.

(continued)

Table 4-1 *(continued)*

Link Relationship	Description
Physical	Select this check box if you've met the person you're linking to face to face. Sharing pictures over the Internet doesn't count. This selection identifies a person you've physically met.
Professional	Select one of these check boxes if the person you're linking to is a co-worker or colleague.
Geographical	Select Co-Resident if the person you're linking to lives with you. Or select Neighbor or None, depending on which option applies to your relationship with the person you're linking to.
Family	If the blogger you're linking to is a family member, select the option that tells how the person is related to you.
Romantic	Select the option that applies to the type of romantic relationship you have with the person you're linking to. Do you have a crush on him? Is she your creative muse? Is he someone you consider to be a sweetheart? Select the option that most closely identifies the romantic relationship, if any.

You can find more information on XFN at `http://gmpg.org/xfn`.

Revisit the Manage Links page any time you want to add a new link, edit an old link, or delete an existing link. You can create an unlimited amount of blogroll categories to sort your blogrolls by topics. I know one blogger who has 50 categories for his links, so the options are limitless.

Managing and Inviting Users

What's a blog without blog users? Of course, your WordPress.com blog always has at least one user: you. To see your list of users, click the Users link that is in the navigation menu. The Users page opens and the Users menu expands to show three different links:

- Authors & Users
- Your Profile (See Chapter 3 for information on the Profile page.)
- Invites

Managing authors and users

The Users page tells you about all the users on your blog. It lists each user's username, name, e-mail address, role on your blog, and number of posts made to your blog. This page also has the Add User from Community section, where you can add a new user to your blog. (By *user,* WordPress means simply a person who is a member of your blog as a contributor, an author, an editor, or an administrator. You can have an unlimited amount of users on one WordPress.com blog.)

To manage user roles, you need to understand the distinct differences among the roles. The following list explains the type of access each role provides:

- ✔ **Contributor:** A Contributor can upload files and write/edit/manage her own posts. When a Contributor writes a post, however, that post is saved as a draft to await administrator approval; Contributors can't publish their posts. This feature is a nice way to moderate content written by new authors.

- ✔ **Author:** In addition to having the access and permissions of a Contributor, an Author can publish his own posts without administrator approval. Authors can also delete their own posts.

- ✔ **Editor:** In addition to having the access and permissions of an Author, an Editor can moderate comments, manage categories, manage links, edit pages, and edit other Authors' posts. Editors can also read and edit private posts.

- ✔ **Administrator:** An Administrator has the authority to change any of the Administration options and settings in the WordPress blog. You, as the account owner, are listed as an Administrator already. You can also assign other users as Administrators.

WordPress.com lets you have an unlimited amount of users and authors on one blog, which is a nice feature if running a multiauthor blog is something you'd like to do.

At the bottom of the Authors & Users page, in the Add User from Community section, you can add new users to your blog. Enter the person's e-mail address, assign a user role, and click the Add User button. The user you add must be a registered user in the WordPress.com system. If you enter someone who isn't registered, WordPress.com gives you the option to send that person an invitation to become a member. (The WordPress people have thought of everything, haven't they?)

To change a user's role, follow these steps:

1. **Find that person's username on the Users page.**

2. **Select the box next to the username.**

3. **From the Change Role To drop-down menu at the top the page, choose the role you want to assign; then click the Change button.**

    The Users page refreshes with the new role assignment applied.

To view all the posts made by an author, click the number that appears below the Posts column for that user.

Inviting friends to WordPress.com

Now that you've experienced the fun, ease, and excitement of having your very own WordPress.com blog, why not tell your friends, so that they can tell their friends, and their friends can tell their friends, and so on?

Click the Invites link on the Links menu, and you can do just that. Figure 4-10 shows the form that lets you invite people you know to sign up for WordPress.com accounts. You can also tell WordPress to add a user to your blogroll after she joins. Additionally, you can tell WordPress to add the new member to your own blog as a Contributor, if you want. (This option is especially helpful if you're setting up new users or authors for your own WordPress.com blog.)

Follow these instructions to invite as many people as you want to join WordPress.com:

1. **Click the Invites link on the Users menu.**

    The Invites page opens.

2. **In the appropriate text boxes, type the user's first name, last name, and e-mail address.**

3. **Type a personal message to the prospective member in the Personal Message text box, or use the default message WordPress.com provides.**

4. **(Optional) Select the Add to My Blogroll after Signup check box if you also want to add this person to your own WordPress.com blogroll.**

5. **(Optional) Select the Add User to My Blog as a Contributor check box if you want to add this user to your blog as a Contributor after he signs up.**

6. Click the Send Invite button to send the invitation to the prospective member via e-mail.

When you complete these steps, WordPress sends you confirmation that the invitation was sent.

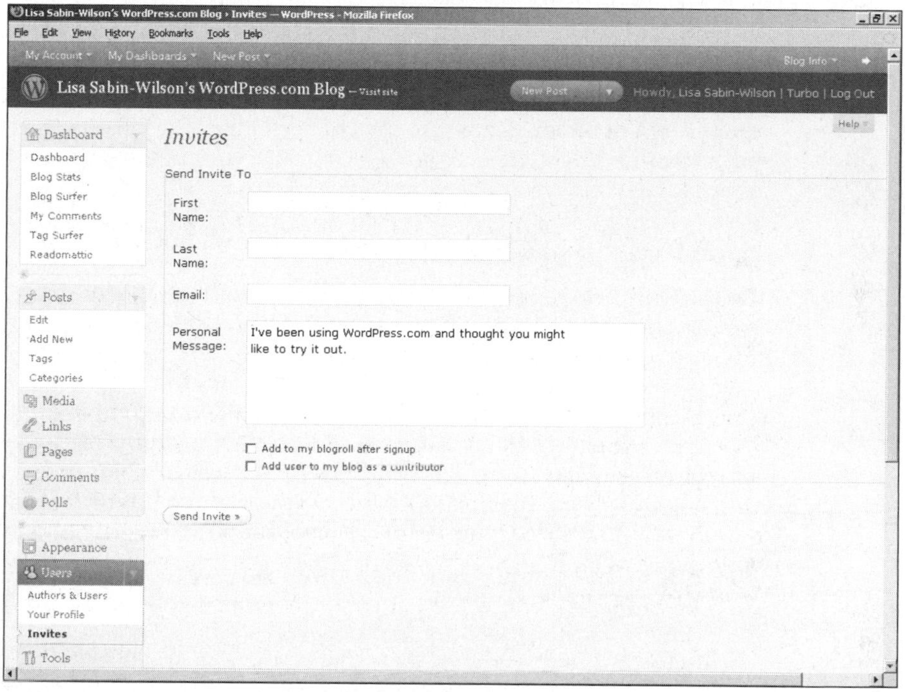

Figure 4-10:
WordPress.
com Invites
page.

Managing Comments and Comment Spam

As I describe in Chapter 2, comments provide a great way for readers to interact with you, and vice versa. Readers of your blog can post comments by using the comment form that appears on the same page as each of the published posts on your blog. You need to be able to exercise control over the comments that appear, however.

Setting discussion options for your blog

Click the Discussion link on the Settings menu. On the Discussion Settings page, you can set the options, such as notification settings, for your posts; determine how comments and comment spam are handled on your WordPress.com blog; and specify whether you want to use avatars on your blog. The Discussion Settings page has six settings you can configure for your blog, each of which I discuss in the following sections.

When you're done setting up your options, click the Save Changes button at the bottom of the page to make the changes take effect. You can revisit this page as often as you need to so you can keep your settings current and to your liking.

Default Article Settings

The Default Article Settings section is where you tell WordPress.com how to handle post notifications. Three options are available to you:

- **Attempt to Notify Any Blogs Linked to from the Article (Slows Down Posting):** Enabled by default, this option makes your blog send a notification, via a ping, to any site you've linked to in your blog post. This feature is very similar to a trackback (which I discuss in Chapter 2) and can slow the process of posting just a bit, because of the time it takes for your blog to talk to another blog to let it know that you're talking about it.

- **Allow Link Notifications from Other Blogs (Pingbacks and Trackbacks):** Enabled by default, this option tells WordPress that you want your blog to be notified via pings and trackbacks that other people have linked to you. WordPress lists any ping and trackback notifications on your site as comments in the Comments section. If you deselect this option, your ears may tingle, but you won't know when other people are talking about, or linking to, you on other blogs.

- **Allow People to Post Comments on the Article:** Enabled by default, this option lets people leave comments on your blog.

Other Comment Settings

The Other Comment Settings tell WordPress how to handle comments:

- **Comment Author Must Fill Out Name and E-Mail:** Enabled by default, this option requires the comment author to fill in the name and e-mail fields on your comment form in order to leave a comment on your blog.

- **Users Must Be Registered and Logged In to Comment:** With this selected, anyone who wants to leave a comment on your blog must be a registered user of your blog, and must be logged in before they can leave a comment. This option is deselected by default.

> ✔ **Automatically Close Comments on Articles Older Than *X* days**: This option helps decrease spam comments on older posts. You can select this option and then enter the number of days (for example: 30) in the text box provided.

E-Mail Me Whenever

The two options in the E-Mail Me Whenever section, Anyone Posts a Comment and A Comment Is Held for Moderation, are selected by default. This feature tells WordPress that you want to receive an e-mail any time anyone leaves a comment on your blog and/or any time a comment is awaiting your approval in the moderation queue. This feature can be very helpful, particularly if you don't visit your blog daily. Everyone likes to get comments on his blog posts, and it's good to be notified when it happens so that you can revisit that post, respond to your readers, and keep the conversation active. You can disable this feature, however, by deselecting these options.

Before a Comment Appears

The three options in the Before a Comment Appears section tell WordPress how you want WordPress to handle comments before they appear in your blog:

> ✔ **An Administrator Must Always Approve the Comment:** Selecting this option holds every new comment on your blog in the moderation queue until you log in and approve it. This feature is particularly helpful if you want to review the content of comments before they're published to your blog.

> ✔ **Comment Author Must Have a Previously Approved Comment:** When this box is selected, the only comments that are approved and published on your blog are those that have been left by commenters who have already been approved by you. Their e-mail addresses are stored in the database, and WordPress runs a check on their e-mails. If the e-mail address matches a previously approved comment, the new comment is published automatically. If no match occurs, WordPress places the comment in the moderation queue, awaiting your approval. This measure is yet another feature that helps prevent comment spam.

Comment Moderation

In the Comment Moderation section, you can set options to specify what types of comments are held in the moderation queue to await your approval. Frequently, comment spammers try to spam your blog with a *ton* of links in the hope of promoting their own sites through your comment form. You can set the number of links that are allowed in a comment before it is tossed into the moderation queue to await approval. The default is 2. Give that a try, and if you find that you're getting lots of spam comments with multiple links, you may want to revisit this page and increase that number.

The text box below the link setting is where you can set keywords, URLs, e-mail addresses, or IP addresses to be flagged for moderation. One popular topic that comment spammers like to spam with is Viagra; they fill their comments with links to sites where you can purchase Viagra. Really, if you wanted to know about those sites, wouldn't you seek them out? Well, that's beside the point. If you're getting a lot of Viagra spam, you can enter **Viagra** in the Comment Moderation list rather than in the Comment Blacklist list, because you might actually receive a legitimate comment with the word *Viagra* in it that you would like to approve. A visitor to my blog left a comment — "Espresso is Viagra for my brain!" — in response to a post I made about my love for espresso. That comment is legitimate but probably got thrown into my moderation queue because I have that term in my Comment Moderation list.

By default, WordPress.com automatically discards spam on older posts on your blog. You can switch this option off by checking the Don't Discard Spam on Old Posts box at the top of this section.

Comment Blacklist

In contrast to the Comment Moderation list, the Comment Blacklist is a list of words, URLs, e-mail addresses, and IP addresses that you want to flat-out ban from ever making it to your blog. Items placed here don't even make it into your Comment Moderation queue; they're filtered as spam by the system and completely disregarded. The words I have placed in my Blacklist are not family friendly and have no place in a nice book like this.

Are you getting the feeling that comment spam is a real issue for bloggers? It's huge — probably bigger than you imagine it to be. Much of the comment-spam prevention is done behind the scenes, so you don't even see half of what's going on. All the options on the Discussion Settings page are geared toward decreasing or eliminating comment or trackback spam from your blog. If, during the course of your blogging experience on WordPress.com, you find that you're having an issue with spam, you may want to revisit these options and make adjustments.

Avatars

Avatars are photos or images that represent your commenters (and you) on your blog. Figure 4-12, later in this chapter, shows a small avatar to the left of the comment. You can choose to display avatars on your blog by selecting the Show Avatars option. You can also set the maximum rating for the avatars, much like the movie rating system we're all used to. If your site is family friendly, you probably don't want to display R- or X-rated avatars on your site. You can select G, PG, R, or X ratings for the avatars that display on your site. You can also select an image to use as the default avatar for those users who do not yet have avatars assigned to their e-mail.

For WordPress.com users, the avatars displayed are the images they uploaded to their profiles (see Chapter 3). Users who are not registered with WordPress.com still have the option of having an avatar displayed when they comment on your blog by signing up for one at `http://gravatar.com`.

Viewing comments

You open the Edit Comments page by clicking the Comments menu. The Edit Comments page shows all the comments on your blog, from the very first day you started. Here, you can view the comments, edit them, mark them as spam, or flat-out delete them.

If you've set your Comments options so that comments aren't published until you approve them, you can approve comments in this section as well. To accomplish this task, of course, you have to have comments on your blog, and if your blog is new, you may not have any yet. Figure 4-11 shows what a comment looks like in this area.

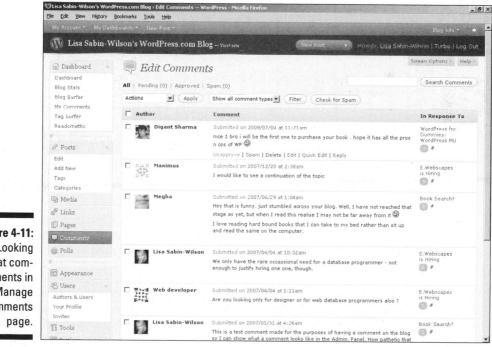

Figure 4-11: Looking at comments in the Manage Comments page.

To manage a comment, find one that you want to edit, delete, unapprove (or remove it from your blog page), or mark as spam. If you need to, you can find a specific comment by using the search feature. Just type a keyword in the search box located in the top-right corner of the page and click the Search Comments button.

When you've found the comment you want to manage, hover your mouse over the comment and six different links appear beneath the comment text, and include:

- **Approve or Unapprove:** If the comment has not yet been approved, the Approve link appears here. Click Approve to publish the comment to your blog. If the comment was approved, click the Unapprove link to . . . well, unapprove it. This link puts the comment back into the moderation queue.

- **Spam:** This link tells WordPress that this comment is spam and removes it from your blog.

- **Delete:** This link deletes the comment from your blog.

- **Edit:** Clicking this link takes you to the Edit Comment page where you can edit the text of the comment, if you need to (correcting typos anyone??)

- **Quick Edit**: This link accomplishes the same as the Edit link except instead of taking you to a new Edit Comment page, it drops down a quick edit text box that allows you to do a fast edit right on the same page.

- **Reply:** This link drops down a text box on the same page to allow you to reply to the comment right from the Edit Comments page.

Managing comment spam with Akismet

Comment spam, as I discuss in Chapter 2, is a sneaky method that spammers are fond of using to post links to their sites on yours. Akismet is the answer to combating comment and trackback spam; it kills spam dead. Created by the Automattic team, headed by Matt Mullenweg, Akismet is a "collaborative effort to make comment and trackback spam a non-issue and restore innocence to blogging, so you never have to worry about spam again," according to Akismet.com.

Click the Spam link on the Edit Comments page to view the comments and trackbacks that were caught by Akismet's spam filters. Akismet keeps the past two weeks' worth of comments and trackbacks that were stopped by its filters because the rare legitimate comment can get caught up in the spam filters. If that happens, you can visit this section and de-spam the comment by clicking the Not Spam button.

I usually don't have to visit the Akismet Spam page. My readers usually are pretty quick to let me know if they've left a comment that didn't get published. In such a case, I check the Akismet Spam page to see whether it was caught in the spam filters. Then I de-spam it and move on.

Creating a Static Page

You can create pages on your blog that are treated differently from posts. These pages, called *static pages,* appear as separate pages on your blog rather than posts within your blog. You use nearly the same process of writing a static page as you do to write a post. You can easily create an unlimited number of static pages, which can serve as nice complements to your overall site content.

You can use this feature to write, for example, an About Me page, on which you give all the wild and wooly details about yourself. (See Figure 4-12 for an example of an About page.) If you use the Page Sidebar widget, the pages you create are listed in your sidebar. (See Chapter 5 for more about widgets.)

Figure 4-12:
The author's
About page.

You can create these pages by logging into your WordPress.com Administration panel and following these steps:

1. **Click the Add New link in the Pages menu.**

   The Add New Page page appears where you can compose your static page.

2. **Type the title of your page in the Title text box.**

3. **Type the body of your page in the Page text box.**

   You can use the Virtual Text Editor and insert media files into your page by using the same techniques discussed in the "Ready? Set? Blog!" section, earlier in this chapter.

4. **Set the options for your page by using the option boxes below the Page text box.**

   To display these boxes, click the white arrow to the left of each option title. The following options appear:

   - *Discussion:* By default, the Allow Comments and Allow Pings boxes are selected. Deselect them if you don't want to allow comments or pings.

   - *Parent:* Choose the page parent from the drop-down menu if you want to make the static page a subpage of another page you've created.

   - *Template:* If the WordPress.com theme you're using has page templates available, choose from this drop-down menu the template you want to use for the page.

   - *Order:* Enter a number in the text box that reflects the order in which you want this page to display on your site. If you want this page to be the third page listed, for example, enter **3**.

   - *Page Author:* Choose the author of this blog from the drop-down menu. This step isn't necessary if you're the only author of this blog; if you have multiple authors, however, you may find this option helpful.

5. **Scroll back to the top of the page, and choose options from the Publish Status drop-down menu.**

   These options are the same as the Publish Status options that are available when you're writing a new blog page. I covered the available options in the "Ready? Set? Blog!" section earlier in this chapter.

6. **Click the Save or Publish button when you're done to save your work.**

Your static pages aren't included in your Recent Posts list, in categories, or in your monthly archive.

Setting Up Your Front Page

On the Reading Settings page (click the Reading link in the Settings menu), you can set how many blog posts show up on the front page of your blog and/or change your front page to display a static page rather than displaying your most recent blog posts. (See the "Creating a Static Page" section, earlier in this chapter, for more information on creating static pages.) You can also determine how many blog posts your readers can see in your RSS feed. Figure 4-13 shows the options that are available.

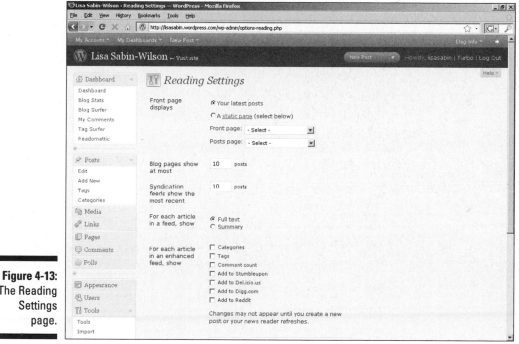

Figure 4-13: The Reading Settings page.

The Reading Settings page gives you control of the settings that let you make these decisions for your blog:

- **Front Page Displays:** This setting determines what appears on the front page of your site.

  - *Your Latest Posts:* Select this option if you want your blog posts to display on the front page of your blog.

  - *A Static Page:* Select this option if you want a static page to display on the front page of your blog.

- *Front Page:* If you choose to display a static page, choose from this drop-down menu which page to display.

- *Posts Page:* If you choose to display a static page, use this drop-down menu to tell WordPress which page to display your posts on.

✔ **Blog Pages Show at Most *X* Posts:** If you choose to display your blog posts on your front page, this step is where you set the number of blog posts to display per page. Figure 4-14, in the following section, shows that I've decided to display ten posts on my front page.

✔ **Syndication Feeds Show the Most Recent *X* Posts:** This setting determines how many posts show in your RSS feed at one time. See the next section for details.

✔ **For Each Article in a Feed, Show:** Indicate here which portion of each article you want to show in your feed:

- *Full Text:* Select this radio button if you want the entire text of each post to be displayed in your RSS feed.

- *Summary:* Select this radio button if you want only excerpts of your posts to be displayed in your RSS feed.

✔ **For Each Article in an Enhanced Feed, Show:** Here, you have the option of showing several more details about your blog, as well as giving the reader the opportunity to add your article to several social bookmark sites:

- Categories

- Tags

- Comment Count

- Add to Stumbleupon

- Add to Del.icio.us

- Add to Digg.com

- Add to Reddit

✔ **Encoding for Pages and Feeds**: UTF-8 is the default, and recommended, character encoding for your blog. *Character encoding* is code that handles the storage and transmission of the text from your blog through the Internet connection. Your safest bet is to leave the default in place, because it is the most commonly accepted character encoding and supports a wide range of languages.

When you change any settings in the Reading Settings page, make sure that you click the Save Changes button in the bottom-left corner to save your preferences.

Publishing a Public or Private Blog

This section contains one very simple option for you to set; this option lets you determine how you want to deal with publicity on your blog. Figure 4-14 shows your choices. To access the privacy options for your blog, click the Privacy link on the Settings menu. You can choose one of these three options in the Privacy Settings page:

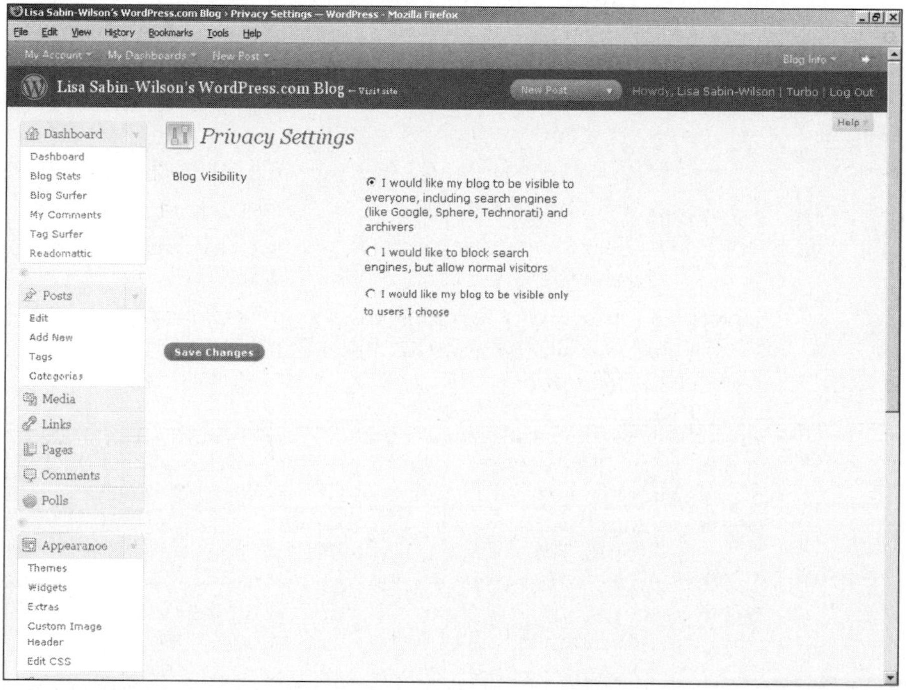

Figure 4-14: Blog Visibility options in the Privacy Settings page.

✔ **I Would Like My Blog to Be Visible to Everyone, Including Search Engines (Like Google, Sphere, Technorati) and Archivers:** Select this option if you want to freely allow search engines to visit your blog and include its content in their search directories.

✔ **I Would Like to Block Search Engines, but Allow Normal Visitors:** Select this option if you don't want search engines to visit and include your site in their directories. This option is helpful if you want normal (read: human) visitors but don't want the publicity that search engines provide.

> ✓ **I Would Like My Blog to Be Visible Only to Users I Choose:** Select this option if you want to make your blog available only to the people you choose. This option keeps your blog completely private and away from prying eyes — except for those users you allow.
>
> When you select and save this option, WordPress.com provides a form where you can enter the WordPress.com usernames for the people you want to invite to view your private blog. (WordPress.com lets you add up to 35 users at no cost; you can pay an annual fee to add more.)

When you finish making your decision, be sure to click the Save Changes button to make the changes take effect.

Establishing Trust Relationships with OpenID

OpenID is a third-party, Internet-community identification system that lets an Internet user create an online identity that she can use anywhere on the Web where OpenID is supported. With WordPress.com, you already have an OpenID identity.

In the WordPress Administration panel, click the OpenID link on the Settings menu to see the OpenID Trusted Sites page, which tells you what your OpenID is. (It's usually your main WordPress.com domain: `http://user name.wordpress.com`.) You can also add the URLs of what you consider to be trusted sites. After you enter the URL of a trusted site and click the Add to List button, you aren't asked whether you trust the site when you attempt to log in to it. In a nutshell, this setting means that you can use your WordPress.com OpenID to log in to any Web site that supports OpenID.

Chapter 5

Enhancing Your Blog with Themes, Widgets, and Upgrades

You don't want your blog to look identical to everyone else's, do you? Although WordPress.com doesn't give you the vast array of design options that you'd have by hosting your own blog, you do have some flexibility.

The great thing about the WordPress hosted service is how easily you can change your theme to one of the alternative designs available. What's not so hot is that you can't create your own custom theme. As noted later in this chapter, you can pay a fee to customize the CSS of the template you've chosen to use, but you need to be familiar with CSS to use this upgrade — and there again, you're limited to customizing only the templates that WordPress provides.

In this chapter, you discover the WordPress.com themes that let you choose a design and format for your blog. You have some fabulous themes to choose among, all created by WordPress users. At this writing, 77 themes are available. You also explore the fun of using sidebar widgets to rearrange how your blogroll, category and monthly archive lists, and page lists are displayed.

This chapter also discusses enhancing your blog with custom CSS (Cascading Style Sheets), choosing a domain name, and increasing the amount of hard drive space on your WordPress.com account through its upgrade feature (for a fee).

Changing Your Blog's Look

It's time to choose a theme for your WordPress.com blog. In this case, the word *theme* is synonymous with the words *design* and *template*. All three words describe the very same things: the visual layout and appearance of your blog.

Follow these steps to find your theme:

1. **In your Administration panel, click the Themes link on the Appearance menu.**

   A page full of themes appears (as shown in Figure 5-1), along with a thumbnail image of the theme so that you can get a basic idea of what it looks like.

2. **Scroll through the themes, and when you find a theme you like, click its name or the thumbnail image associated with it.**

   You can page through the list of available themes by using the handy buttons at the top-right and bottom-right corners of the Available Themes section. Or you can use the drop-down menu in the top-left corner of the Available Themes section to filter your theme choices by color, columns, width, and option (refer to Figure 5-1).

   What happens next is pretty nifty! A box pops up, showing you a preview of what your own blog would look like with that particular theme.

3. **Click the Activate link in the top-right corner to activate the theme on your own blog, or click the X in the top-left corner if you decide you'd rather not use that theme.**

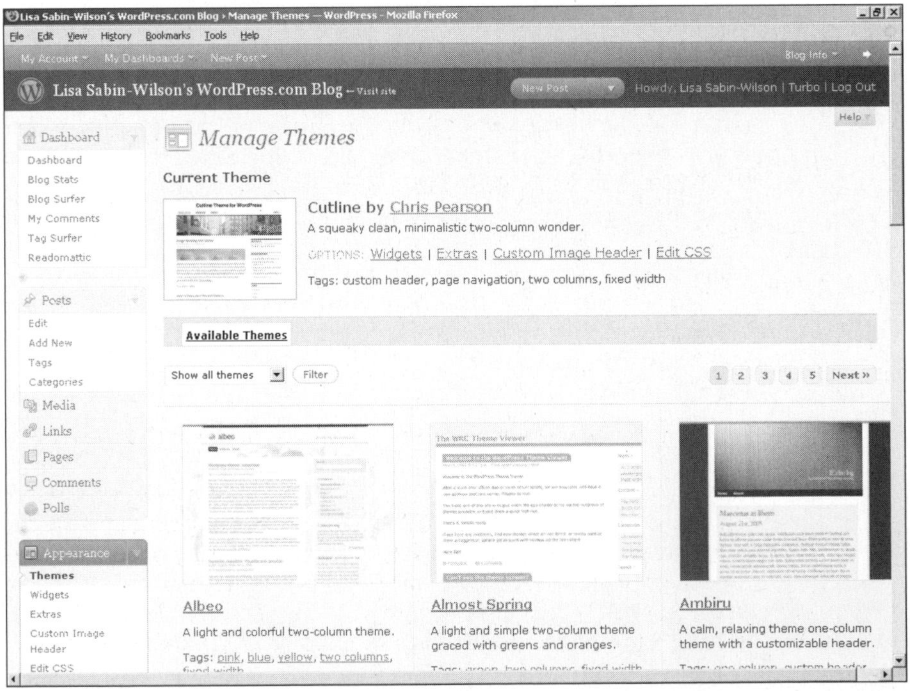

Figure 5-1:
Choose a look for your blog.

No, really — it's just that easy. If you get tired of that theme, go to the Design tab and click a different theme name, and you're done.

It really is that easy!

Widget Wonder: Adding Handy Tools to Your Sidebar

WordPress widgets are very helpful tools built into the WordPress.com application. They allow you to easily arrange the display of content in your blog sidebar, such as your blogroll(s), recent posts, and monthly and category archive lists. With widgets, arrange and display the content in the sidebar of your blog without having to know a single bit of PHP or HTML.

Selecting and activating widgets

Click the Widgets link on the Appearance menu in your Administration panel. The Widgets page displays the available widgets, as shown in Figure 5-2. This feature is a big draw because it lets you control what features you use and where you place them — all without having to know a lick of code.

On the left side of the Widgets page is a listing of all widgets available for your WordPress.com blog.

On the right side of the Widgets page are the widgets you're using in your sidebar. Figure 5-2 shows that I am using the following widgets in my sidebar:

✔ Recent Posts

✔ Categories

✔ Archives

The Widgets page also includes a drop-down menu in the Current Widgets section (refer to Figure 5-2). If you're using a theme that has only one sidebar, the Widgets page has only one sidebar for you to configure. If you are using a theme with two sidebars (usually called a three-column layout), use the drop-down menu to toggle between Sidebar 1 and Sidebar 2. When you want to configure widgets for Sidebar 1, be sure that Sidebar 1 is selected in the drop-down menu; when you want to configure widgets for the second sidebar, choose Sidebar 2. Click the Show button to load the widgets for that sidebar on your screen.

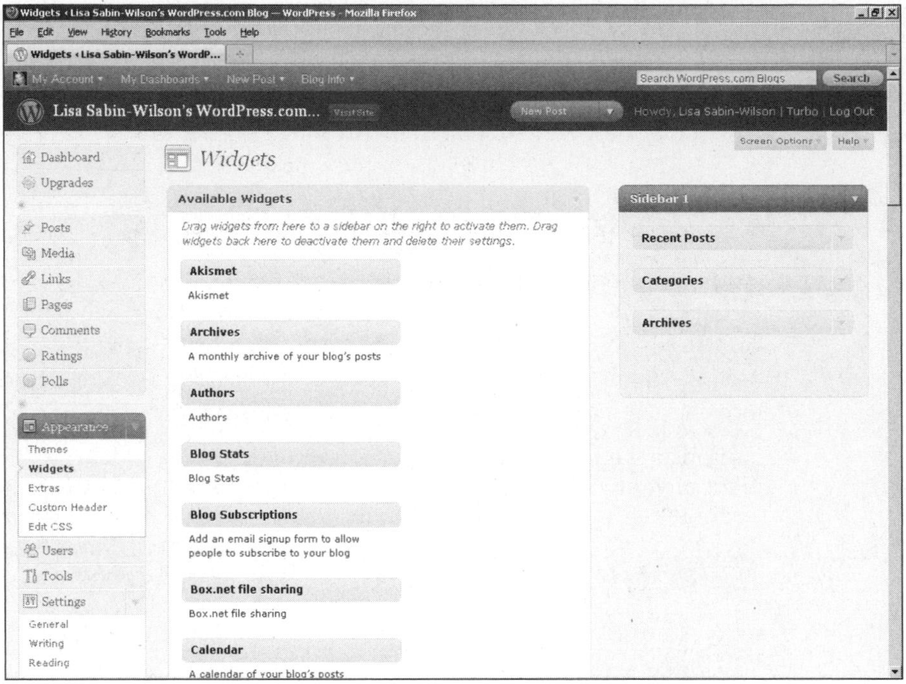

Figure 5-2:
WordPress.
com
Widgets
page.

To add a new widget to your sidebar, follow these steps:

1. **Choose the widget you want to use.**

   You find all the widgets are listed in the Available Widgets section. For the purpose of these steps, choose the Archives widget.

2. **Click on the widget menu bar.**

   While holding your mouse button down on the widget menu bar, drag it over to the Sidebar section on the right side of the page, then release the mouse button. This action drops the widget into your sidebar and the content of the widget now appears on your site in the sidebar.

3. **Click the arrow you see to the right of the widget title.**

   Clicking the arrow drops down the options menu for that widget.

   Each widget has different options that you can configure. The Archives widget, for example, lets you configure the title, the display of the post counts, and the display of the archives (see Figure 5-3).

4. **Select your options and click the Save button.**

   This saves the options you've set. Now, click the Close link to close the widget options menu.

5. **Arrange your widgets in the order in which you want them to appear on your site by clicking a widget and dragging it above or below another widget.**

   Repeat this step until your widgets are arranged the way you want them.

To remove a widget from your sidebar, click the arrow to the right of the widget title to open the options menu and then click the Delete link. WordPress removes the widget from the Current Widgets list on the right side of this page and places it back in the Available Widgets list.

After you've selected and configured all your widgets, click the Visit Site button at the top of your WordPress Administration panel (you'll see it to the right of your site name), and your blog's sidebar matches the content (and order of the content) you've arranged in the sidebar on the Widgets page. How cool is that? You can go back to the Widgets page and rearrange the items, as well as add and remove items, to your heart's content.

Figure 5-3: Configuring widget options.

Using Text widgets

The Text widget in WordPress.com is a little bit different from the rest of the widgets you encounter on the Widgets page. Add the Text widget just as you would any other, using the steps I outline in the preceding section. After you have it settled in the sidebar, click the arrow to the right of the widget title. A text box drops down to let you type text or insert code (see Figure 5-4).

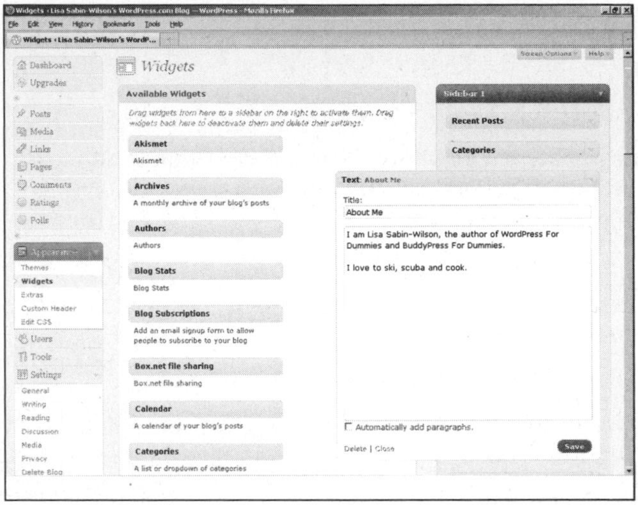

Figure 5-4:
Text widget
text box.

You have no real options to configure, but you can use this simple text box for several things. Here are a couple of examples of what you can use a Text widget for:

- Type a short paragraph of text, such as a bio.
- Insert the HTML code to display an image in your sidebar. (See Chapter 13 for some information on basic HTML codes you can use.)

Using the RSS widget

The RSS widget lets you display content from another blog in your sidebar. If I wanted to display a list of recent posts from another blog that I have somewhere else, for example, I would use the RSS widget to accomplish this task. Follow these steps to add the RSS widget to your blog:

1. **Add the RSS widget to your sidebar on the Widgets page.**

   Follow the steps in the "Selecting and activating widgets" section, earlier in this chapter, to add the widget.

2. **Click the Edit link to the right of the RSS widget's name.**

   A box drops down, displaying the different options you can configure for the RSS widget.

3. **In the Enter the RSS URL Here text box, type the RSS URL of the blog you want to add.**

   You can usually find the RSS Feed URL of a blog listed in the sidebar.

4. **Type the title of the RSS widget.**

This title is what will appear in your blog above the links from this blog. If I wanted to add the RSS feed from my personal blog, for example, I would type **Lisa Sabin-Wilson's blog**.

5. **(Optional) Select the Display the Item Content box.**

   Checking this box tells WordPress that you also want to display the content of the feed (usually, the content of the blog post from the feed URL). If you want to display only the title, leave the box unchecked.

6. **(Optional) Select the Display Item Author, If Available box.**

   Select this option if you want to display the author's name along with the item's title.

7. **(Optional) Select the Display Item Date box.**

   Select this option if you want to display the date the item was published, along with the item title.

8. **Click the Save Changes button.**

   WordPress saves all the options you've just set and reloads the Widgets page with your RSS widget intact.

Figure 5-5 shows my WordPress.com blog displaying the content from my personal blog in the sidebar. I used the RSS widget to make this happen!

Figure 5-5:
Content
from
another blog
shown in
my sidebar
via the RSS
widget.

Upgrading Your Hosted Service (For a Fee)

Although WordPress.com is a free service, it offers enhancements for a fee. WordPress.com calls these items *upgrades*, and you can purchase credits for them at the cost of $1 (USD) per credit. (The prices I give here are current as of this book's printing, but they are, of course, subject to change.) Click the Upgrades link in the Upgrades menu to display the Upgrades page, shown in Figure 5-6.

Following is a list of the current upgrades you can purchase to enhance your WordPress.com account, with the prices reflecting the annual cost:

- ✔ **Add a Domain:** This upgrade allows you to add your own domain name to your WordPress.com account; see the Naming Your Domain section later in this chapter. This service costs $5 for the domain registration and $9.97 for the domain mapping.

- ✔ **VideoPress:** This upgrade equips you with the ability to upload, store, and share your videos from your WordPress.com account. This service covers the storage space that your video files take up on the WordPress.com servers and costs $59.97 per year.

- ✔ **Custom CSS:** This upgrade lets you customize the Cascading Style Sheets (CSS) for the theme you're currently using in the WordPress.com system. Recommended for users who understand the use of CSS, this upgrade currently costs $14.97 per year.

- ✔ **Unlimited Private Users:** With a free account, you're limited to 35 private users — if you choose to publish your WordPress.com blog as a private blog — giving access to only those users whom you authorize. This upgrade removes that limit, letting you have unlimited private users for your blog (provided that those users are already WordPress.com account holders). The cost is $29.97 per year.

- ✔ **Additional Space:** With the free WordPress.com blog, you have 3GB of hard drive space for use in your upload directory. The various space upgrades add more, letting you upload more files (images, videos, audio files, and so on). Currently, you can add 5GB for $19.97, 15GB for $49.97, or 25GB for $89.97 annually.

- ✔ **No Ads:** For the cost of $29.97 per year, you can ensure that your WordPress.com blog is ad-free. Occasionally, WordPress.com does serve ads on your blog pages to try and defray the costs of running a popular service. If you'd rather not have those ads appearing on your blog, pay for the No Ads upgrade and you'll be ad-free!

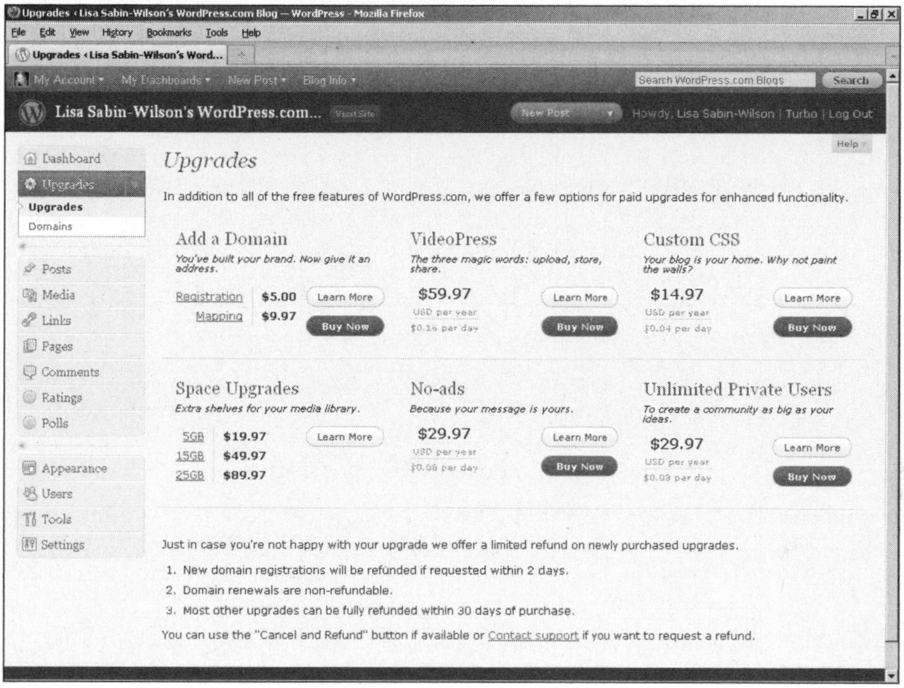

Figure 5-6:
The
WordPress.
com
Upgrades
page.

Naming Your Domain

The URL for your WordPress.com blog is `http://username.wordpress.com`, with *username* being your username. My username is `designs`; therefore, my WordPress.com domain is `http://designs.wordpress.com`.

WordPress.com lets you use your own domain name for your WordPress.com blog. Using the Domains feature in WordPress.com is not free, however. At this writing, this feature costs $5 for the domain registration and $9.97 for the domain mapping.

When you have your domain registered, go to your WordPress.com Administration panel, click the Domains link on the Upgrades menu, click the Domains tab, and type your domain name in the Add a Domain text box (see Figure 5-7). Then follow the prompts to fully set up your domain name.

Figure 5-7:
Use your own domain in WordPress. com by upgrad- ing on the Domains page.

When you've configured your domain name correctly, your old WordPress. com URL redirects to your new domain name. If my domain name is LisaSabin-Wilson.com, my WordPress.com blog at `http://designs.wordpress.com` redirects to `http://lisasabin-wilson.com`.

Part III
Self-Hosting with WordPress.org

The 5th Wave   By Rich Tennant

"He should be all right now. I made him spend two-
and-a-half hours reading prisoner blogs on the
state penitentiary Web site."

In this part . . .

In this part, you dig into the guts of WordPress.org. I tell you how to get your own domain name and Web host and take you through the installation procedure and features of the Administration panel that you'll want to know about when getting started.

Chapter 6

Setting Up Blogging Base Camp

• •

• •

*B*efore you can start blogging with WordPress.org, you have to set up your base camp. Doing so involves more than simply downloading and installing the WordPress software. You also need to establish your *domain* (your blog address) and your *Web hosting service* (the place that houses your blog). Although you initially download your WordPress software onto your hard drive, your Web host is where you install it.

Obtaining a Web server and installing software on it are much more involved projects than simply obtaining an account with the hosted version of WordPress that's available at WordPress.com (covered in Part II). You have to consider many factors in this undertaking, as well as cope with a learning curve, because setting up your blog through a hosting service involves using some technologies that you may not feel comfortable with at first. This chapter takes you through the basics of those technologies, and by the last page of this chapter, you'll have WordPress successfully installed on a Web server with your own domain name.

Establishing Your Domain

You've read all the hype. You've heard all the rumors. You've seen the flashy blogs on the Web powered by WordPress. But where do you start?

The first steps toward installing and setting up a WordPress blog are making a decision about a domain name and then purchasing the registration of that name through a domain registrar. A *domain name* is the *unique* Web address that you type in a Web browser's address bar to visit a Web site. Some examples of domain names are WordPress.org and Google.com.

Domain names: Do you own or rent?

In reality, when you "buy" a domain name, you don't really own it. Rather, you're purchasing the right to use that domain name for the period of time specified in your order. You can register a domain name for one year or up to ten years. Be aware, however, if you don't renew the domain name when your registration period ends, you lose it — and most often, you lose it right away to someone who preys on abandoned or expired domain names. Some people keep a close watch on expiring domain names, and as soon as the buying window opens, they snap the names up and start using them for their own Web sites, in the hope of taking full advantage of the popularity that the previous owners worked so hard to attain for those domains.

I emphasize the word *unique* because no two domain names can be the same. If someone else has registered the domain name you want, you can't have it. With that in mind, it sometimes takes a bit of time to find a domain that isn't already in use and is available for you to use. You have alternatives, of course. You could contact the owner of the domain name you want and find out whether it's for sale and how much the owner will sell it for. With this approach, however, chances are that you'll pay *way* more for the domain name than if you'd purchased an available domain name through a domain registrar.

Understanding domain name extensions

When registering a domain name, be aware of the *extension* that you want. The `.com`, `.net`, `.org`, `.info`, or `.biz` extension that you see tagged onto the end of any domain name is the *top-level domain extension*. When you register your domain name, you're asked to choose the extension you want for your domain (as long as it's available, that is).

A word to the wise here: Just because you have registered your domain as a `.com` doesn't mean that someone else doesn't, or can't, own the very same domain name with a `.net`. So if you register MyDogHasFleas.com, and it becomes a hugely popular site among readers with dogs that have fleas, someone else can come along and register MyDogHasFleas.net, and run a similar site to yours in the hope of riding the coattails of your Web site's popularity and readership.

You can register your domain name with all available extensions if you want to avert this problem. My business Web site, for example, has the domain name EWebscapes.com; however, I also own EWebscapes.net, EWebscapes.biz, and EWebscapes.info.

Considering the cost of a domain name

Registering a domain costs you anywhere from $3 to $30 per year, depending on what service you use for a registrar and what options (such as privacy options and search-engine submission services) you apply to your domain name during the registration process.

When you pay the domain registration fee today, you need to pay another registration fee when the renewal date comes up again in a year, or two, or five — however many years you chose to register your domain name for. (See the "Domain names: Do you own or rent?" sidebar.) Most registrars give you the option of signing up for a service called Auto Renew. This service automatically renews your domain name and bills the charges to the credit card you have set up on that account. The registrar sends you a reminder a few months in advance, telling you it's time to renew. If you do not have Auto Renew set up, you need to log in to your registrar account before it expires and manually renew your domain name.

Registering your domain name

Domain registrars are certified and approved by the Internet Corporation for Assigned Names and Numbers (ICANN). Although hundreds of domain registrars exist today, the ones in the following list are popular because of their longevity in the industry, competitive pricing, and variety of services they offer in addition to domain name registration (such as Web hosting and Web site traffic builders):

- **GoDaddy:** `http://GoDaddy.com`
- **Register.com:** `http://register.com`
- **Network Solutions:** `http://networksolutions.com`
- **NamesDirect:** `http://namesdirect.com`

No matter where you choose to register your domain name, here are the steps you can take to accomplish this task:

1. **Decide on a domain name.**

   Doing a little planning and forethought here is necessary. Many people think of a domain name as a *brand* — a way of identifying their Web sites or blogs. Think of potential names for your site; then you can proceed with your plan.

2. **Verify the domain name's availability.**

In your Web browser, enter the URL of the domain registrar of your choice. Look for the section on the registrar's Web site that lets you enter the domain name (typically, a short text field) to see whether it's available. If the domain name isn't available as a .com, try .net or .info.

3. **Purchase the domain name.**

Follow the domain registrar's steps to purchase the name using your credit card. After you complete the checkout process, you receive an e-mail confirming your purchase, so be sure to use a valid e-mail address during the registration process.

The next step is obtaining a hosting account, which I cover in the next section.

Some of the domain registrars have hosting services that you can sign up for, but you don't have to use those services. Often, you can find hosting services for a lower cost than most domain registrars offer. It just takes a little research.

Finding a Home for Your Blog

When you have your domain registered, you need to find a place for it to live — a Web host. Web hosting is the second piece of the puzzle that you need to complete before you begin working with WordPress.org.

A *Web host* is a business, group, or individual that provides Web server space and bandwidth for file transfer to Web site owners who don't have it. Usually, Web hosting services charge a monthly or annual fee — unless you're fortunate enough to know someone who's willing to give you server space and bandwidth for free. The cost varies from host to host, but you can obtain quality Web hosting services for $3 to $10 per month to start.

Web hosts consider WordPress to be a *third-party application*. What this means to you is that the host typically won't provide technical support on the use of WordPress (or any other software application), because support isn't included in your hosting package. Although most Web hosts attempt to assist you with the use of the software, ultimately, the responsibility for running it on your server account is all yours. This condition is one of the big reasons that some folks opt to run a WordPress-powered blog on the hosted version at WordPress.com. If you've chosen to go the self-hosted route with the WordPress.org software, you can find help and support on the use of WordPress in the WordPress support forums located at http://word press.org/support/.

Several Web hosting providers also have WordPress-related services available for additional fees. These services can include technical support, plugin installation and configuration, and theme design services.

Hosting services generally provide (at least) these services with your account:

- ✔ Hard drive space
- ✔ Bandwidth (transfer)
- ✔ Domain e-mail with Web mail access
- ✔ File Transfer Protocol (FTP) access
- ✔ Comprehensive Web site statistics
- ✔ MySQL database(s)
- ✔ PHP

Because you intend to run WordPress on your Web server, you need to look for a host that provides the minimum requirements needed to run the software on your hosting account, which are

- ✔ PHP version 4.3 (or greater)
- ✔ MySQL version 4.0 (or greater)

The easiest way to find out whether a host meets the minimum requirement is to check the FAQ (Frequently Asked Questions) section of the host's Web site, if it has one. If not, find the contact information for the hosting company, and fire off an e-mail requesting information on exactly what it supports. Any Web host worth dealing with will answer your e-mail within a reasonable amount of time (12–24 hours is a good barometer).

Getting help with hosting WordPress

The popularity of WordPress has given birth to services on the Web that emphasize the use of the software. These services include WordPress designers, WordPress consultants, and — yes — Web hosts that specialize in using WordPress.

Many of these hosts offer a full array of WordPress features, such as an automatic WordPress installation included with your account, a library of WordPress themes, and a staff of support technicians who're very experienced in using WordPress.

Here is a list of some of those providers:

- ✔ **Blogs About Hosting:** `http://blogs-about.com`
- ✔ **Laughing Squid:** `http://laughingsquid.net`
- ✔ **AN Hosting:** `http://anhosting.com`
- ✔ **DreamHost:** `http://dreamhost.com`

A word about Web hosts and domain registration: A few Web hosting providers offer free domain name registration when you sign up for their hosting services. Research this topic and dig through those hosting providers' terms of service, because that free domain name sometimes comes with a few conditions.

Many of my clients have gone this route, only to find out a few months later — when they're unhappy with the unreliable hosting service and would like to change to another host — that the Web hosting provider has full control of the domain name, and they aren't allowed to move that domain off the host's servers, either for a set period (usually, a year or two) or for infinity. I feel that it's always best to have the control in *your* hands, not someone else's, so I recommend registering your domain name yourself with an independent domain registrar, such as GoDaddy.

Dealing with disk space and bandwidth

Web hosting services provide two very important things with your account:

- ✔ Disk space
- ✔ Bandwidth transfer

Think of your Web host as a garage that you pay to park your car in. The garage gives you the place to store your car (disk space). It even gives you the driveway so that you, and others, can get to and from your car (bandwidth). It won't, however, fix your rockin' stereo system (WordPress or any other third-party software application) that you've installed — unless you're willing to pay a few extra bucks for that service.

Managing disk space

Disk space is nothing more complicated than the hard drive on your own computer. Each hard drive has the capacity, or space, for a certain amount of files. An 80GB (gigabyte) hard drive can hold 80GB of data — no more. Your hosting account provides you a limited amount of disk space, and the same concept applies. If your Web host provides you 10GB of disk space, that's the limit on the file size that you're allowed to have. If you want more disk space, you need to upgrade your space limitations. Most Web hosts have a mechanism in place for you to upgrade your allotment.

Starting out with a self-hosted WordPress blog doesn't take much disk space at all. A good starting point for disk space is between 3–5GB of storage space. If you find that you need additional space in the future, contact your hosting provider for an upgrade in space.

Time for a public-service announcement: A good Web host has a system in place that sends you a warning (via e-mail) when you reach at least 80 percent of your total disk space capacity. This warning helps you manage the space in your hosting account. With this warning, you can plan on either doing some account maintenance of your own and clearing out some unnecessary files that may be taking up space, or getting in contact with your Web host to upgrade your account.

Choosing the size of your bandwidth pipe

Bandwidth refers to the amount of data that is carried from point A to point B within a specific period (usually, only a second or two). I live out in the country — pretty much the middle of nowhere. The water that comes to my house is provided by a private well that lies buried in the backyard somewhere. Between my house and the well are pipes that bring the water to my house. The pipes provide a free flow of water to our home so that everyone can enjoy their long, hot showers while I labor over dishes and laundry, all at the same time. Lucky me!

The very same concept applies to the bandwidth available with your hosting account. Every Web hosting provider offers a variety of bandwidth limits on the accounts it offers. When I want to view your Web site in my browser window, the bandwidth is essentially the pipe that lets your data flow from your "well" to my computer and appear on my monitor. The bandwidth limit is kind of like the pipe connected to my well: It can hold only a certain amount of water before it reaches maximum capacity and won't bring the water from the well any longer. Your bandwidth pipe size is determined by how much bandwidth your Web host allows for your account — the larger the number, the bigger the pipe. A 50MB bandwidth limit makes for a smaller pipe than does a 100MB limit.

Web hosts are pretty generous with the amount of bandwidth they provide in their packages. Like disk space, bandwidth is measured in gigabytes (GB). Bandwidth provision of 10–50GB is generally a respectable amount to run a Web site with a blog.

Web sites that run large files — such as video, audio, or photo files — generally benefit from higher disk space compared with sites that don't involve large files. Keep this point in mind when you're signing up for your hosting account. Planning now will save you a few headaches down the road.

Transferring Files from Point A to Point B

This section introduces you to the basic elements of File Transfer Protocol (FTP). The ability to use FTP with your hosting account is a given for almost every Web host on the market today. FTP is the method you use to move files from one place to another — for example, from your computer to your Web hosting account. This method is referred to as *uploading*.

Using FTP to transfer files requires an FTP client. Many FTP clients are available for download. Following are some good (and free) ones:

- **WS_FTP:** www.ipswitch.com/_download/wsftphome.asp
- **SmartFTP:** www.smartftp.com/download
- **FileZilla:** http://sourceforge.net/projects/filezilla
- **FTP Explorer:** www.ftpx.com

Earlier in this chapter, in "Finding a Home for Your Blog," you find out how to obtain a Web hosting account. Your Web host gives you a username and password for your account, including an FTP IP address. (Usually, the FTP address is the same as your domain name, but check with your Web host, as addresses may vary.) It is this information — the username, password, and FTP IP address — that you insert into the FTP program to connect it to your hosting account.

Figure 6-1 shows my FTP client connected to my hosting account. The directory on the left is the listing of files on my computer; the directory on the right shows the listing of files on my hosting account.

FTP clients make it easy to transfer files from your computer to your hosting account by using a drag-and-drop method. You simply click the file on your computer that you want to transfer, drag it over to the side that lists the directory on your hosting account, and drop it. Depending on the FTP client you've chosen to work with, you can refer to its user manuals or support documentation for detailed information on how to use the program.

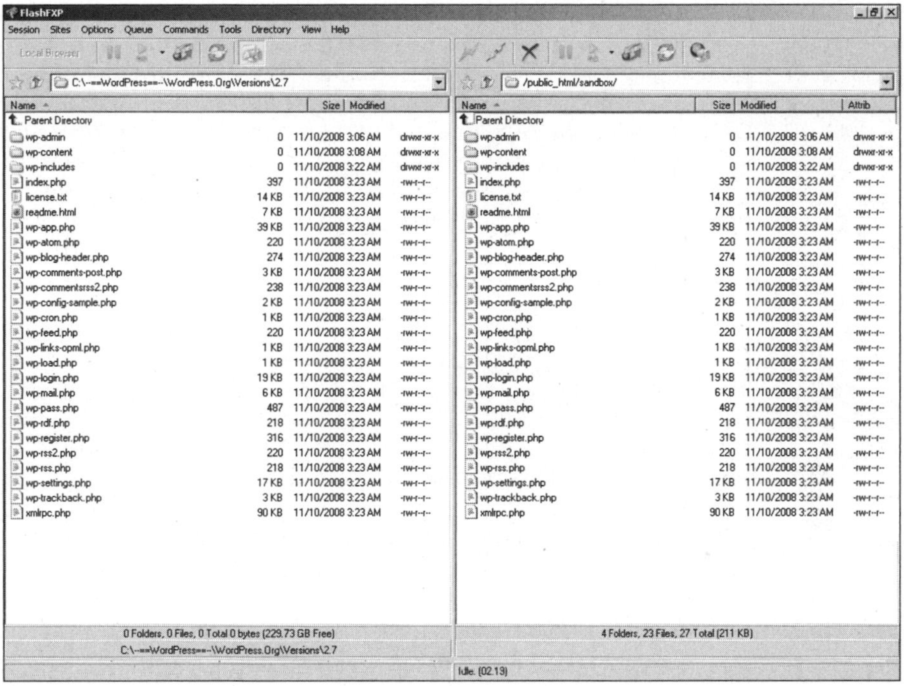

Figure 6-1:
Using an
FTP client
makes file
transfers
easy.

Installing WordPress

By the time you're finally ready to install WordPress.org, you should have done the following things:

- ✔ Purchased the domain name registration for your account
- ✔ Obtained a hosting service on a Web server for your blog
- ✔ Established your hosting account username, password, and FTP address
- ✔ Acquired an FTP client for transferring files to your hosting account

If you've missed any of the items listed, you can go back to the beginning of this chapter to reread the portions you need.

Some Web hosts now offer a one-click installation process for WordPress. If this is the case for you, you can simply follow the instructions provided by your Web host. The instructions in this section are for those of you who are doing a manual install of WordPress on your Web server.

If you have to install WordPress manually, here's where the rubber meets the road — that is, you're putting WordPress's famous five-minute installation to the test. Set your watch, and see whether you can meet that five-minute mark.

The famous five-minute installation includes the time it takes to install the software only. It does not include the time to register a domain name; the time to obtain and set up your Web hosting service; or the time to download, install, configure, and learn how to use the FTP software.

Without further ado, go get the latest version of the WordPress software here: `http://wordpress.org/download`.

WordPress gives you two compression formats for the software: `zip` and `tar.gz`. I recommend getting the zip file, as it's the most common format for compressed files.

Download the WordPress software to your computer, and decompress (or unpack, or unzip) it to a folder on your computer's hard drive. These steps are the first in the installation process for WordPress. Having the program on your own computer isn't enough, however; you also need to *upload* (transfer) it to your Web server account (the one you obtained in "Finding a Home for Your Blog," earlier in this chapter). Before installing WordPress on your Web server, you need to make sure that you have a MySQL database all set up and ready to accept the WordPress installation. The next section tells you what you need to know about MySQL.

Setting up the MySQL database

The WordPress software is a personal publishing system that uses a PHP-and-MySQL platform, which provides everything you need to create your own blog and publish your own content dynamically without having to know how to program those pages yourself. In short, all your content (options, posts, comments, and other pertinent data) is stored in a MySQL database in your hosting account.

Every time visitors go to your blog to read your content, they make a request that's sent to your server. The PHP programming language receives that request, obtains the requested information from the MySQL database, and then presents the requested information to your visitors through their Web browsers.

Every Web host is different in how it gives you access to set up and manage your MySQL database(s) for your account. A popular account administration interface in use today is called cPanel (shown in Figure 6-2), and in this section, I use cPanel. If your host provides a different interface, the same basic steps apply; just the setup in the interface that your Web host provides may be different.

Figure 6-2:
cPanel is a
Web host-
ing account
manager
provided
by several
Web hosting
companies.

To set up the MySQL database for your WordPress blog with cPanel, follow these steps:

1. **Log in to the administration interface with the username and password assigned to you by your Web host.**

   I'm using the cPanel administration interface, but your host may provide NetAdmin or Plesk, for example.

2. **Locate the MySQL Database Administration section.**

   In cPanel, click the MySQL Databases icon.

3. **Choose a name for your database, and enter it in the Name text box.**

   Be sure to make note of the database name, because you will need it during the installation of WordPress later.

   It doesn't really matter what you choose for the database name, username, or password. For security reasons, however, make sure that your password isn't something that sneaky hackers can easily guess. Usually, I give my database a name that I will easily recognize later. This practice is especially helpful if you're running more than one MySQL database in your account. If I name this database something like *WordPress* or *wpblog,* I can be reasonably certain — a year from now, when I want to access my database to make some configuration changes — that I know exactly which one I need to deal with.

4. **Click the Create Database button.**

   You get a message confirming that the database has been created.

5. **Click the Go Back link or the Back button on your browser toolbar.**

6. **Choose a username and password for your database, enter them in the Add New User text boxes, and then click the Create User button.**

   You get a confirmation message that the username was created with the password you specified.

   Make absolutely sure that you note the database name, username, and password that you set up during this process. You *will* need them in the next section before officially installing WordPress on your Web server. Jot them down on a piece of paper, or copy and paste them into a text-editor window; either way, just make sure that you have them immediately handy.

7. **Click the Go Back link or the Back button on your browser toolbar.**

8. **In the Add Users to Database section, choose the user you just set up from the User drop-down menu; then choose the new database from the Database drop-down menu.**

   The MySQL Account Maintenance, Manage User Privileges page appears in cPanel.

9. **Assign user privileges by selecting the All Privileges check box.**

   Because you're the administrator (owner) of this database, you need to make sure that you assign all privileges to the new user you just created.

10. **Click the Make Changes button.**

    A page opens with a confirmation message that you've added your selected user to the selected database.

11. **Click the Go Back link.**

    You go back to the MySQL Databases page.

Uploading the WordPress files

To upload the WordPress files to your host, return to the folder on your computer where you unpacked the WordPress software that you downloaded earlier. You'll find all the files you need (shown in Figure 6-3) in a folder called /wordpress.

Using your FTP client, connect to your Web server, and upload all these files to your hosting account, into the root directory.

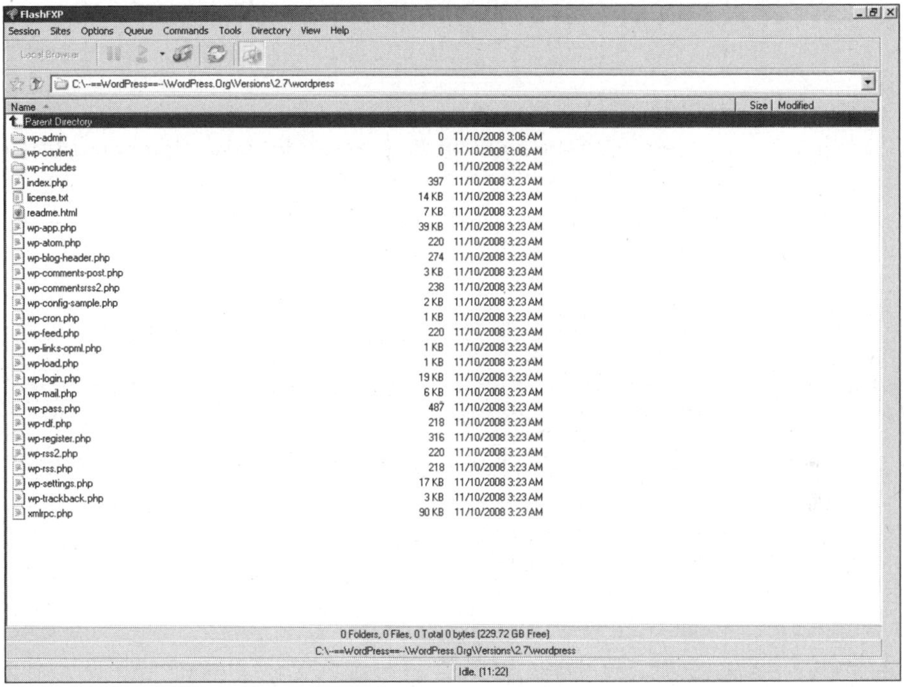

Figure 6-3:
WordPress
software
files to be
uploaded to
your Web
server.

If you don't know what your root directory is, contact your hosting provider and ask, "What is my root directory for my account?" Every hosting provider's setup is different. On my Web server, my root directory is the `public_html` folder; some of my clients have a root directory in a folder called `httpdocs`. The answer really depends on what type of setup your hosting provider has. When in doubt, ask!

Here are a few things to keep in mind when you're uploading your files:

✔ **Upload the *contents* of the `/wordpress` folder to your Web server — not the folder itself.** Most FTP client software lets you select all the files and drag 'n' drop them to your Web server. Other programs have you highlight the files and click a Transfer button.

✔ **Choose the correct transfer mode.** File transfers via FTP have two different forms: ASCII and binary. Most FTP clients are configured to auto-detect the transfer mode. Understanding the difference as it pertains to this WordPress installation is important, so that you can troubleshoot any problems you have later:

 • *Binary transfer mode* is how images (such as `.jpg`, `.gif`, `.bmp`, and `.png` files) are transferred via FTP.

• *ASCII transfer mode* is for everything else (text files, PHP files, JavaScript, and so on).

For the most part, it's a safe bet to make sure that the transfer mode of your FTP client is set to autodetect. But if you experience issues with how those files load on your site, retransfer the files using the appropriate transfer mode.

✔ **You can choose a different folder from the root.** You aren't required to transfer the files to the root directory of your Web server. You can make the choice to run WordPress on a subdomain, or in a different folder, on your account. If you want your blog address to be `http://your domain.com/blog`, you would transfer the WordPress files into a folder named `/blog`.

✔ **Choose the right file permissions.** You need to pay attention to file permissions when you're transferring files to your Web server. *File permissions* tell the Web server how these files can be handled on your server — whether they're files that can be written to. As a general rule, PHP files need to have a permission (`chmod`) of 666, whereas file folders need a permission of 755. Almost all FTP clients let you check and change the permissions on the files, if you need to. Typically, you can find the option to change file permissions within the menu options of your FTP client.

Some hosting providers run their PHP software in a more secure format called *safe mode.* If this is the case with your host, you need to set the PHP files to 644. If you're unsure, ask your hosting provider what permissions you need to set for PHP files.

Last step: Running the install script

The final step in the installation procedure for WordPress is connecting the WordPress software you uploaded to the MySQL database. Follow these steps:

1. **Type this URL in the address window of your browser, replacing *your-domain.com* with your own domain name:**

   ```
   http://yourdomain.com/wp-admin/install.php
   ```

   If you chose to install WordPress in a different folder from the root directory of your account, make sure you indicate this fact in the URL for the install script. If you transferred the WordPress software files to a folder called `/blog`, for example, you would point your browser to the following URL to run the installation: `http://yourdomain.com/blog/wp-admin/install.php`.

   Assuming that you did everything correctly (see Table 6-1 for help with common installation problems), you see the message shown in Figure 6-4.

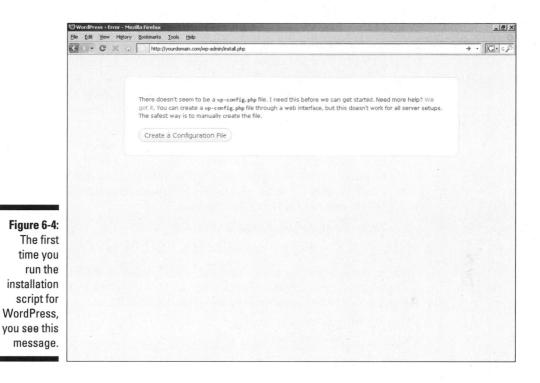

Figure 6-4:
The first
time you
run the
installation
script for
WordPress,
you see this
message.

2. **Click the Create a Configuration File button.**

   The next page that opens is a Welcome to WordPress message, which gives you the information you need to proceed with the installation.

3. **Click the Let's Go button at the bottom of that page.**

4. **Dig out the database name, username, and password that you saved earlier, and use that information to fill in the following fields (shown in Figure 6-5):**

   • *Database Name:* Type the database name you used when you created the MySQL database before this installation. Because hosts differ in configurations, you need to enter either the database name or the database name with your hosting account username appended.

   If you named your database *wordpress,* for example, you would enter that in this text box. Or if your host requires you to append the database name with your hosting account username, you would enter ***username*_wordpress**, substituting your hosting username for *username.* My username is *lisasabin,* so I entered **lisasabin_wordpress**.

- *User Name:* Type the username you used when you created the MySQL database before this installation. Depending on what your host requires, you may need to append this username to your hosting account username.

- *Password:* Type the password you used when you set up the MySQL database. You don't need to append the password to your hosting account username here.

- *Database Host:* Ninety-nine percent of the time, you'll leave this field set to *localhost*. Some hosts, depending on their configurations, have different hosts set for the MySQL database server. If *localhost* doesn't work, you need to contact your hosting provider to find out the MySQL database host.

- *Table Prefix:* Leave this field set to *wp_*.

5. **When you have all that information filled in, click the Submit button.**

   You see a message that says, "All right, sparky! You've made it through this part of the installation. WordPress can now communicate with your database. If you're ready, time now to run the install!"

6. **Click the Run the Install button.**

   You see another welcome page with a message welcoming you to the famous five-minute WordPress installation process.

7. **Enter or possibly change this information:**

   - *Blog Title:* Enter the title you want to give your blog. The title you enter isn't written in stone; you can change it at a later date, if you like.

   - *Your E-Mail Address:* Enter the e-mail address you want to use to be notified of administrative information about your blog. You can change this address at a later date, too.

   - *Allow My Blog to Appear in Search Engines Like Google and Technorati:* By default, this check box is selected, which lets the search engines index the content of your blog and include your blog in search results. To keep your blog out of the search engines, deselect this check box.

8. **Click the Install WordPress button.**

   The WordPress installation machine works its magic and creates all the tables within the database that contain the default data for your blog. WordPress gives you the login information you need to access the WordPress Administration panel (see Figure 6-6). Make note of this username and password before you leave this page. Scribble it down on a piece of paper or copy it into a text editor such as Notepad.

After you click the Install WordPress button, you're sent an e-mail with the login information and login URL. This information is handy if you're called away during this part of the installation process. So go ahead and let the dog out, answer the phone, brew a cup of coffee, or take a 15-minute power nap. If you somehow get distracted away from this page, the e-mail sent to you contains the information you need to successfully log in to your WordPress blog.

9. **Click the Log In button to log in to WordPress.**

If you happen to lose this page before clicking the Log In button, you can always find your way to the login page by entering your domain followed by the call to the login file (for example, `http://yourdomain.com/wp-login.php`).

You know that you're finished with the installation process when you see the login page, as shown in Figure 6-7. Check out Table 6-1 if you experience any problems during this installation process; it covers some of the common problems users run into.

So do tell — how much time does your watch show for the installation? Was it five minutes? Stop by my blog sometime (`http://lisasabin-wilson.com`), and let me know whether WordPress stood up to its famous five-minute-installation reputation. I'm a curious sort.

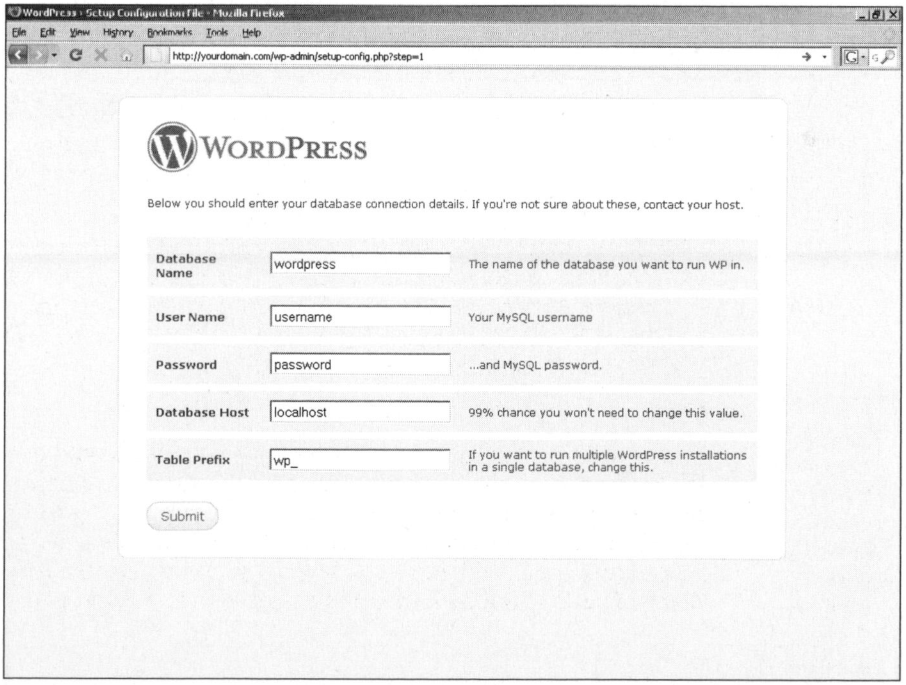

Figure 6-5:
At this step of the WordPress installation phase, you need to enter the database name, username, and password.

WordPress › Setup Configuration File · Mozilla Firefox

File Edit View History Bookmarks Tools Help

http://yourdomain.com/wp-admin/setup-config.php?step=1

WORDPRESS

Below you should enter your database connection details. If you're not sure about these, contact your host.

Database Name	wordpress	The name of the database you want to run WP in.
User Name	username	Your MySQL username
Password	password	...and MySQL password.
Database Host	localhost	99% chance you won't need to change this value.
Table Prefix	wp_	If you want to run multiple WordPress installations in a single database, change this.

Submit

Figure 6-6:
This step of the installation process assigns a username and password. Be sure to keep them handy!

Figure 6-7:
You know you've run a successful WordPress installation when you see the login page.

The good news is — you're done! Were you expecting a marching band? WordPress isn't that fancy . . . yet. Give them time, though; if anyone can produce it, the folks at WordPress can.

Table 6-1	Common WordPress Installation Problems	
Error Message	*Common Cause*	*Solution*
Error Connecting to the Database	The database name, username, password, or host was entered incorrectly.	Revisit your MySQL database to obtain the database name, username, and password, and reenter that information.
Headers Already Sent Error Messages	A syntax error occurred in the `wp-config.php` file.	Open the `wp-config.php` file in a text editor. The first line should contain only this line: `<?php`. The last line should contain only this line: `?>`. Make sure that those lines contain nothing else — not even white space. Save the file changes.
500: Internal Server Error	Permissions on PHP files are set incorrectly.	Try setting the permissions (`chmod`) on the PHP files to 666. If that change doesn't work, set them to 644. Each Web server has different settings for how it lets PHP execute on its servers.
404: Page Not Found	The URL for the login page is incorrect.	Double-check that the URL you're using to get to the login page is the same as the location of your WordPress installation (such as `http://yourdomain.com/wp-login.php`).
403: Forbidden Access	An `index.html` or `index.htm` file exists in the WordPress installation directory.	WordPress is a PHP application, so the default home page is `index.php`. Look in the WordPress installation folder on your Web server. If there is an `index.html` or `index.htm` file in there, delete it.

Let me be the first to congratulate you on your newly installed WordPress blog! When you're ready, log in and familiarize yourself with the Administration panel, which I describe in Chapter 7.

Chapter 7

Understanding the WordPress.org Administration Panel

*W*ith WordPress.org successfully installed, you can explore your new blogging software. This chapter guides you through the preliminary setup of your new WordPress blog using the Administration panel. When you blog with WordPress, you spend a lot of time in the Administration panel, which is where you make all the exciting, behind-the-scenes stuff happen. In this panel, you find all the settings and options that enable you to set up your blog just the way you want it. (If you still need to install and configure WordPress, check out Chapter 6.)

Feeling comfortable with the Administration panel sets you up for successful entrance into the WordPress blogging world. You will tweak your WordPress settings several times throughout the life of your blog. In this chapter, as I go through the various sections, settings, options, and configurations available to you, understand that nothing is set in stone. You can set options today and change them at any time.

Logging In to the Administration Panel

I find that the direct approach (also known as jumping in) works best when I want to get familiar with a new software tool. To that end, just follow these steps to log in to WordPress and take a look at the guts of the Administration panel:

1. **Open your Web browser, and type the WordPress login-page address (or URL) in the address box.**

   The login-page address looks something like this:

   `http://www.`*yourdomain*`.com/wp-login.php.`

   If you installed WordPress in its own folder, include that folder name in the login URL. If you installed WordPress in a folder ingeniously named `wordpress`, the login URL becomes `http://www.`*yourdomain*`.com/wordpress/wp-login.php`.

2. **Type your username in the Username text box and your password in the Password text box (see Figure 7-1).**

   In case you forget your password, WordPress has you covered. Click the Lost Your Password? link (located near the bottom of the page), enter your username and e-mail address, and then click the Submit button. WordPress resets your password and e-mails the new password to you.

   After you request a password, you receive two e-mails from your WordPress blog. The first e-mail contains a link that you click to verify that you requested the password. After you verify your intentions, you receive an e-mail containing your new password.

3. **Select the Remember Me check box if you want WordPress to place a cookie in your browser.**

   The cookie tells WordPress to remember your login credentials the next time you show up. The cookie set by WordPress is harmless and stores your WordPress login on your computer. Because of the cookie, WordPress remembers you the next time you visit.

   Note: Before you set this option, make sure that your browser is configured to allow cookies. (If you aren't sure how to do this, check the help documentation of the Internet browser you're using.)

4. **Click the Log In button.**

Figure 7-1:
Log in to the Administration panel to manage your options and settings.

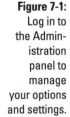

After you've logged in to your WordPress Administration panel, you see the Dashboard page.

Navigating the Dashboard

You can consider the Administration panel to be a Control Panel of sorts, because it offers several quick links and areas that provide information about your blog, starting with the actual Dashboard page, shown in Figure 7-2.

You can change how the WordPress Dashboard looks, at least in terms of the order the modules appear on it. You can expand (open) and collapse (close) the individual modules by clicking your mouse anywhere within the grey title bar of the module. This feature is really nice because you can utilize the Dashboard for just those modules that you use regularly. The concept is easy: Keep the modules you use all the time open and close the ones that you only use occasionally — you can open those modules only when you really need them. You save space and you can customize your Dashboard to suit your own needs.

When you view your Dashboard for the very first time, all of the modules in the Dashboard appear in the expanded (open) position by default (refer to Figure 7-2).

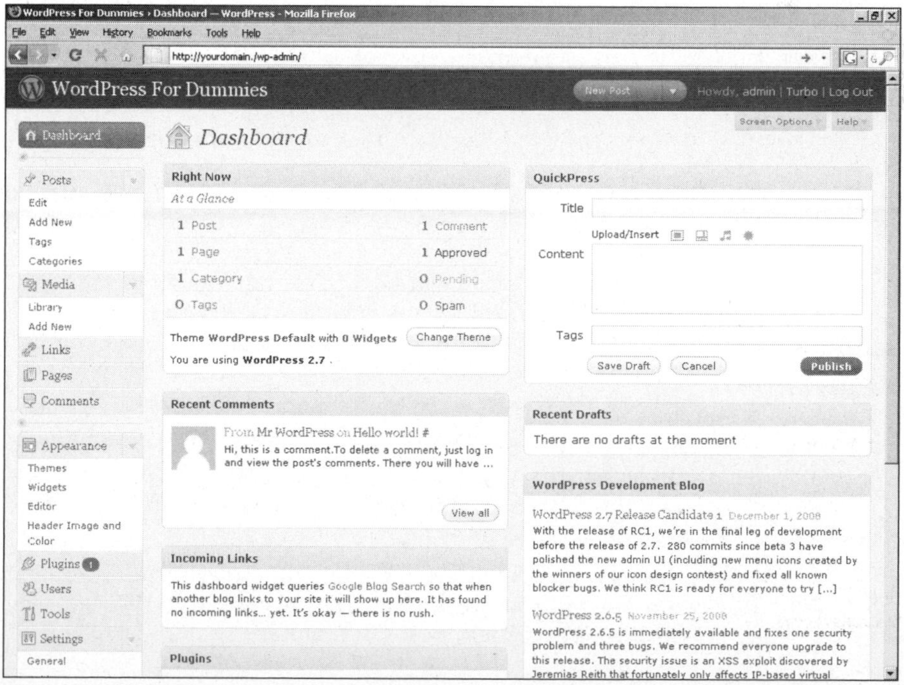

Figure 7-2: The WordPress Dashboard page is the screen you see the first time you log in to your WordPress Administration panel.

The navigation menu in the WordPress Dashboard appears on the left side of your browser window. When you need to get back to the WordPress Dashboard, click the Dashboard link that appears at the top of the navigation menu of any of the pages within your WordPress Administration panel.

In the following sections, I cover the Dashboard page as it appears when you login to your WordPress Administration panel for the very first time; later in this chapter, I show you how to configure the appearance of your Dashboard so that it best suits how you use the available modules.

Right Now

The Right Now module in the Dashboard shows what is going on in your blog right now, right this very second! Figure 7-3 shows the expanded Right Now module in my brand-spanking-new WordPress blog.

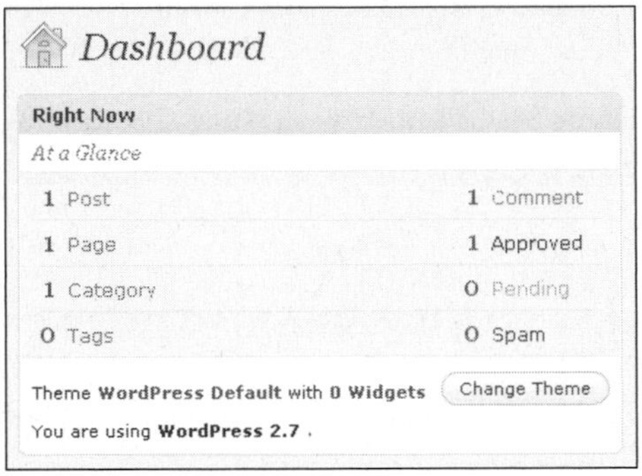

Figure 7-3:
The Right Now module in the Dashboard, expanded to see the available features.

> 🏠 *Dashboard*
>
> **Right Now**
> *At a Glance*
>
> | | | |
> |---|---|---|
> | 1 Post | | 1 Comment |
> | 1 Page | | 1 Approved |
> | 1 Category | | 0 Pending |
> | 0 Tags | | 0 Spam |
>
> Theme **WordPress Default** with 0 Widgets   (Change Theme)
> You are using **WordPress 2.7** .

The Right Now module shows the following default information under the At a Glance header:

✔ **The number of posts you have:** This number reflects the total number of posts you currently have in your WordPress blog; I have 1 post on my blog. The number is blue, which means it's a link that you can click. When you do, you go to the Edit Posts page, where you can edit the posts on your blog. I cover editing posts in Chapter 8.

✔ **The number of pages:** This is the current number of pages on your blog, which changes as you add or delete pages. (*Pages,* in this context, refer to the static pages you have created in your blog.) Figure 7-3 shows that my blog has 1 page.

Clicking this link takes you to the Edit Pages page, where you can view, edit, and delete your current pages. (Find the difference between WordPress posts and pages in Chapter 8.)

✔ **The number of categories:** This is the current number of categories you have on your blog, which changes as you add and delete categories. Figure 7-3 shows that I have 1 category for my blog.

Clicking this link takes you to the Categories Page, where you can view, edit, and delete your current categories; or add brand new ones. (For details about the management and creation of categories, see Chapter 8.)

✔ **The number of tags:** This is the current number of tags you have in your blog, which changes as you add and delete categories in the future. Figure 7-3 shows that I have 0 tags.

Clicking this link takes you to the Tags page, where you can add new tags and view, edit, and delete your current tags. (You can find more information about tags in Chapter 8.)

✔ **The number of comments:** This is the total number of the comments that are currently on your blog. Figure 7-3 shows that I have 1 Comment, 1 Approved, 0 Pending, and 0 marked as spam.

Clicking any of these four links takes you to the Edit Comments page, where you can manage the comments on your blog. I cover the management of comments in the "Comments" section, later in this chapter.

The last section of the Dashboard's Right Now module in the Dashboard shows the following information:

✔ **Which WordPress theme you are using:** Figure 7-3 shows that I'm using the WordPress Default theme. The theme name is a link that, when clicked, takes you to the Manage Themes page where you can view and activate themes on your blog.

✔ **How many widgets you've added to your blog:** This is the number of WordPress widgets you're using in your blog. Figure 7-3 shows that I have 0 widgets. The number 0 is a link that, when clicked, takes you to the Widgets page, where you can change your widget options by editing them, moving them, or removing them. (I cover widgets in detail in Chapter 5 if you want to check that out — although that chapter is in the WordPress.com part of this book, the method of using sidebar widgets is the same for self-hosted WordPress.org blogs.)

✔ **Change Theme:** Clicking this button takes you to the Manage Themes page, which lists your currently active and all available themes for your WordPress blog. Your active theme (the theme that's visible on your active blog) is shown at the top below the Current Theme header. All other available themes are listed below Available Themes. Click any theme on this page to use it on your blog.

✔ **The version of WordPress you're using:** This is the last statement in the Right Now section. Figure 7-3 shows that I'm using WordPress version 2.7. In the future, this version announcement will change if you are using an older version of WordPress. When WordPress software is upgraded, this statement will tell you that you are using an outdated version of WordPress and encourage you to upgrade to the latest version.

Recent Comments

The next module is called Recent Comments — within this module, you find:

- **Most recent comments published to your blog:** WordPress displays a maximum of five comments in this area.

- **The author of each comment:** The name of the person who left the comment appears below it. This section also displays the author's picture (or avatar), if they have one.

- **A link to the post the comment was left on:** The post title appears to the right of the commenter's name. Click the link, and you go to that post in the Admin panel.

- **An excerpt of the comment:** This is a short snippet of the comment this person left on your blog.

- **Comment management links:** When you hover over the comment with your mouse cursor, five links appear underneath the comment that give you the opportunity to manage those comments right from your Dashboard: Unapprove (this link appears only if you have comment moderation turned on. Find out more about moderating comments in the "Comments" section, later in this chapter), Edit, Reply, Spam, and Delete.

- **View All button:** This button invites you to see all the comments that have been left on your blog. Clicking the View All button takes you to the Edit Comments page, where you can view and edit, moderate, or delete any comments that have been left for your blog.

You'll find even more information on managing your comments in the "Comments" section, later in this chapter.

Incoming Links

The next module visible in the Dashboard is Incoming Links. It lists all the blog-savvy people who wrote a blog post that links to your blog. When your blog is brand new, you won't see any incoming links listed in this section. Don't despair, however; as time goes on, you will see this listing of links fill up as more and more people discover you and your inspired writings!

In the meantime, the Incoming Links module shows *"This dashboard widget queries Google Blog Search so that when another blog links to your site it will show up here. It has found no incoming links ... yet. It's okay — there is no rush."* The phrase *Google Blog Search* is a link; when you click it, you go the Google Blog Search directory, which is a search engine for blogs only.

The following steps show you what how you can edit the Incoming Links module:

1. **Hover your mouse over the title of the Incoming Links module and a new link appears directly to the right of the Configure title. Click that link.**

   Now you can change the settings of the Incoming Links module (see Figure 7-4).

2. **Add a URL in the Enter the RSS Feed URL Here box.**

   You can enter the URL of any RSS feed you want to display incoming links to your site. Feeds you can use include Technorati (`http://technorati.com`) and Yahoo! Search (`http://search.yahoo.com`). You're not restricted to using the Google Blog Search engine (`http://blogsearch.google.com`) to provide your Incoming Links information.

3. **Specify how many items you want to display.**

   The default number is 5, but making a different choice from the drop-down menu lets you display up to 20 items (incoming links).

4. **Specify whether to display the item date.**

   Check the Display Item Date? box if you want each incoming link to display the date the link was created. If you don't want the date display, leave that box blank.

5. **Click the Submit button to save all your preferences.**

   Clicking Submit resets the Incoming Links module with your new settings saved.

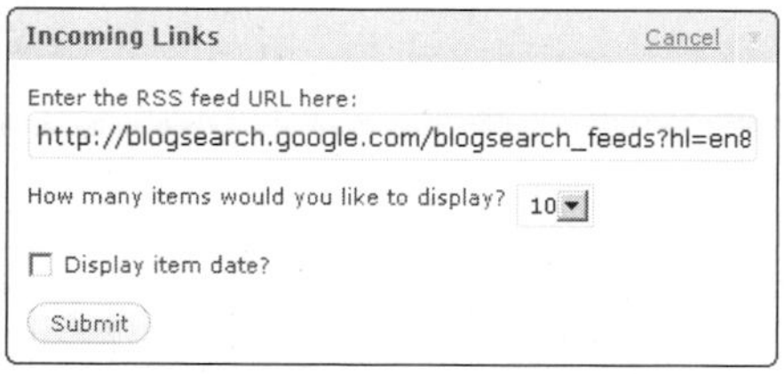

Figure 7-4:
Changing the settings of the Incoming Links module by clicking the Edit link.

Incoming Links	Cancel
Enter the RSS feed URL here:	
http://blogsearch.google.com/blogsearch_feeds?hl=en8	
How many items would you like to display? 10	
☐ Display item date?	
Submit	

Plugins

I cover the management and use of WordPress plugins in detail in Chapter 10; however, for the purposes of this section, I discuss the functions of the Plugins module in the Dashboard so you know what to do with it now!

The Plugins module includes three titles of WordPress plugins that are linked to its page within the WordPress Plugin Directory. The Plugins module pulls information via RSS feed from the official WordPress Plugin Directory at `http://wordpress.org/extend/plugins`. This module displays a plugin from three different plugin categories in the official WordPress Plugin Directory: Most Popular, Newest Plugins and Recently Updated.

The Plugins module doesn't have an Edit link, so you can't customize the information that it displays. Use this box to discover new plugins that can help you do fun and exciting things with your blog.

The Plugins module does have a very exciting feature that you can use to install, activate, and manage plugins on your blog. Just follow these steps to make it happen:

1. **Click the Install link next to the title of the plugin.**

   The Plugin Information popup window opens (see Figure 7-5). It displays the various bits of information about the plugin you've chosen, such as title, description, version, author, date last updated, and the number of times the plugin was downloaded.

2. **Click the Install Now button.**

   This button is at the top right of the Plugin Information page, as seen in Figure 7-5.

   The Plugin Information popup window closes and the Install Plugins page in your WordPress Administration panel opens, where you see a confirmation message that the plugin has been downloaded, unpacked, and successfully installed.

3. **Specify whether to install the plugin or proceed to the Plugins page.**

   Two links are shown under the confirmation message:

   - *Activate Plugin:* Click this link to activate the plugin you just installed on your blog.

   - *Return to Plugins Page:* Click this link to go to the Manage Plugins page.

   I cover the installation, installation, and activation of WordPress plugins in further depth in Chapter 10.

4. **Click the Dashboard link to return to the Dashboard.**

   The Dashboard link is located at the top of the left menu on every page of your WordPress Administration panel.

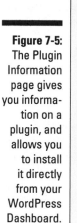

Figure 7-5:
The Plugin Information page gives you information on a plugin, and allows you to install it directly from your WordPress Dashboard.

QuickPress

The QuickPress module is a handy form that allows you to write, save, and publish a blog post right from your WordPress Dashboard. The options are similar to the ones I cover in the section on writing posts in Chapter 8.

Recent Drafts

If you're using a brand new WordPress blog and this is a new installation, the Recent Drafts module displays the message: *There are no drafts at the moment.* That is because you have not written any drafts. As time goes on, however, and you have written a few posts in your blog, you may save some of those posts as Drafts — to be edited and published at a later date. Those drafts show up in the Recent Drafts module.

WordPress displays up to five drafts and displays the title of the post, the date it was last saved, and a short excerpt. A View All link also displays; click that link to go the Manage Posts page where you can view, edit, and manage your blog posts. Check out Chapter 8 for more information.

WordPress Development Blog

When you first install WordPress, the WordPress Development Blog module is by default populated with the two most recent updates from the official WordPress development blog at `http://wordpress.org/development`. You see the title of the last post, the date it was published, and a short excerpt of the post. Click a title, and you go directly to that post on the WordPress Development Blog.

Following the updates of the WordPress Development Blog is very useful, and I highly recommend it. Why? Every single time you log in to your WordPress Dashboard, a glance at this section informs you about any news, updates, or alerts from the makers of WordPress. You can find out about any new versions of the software, security patches, or other important news regarding the software you are using to power your blog.

Although I recommend that you keep the WordPress Development Blog updates in this section, the WordPress platform lets you change this box to display posts from another blog of your choosing. You can accomplish this change by following these steps:

1. **Hover your mouse over the WordPress Development module title. Click the Configure link shown to the right of the WordPress Development Blog title.**

   The module changes to display several options to change the information contained in the box (see Figure 7-6).

2. **Type your preferred RSS feed in the Enter the RSS feed URL Here box.**

3. **Type your preferred title in the Give the Feed a Title (Optional) box.**

4. **Specify the number of items you want to display.**

   The default number of items is 2, but you can display up to 20 by making a different choice from the drop-down menu.

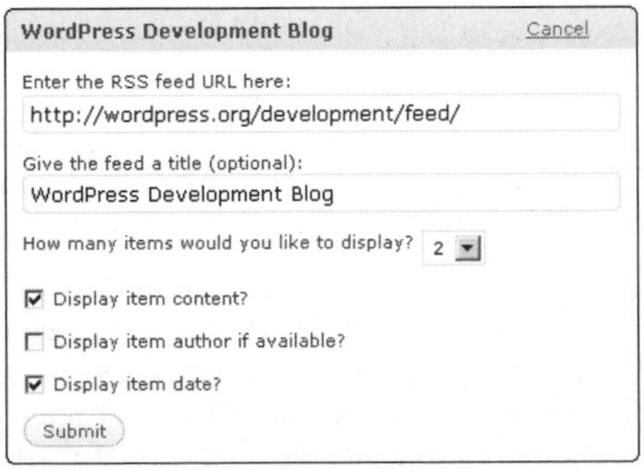

Figure 7-6:
Options to change the Feed Title and URL of the WordPress Development Blog module.

> **WordPress Development Blog**   Cancel
>
> Enter the RSS feed URL here:
> `http://wordpress.org/development/feed/`
>
> Give the feed a title (optional):
> `WordPress Development Blog`
>
> How many items would you like to display? 2 ▾
>
> ☑ Display item content?
> ☐ Display item author if available?
> ☑ Display item date?
>
> (Submit)

5. **Specify whether you want to display the item's content.**

   Item content refers to the text content of the post. If you don't check the Display Item Content? box, WordPress doesn't display an excerpt of the post — only the post title.

6. **Specify whether you want to display the name of the person who wrote the post.**

   Leave the Display Item Author If Available? box unchecked if you don't want the author's name displayed.

7. **Specify whether you want to display the date.**

   Leave the Display Item Date? box unchecked if you don't want the date displayed.

8. **Click the Submit button to save your changes.**

   The Dashboard page refreshes with your new changes. Click the title of the box to collapse it.

If you change your mind, click the Cancel link shown to the right of the WordPress Development Blog title. Clicking Cancel discards any changes you made and keeps the original settings intact.

The title of the WordPress Development Blog module changes to the title you chose in Step 3. Figure 7-7 shows that I changed the title to Lisa's Blog.

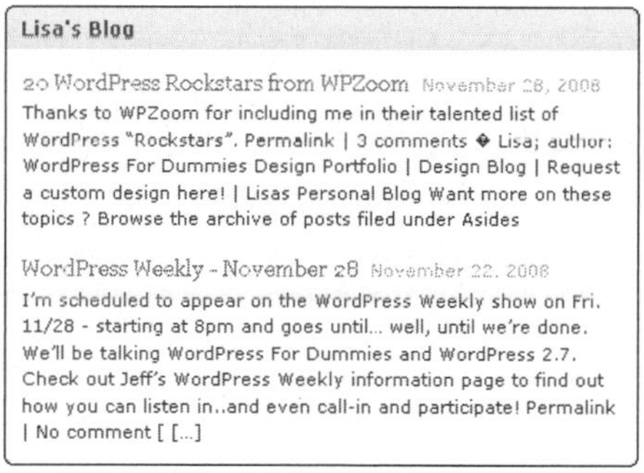

Figure 7-7:
The WordPress Development Blog module changes based on the options you set.

> **Lisa's Blog**
>
> 20 WordPress Rockstars from WPZoom November 28, 2008
> Thanks to WPZoom for including me in their talented list of
> WordPress "Rockstars". Permalink | 3 comments ◆ Lisa; author:
> WordPress For Dummies Design Portfolio | Design Blog | Request
> a custom design here! | Lisas Personal Blog Want more on these
> topics ? Browse the archive of posts filed under Asides
>
> WordPress Weekly - November 28 November 22, 2008
> I'm scheduled to appear on the WordPress Weekly show on Fri.
> 11/28 - starting at 8pm and goes until... well, until we're done.
> We'll be talking WordPress For Dummies and WordPress 2.7.
> Check out Jeff's WordPress Weekly information page to find out
> how you can listen in..and even call-in and participate! Permalink
> | No comment [[...]

Other WordPress News

The Other WordPress News module of the Dashboard pulls in posts from a site called WordPress Planet (`http://planet.wordpress.org`). By keeping the default setting in this area the same, you stay in touch with several posts made by folks who are involved in WordPress development, design, and troubleshooting. You can find lots of interesting and useful tidbits if you keep this area intact. Quite often, I find great information about new plugins or themes, problem areas and support, troubleshooting, and new ideas, so I tend to stick with the default setting.

WordPress is all about user experience, however, so you can change the options to specify what displays in this area. You can change the items in this module the same way that you change the options for the WordPress Development Blog module (see the preceding section).

Arranging the Dashboard to Your Tastes

You have the ability to arrange the order of the modules in your Dashboard to suit your tastes. WordPress places a great deal of emphasis on user experience and a big part of that effort results in your ability to create a Dashboard that you find most useful. Changing the modules that are displayed, and the order they are displayed in, is very easy.

In the following steps, I show you how to move the Right Now module so that it displays on the right side of your Dashboard page:

1. **Hover your mouse over the title bar of the Right Now module.**

   When hovering over the box title, your mouse cursor changes to the Move cursor (a cross with arrows on a PC or the hand cursor on a Mac).

2. **Click and hold your mouse button and drag the Right Now module to the right side of the screen.**

   As you drag the box, a light gray box with a dotted border appears on the right side of your screen. That gray box is a guide that shows you where you should drop the module. See Figure 7-8.

3. **Release the mouse button when you have the Right Now module in place.**

   The Right Now module is now positioned on the right side of your Dashboard page.

   The other modules on the left side of the Dashboard have now shifted down and the Recent Comments Module is the first module shown at the top of the left side on the Dashboard page.

4. **(Optional) Click once on the title bar of the Right Now module.**

   The module collapses. Click the title bar again and the module expands. You can keep that module opened or closed based on your own preference.

Figure 7-8:
A light gray box appears as a guide when dragging and dropping modules in the WordPress Dashboard.

Repeat these steps with each module you see on the Dashboard by dragging and dropping them so they appear in the order you prefer.

When you navigate away from the Dashboard, WordPress remembers the changes you've made. When you return, you still see your customized Dashboard and you don't need to redo these changes in the future.

If you find that your Dashboard contains a few modules you just never use, you can completely get rid of them altogether by following these steps:

1. **Click the Screen Options button at the top of the Dashboard.**

   The Screen Options menu opens, displaying the title of each module with check boxes to the left of each title.

2. **De-select the module you want to hide on your Dashboard.**

   The check mark is removed from the box and the module disappears from your Dashboard. Figure 7-9 shows my customized Dashboard.

If you miss a module you've hidden, you can simply enable that module by selecting the module from the Screen Options menu.

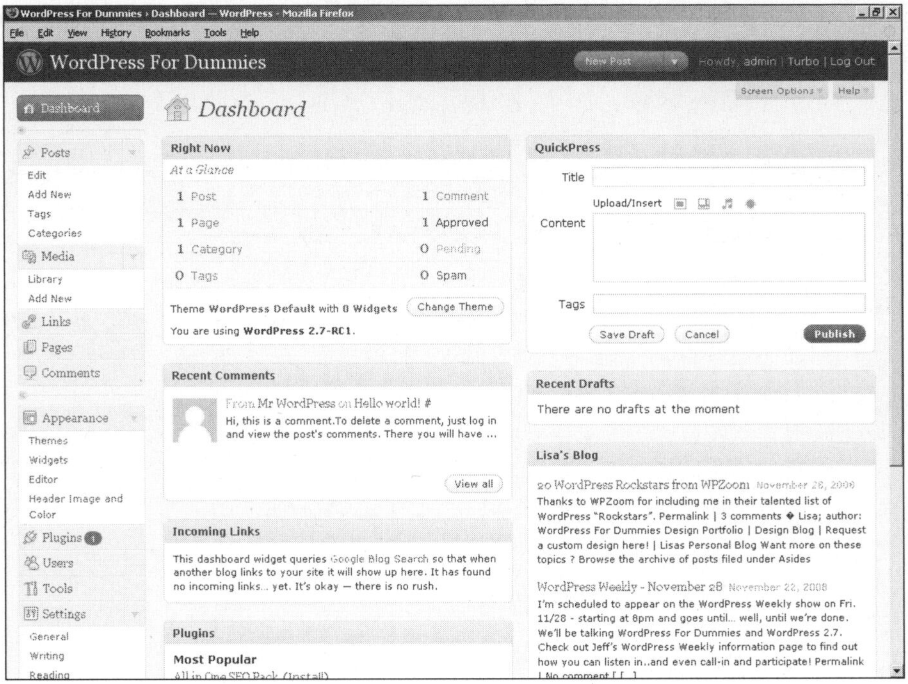

Figure 7-9:
My
WordPress
Dashboard
after I cus-
tomized it.

Setting Options in the Administration Panel

The navigation menu is located on the left side of every page within the WordPress Administration panel. You'll find it there everywhere you go — like a loyal friend, it's always there for you when you need it!

The navigation menu is divided into ten different menus. Hover your mouse over a menu and a down arrow appears to the right; click the down arrow to reveal the submenu. The submenus take you to areas within your Administration panel that allow you to perform tasks such as publishing a new blog post, adding a new link, or managing your comments.

When you expand a menu in the navigation menu, WordPress remembers and keeps that menu expanded as you navigate through different pages in the Administration panel. Likewise, if you collapse the menu, WordPress remembers that you've closed that menu, and the menu stays closed as you browse through your WordPress Administration panel.

The settings that allow you to personalize your blog are the first ones that I cover in the next part of this chapter. Some of the menu items, like creating and publishing new posts, are covered in detail other chapters, but they're well worth a mention here as well so that you know what you're looking at. (Each section contains a cross-reference telling you where you can find more in-depth information on that topic in this book.)

Configuring the Settings

At the very bottom of the navigation menu is the Settings menu. Click the Settings link and a submenu drops down that contain the following links, which I discuss in the sections that follow:

- ✔ General
- ✔ Writing
- ✔ Reading
- ✔ Discussion
- ✔ Media
- ✔ Privacy
- ✔ Permalinks
- ✔ Miscellaneous

General

After you install the WordPress software and log in, you can put a personal stamp on your blog by giving it a title and description, setting your contact e-mail address, and identifying yourself as the author of the blog. You take care of these and other settings on the General Settings page.

To begin personalizing your blog, start with your general settings by following these steps:

1. **Click the General link in the Settings menu.**

   The General Settings page appears (see Figure 7-10).

2. **Enter the name of your blog in the Blog Title text box.**

   The title you enter here is the one that you've given your blog to identify it as your own. In Figure 7-10, I gave my new blog the title *WordPress For Dummies,* which appears on the blog as well as in the title bar of the viewer's Web browser. But I chose to title my personal blog *Lisa Sabin-Wilson* to identify it as mine. Mine! MINE! And with it, I shall rule the world! Ahem . . . moving on!

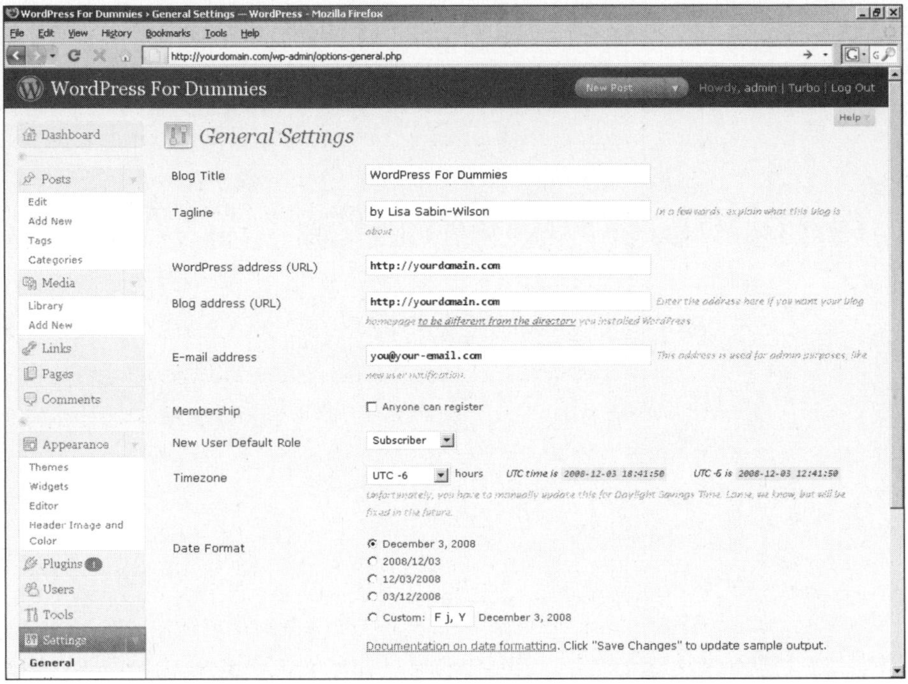

Figure 7-10:
Personalize
the settings
of your
WordPress
blog on the
General
Settings
page.

Give your blog an interesting and identifiable name. You could use
Fried Green Tomatoes, for example, if you're blogging about the topic,
the book or the movie, or even anything remotely related to the lovely
Southern dish.

**3. In the Tagline text box, enter a five- to ten-word phrase that describes
your blog.**

Figure 7-10 shows that my tagline is *by Lisa Sabin-Wilson.* So my blog
displays my blog title followed by the tagline: *WordPress For Dummies by
Lisa Sabin-Wilson.*

The general Internet-surfing public can view your blog title and tagline,
which various search engines (such as Google, Yahoo!, and MSN) grab for
indexing, so choose your words with this fact in mind. (You can find more
information about search engine optimization, or SEO, in Chapter 14.)

**4. In the WordPress Address (URL) text box, enter the location where
you installed your WordPress blog software.**

Be sure to include the `http://` portion of the URL and the entire path to
your WordPress installation — for example, `http://yourdomain.com.`
If you installed WordPress in a folder in your directory — in a folder called

wordpress, for example — you need to make sure to include it here. If I had installed WordPress in a folder called wordpress, the WordPress address would be http://*yourdomain*.com/wordpress.

5. **In the Blog Address (URL) text box, enter the Web address where people can find your blog by using their Web browsers.**

Typically, what you enter here is the same as your domain name (http://*yourdomain*.com). If you install WordPress in a subdirectory of your site, the WordPress installation URL is different from the blog URL. If you install WordPress at http://*yourdomain*.com/word press/ (WordPress URL), you need to tell WordPress that you want the blog to appear at http://*yourdomain*.com (the blog URL).

6. **Enter your e-mail address in the E-Mail Address text box.**

WordPress sends messages about the details of your blog to this e-mail address. When a new user registers for your blog, for example, WordPress sends you an e-mail alert.

7. **Select a Membership option.**

Select the Anyone Can Register box if you want to keep registration on your blog open to anyone who wants to. Keep the box unchecked if you'd rather not have open registration on your blog.

8. **From the New User Default Role drop-down menu, choose the role that you want new users to have when they register for user accounts in your blog.**

You need to understand the differences among the user roles, because each user role is assigned a different level of access to your blog, as follows:

- *Subscriber:* Subscriber is the default role. It's a good idea to maintain this role as the one assigned to new users, particularly if you don't know who is registering. Subscribers are given access to the Dashboard page, and they can view and change the options in their profiles on the Your Profile and Personal Options page. (They don't have access to your account settings, however — only to their own). Each user can change his username, e-mail address, password, bio, and other descriptors in his user profile. Subscribers' profile information is stored in the WordPress database, and your blog remembers them each time they visit, so they don't have to complete the profile information each time they leave comments on your blog.

- *Contributor:* In addition to the access Subscribers have, Contributors can upload files and write, edit, and manage their own posts. Contributors can write posts, but they can't publish the posts; the administrator reviews all Contributor posts and decides whether to publish them. This setting is a nice way to moderate content written by new authors.

- *Author:* In addition to the access Contributors have, Authors can publish and edit their own posts.

- *Editor:* In addition to the access Authors have, Editors can moderate comments, manage categories, manage links, edit pages, and edit other Authors' posts.

- *Administrator:* Administrators can edit all the options and settings in the WordPress blog.

9. In the Timezone section, choose your UTC time from the drop-down menu.

This setting refers to the number of hours that your local time differs from Coordinated Universal Time (UTC). This setting ensures that all your blog posts and comments left on your blog are time-stamped with the correct time. If you're lucky enough, like me, to live on the frozen tundra of Wisconsin, which is in the Central time zone (CST), you would choose **–6** from the drop-down menu because that time zone is 6 hours off UTC.

If you're unsure what your UTC time is, you can find it at the Greenwich Mean Time (`http://wwp.greenwichmeantime.com`) Web site. GMT is essentially the same thing as UTC.

10. In the Date Format text box, enter the format in which you want the date to be displayed in your blog.

This setting determines the style of the date display. The default format is already selected, and displayed for you: **F j, Y** (F = the full month name; j = the two-digit day; Y = the four-digit year), which gives you the date output. This default date format displays the date like this: January 1, 2008.

Select a different format by clicking the circle to the left of the option. You can also customize the date display by selecting the Custom option and entering your preferred format in the text box provided. If you're feeling adventurous, you can found out how to customize the date format here: `http://codex.wordpress.org/Formatting_Date_and_Time`.

11. In the Time Format text box, enter the format in which you want the time to be displayed in your blog.

This setting is the style of the time display. The default format is already inserted for you: **g:i a** (g = the two-digit hour; i = the two-digit minute; a = lowercase ante meridiem and post meridiem, or a.m. or p.m.), which gives you the output of 12:00 a.m.

Select a different format by clicking the circle to the left of the option. You can also customize the date display by selecting the Custom option and entering your preferred format in the text box provided; find out how at `http://codex.wordpress.org/Formatting_Date_and_Time`.

The Timezone option does not update automatically for daylight saving time (DST). If you live in an area of the world that practices DST, you have to update the Timezone option manually when it occurs.

You can format the time and date in several ways. Go to `http://us3.php.net/date` to find potential formats at the PHP Web site.

12. **From the drop-down menu, choose the day the week starts in your calendar.**

    The display of the calendar in the sidebar of your blog is optional. If you choose to display the calendar, you can select the day of the week you want your calendar to start with.

Click the Save Changes button at the bottom of any page where you set new options. If you don't click Save Changes, your settings aren't saved, and WordPress reverts to the preceding options. Each time you click the Save Changes button, WordPress reloads the current page, displaying the new options that you just set.

Writing

Click the Writing link in the Settings menu; the Writing Settings page opens (see Figure 7-11).

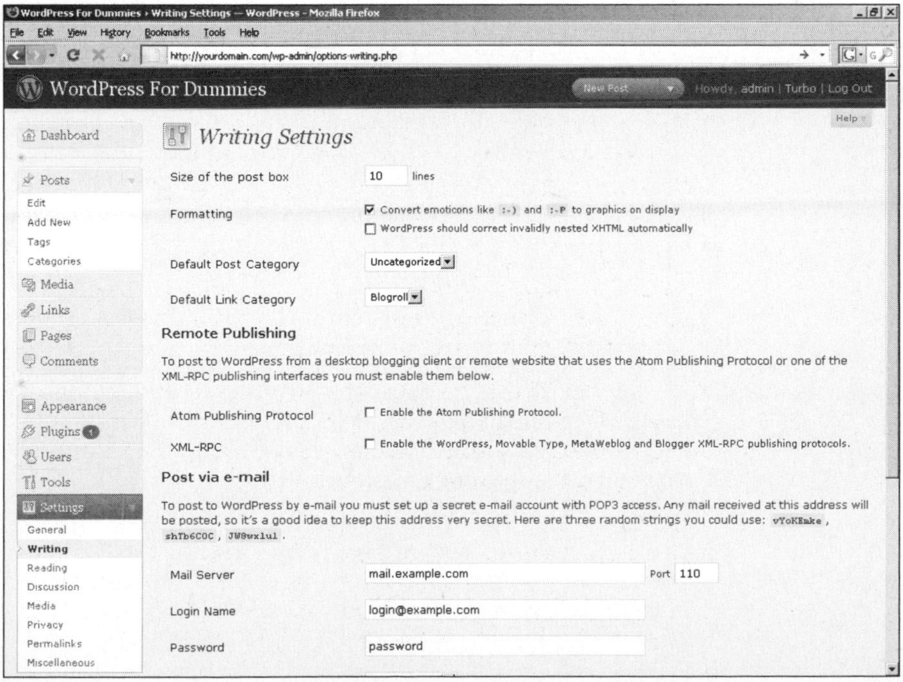

Figure 7-11:
The Writing
Settings
page.

This page lets you set some basic options for writing your posts. Table 7-1 gives you some information on choosing how your posts look and how WordPress handles some specific conditions.

After you set your options, be sure to click the Save Changes button; otherwise, the changes won't take effect.

Table 7-1	Writing Settings Options	
Option	*Function*	*Default*
Size of Post Box	Determines the size of the text edit box on the Write Post page. The bigger the number, the taller the box.	Ten lines
Formatting	Determines whether WordPress converts emoticons to graphics and whether WordPress corrects invalidly nested XHTML automatically. In general, I recommend selecting this option. (You can find more information about valid XHTML code at `http://validator.w3.org/docs/#docs_all`.)	Convert emoticons — such as :-) and :-P — to graphics and correct invalidly nested XHTML
Default Post Category	Lets you select the category that WordPress defaults to any time you forget to choose a category when you publish a post.	Uncategorized
Default Link Category	Lets you select the category that WordPress defaults to any time you forget to categorize a link.	Blogroll
Remote Publishing	Lets you enable Atom Publishing Protocol or one of the XML-RPC publishing interfaces that enable you to post to your WordPress blog from a remote Web site or desktop-publishing application.	Disabled
Post via E-Mail	Lets you publish blog posts from your e-mail account by letting you enter the e-mail and server information for the account you'll be using to send posts to your WordPress blog.	N/A

Option	Function	Default
Update Services	Lets you indicate which ping service you want to use to notify the world that you've made updates, or new posts, to your blog. These update services include blogrolling.com and weblogs.com. The default, rpc. pingomatic.com, updates all the popular services simultaneously.	`http://rpc.` `pingomatic.com`
Press This	A handy link that you can click and drag to your browsers toolbar or your Favorites. It creates a quick and easy post shortcut for posting interesting things you find on the Internet to your blog directly from your browser.	No defaults

Go to `http://codex.wordpress.org/Update_Services` for comprehensive information on update services.

Reading

The third link in the Settings menu is Reading (see Figure 7-12).

You can set the following options in the Reading Settings page:

- **Front Page Displays:** Choose what you want to display on the front page of your blog: your latest posts or a static page. You can find detailed information about using a static page for your front page in Chapter 14.

- **Blog Pages Show at Most:** Enter the maximum number of posts you want to display on each blog page.

- **Syndication Feeds Show the Most Recent:** In the Posts box, enter the maximum number of posts you want to show in your RSS feed at any time.

- **For Each Article in a Feed, Show:** Select either Full Text or Summary. Full Text publishes the entire post to your RSS feed, whereas Summary publishes only an excerpt. (Check out Chapter 8 for more information on WordPress RSS feeds.)

- **Encoding for Pages and Feeds:** UTF-8 is the default, and recommended, character encoding for your blog. *Character encoding* is code that handles the storage and transmission of the text from your blog through the Internet connection. Your safest bet is to leave the default setting in place, because UTF-8 is the most commonly accepted character encoding and supports a wide range of languages.

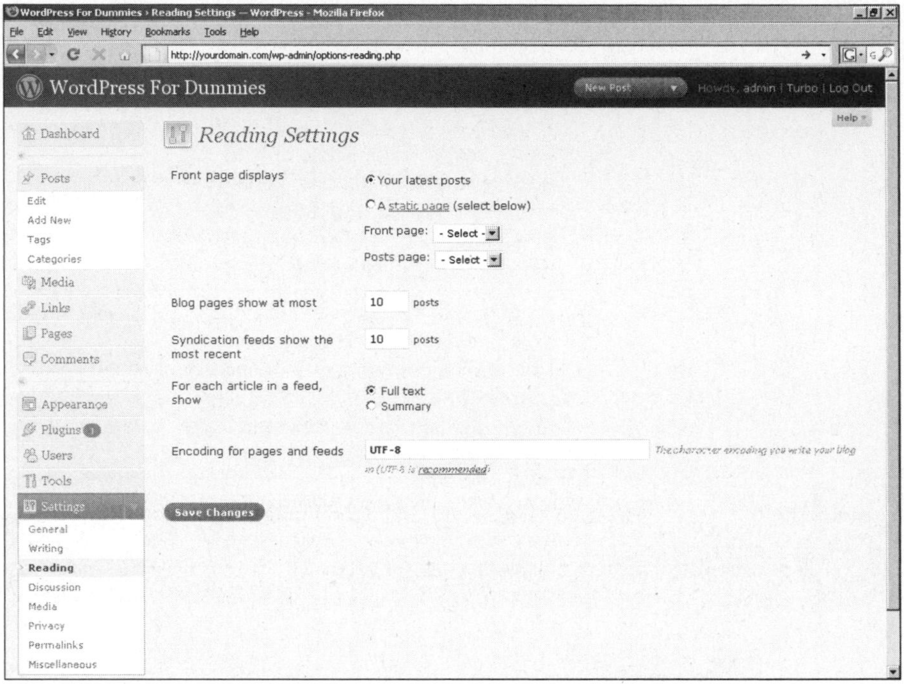

Figure 7-12:
The Reading
Settings
page.

Be sure to click the Save Changes button when you've set all your options in
the Reading Settings page to make the changes take effect.

Discussion

Discussion is the fourth link in the Settings menu; click it to open the
Discussion Settings page (see Figure 7-13). The sections on this tab let you
set options for handling comments and publishing of posts to your blog.

The following sections cover the options available to you in the Discussion
Settings page, which deals mainly with how comments and trackbacks are
handled in your blog.

Default Article Settings

In the Default Article Settings sections, you can tell WordPress how to handle
post notifications. Here are your options:

✔ **Attempt to Notify Any Blogs Linked to from the Article (Slows Down Posting):** Check this box, and your blog sends a notification (or *ping*) to any site you have linked to in your blog posts. This notification is also commonly referred to as a *trackback* (I discuss trackbacks in Chapter 2). Clear this box if you don't want these notifications to be sent.

✔ **Allow Link Notifications from Other Blogs (Pingbacks and Trackbacks):** By default, this box is checked, and your blog is open to be notified via a ping or trackback from another blog that has linked to yours. Any trackbacks or pings sent to your blog are listed on your site in the comments section of the blog post. If you clear this box, your blog won't accept pingbacks or trackbacks from other blogs.

✔ **Allow People to Post Comments on the Article:** By default, this box is checked, and people can leave comments on your blog posts. If you clear this box, no one can leave comments on your blog.

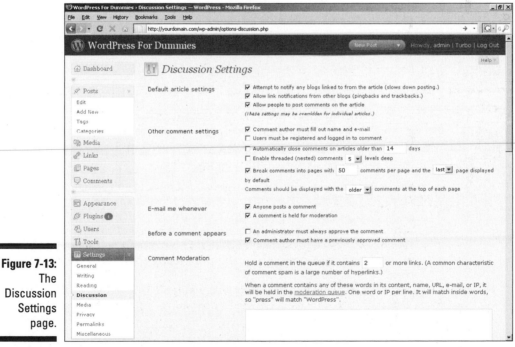

Figure 7-13:
The
Discussion
Settings
page.

Other Comment Settings

The Other Comment Settings tell WordPress how to handle comments:

- ✔ **Comment Author Must Fill Out Their Name and E-Mail:** Enabled by default, this option requires all commenters on your blog to fill in the Name and E-Mail field when leaving a comment. This option is very helpful in combating comment spam. (See Chapters 2 and 10 for information on comment spam.) Clear this check box to disable this option.

- ✔ **Users Must Be Registered and Logged in to Comment:** Not enabled by default, this option allows you to accept comments on your blog from only those people who have registered and are currently logged in as a user on your blog. If the user is not logged in, they see a message that says: *You must be logged in in order to leave a comment.*

- ✔ **Automatically Close Comments on Articles Older Than *X* Days:** Check the box next to this option to tell WordPress you would like comments on older articles to be automatically closed. Fill in the text box provided with the number of days you would like to wait before WordPress closes comments on older articles.

   This is a very effective anti-spam technique that many bloggers use to keep the comment and trackback spam on their blog down.

- ✔ **Enable Threaded (Nested) Comments *X* Levels Deep:** The drop-down menu allows you to choose the level of threaded comments you'd like to have on your blog. The default is 1; you can choose up to 10 levels. Instead of all comments being displayed on your blog in chronological order (as it is by default), nesting them allows you and your readers to reply to comments within the comment itself.

- ✔ **Break Comments into Pages with *X* Comments Per Page:** Fill in the text box with a number of comments you want to display on one page. This is very helpful for blogs that receive a large number of comments. It provides you with the ability to break the long string of comments into several pages, which makes it easier to read and helps speed up the load time of your site, because the page isn't loading such a large number of comments at once.

- ✔ **Comments Should Be Displayed with the Older/Newer comments at the Top of Each Page:** Use the drop-down menu to select Older or Newer. Selecting Older displays the comments on your blog in the order of oldest to newest. Selecting Newer does the opposite: displays the comments on your blog in the order of newest to oldest.

E-Mail Me Whenever

The two options in the E-Mail Me Whenever section are enabled by default:

- ✔ **Anyone Posts a Comment:** This option lets you receive an e-mail notification whenever anyone leaves a comment on your blog. Clear the box if you don't want to be notified by e-mail about every new comment.

> ✔ **A Comment Is Held for Moderation:** This option lets you receive an e-mail notification whenever a comment is awaiting your approval in the comment moderation queue. (See Chapter 8 for more information about the comment moderation queue.) You need to deselect this option if you don't want this notification.

Before a Comment Appears

The two options in the Before a Comment Appears section tell WordPress how you want WordPress to handle comments before they appear in your blog:

> ✔ **An Administrator Must Always Approve the Comment:** Disabled by default, this option keeps every single comment left on your blog in the moderation queue until you, the administrator, log in and approve it. Check this box to enable this option.

> ✔ **Comment Author Must Have a Previously Approved Comment:** Enabled by default, this option requires comments posted by all first-time commenters to be sent to the comment moderation queue for approval by the administrator of the blog. After comment authors have been approved for the first time, they remain approved for every comment thereafter. WordPress stores their e-mail addresses in the database, and any future comments that match any stored e-mails are approved automatically. This feature is another measure that WordPress has built in to combat comment spam.

Comment Moderation

In the Comment Moderation section, you can set options to specify what types of comments are held in the moderation queue to await your approval.

To prevent spammers from spamming your blog with a *ton* of links check the Hold a Comment in the Queue If It Contains X or More Links box. The default number of links allowed is 2. Give that setting a try, and if you find that you're getting lots of spam comments with multiple links, you may want to revisit this page and increase that number. Any comment with a higher number of links goes to the comment moderation area for approval.

The large text box in the Comment Moderation section lets you type keywords, URLs, e-mail addresses, and IP addresses in comments that you want to be held in the moderation queue for your approval.

Comment Blacklist

In this section, type a list of words, URLs, e-mail addresses, and/or IP addresses that you want to flat-out ban from your blog. Items placed here don't even make it into your comment moderation queue; the WordPress system filters them as spam. Let me just say that the words I have placed in my blacklist are not family-friendly and have no place in a nice book like this.

Avatars

The final section of the Discussion Settings page is Avatars. (See the nearby sidebar "What are avatars, and how do they relate to WordPress?" for information about avatars.) In this section, you can select different settings for the use and display of avatars on your site:

1. **In the Avatar Display section, decide how to display avatars on your site.**

   - *Don't Show Avatars:* Choose this option, and your blog won't display avatars.

   - *Show Avatars:* Choose this option to have your blog display avatars.

2. **In the Maximum Rating section, set the rating for the avatars that do display on your site.**

   This feature works much like the movie rating system you're used to. You can select G, PG, R, and X ratings for the avatars that display on your site. If your site is family-friendly, you probably don't want it to display R- or X-rated avatars.

3. **Choose a default avatar in the Default Avatar section (see Figure 7-14):**

   - Mystery Man

   - Blank

   - Gravatar Logo

   - Identicon (Generated)

   - Wavatar (Generated)

   - MonsterID (Generated)

4. **Click the Save Changes button.**

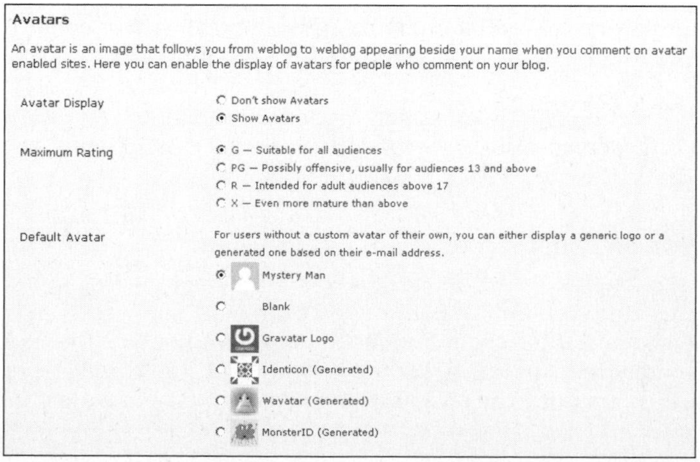

Figure 7-14: Default avatars you can display in your blog.

What are avatars, and how do they relate to WordPress?

An *avatar* is an online graphical representation of an individual. It's a small graphic icon that people use to visually represent themselves on the Web in areas they participate in conversations such as discussion forums and blog comments. *Gravatars* are globally recognized avatars; it's an avatar that you can take with you wherever you go. It appears alongside blog comments, blog posts, and discussion forums as long as the site you are interacting with is Gravatar-enabled. In

October 2007, Automattic, the core group behind the WordPress platform, purchased the Gravatar service and integrated it into WordPress so that all could enjoy and benefit from the service. Gravatars are not automatic; you need to sign up for an account with Gravatar so that you can assign an avatar to you, via your e-mail address. Find out more about Gravatar by visiting `http://gravatar.com`.

Avatars display in a couple places:

- ✔ **The Comments page in the Administration panel:** In Figure 7-15, the first three comments have the commenter's avatar displayed next to them.
- ✔ **The comments on individual blog posts to your blog:** Figure 7-16 shows a list of comments on my own personal blog.

Figure 7-15: Comment authors' avatars appear in the Comments page in the WordPress Administration panel.

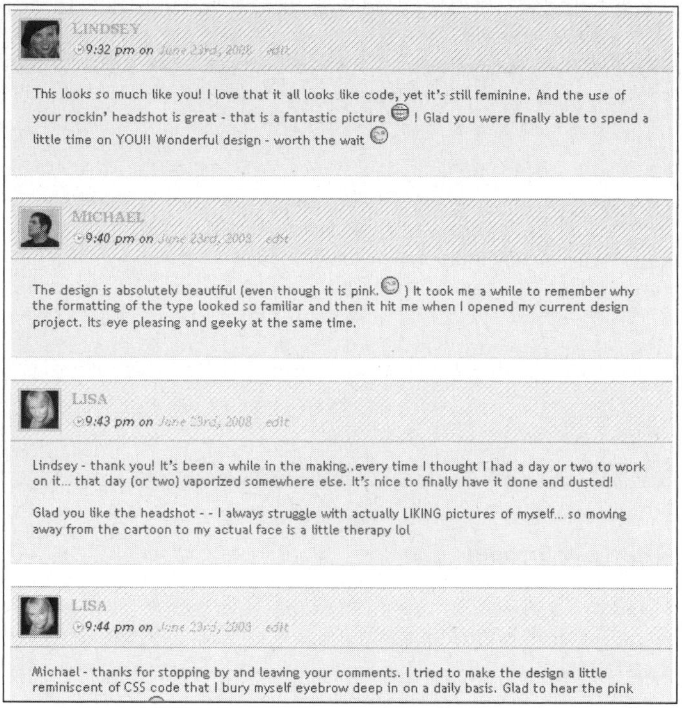

LINDSEY
9:32 pm on *June 23rd, 2008* / *edit*

This looks so much like you! I love that it all looks like code, yet it's still feminine. And the use of your rockin' headshot is great - that is a fantastic picture 😊 ! Glad you were finally able to spend a little time on YOU!! Wonderful design - worth the wait 😊

MICHAEL
9:40 pm on *June 23rd, 2008* / *edit*

The design is absolutely beautiful (even though it is pink. 😊) It took me a while to remember why the formatting of the type looked so familiar and then it hit me when I opened my current design project. Its eye pleasing and geeky at the same time.

LISA
9:43 pm on *June 23rd, 2008* / *edit*

Lindsey - thank you! It's been a while in the making..every time I thought I had a day or two to work on it... that day (or two) vaporized somewhere else. It's nice to finally have it done and dusted!

Glad you like the headshot - - I always struggle with actually LIKING pictures of myself... so moving away from the cartoon to my actual face is a little therapy lol

LISA
9:44 pm on *June 23rd, 2008* / *edit*

Michael - thanks for stopping by and leaving your comments. I tried to make the design a little reminiscent of CSS code that I bury myself eyebrow deep in on a daily basis. Glad to hear the pink

Figure 7-16:
Comments on a post, showing the comment author's avatars.

To enable the display of avatars in comments on your blog, the Comments Template (`comments.php`) in your active theme has to contain the code to display them. Hop on over to Chapter 12 to find out how to do that.

Click the Save Changes button after you've set all your options on the Discussion Settings page to make the changes take effect.

Media

The next link in the Settings menu is Media; click the Media link and the Media Settings page opens (see Figure 7-17.)

On the Media Settings page, you can configure the options for how the display of your media (images, documents, video, and audio) files are displayed on your blog.

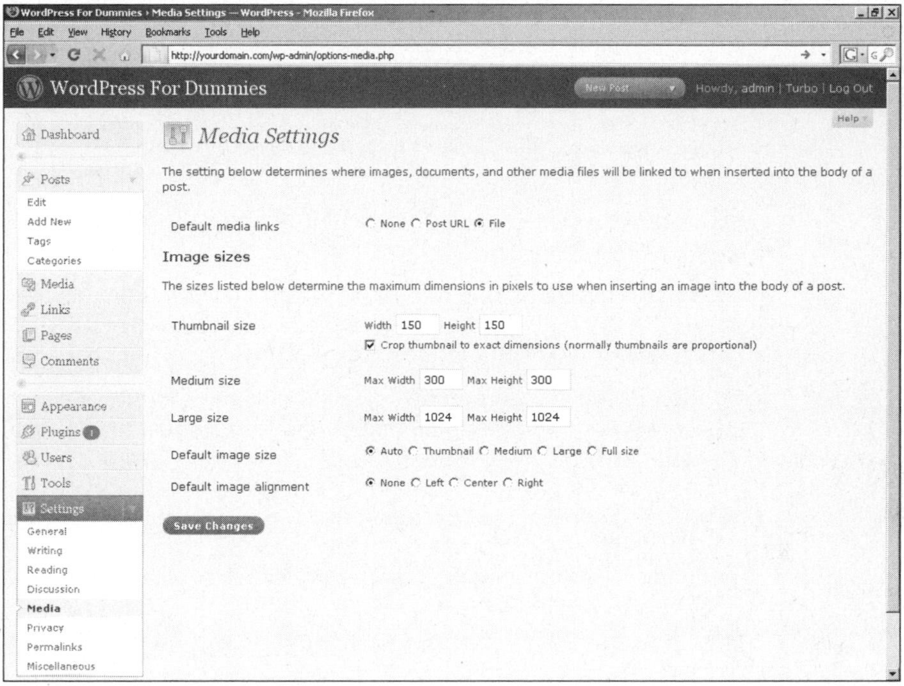

Figure 7-17:
The Media
Settings
page.

The first one is easy! For the Default Media Links settings, you have three
options on how you want your media files linked (where should a link take
your visitors?) when you insert one into the body of your blog post:

✔ **None:** Select this option if you don't want your media files to be linked
  to anything.

✔ **Post URL:** Select this option to link the media file to the permalink URL
  of the post the file appears in.

✔ **File:** Select this option to link the media file to the actual file. When a
  reader clicks the media file, the file opens in a new browser window;
  whether it is a Microsoft Word document or a photograph, the actual file
  opens when clicked.

The next set of options on the Media Settings page deals with images.
WordPress automatically resizes your images for you in three different sizes.
The dimensions are referenced in pixels by width, then height. (For example:
50 x 50 means 50 pixels in width by 50 pixels in height.)

- ✔ **Thumbnail Size:** The default is 150 x 150; enter the width and height of your choice. Select the Crop Thumbnail to Exact Dimensions box to resize the thumbnail exactly to the width and height you specified. Clear this box and WordPress resizes the image proportionally.

- ✔ **Medium Size:** The default is 300 x 300; enter the width and height numbers of your choice.

- ✔ **Large Size:** The default is 1024 x 1024; enter the width and height numbers of your choice.

- ✔ **Default Image Size:** Select Auto, Thumbnail, Medium, or Large to tell WordPress the default image size you want to use in your posts. You can override this default choice on a per post basis if you need to.

- ✔ **Default Image Alignment:** Select None, Left, Center, or Right to tell WordPress the default alignment you want to use for the images in your post. You can override this default choice on a per post basis.

Be sure to click the Save Changes button to save your configurations!

In Chapter 9, I go into much greater detail on how to insert images in your WordPress posts and pages;

Privacy

The next Settings menu option is Privacy; click it to display the Privacy Settings page (see Figure 7-18).

This page contains only two options, both of which concern visibility on your blog:

- ✔ **I Would Like My Blog to Be Visible to Everyone, Including Search Engines (Like Google, Sphere, Technorati) and Archivers.** This option is the default setting and means that you are freely allowing search engines to visit your blog and to list you in their search results, and letting your site be indexed in blog archive services such as Technorati.

- ✔ **I Would Like to Block Search Engines, but Allow Normal Visitors.** If you are one of those rare bloggers who *doesn't* want that type of exposure for your blog, but you do want to let normal visitors (read: no search engines) see your blog, select this option.

Be sure to click the Save Changes button after you set all your options on the Privacy Settings page to make the changes take effect.

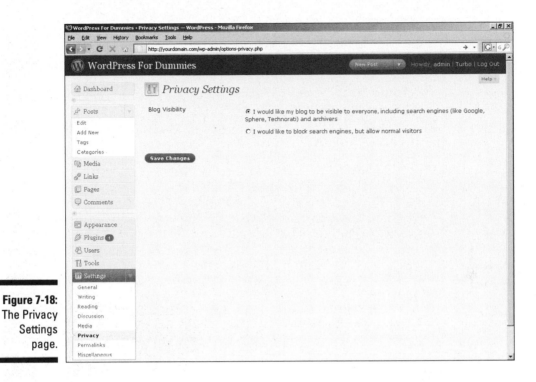

Figure 7-18:
The Privacy
Settings
page.

Permalinks

The next link on the Settings menu is Permalinks. Clicking this link loads the Permalink Settings page (see Figure 7-19).

Each of the posts you create on your blog has a unique URL called a *permalink,* which is permanent link (URL) for all your blog posts, pages, and archives. I cover permalinks extensively in Chapter 8 by explaining what they are, how you can use them, and how you set the options in this page.

Miscellaneous

The final link on the Settings menu is Miscellaneous; click it to display the Miscellaneous Settings page (see Figure 7-20).

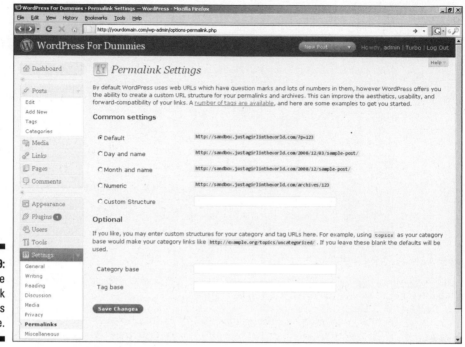

Figure 7-19:
The
Permalink
Settings
page.

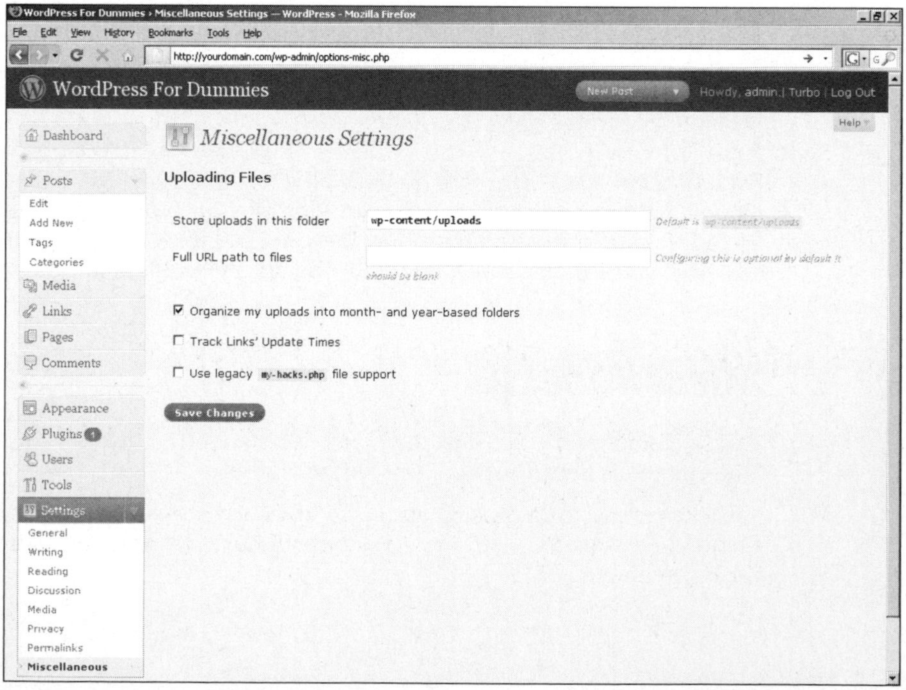

Figure 7-20:
The Miscel-
laneous
Settings
page.

You can change the following settings on this page:

- ✔ **Store Uploads in This Folder:** Type the server path to the folder on your Web server where you want your file uploads to be stored. The default is `wp-content/uploads`. You can specify any folder you want, however; just be sure that the folder you specify has permissions (`chmod`) set to 755 so that it is writeable. (See Chapter 6 for more information on setting file permissions.)

- ✔ **Full URL Path to Files (optional):** You can also type the full URL path to the uploads folder as an optional setting. (The full URL path would be something like `http://yourdomain.com/wp-content/uploads`.)

- ✔ **Organize My Files into Month and Year-Based Folders:** Select this box to have WordPress organize your uploaded files in folders by month and by year. Files you upload in January 2009, for example, would be in the following folder: `/wp-content/uploads/2009/01/`. Likewise, files you upload in February 2009 would be in `/wp-content/uploads/2009/02/`.

  This box is deselected by default; leave it that way if you do not want WordPress to organize your files in month and year-based folders.

- ✔ **Track Links' Update Times:** Check this box to have WordPress track the update times on links that you have listed in your link lists. For this feature to work, the blogs you have listed need to ping (or notify) an update service such as blogrolling.com. WordPress can be configured to display a special notation, such as an asterisk, for updated links in your blogroll.

- ✔ **Use Legacy my-hacks.php File Support:** This feature, for small hacks, is rarely used by anyone other than true WordPress code jockeys. If you don't know whether you are using the `my-hacks.php` file, you probably aren't and would be safer leaving it alone.

Click the Save Changes button to save your configured options.

Creating Your Personal Profile

The next place to visit to really personalize your blog is your profile page in your WordPress Administration panel.

To access your profile page, click the down arrow to the right of the Users menu; then click the Your Profile submenu link; you're taken to the Profile page (see Figure 7-21).

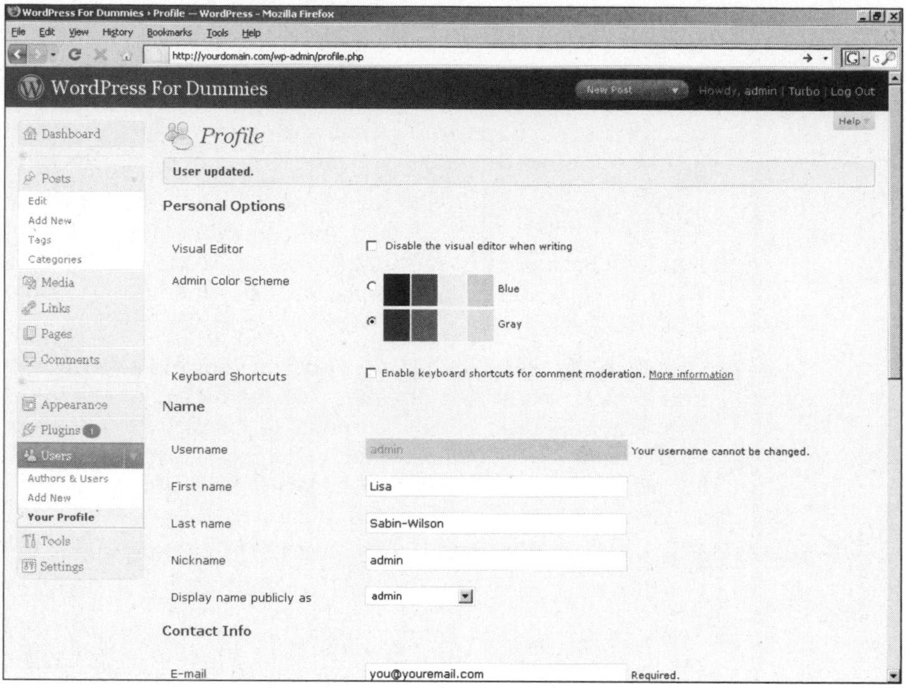

Figure 7-21:
Establish
your profile
details here.

Here are the settings on this page:

✔ **Personal Options:** The Personal Options section is where you can set two preferences for your blog:

- *Visual Editor:* Check this box to indicate that you want to use the Visual Editor when writing your posts. The Visual Editor refers to the formatting options you find in the Write Post page (discussed in detail in Chapter 8). By default, the box is checked, which means that the Visual Editor is on. To turn it off, clear the box.

- *Admin Color Scheme:* These options set the colors in your Administration panel. The default is the Gray color scheme. If you have been using WordPress since before March 2007, the Blue color scheme will be familiar to you as the colors used in previous versions of the Administration panel.

- *Keyboard Shortcuts:* This enables you to use keyboard shortcuts for comment moderation. To learn more about keyboard shortcuts, click the More Information link; you're taken to the Keyboard Shortcuts page (http://codex.wordpress.org/Keyboard_Shortcuts) in the WordPress Codex with some helpful information.

✔ **Name:** This section is where you can input personal information such as your first name, last name, and nickname, and specify how you want your name to be displayed publicly. Fill in the text boxes with the requested information.

✔ **Contact Info:** In this section, you provide your e-mail address and other contact information to tell your visitors who you are and where they may contact you. Aside from e-mail, you can provide your ID for various Internet chat programs such as Yahoo! IM, AIM (AOL Instant Messenger), and Jabber/Google Talk.

Note that your e-mail address is the only required entry here. This address is the one WordPress uses to notify you when you have new comments or new user registrations on your blog. Make sure to use a real e-mail address so that you get these notifications.

✔ **About Yourself:** This section is where you can provide a little bio for yourself and change the password for your blog.

When your profile is published to your Web site, it not only can be viewed by anyone — it also gets picked up by search engines like Google and Yahoo! Always be careful with the information in your profile. Think hard about the information you want to share with the rest of the world!

- *Biographical Info:* Type a short bio in the Biographical Info text box. This information can be shown publicly if you are using a theme that displays your bio, so be creative!

- *New Password:* When you want to change the password for your blog, type your new password in the first text box in the New Password section. To confirm your new password, type it again in the second text box.

Directly below the two text boxes is a little password helper. WordPress helps you create a secure password by alerting you if the password you've chosen is too short or not secure enough by telling you that it is Bad. When creating a new password, use a combination of letters, numbers, and symbols to make it hard for anyone to guess (for example, aty89!#4j). When you create a password that WordPress thinks is a good one, it lets you know by saying that the password is Strong.

Change your password frequently. I can't recommend this practice strongly enough. Some people on the Internet make it their business to attempt to hijack blogs for their own malicious purposes. If you change your password monthly, you lower your risk by keeping hackers guessing.

When you finish setting all the options on the Profile page, don't forget to click the Update Profile button to save your changes.

Setting Your Blog's Format

In addition to setting your personal settings in the Administration panel, you can manage the day-to-day maintenance of your blog. This next section takes you through the links to these sections in the navigation menu, directly underneath the Dashboard link.

Posts

Click the down arrow to the right of the Pages menu and a submenu drops down with four links: Edit, Add New, Tags, and Categories. Each link gives you the tools you need to publish content to your blog:

✔ **Edit:** This link opens the Edit Posts page where you see a listing of all the saved posts you've written on your blog. On this page, you can search for posts by date, category, or keyword. You can view all posts, only posts that have been published, or just those posts that have been saved, but not yet published (*drafts*). You can also edit and delete posts from this page. Check out Chapter 8 for more information on editing posts on your blog.

✔ **Add New:** This link opens the Add New Post page, which is where you compose your blog posts, set the options for each post (such as assigning a post to a category, making it a private or public post), and publish the post to your blog. You can find more information on posts, post options, and publishing in Chapter 8.

You can also get to the Add New Post page by clicking the Posts menu.

✔ **Post Tags:** This link opens the Tags page in your WordPress Administration panel where you can view, add, edit, and delete tags on your blog. Chapter 8 provides you with more information about what tags are and why you use them on your blog.

✔ **Categories:** This link opens the Categories page where you can view, edit, add, and delete categories on your blog. Find more information on categories in Chapter 8.

Media

Click the Media menu to expand the submenu of links for this section:

✔ **Library:** This link opens the Media Library page. On this page, you view, search, and manage all the media files you've ever uploaded to your WordPress blog.

✔ **Add New:** This link opens the Upload New Media page where you can use the built-in uploader to transfer media files from your computer to the media directory in WordPress. Chapter 9 takes you through the details of how to upload images, videos, audio, and other media files (such as Microsoft Word or PowerPoint documents) using the WordPress upload feature.

You can also get to the Upload New Media page by clicking the Media menu.

Links

The next menu header in the navigation menu is Links. Expand the Links submenu by clicking the down arrow to the right of the Links menu:

✔ **Edit:** This link opens the Edit Links page, where you can view, search, edit, and delete existing links in your WordPress blog. Chapter 8 gives you detailed information about links, link lists, and blogrolls.

✔ **Add New:** This link opens the Add New Link page, where you can add new links to your link lists. (You can find more information about creating and managing link lists in Chapter 8.)

You can also get to the Add New Link page by clicking the Links menu.

✔ **Link Categories:** This link opens the Link Categories page where you can add new, view, edit, and delete existing link categories (see Chapter 8).

Pages

People use this feature to create pages on their sites such as an About Me or Contact Me page. Flip to Chapter 8 for more information on pages. Click the Pages menu to reveal the submenu links:

✔ **Edit:** This link opens the Edit Pages page where you have the ability to search, view, edit, and delete pages in your WordPress blog,

✔ **Add New:** This link opens the Add New Page page where you can compose, save, and publish a new page on your blog. Table 7-2 describes the difference between a post and a page — it's subtle, but posts and pages are very different from one another!

You can also get to the Add New Page page by clicking the Pages menu.

Table 7-2	The Differences between a Post and a Page	
WordPress Options	*Page*	*Post*
Appears in blog post listings	No	Yes
Appears as a static page	Yes	No
Appears in category archives	No	Yes
Appears in monthly archives	No	Yes
Appears in Recent Posts listings	No	Yes
Appears in search results	No	Yes

Comments

Clicking the down arrow to the right of the Comments menu expands the Comments submenu. Click the Comments link and the Edit Comments page opens, where WordPress gives you the options to view:

✔ **All:** This shows all comments that currently exist on your blog. This includes approved, pending, and spam comments.

✔ **Awaiting Moderation:** This shows comments that are not yet approved by you but are pending in the moderation queue.

✔ **Approved:** This shows all comments that have been previously approved by you.

✔ **Spam:** This shows all of the comments that are marked as spam.

✔ **Trash:** This shows comments that you have marked as Trash but have not yet been deleted permanently from your blog.

You can find information in Chapter 2 about the purpose of comments. In Chapter 8, I give you details on how to use the Manage Comments section of your WordPress Administration panel.

Appearance

When you click the Appearance menu in the navigation menu, a submenu drops down with the following links:

✔ **Themes:** Click this link to open the Manage Themes page where you can manage the themes available on your blog. Check out Chapter 11 to learn about using themes on your WordPress blog, and how to manage those themes on this page.

You can also navigate to this page by clicking the Themes menu.

- ✔ **Widgets:** This link opens the Widgets page where you can add, delete, edit, and manage the widgets you use on your blog.

- ✔ **Editor:** This link opens the Theme Editor page where you can edit your theme templates. Chapters 11, 12, and 13 have extensive information on themes and templates.

- ✔ **Header Image and Color:** This link opens the Customize Header page; however, this menu item and page exist only if you have the WordPress Default theme activated. Not all WordPress themes use the Customize Header feature, so you don't see this menu item if your theme doesn't take advantage of that feature.

- ✔ **Add New Themes:** This link opens the Install Themes page where you are able to browse the official Themes Directory from within your WordPress Dashboard. You can find, preview, and install new themes on your blog on the Install Themes page.

Chapter 11 gives you a great deal of information about how to use WordPress themes (including where to find, install, and activate them in your WordPress blog), as well as detailed information on using WordPress widgets to display the content you want.

Part V provides information about WordPress themes and templates. You can dig deep into WordPress template tags and tweak an existing WordPress theme by using Cascading Style Sheets (CSS) to customize your theme a bit more to your liking.

Plugins

The next menu in the navigation menu is Plugins. Click the Plugins menu to expand the submenu of links:

- ✔ **Installed**: Click this link and open the Manage Plugins page where you can view all the plugins currently installed on your blog. On this page, you also have the ability to activate, deactivate, and delete plugins on your blog (see Chapter 10). If you click the Plugins menu, you also go to the Manage Plugins page.

- ✔ **Add New**: This link opens the Install Plugins page where can search for plugins from the official WordPress Plugin Directory by keyword, author, or tag. You can also install plugins directly to your blog from the Plugin Directory — you find out all about this exciting feature in Chapter 10!

- ✔ **Editor:** This link opens the Edit Plugins page where you can edit the plugin files in a text editor. I very strongly advise against editing plugin files unless you know what you are doing (read: you are familiar with PHP and WordPress functions). Head over to Chapter 10 to read more information on editing plugin files.

Users

The Users menu has two links:

- **Authors & Users:** Click this link to go to the Users page where you can view, edit, and delete on your WordPress blog. Each user has a unique login name and password as well as having an e-mail address assigned to their account. You can view and edit their information on the Users page.

- **Add New:** This link opens the Add New User page where you can add new users to your WordPress blog. You simply type in the username, first name, last name, e-mail (required), Web site, and password in the fields provided and click the Add User button. You can also select whether you want WordPress to e-mail the login information to the user when the new user account is created.

- **Your Profile:** Turn to the "Creating Your Personal Profile" section, earlier this chapter, for more information about creating a profile page.

Tools

The last menu item in the navigation menu (and subsequently in this chapter!) is Tools. Click the Tools menu to drop down the submenu of links that includes:

- **Import:** WordPress gives you the ability to import from a different blog platform. This feature is covered in depth in the appendix.

- **Export:** WordPress also allows you to export your content from WordPress so you can import it into a different platform, or to another WordPress blog. This information is also covered in the appendix.

 In order to use Google Gears, you need a Google account and you need to give authorization for Gears to access your blog files.

- **Upgrade:** This link takes you to the Upgrade WordPress page where you can automatically upgrade your WordPress software whenever a new upgrade is available. Click the Upgrade Automatically button and you are effortlessly taken through the upgrade process. Some Web host server configurations do not allow WordPress to access the automatic upgrade from within the Administration panel. If this is the case with your Web hosting situation, click the Download Nightly Build button to download the latest version of WordPress to your computer; then you can upload the files to your Web server via FTP. (See Chapter 6 for information on using FTP to upload WordPress files.)

Chapter 8

Establishing Your Blog Routine

*W*ordPress is a powerful publishing tool, especially when you use the full range of options available. With the basic settings configured (which you do in Chapter 7), now is the time to go forth and blog! You can, at this point, skip to the "Blog It!: Writing Your First Entry" section in this chapter and jump right into creating new posts for your blog. Or you can stay right here with me and discover some of the options you can set to make your blog a bit more organized and logical from the get-go.

A blog can become unwieldy and disorganized, requiring you to revisit these next few features sometime in the near future so that you can get the beast under control. So why not do a little planning and get the work over with now? I promise it won't take that long, and you'll thank me for it later.

Staying on Topic with Categories

In WordPress, a *category* is what you determine to be the main topic of a blog post. Through the use of categories, you can file your blog posts into topics, by subject. To improve your readers' experiences in navigating through your blog, WordPress organizes posts by the categories you assign to them.

Visitors can click the categories they're interested in to see the blog posts you've written on those particular topics. You should know ahead of time that the list of categories you set up is displayed on your blog in a few different places, including the following:

- **Body of the post:** In most WordPress themes, you see the title followed by a statement such as Filed In: *Category 1*, *Category 2*. The reader can click the category name to go to a page that lists all the posts you've made in that particular category. You can assign a single post to more than one category.

- **Sidebar of your blog theme:** You can place a full list of category titles in the sidebar. A reader can click any category and get taken to a page on your site that lists the posts you've made within that particular category.

Subcategories (also known as *category children*) can further refine the main category topic by listing specific topics related to the main (parent) category. In your WordPress Administration panel, on the Manage Categories page, subcategories are listed directly below the main category. Here's an example:

Books I Enjoy (main category)

    Fiction (subcategory)

    Nonfiction (subcategory)

    Trashy romance (subcategory)

    Biographies (subcategory)

    For Dummies (subcategory)

Changing the name of a category

Upon installation, WordPress gives you one default category called Uncategorized (see the Categories page shown in Figure 8-1). That category name is pretty generic, so you'll definitely want to change it to one that's more specific to you. (On my blog, I changed it to Life in General. Although that name's still a bit on the generic side, it doesn't sound quite so . . . well, uncategorized.)

The default category also serves as kind of a fail-safe. If you publish a post to your blog and don't assign that post to a category, the post automatically gets assigned to the default category, no matter what you name the category.

So how do you change the name of that default category? When you're logged in to your WordPress Dashboard, just follow these steps:

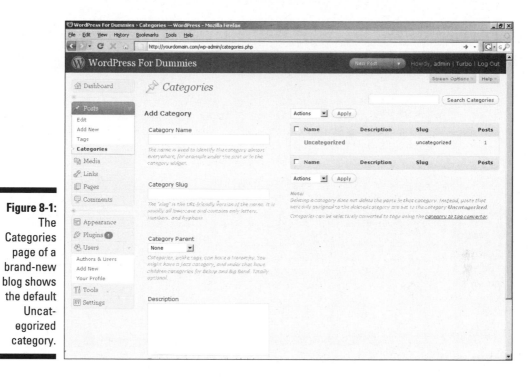

Figure 8-1:
The
Categories
page of a
brand-new
blog shows
the default
Uncat-
egorized
category.

1. **Click the down arrow to the right of the Posts menu, and then click the Categories link.**

   The Categories page opens, containing all the tools you need to set up and edit category titles for your blog.

2. **Click the title of the category you would like to edit.**

   If you want to change the Uncategorized category, click the word Uncategorized and you go to the Edit Category page (see Figure 8-2).

3. **Type the new name for the category in the Category Name text box.**

4. **Type the new slug in the Category Slug text box.**

   The term slug refers to the word(s) used in the Web address for the specific category. For example, the category of Books has a Web address of `http://yourdomain.com/category/books`; if you change the Category Slug to Books I Like, then the Web address is `http://your domain.com/category/books-i-like` (WordPress automatically inserts a dash between the slug words in the Web address).

5. **Choose a parent category from the Category Parent drop-down menu.**

   If you want this category to be a main category, not a subcategory, choose None.

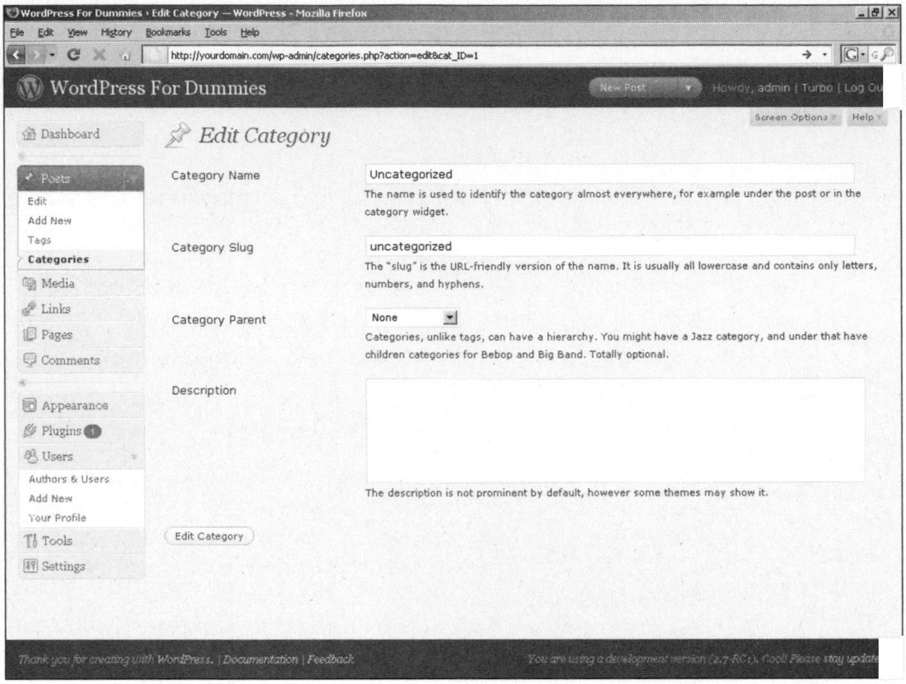

Figure 8-2:
Editing a
category in
WordPress
on the Edit
Category
page.

6. **(Optional) Type a description of the category in the Description text box.**

   Use this description to remind yourself what your category is about. Some WordPress themes display the category description right on your site, too, which can be helpful for your visitors. (See Chapter 12 for more about themes.) You'll know if your theme is coded in this way if your site displays the category description on the category page(s).

7. **Click the Edit Category button.**

   The information you just edited is saved, and the Categories page reloads, showing your new category name.

Creating new categories

Today, tomorrow, next month, next year — as your blog grows in size and age, you will continue adding new categories to further define and archive the history of your blog posts. You aren't limited in the number of categories and subcategories you can create in your blog.

Creating a new category is as easy as following these steps:

1. **Click the down arrow to the right of the Posts menu, and then click the Categories link.**

   The Categories page opens.

2. **The left side of the Categories page displays the Add Category section.**

   See Figure 8-3.

3. **Type the name of your new category in the Category Name text box.**

   Suppose that you want to create a category in which you file all your posts about the books you read. In the Category Name text box, type something like **Books I Enjoy**.

4. **Type a name in the Category Slug text box.**

   The category slug creates the link to the category page that lists all the posts you've made in this category. If you leave this field blank, WordPress automatically creates a slug based on the category name. If the category is Books I Enjoy, WordPress automatically creates a category slug like this: `http://yourdomain.com/category/books-i-enjoy`. If you want to shorten it, however, you can! Type **books** in the Category Slug text box, and the link to the category becomes this: `http://yourdomain.com/category/books`.

Add Category

Category Name

The name is used to identify the category almost everywhere, for example under the post or in the category widget.

Category Slug

The "slug" is the URL-friendly version of the name. It is usually all lowercase and contains only letters, numbers, and hyphens.

Category Parent

None

Categories, unlike tags, can have a hierarchy. You might have a Jazz category, and under that have children categories for Bebop and Big Band. Totally optional!

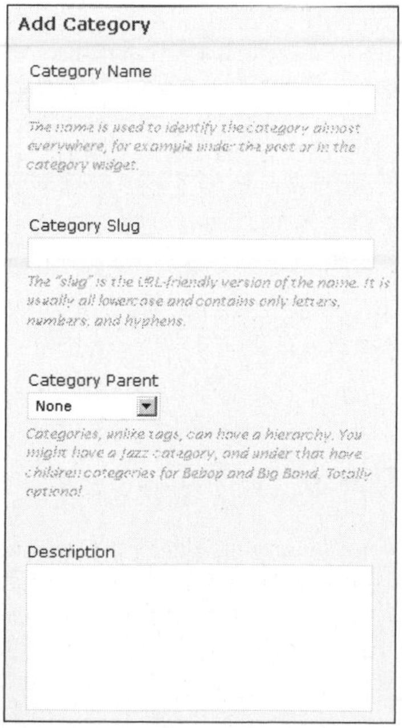

Figure 8-3:
Create a
new cat-
egory on
your blog.

Description

5. **Choose the category's parent from the Category Parent drop-down menu.**

   Choose None if you want this new category to be a parent category. If you'd like this category to be a subcategory of another category, choose the category you want to be the parent of this one.

6. **(Optional) Type a description of the category in the Description text box.**

   Some WordPress templates are set up to actually display the category description directly beneath the category name (see Chapter 12). Providing a description helps you to further define the category intent for your readers. The description can be as short or as long as you like.

7. **Click the Add Category button.**

   That's it! You've added a new category to your blog. Armed with this information, you can add an unlimited number of categories to your blog.

You can delete a category on your blog by selecting the box to the left of the category name on the Categories page, and then select Delete in the Actions drop-down menu.

Deleting a category doesn't delete the posts and links in that category. Instead, posts in the deleted category are assigned to the Uncategorized category (or whatever you've named the default category).

If you have an established WordPress blog with categories already created, you can convert some or all of your categories to tags. To do so, scroll to the bottom of the Categories page in the WordPress Administration panel, and click the category to Tag Converter link. (See the nearby sidebar "What are tags, and how/why do I use them?" for more information on tags.)

What are tags, and how/why do I use them?

Tags are not to be confused with categories, but a lot of people do confuse them. *Tags* are clickable, comma-separated keywords that help you microcategorize a post by defining the topics in it. Unlike WordPress categories, tags do not have a hierarchy; there are no parent tags and child tags. If you write a post about your dog, for example, you can put that post in the Pets category — but you can also add some specific tags that let you get a whole lot more specific, such as poodle, small dogs. If someone clicks your poodle tag, he finds all the posts you've ever made that contain the poodle tag.

Another reason to use tags: Search-engine spiders harvest tags when they crawl your site, so tags help other people find your site when they search for specific words.

You can manage your tags in the WordPress Administration panel by clicking the Tags link on the Pages menu. The Tags page opens where you can view, edit, delete, and add new tags.

Link Lists: Sharing Your Favorite Sites

A *link list,* commonly referred to as a *blogroll,* is a list of links to other Web sites and blogs that you've collected and want to share with your readers. The link list is displayed in your blog, usually in the sidebar, through the use of widgets, or on a dedicated page of links, if your theme has a links page template (see Chapter 12 to find out how to create a template).

You can use a link list in various ways:

- ✔ Share links with other blogs that have linked to your blog.
- ✔ Provide additional resources that you think your readers will find useful.
- ✔ Provide links to other sites you own.

Organizing your links

As with posts, you can create multiple categories for your links in the WordPress Administration panel if you want to have more than one link list. Sometimes, having a large list of links below the heading Blogroll is just too generic, and you may want to display groups of links with different headings that further define them.

By default, WordPress provides one link category called Blogroll. You can keep this name as is or change it in the same way that you change a post category name (refer to "Changing the name of a category," earlier in this chapter). Just click the name of the category and edit the details as you need to.

You can define your links by creating link categories in the Administration panel and then assigning links to the appropriate categories. To create link categories, follow these steps:

1. **Click the down arrow to the right of the Links menu, and then click the Link Categories link.**

   The Link Categories page opens, as shown in Figure 8-4. The left side of the Link Categories page displays the Add Category section.

2. **Type the name of the link category in the Category Name box.**

3. **Type the slug of the link category in the Category Slug box.**

   This entry is the same as the category slug described previously in the "Changing the name of a category" section in this chapter.

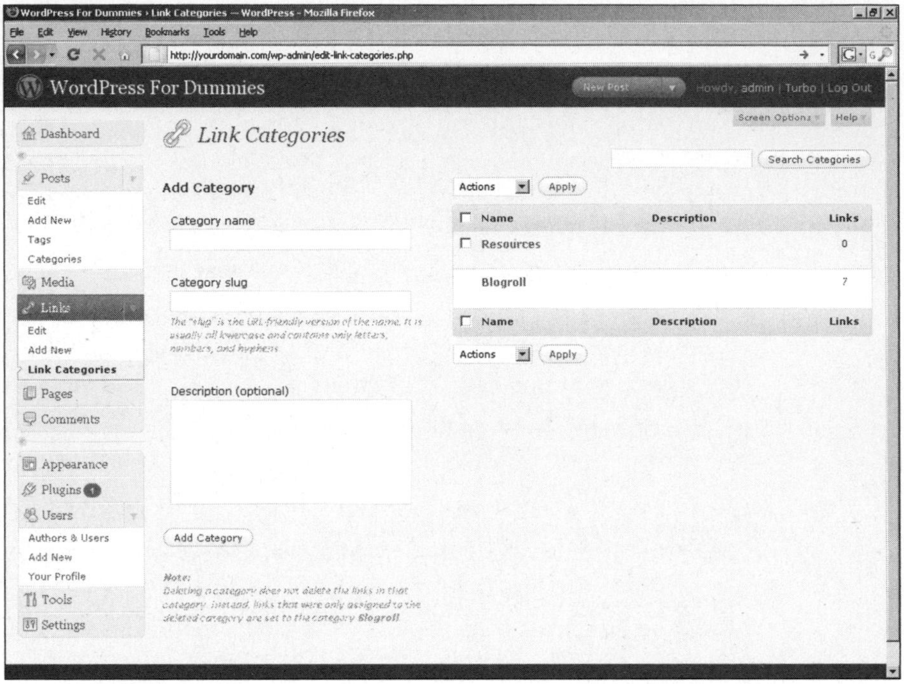

Figure 8-4:
The Link
Categories
page.

4. (Optional) Type a description of the link category in the Category Description box.

Providing a description helps you further define the category intent for your readers. The description can be as short or as long as you like. Some WordPress templates are set up to actually display the category description directly beneath the category name.

5. Click the Add Category button.

The Link Categories page refreshes and displays your new link category.

Revisit the Link Categories page any time you want to add, edit, or delete a link. To edit or delete a link category, you would follow the same steps as you did in the previous section for post categories. You can create an unlimited amount of link categories to sort your link lists by topics. (I know one blogger who has 50 categories for his links.)

In Chapter 5, I show you how to display your link lists by using WordPress widgets, and in Chapter 12, I provide information about different ways you can display your link lists by using template tags.

Adding new link loves

You've created your link categories; now you just need to add some new links! To add a new link, follow these steps:

1. **Click the Add New link on the Links menu.**

   The Add New Links page opens, as shown in Figure 8-5.

2. **Type the name of the link in the Name text box.**

   This is the actual name of the site that you are adding to your link list.

3. **Type the URL of the link in the Web Address box.**

   This is the destination you want your visitors to go to when they click the name of the site. Don't forget to include the `http://` part of the Web address; for example, `http://lisasabin-wilson.com`.

4. **(Optional) Type a description of the site in the Description box.**

   Providing a description helps further define the site for your readers. Some WordPress templates are coded to display the link description directly below the link name through the use of a specific WordPress template tag.

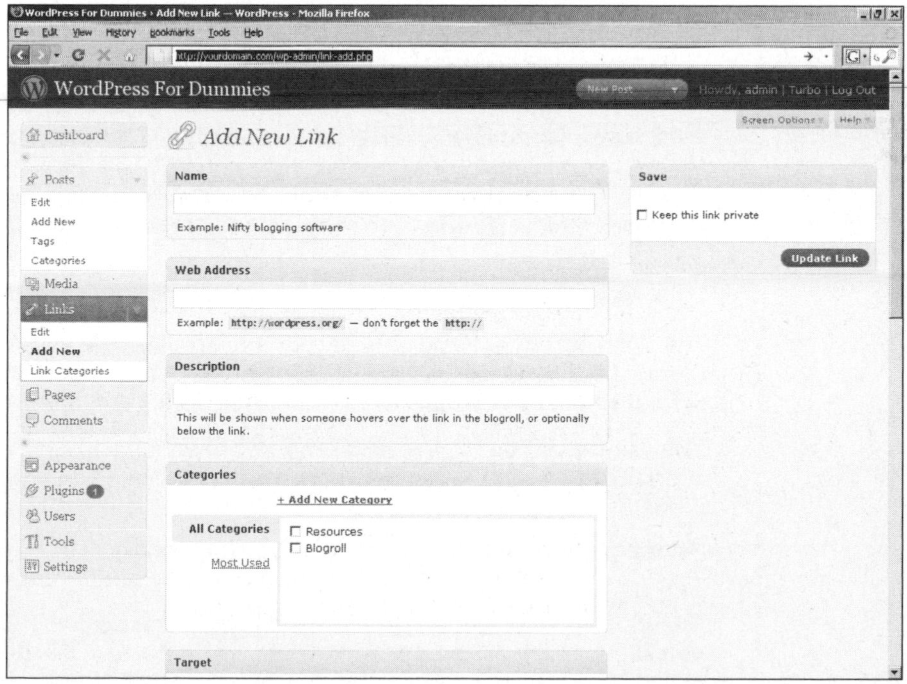

Figure 8-5: Add a new link with the Add New Links page.

5. (Optional) Select a category.

Assign your new link to a category by checking the box to the left of the category you've chosen in the Categories module. If you don't select a category for your new link, it's automatically assigned to the default category. Figure 8-6 shows the list of link categories I have in my blog.

If you find that the Link Category is not an option you use regularly, you can collapse (close) this module by clicking anywhere in the Categories title bar. You can also move the Categories module to a different position on the Add New Link page by dragging and dropping it to a new location.

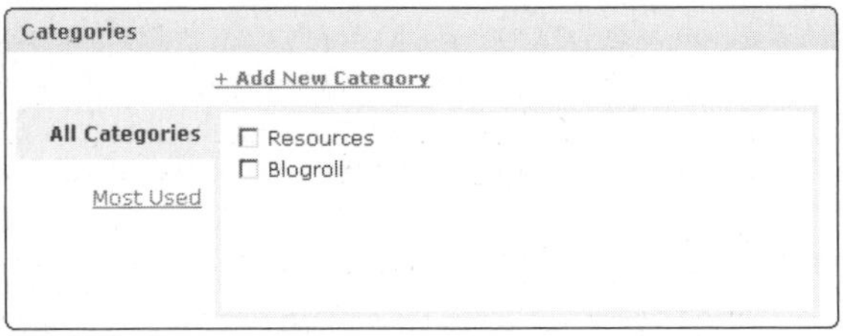

Figure 8-6:
You can
assign a
link to an
existing
category or
add a new
category
here.

6. (Optional) Select a target for your new link.

Click one of the following radio buttons in the Target section:

- *_blank:* Loads the link in a new browser window

- *_top:* Loads the link in the top frame (if your site is designed with frames)

- *None:* Loads the link in the same browser window

The third option — None — is my personal preference and recommendation. I like to let my visitors decide whether they want a bunch of new browser windows opening every time they click a link on my site.

You can reposition the Target module by dragging and dropping it to a new location on the Add New Link page. You can also collapse this module.

7. Set the Link Relationship (XFN) options (Optional).

XFN stands for XHTML Friends Network and allows you to indicate the relationship you have with the people you are linking to by defining how you know, or are associated with, them. Table 8-1 lists the different relationships you can assign to your links. Link Relationship (XFN) is kind of a silly bookmark-type assignment that indicates how well you know the person whose site or blog you're linking to by defining your relationship with her. You can find more information on XFN at http://gmpg.org/xfn.

You can reposition the Link Relationship module by dragging and dropping it to a new location on the Add New Link page. You can also collapse (close) this module.

Table 8-1	Link Relationships Defined
Link Relationship	*Description*
Identity	Check this box if the link is to a Web site you own.
Friendship	Choose the option (Contact, Acquaintance, Friend, or None) that most closely identifies the friendship, if any.
Physical	Check this box if you've met the person you're linking to face to face. Sharing pictures over the Internet doesn't count; this selection identifies a person you've physically met.
Professional	Check one of these boxes if the person you're linking to is a co-worker or colleague.
Geographical	Choose Co-Resident if the person you're linking to lives with you, or choose Neighbor or None, depending on which option applies to your relationship with the person you're linking to.
Family	If the blogger you're linking to is a family member, choose the option that tells how the person is related to you.
Romantic	Choose the option that applies to the type of romantic relationship, if any, you have with the person you're linking to. Do you have a crush on him? Is she your creative muse or someone you consider to be a sweetheart?

8. **Set the advanced options for your new link (see Figure 8-7).**

   You have four options in the Advanced module:

   - *Image Address:* Type the URL of the picture that you want to appear next to the link in your link list.

     This option associates an image with the link. To use it, you need to know the direct URL to the image source (such as http://yourdomain.com/images/image.jpg).

     To find the URL for an image displayed on a Web site, right-click the image and choose Properties from the shortcut menu. Copy and paste all the text from the Address (URL) field to the Image Address box in the WordPress options box.

   - *RSS Address:* Add the site's RSS feed alongside the link that appears on your site. (Not all WordPress themes accommodate this feature.)

To find the RSS URL of the site you're linking to, visit that site, and locate the RSS link. (It's usually listed in the sidebar or footer of the site.) Right-click the link, and from the shortcut menu, choose Copy Shortcut (in Internet Explorer) or Copy Link Location (in Firefox). Then, in WordPress, paste the link in the RSS Address field.

- *Notes:* Type your notes in the Notes field.

  These notes aren't displayed on your site, so feel free to enter whatever notes you need to further define the details of this link. A month from now, you may not remember who this person is or why you linked to her, so here is where you can add notes to remind yourself.

- *Rating:* Use the Rating drop-down menu to rate the link from 0–10, 0 being the worst and 10 being the best. Some WordPress themes display your link list in the order in which you've rated your links, from best to worst.

You can reposition the Advanced module by dragging and dropping it to a new location on the Add New Link page. You can also collapse (close) this module.

9. **To save your changes, scroll up to the top of the Add New Links page and click the Save button. Choose whether to make the link public or private.**

To keep the link private, select the Keep This Link Private box. No one you can see the link. If you want the link to be publicly displayed on your blog, leave that box unchecked.

You can reposition the Save module by dragging and dropping it to a new location on the Add New Link page. You can also collapse (close) this module.

A blank Add New Links page opens, ready for you to add another new link!

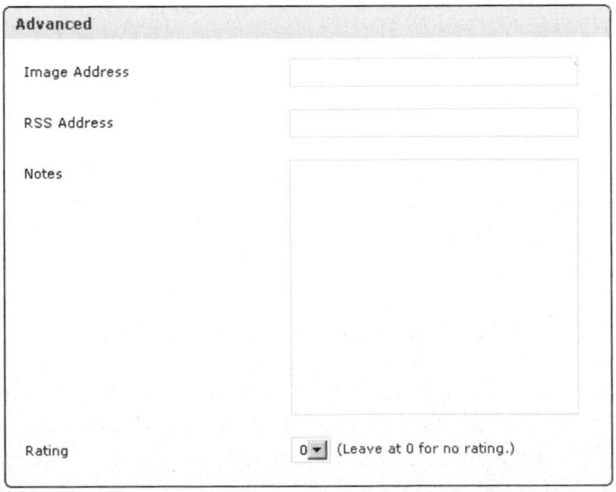

Figure 8-7:
Advanced
link options
give you
settings
to further
manage the
individual
links in your
blogroll.

Advanced	
Image Address	
RSS Address	
Notes	
Rating	0 ▾ (Leave at 0 for no rating.)

Editing existing links

You can edit the links in your blog by clicking the Edit link on the Links menu; the Edit Links page opens.

When you first view the Edit Links page, some links are already assigned to your blog. By default, WordPress provides seven links in your link list. These links go to some helpful Web sites that contain information and resources for the WordPress software. You can delete these links, but I recommend saving them for future reference.

Here's what you can do with your links:

✔ **Edit an existing link:** Click the name of the link you'd like to edit. The Edit Link page opens. Edit the fields you need to change; click the Save button at the top right of the page.

✔ **Sort the links:** You can sort by Link ID, Name, Address, or Rating by using the Order by Name drop-down menu. Likewise, you can sort your links by category by using the View All Categories drop-down menu and selecting the Link Category you'd like to filter your links by.

✔ **Search for specific links using keywords and phrases:** Enter your keyword in the text box at the top right hand side of the Edit Links page and click the Search Links button. If any links match the keywords and/or phrase you typed, they display on the page.

Examining a Blog Post's Address: Permalinks

Each WordPress blog post is assigned its own Web page, and the address (or URL) of that page is called a *permalink*. Posts that you see in WordPress blogs usually have the post permalink in four typical areas:

✔ The title of the blog post

✔ The Comments link below the post

✔ A Permalink link that appears (in most themes) below the post

✔ The titles of posts appearing in a Recent Posts sidebar

Permalinks are meant to be permanent links to your blog posts (which is where the *perma* part of that word comes from, in case you're wondering). Other bloggers can use a post permalink to refer to that particular blog post. So ideally, the permalink of a post never changes. WordPress creates the permalink automatically when you publish a new post.

By default, a blog post permalink in WordPress looks like this:

```
http://yourdomain.com/?p=100/
```

The `p` stands for *post,* and `100` is the ID assigned to the individual post. You can leave the permalinks in this format, if you don't mind letting WordPress associate each post with an ID number.

WordPress, however, lets you take your permalinks to the beauty salon for a bit of makeover so you can create pretty permalinks. I'll bet you didn't know that permalinks could be pretty, did you? They certainly can. Allow me to explain.

Making your post links pretty

Pretty permalinks are links that are more pleasing to the eye than standard links and, ultimately, more pleasing to search-engine spiders. (See Chapter 14 for an explanation of why search engines like pretty permalinks.) Pretty permalinks look something like this:

```
http://yourdomain.com/2008/01/01/pretty-permalinks/
```

Break down that URL, and you see the date when the post was made, in year/month/day format. You also see the topic of the post.

To choose how your permalinks look, click Permalinks in the Settings menu. The Permalink Settings page opens (see Figure 8-8).

In this page, you find several options for creating permalinks:

- **Default** (ugly permalinks): WordPress assigns an ID number to each blog post and creates the URL in this format: `http://yourdomain.com/?p=100`.

- **Day and Name** (pretty permalinks): For each post, WordPress generates a permalink URL that includes the year, month, day, and post slug/title: `http://yourdomain.com/2008/01/01/sample-post/`.

- **Month and Name** (also pretty permalinks): For each post, WordPress generates a permalink URL that includes the year, month, and post slug/title: `http://yourdomain.com/2008/01/sample-post/`.

- **Numeric** (not so pretty): WordPress assigns a numerical value to the permalink. The URL is created in this format: `http://yourdomain.com/archives/123`.

- **Custom Structure:** WordPress creates permalinks in the format you choose. You can create a custom permalink structure by using tags or variables, as I discuss in the next section.

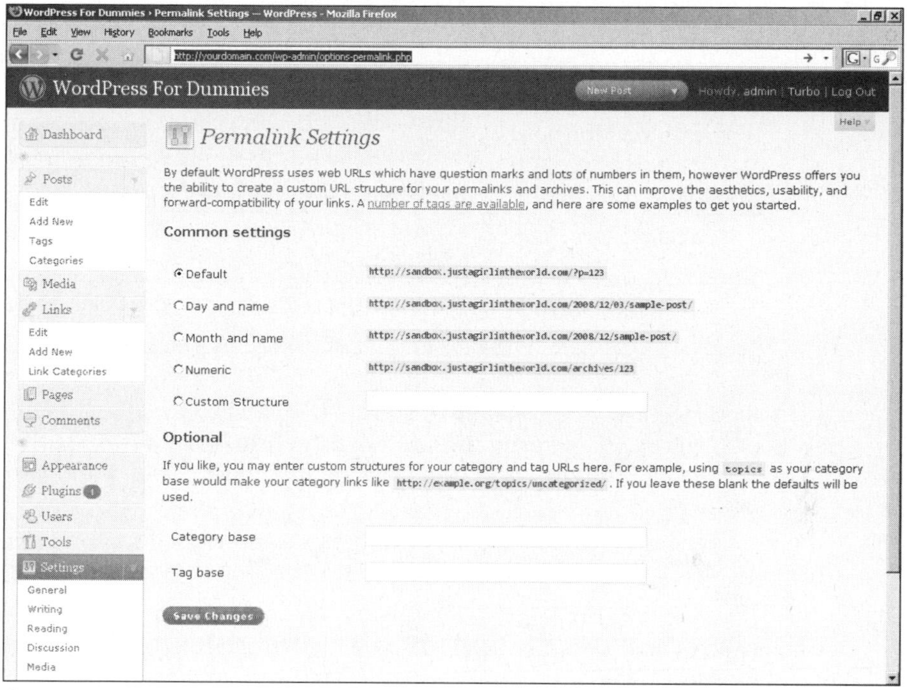

Figure 8-8:
Make your
permalinks
pretty.

To create the pretty-permalink structure, select the Day and Name radio button; then click the Save Changes button at the bottom of the page.

Customizing your permalinks

A *custom permalink structure* is one that lets you define which variables you want to see in your permalinks by using the tags in Table 8-2.

Table 8-2	Custom Permalinks
Permalink Tag	*Results*
%year%	4-digit year (such as 2007)
%monthnum%	2-digit month (such as 02 for February)
%day%	2-digit day (such as 30)
%hour%	2-digit hour of the day (such as 15 for 3 p.m.)
%minute%	2-digit minute (such as 45)
%second%	2-digit second (such as 10)

(continued)

Table 8-2 *(continued)*

Permalink Tag	Results
%postname%	Text — usually, the post name — separated by hyphens (such as `making-pretty-permalinks`)
%post_id%	The unique numerical ID of the post (such as `344`)
%category%	The text of the category name that you filed the post in (such as `books-i-read`)
%author%	The text of the post author's name (such as `lisa-sabin-wilson`)

If you want your permalink to show the year, month, day, category, and post name, you'd select the Custom Structure radio button in the Customize Permalink Structure page and type the following tags in the Custom Structure text box:

```
/%year%/%monthnum%/%day%/%category%/%postname%/
```

Under this permalink format, the link for a post made on February 1, 2008, called WordPress For Dummies and filed in the Books I Read category, would look like this:

```
http://yourdomain.com/2008/01/01/books-i-read/wordpress-for-dummies/
```

Be sure to include the slashes before tags, between tags, and at the very end of the string of tags. This format ensures that WordPress creates correct, working permalinks by using the correct `re_write` rules located in the `.htaccess` file for your site. (See the following section for more information on `re_write` rules and `.htaccess` files.)

Changing the structure of your permalinks in the future affects the permalinks for all the posts on your blog . . . new and old. Keep this fact in mind if you ever decide to change the permalink structure. An especially important reason: Search engines (such as Google and Yahoo!) index the posts on your site by their permalinks, so changing the permalink structure makes all those indexed links obsolete.

Don't forget to click the Save Changes button at the bottom of the Customize Permalink Structure page; otherwise your permalink changes aren't saved!

Making sure that your permalinks work with your server

After you set the format for the permalinks for your site by using any options other than the default, WordPress writes specific rules, or directives, to the .htaccess file on your Web sever. The .htaccess file in turn communicates to your Web server how it should serve up the permalinks, according to the permalink structure you've chosen to use.

To use an htaccess file, you need to know the answers to two questions:

- ✔ Does your Web server configuration use and give you access to the .htaccess file?
- ✔ Does your Web server run Apache with the mod_rewrite module?

If you don't know the answers, contact your hosting provider to find out.

If the answer to both questions is yes, proceed to the next section. If the answer is no, skip to the "Working with servers that don't use Apache mod_rewrite" section, later in this chapter.

Creating .htaccess files

You and WordPress work together in glorious harmony to create the .htaccess file that lets you use a pretty permalink structure in your blog. The file works like this:

1. Using a plain-text editor (such as Notepad for Windows or TextEdit for a Mac), create a blank file; name it htaccess.txt; and upload it to your Web server via FTP. (See Chapter 6 for more information about FTP.) When the file is on your Web server, rename the file .htaccess (notice the period at the beginning), and make sure that it is writable by the server by changing permissions to either 755 or 777. (See Chapter 6 for information on changing permissions on server files.)

   If .htaccess already exists, you can find it in the root of your directory on your Web server — that is, the same directory where you find your wp-config.php file. If you don't see it in the root directory, try changing the options of your FTP client to show hidden files. (Because the .htaccess file starts with a period [.], it may not be visible until you configure your FTP client to show hidden files.)

2. Create the permalink structure in the Customize Permalink Structure page in your WordPress Administration panel.

3. Click the Save Changes button at the bottom of the Customize Permalink Structure page.

   WordPress inserts into the `.htaccess` file the specific rules necessary for making the permalink structure functional in your blog.

If you followed these steps correctly, you have an `.htaccess` file on your Web server that has the correct permissions set so that WordPress can write the correct rules to it. Your pretty permalink structure works flawlessly. Kudos!

If you open the `.htaccess` file and look at it now, you'll see that it's no longer blank. It should have a set of code in it called *rewrite rules,* which looks something like this:

```
# BEGIN WordPress
<IfModule mod_rewrite.c>
RewriteEngine On
RewriteBase /
RewriteCond %{REQUEST_FILENAME} !-f
RewriteCond %{REQUEST_FILENAME} !-d
RewriteRule . /index.php [L]
</IfModule>

# END WordPress
```

I could delve deeply into `.htaccess` and all the things you can do with this file, but I'm restricting this section to how it applies to WordPress permalink structures. If you'd like to unlock more mysteries about `.htaccess`, check out "Comprehensive Guide to .htaccess" at `http://javascriptkit.com/howto/htaccess.shtml`.

Working with servers that don't use Apache mod_rewrite

Using permalink structures requires that your Web hosting provider has a specific Apache module option called `mod_rewrite` activated on its servers. If your Web hosting provider doesn't have this item activated on its servers, or if you're hosting your site on a Windows server, the custom permalinks work only if you type **index.php** in front of any custom permalink tags.

For example, create the custom permalink tags like this:

```
/index.php/%year%/%month%/%date%/%postname%/
```

This format creates a permalink like this:

```
http://yourdomain.com/index.php/2008/02/01/wordpress-for-
        dummies
```

You don't need an `.htaccess` file to use this permalink structure.

Discovering the Many WordPress RSS Options

In Chapter 2, you can read about RSS feed technology and why it's an important part of publishing your blog. Allow me to quote myself from that chapter: For your blog readers to stay updated with the latest and greatest content you post to your site, they need to subscribe to your RSS feed.

RSS feeds come in different flavors, including RSS 0.92, RDF/RSS 1.0, RSS 2.0, and Atom. The differences among them lie within the base code that makes up the functionality of the syndication feed. What's important is that WordPress supports all versions of RSS — which means that anyone can subscribe to your RSS feed with any type of feed reader available.

I mention many times throughout this book that WordPress is very intuitive, and this section on RSS feeds is a shining example of a feature that WordPress automates. WordPress has a built-in feed generator that works behind the scenes to create feeds for you. This feed generator creates feeds from your posts, comments, and even categories.

The RSS feed for your blog posts is *autodiscoverable,* which means that almost all RSS feed readers and even some browsers (Firefox, Internet Explorer 7, and Safari, for example) automatically detect the RSS feed URL for a WordPress blog. Table 8-3 gives you some good guidelines on how to find the RSS feed URLs for the different sections of your blog.

Table 8-3	URLs for Built-In WordPress Feeds
Feed Type	*Example Feed URL*
RSS 0.92	`http://yourdomain.com/wp-rss.php` or `http://yourdomain.com/?feed=rss`
RDF/RSS 1.0	`http://yourdomain.com/wp-rss2.php` or `http://yourdomain.com/?feed=rdf`
RSS 2.0	`http://yourdomain.com/wp-rss2.php` or `http://yourdomain.com/?feed=rss2`
Atom	`http://yourdomain.com/wp-atom.php` or `http://yourdomain.com/?feed=atom`

(continued)

Table 8-3 *(continued)*

Feed Type	Example Feed URL
Comments RSS	`http://`*yourdomain.*`com/?feed=rss&p=50` `p` stands for *post,* and `50` is the post ID. You can find the post ID in the Administration panel by clicking the Manage tab. The post ID is listed immediately to the left of the post title.
Category RSS	`http://`*yourdomain.*`com/wp-rss2.php?cat=50` `cat` stands for *category,* and `50` is the category ID. You can find the category ID in the Administration panel by clicking the Manage tab and then the Categories subtab. The category ID is listed immediately to the left of the category title.

If you're using custom permalinks (see "Making your post links pretty," earlier in this chapter), you can simply add `/feed` to the end of any URL on your blog to find the RSS feed. Some of your links will look similar to these:

- ✔ `http://`*yourdomain.*`com/feed` — your main RSS feed
- ✔ `http://`*yourdomain.*`com/comments/feed` — your comments RSS feed
- ✔ `http://`*yourdomain.*`com/category/cat-name/feed` — RSS feed for a category

Try it with any URL on your site. Add `/feed` at the end, and you'll have the RSS feed for that page.

RSS feeds are important parts of delivering content from your blog to your readers. RSS feeds are expected these days, so the fact that WordPress has taken care of the feeds for you, is compliant with all RSS formats, and offers so many internal feeds gives the software a huge advantage over any of the other blog-software platforms.

If you intend to use the Atom publishing protocol, you need to enable it manually because it is disabled by default. Click the Writing link on the Settings menu, and then check the two boxes in the Remote Publishing section to enable Atom publishing in WordPress.

Blog It!: Writing Your First Entry

It's finally time to write your first post in your new WordPress blog! The topic you choose to write about and the writing techniques you use to get your message across are all on you; I have my hands full writing this book! I *can* tell you, however, how to write the wonderful passages that could bring you blog fame. Ready?

Composing your blog post

Composing a blog post is a lot like typing an e-mail: You give it a title, you write the message, and you click a button to send your words into the world.

 You can collapse or reposition all the modules on the Add New Posts page to suit your needs. The only section on the Add New Posts page that cannot be collapsed and repositioned is the actual title and post box (where you write your blog post).

Follow these steps to write a basic blog post:

1. **Click the Add New link on the Posts menu.**

   The Add New Post page opens, as shown in Figure 8-9.

2. **Type the title of your post in the Title text box.**

3. **Type the content of your post in the Post text box.**

   You can use the Visual Text Editor to format the text in your post. I explain the Visual Text Editor and the buttons and options after these steps.

4. **Click the Save Draft button in the Publish module, located at the top right side of the Add New Post page.**

   The page refreshed with your post title and content saved, but not yet published to your blog.

By default, the area in which you write your post is in Visual Editing mode, as indicated by the Visual tab that appears above the text. Visual Editing mode is how WordPress provides WYSIWYG (What You See Is What You Get) options for formatting. Rather than have to embed HTML code in your post, you can simply type your post, highlight the text you want to format, and click the buttons (shown in Figure 8-9) that appear above the box in which you type your post.

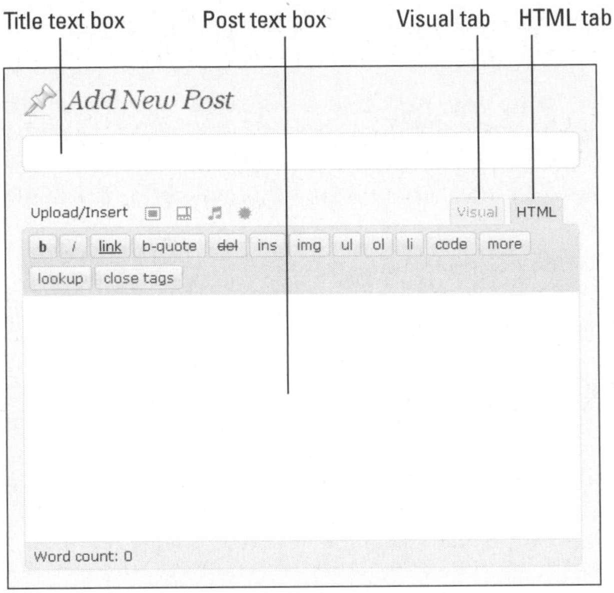

Title text box   Post text box   Visual tab   HTML tab

Figure 8-9:
This page is
where you
give your
blog post
a title and
write your
post body.

If you've ever used a word processing program, such as Microsoft Word, you'll recognize many of these buttons:

- **Bold:** Embeds the `<strong> </strong>` HTML tag to emphasize the text in bold. Example: **Bold Text.**

- **Italic:** Embeds the `<em> </em>` HTML tag to emphasize the text in italics. Example: *Italic Text.*

- **Strikethrough:** Embeds the `<strike> </strike>` HTML tag that puts a line through your text. Example: ~~Strikethrough Text~~.

- **Unordered List:** Embeds the `<ul><li> </li></ul>` HTML tags that create an unordered, or bulleted, list.

- **Ordered List:** Embeds the `<ol><li> </li></ol>` HTML tags that create an ordered, or numbered, list.

- **Blockquote:** Inserts the `<blockquote> </blockquote>` HTML tag that indents the paragraph or section of text you've selected.

- **Align Left:** Inserts the `<p align="left"> </p>` HTML tag that lines up the paragraph or section of text you've selected against the left margin.

- **Align Center:** Inserts the `<p align="center"> </p>` HTML tag that positions the paragraph or section of text you've selected in the center of the page.

✔ **Align Right:** Inserts the `<p align="right"> </p>` HTML tag that lines up the paragraph or section of text you've selected against the right margin.

✔ **Insert/Edit Link:** Inserts the `<a href=" "> </a>` HTML tag around the text you've selected to create a hyperlink.

✔ **Unlink:** Removes the hyperlink from the selected text, if it was previously linked.

✔ **Insert More Tag:** Inserts the `<!--more-->` tag, which lets you split the display on your blog page. It publishes the text written above this tag with a Read More link, which takes the user to a page with the full post. This feature is good for really long posts.

✔ **Toggle Spellchecker:** Perfect for typo enthusiasts! Checking your spelling before you post is always a good idea.

✔ **Toggle Full Screen Mode:** Lets you focus purely on writing, without the distraction of all the other options on the page. Click this button, and the Post text box expands to fill the full height and width of your browser screen. To bring the Post text box back to its normal state, click the Toggle Full Screen button again. Voilà — it's back to normal!

✔ **Show/Hide Kitchen Sink:** I saw this button and thought, "Wow! WordPress does my dishes, too!" Unfortunately, the button's name is a metaphor that describes the advanced formatting options available with the Visual Text Editor. Click this button, and a new formatting menu drops down, providing options for underlining, font color, custom characters, undo and redo, and so on — a veritable kitchen sink full of options!

You can turn off the Visual Text Editor by clicking the Your Profile link on the Users menu. Uncheck the Use the Visual Editor When Writing box to turn off this editor if you'd rather insert the HTML code yourself in your posts.

If you'd rather embed your own HTML code and skip the Visual Text Editor, click the HTML tab that appears to the right of the Visual tab. If you're planning to type HTML code in your post — for a table or video files, for example, — you have to click the HTML tab before you insert that code. If you don't, the Visual Text Editor formats your code, and it most likely will look nothing like you intended it to.

At this point, you can skip to the "Publishing your post" section of this chapter for information on publishing your post to your blog, or continue with the following sections to discover how to refine the options for your post.

WordPress has a nifty, built-in autosave feature that saves your work while you're typing and editing a new post. If your browser crashes or you accidentally close your browser window before you've saved your post, it will be there for you when you get back. Those WordPress folks are so thoughtful!

Dressing up your posts with images, video, and audio

Directly above and to the left of the Visual Text Editor row of buttons is an Add Media area with a row of four icons. These icons let you insert images/ photos, photo galleries, videos, and audio files into your posts. WordPress has an entire Media Library capability, which I describe in great detail in Chapter 9.

Refining your post options

After you write the post, you can choose a few extra options before you publish it for the entire world to see. These settings apply to the post you're currently working on — not to any future or past posts. You can find these options below and to the right of the Post text box (see Figure 8-10). Click the title of each option — the settings for that specific option expand.

You can reposition the different post option modules on the Add New Post page to fit the way you use this page.

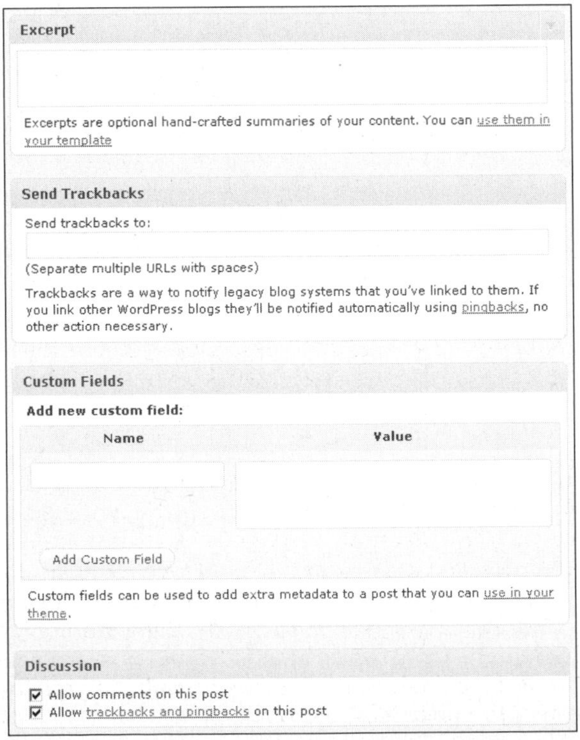

Excerpt

Excerpts are optional hand-crafted summaries of your content. You can <u>use them in your template</u>

Send Trackbacks

Send trackbacks to:

(Separate multiple URLs with spaces)

Trackbacks are a way to notify legacy blog systems that you've linked to them. If you link other WordPress blogs they'll be notified automatically using <u>pingbacks</u>, no other action necessary.

Custom Fields

Add new custom field:

Name	Value

Add Custom Field

Custom fields can be used to add extra metadata to a post that you can <u>use in your theme</u>.

Discussion

☑ Allow comments on this post
☑ Allow <u>trackbacks and pingbacks</u> on this post

Figure 8-10:
Several options are available for your blog post.

Here are the options found underneath the Post text box:

- **Excerpt:** Excerpts are short summaries of your posts. Many bloggers use snippets to show teasers of their blog posts, thereby encouraging the reader to click the Read More links to read the posts in their entirety. Type your short summary in the Excerpt box. Excerpts can be any length, in terms of words; however, the point is to keep it short and sweet and tease your readers into clicking the Read More link.

- **Send Trackbacks:** I discuss trackbacks in Chapter 2, if you'd like to refresh your memory banks on what they are. If you want to send a trackback to another blog, enter the blog's trackback URL in the Send Trackbacks To box. You can send trackbacks to more than one blog; just be sure to separate trackback URLs with spaces.

- **Custom Fields:** Custom fields add extra data to your posts and are fully configurable by you.

- **Discussion:** Decide whether to let readers submit comments through the comment system by checking Allow Comments on this Post box. By default, the box is checked; uncheck it to disallow comments on this post.

Here are the options found to the right of the Post text box:

- **Publish:** These are the publishing options for your post, which I covered in the "Publishing your post" section.

- **Tags:** Type your desired tags in the Add New Tag text box. Be sure to separate each tag with a comma so that WordPress knows where each tag begins and ends. Cats, Kittens, Feline represents three different tags, for example, but without the commas, WordPress would consider those three words to be one tag. See the sidebar "What are tags, and how/why do I use them?" earlier in this chapter for more information on tags.

- **Categories:** You can file your posts in different categories to organize them by subject. (See more about organizing your posts by category in "Staying on Topic with Categories," earlier in this chapter.) Check the box to the left of the category you want to use. You can toggle between listing all categories on your blog, or just the categories you use the most often by clicking the All Categories or Most Used links, respectively. Don't see the category you need listed here? Click the + Add New Category link, and you can add a category right there on the Add New Post page!

- **Privacy Options:** You can password-protect your post by creating a password and entering it in this box. When you do, you can share the password with only the readers you want to let read that post. This feature is perfect for those times when you'd love to make a blog post about all the stupid things your boss did today, but don't want your boss to see it (not that my boss ever does anything stupid; I'm just using an obscure example!). This feature also hides the post from search engines so that it doesn't show up in search results. If you don't want to password-protect the post, leave this box blank.

When you finish setting the options for your post, don't navigate away from this page; your options have not yet been fully saved. The next section on publishing your post covers all the options you need for saving your post settings!

Publishing your post

You have given your new post a title and written the content of your new blog post. Maybe you've even added an image or other type of media file to your blog post (see Chapter 9), and have configured the tags, categories, and other options. Now the question is: Publish? Or not to publish (yet)?

WordPress gives you three options for saving or publishing your post when you're done writing it. The Publish box is located on the right side of the Add New (or Edit) Post page. Just click the title of the Publish box to expand the settings you need. Figure 8-11 shows the available options in the Publish box.

Figure 8-11:
The publish status for your blog posts.

> **Publish**
>
> Save Draft   Preview
>
> Status: **Draft**
> Draft ▼ (OK) Cancel
>
> Visibility: **Public**
> ● Public
>   ☐ Stick this post to the front page
> ○ Password protected
> ○ Private
> (OK) Cancel
>
> 📅 Publish **immediately**
> Dec ▼ 03 , 2008 @ 14 : 52
> (OK) Cancel
>
>   Publish

The Publish module has several options:

- **Save Draft:** Choose this option to save your post as a draft. The Edit Post page reloads with all your post contents and options saved; you can continue editing it now, tomorrow, or the next day. To access your draft posts, click the Edit link on the Posts menu.

- **Preview:** Click the Preview button to view your post in a new window, as it would appear on your live blog if you had published it. Previewing the post doesn't publish it to your site yet. It gives you the opportunity to view it on your site and check it for any formatting or content changes you'd like to make.

✔ **Status:** Click the Edit link to open the settings for this option. A drop-down menu appears and you can select Draft or Pending Review:

   • Select *Draft* to save the post, but not publish it to your blog.

   • Select *Pending Review* and the post shows up in your list of drafts next to a Pending Review header. This option lets the administrator of the blog know that contributors have entered posts that are waiting for administrator review and approval (helpful for blogs with multiple authors).

   Click the OK button to save your settings.

✔ **Stick This Post to the Front Page:** Select this box to have WordPress publish the post to your blog and keep it at the very top of all blog posts until you edit this post and change this setting.

   This is otherwise known as a *sticky post*. Typically, posts are displayed in a chronological order on your blog, displaying the most recent post on top. If you make a post sticky, it remains at the very top no matter how many other posts you make after it. When you want to un-stick the post, deselect the Stick This Post to the Front Page box.

✔ **Publish Immediately:** Click the Edit link and you can set the timestamp for your post. If you want the post have the current time and date, ignore this setting altogether.

   If you'd like to future-publish this post, you can set the time and date for anytime in the future. This feature has come in handy for me many times. For example, when I have a vacation planned and I don't want my blog to go without updates while I'm gone, I'll sit down and write a few posts and set the date for a time in the future. They're published to my blog while I was somewhere tropical, diving with the fishes.

✔ **Publish:** This button wastes no time! It bypasses all the previous draft, pending review and sticky settings and publishes the post directly to your blog immediately.

After you choose an option from the drop-down menu, click the Save button. The Write Post page saves your publishing-status option.

If you want to publish your post right away, skip all the other options in the Publish module, and just click the Publish button. This method eliminates the fuss with the Publish Status options and sends your new post to your blog in all its glory.

If you click Publish and for some reason don't see the post you just published on the front page of your blog, you probably left the Publish Status drop-down menu set to Unpublished. You'll find your new post in the draft posts, which you'll find by clicking the Edit link on the Posts menu.

You are your own editor

While I write this book, I have editors looking over my shoulder, making rec-ommendations, correcting my typos and grammatical errors, and helping me out by telling me when I get too long-winded. You, on the other hand, are not so lucky! You are your own editor and have full control of what you write, when you write it, and how you write it. You can always go back and edit previous posts to correct typos, grammatical errors, and other mistakes by following these steps:

1. **Find the post that you want to edit by clicking the Edit link on the Posts menu.**

   The Edit Posts page opens and lists the 20 most recent posts you've made to your blog.

   You can filter that listing of posts by date by choosing a date from the Show All Dates drop-down menu at the top of the Edit Posts page. For example, if you choose November 2008, the Edit Posts page reloads, displaying only those posts that were published in the month of November 2008.

   You can also filter the post listing by category. Select your desired category from the View All Categories drop down menu.

2. **When you find the post you need, click its title.**

   The Edit Post window opens. In this window, you can edit the post and/or any of its options.

   You can also click the Edit link that appears beneath the post title on the Edit Posts page.

   If you only need to edit the post options, click the Quick Edit link. The post options open and you can configure post options like the title, status, password, categories, tags, comments, and timestamp. Click the Save button to save your changes.

3. **Edit your post; then click the Update Post button.**

   The Edit Post window refreshes with all of your changes saved.

Look Who's Talking on Your Blog

The feature that really catapulted blogging into the limelight is the comments feature, which lets visitors interact with the authors of blogs. I cover the concept of blog comments and trackbacks in Chapter 2. They provide a great way for readers to interact with site owners, and vice versa.

Managing comments and trackbacks

To find your comments, click the Comments link on the Comments menu; the Edit Comments page opens (see Figure 8-12).

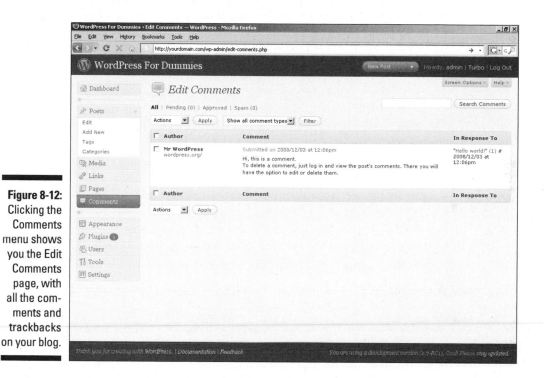

Figure 8-12:
Clicking the
Comments
menu shows
you the Edit
Comments
page, with
all the com-
ments and
trackbacks
on your blog.

When you hover over the comment with your mouse, several links appear that give you the opportunity to manage those comments:

- **Unapprove**: This link only appears if you have comment moderation turned on and appear with approved comments only. The comment is placed in the moderation queue, which you get to by clicking the Awaiting Moderation link that appears below the Manage Comments header. The moderation queue is kind of a holding area for comments that haven't yet been published to your blog. (See the following section for more on the moderation queue.)

- **Spam**: Click this link to mark the comment as spam and toss it into the spam bin where it will never be heard from again!

- **Delete:** This link does exactly what it says; it deletes the link completely from your blog.

✔ **Edit:** Click this link to open the Edit Comment page where you can edit the different fields, such as name, e-mail, URL, and comment content (see Figure 8-13).

✔ **Quick Edit:** Click this link and, without ever leaving the Edit Comments page, the comment options open and you can configure the post options like name, e-mail, URL, and comment content. Click the Save button to save your changes.

✔ **Reply:** Click this link and a text box drops down where you can type and submit your reply to this person. This feature eliminates the need to have to load your live site in order to reply to a comment.

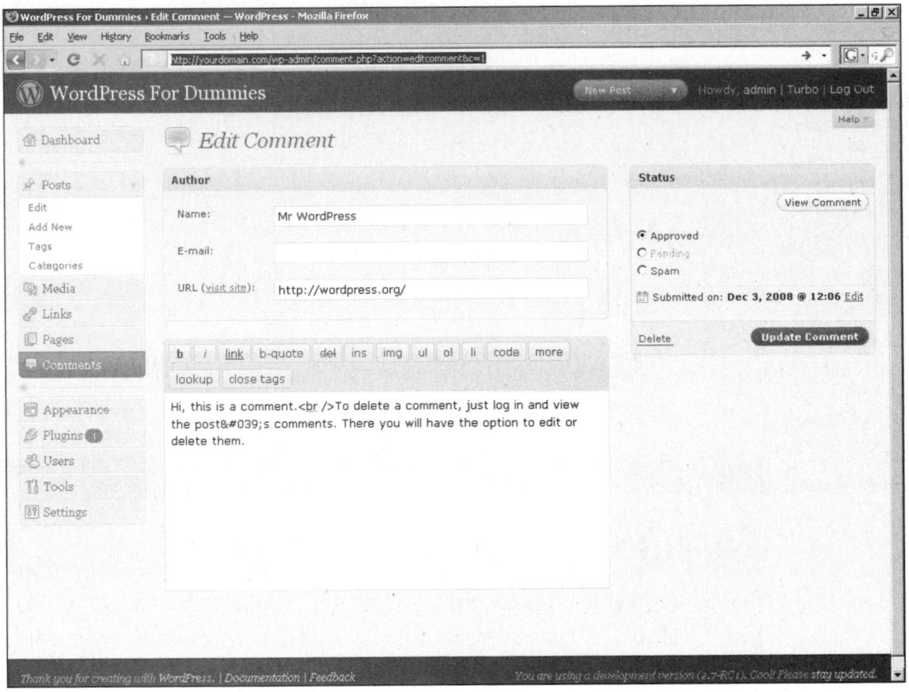

Figure 8-13:
Edit a user's comment in the Edit Comment page.

If you have a lot of comments listed in this page and want to bulk-edit them, check the boxes to the left of all the comments you want to manage; then select one of the following from the Actions drop-down menu at the top left of the Edit Comments page: Approve, Mark As Spam, Unapprove, or Delete.

Moderating comments and trackbacks

If you have your options set so that comments aren't published to your blog until you approve them, you can approve comments from the Edit Comments page as well. Just click the Pending link, and you go to the Edit Comments page. If you have comments and/or trackbacks awaiting moderation, you see them on this page, and you can approve them, mark them as spam, or delete them.

A nice feature of WordPress is that it immediately notifies you of any comments sitting in the moderation queue, awaiting your action. This notification, which appears on every single page, is a small orange conversation bubble that appears in the left navigation menu, to the right of the Comments menu. Figure 8-14 shows that I have 10 comments awaiting moderation. I'd better get busy and deal with those comments!

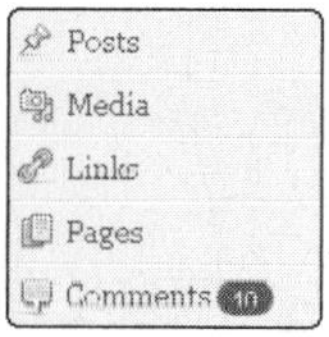

Figure 8-14:
A small con-
versation
bubble tell-
ing me that
I have 10
comments
awaiting
moderation.

- Posts
- Media
- Links
- Pages
- Comments 10

Tackling spam with Akismet

I touch on Akismet a few times throughout this book. Why do I discuss it so much? Only because it's my humble opinion that Akismet is the mother of all plugins and that no WordPress blog is complete without a fully activated version of Akismet running in it.

Apparently WordPress agrees, because the plugin is packaged in every WordPress software release beginning with version 2.0. Akismet was created by the folks at Automattic, the same folks who brought you the WordPress. com hosted version (discussed in Part II of this book). Automattic also works with of some of the original developers of the WordPress software platform.

Akismet is the answer to combatting comment and trackback spam. Matt Mullenweg of Automattic says Akismet is a "collaborative effort to make comment and trackback spam a non-issue and restore innocence to blogging, so you never have to worry about spam again" (from the Akismet Web site at `http://akismet.com`).

I've been blogging since 2002. I started blogging with the Movable Type blogging platform and moved to WordPress in 2003. As blogging became more and more popular, comment and trackback spam became more and more of a nuisance. One morning in 2004, I found that 2,300 pieces of disgusting comment spam had been published to my blog. Something had to be done! The folks at Automattic did a fine thing with Akismet. Since the emergence of Akismet, I've barely had to think about comment or trackback spam except for the few times a month I check my Akismet spam queue.

I talk in greater detail about plugin use in WordPress in Chapter 10, where you find out how to activate Akismet and make sure that it is protecting your blog from trackback and comment spam.

Part IV
Flexing and Extending WordPress

The 5th Wave   By Rich Tennant

FREELANCER NED WILLIS CONSULTS
WITH A MEMBER OF HIS TECHNICAL STAFF

"...and that's pretty much all there is to
migrating your blog to WordPress."

In this part . . .

Ready? Set? Action! This part of the book starts by showing you how to add media files — images, video, and audio — to your site to create a fun, interactive experience for your readers. This part also covers using WordPress plugins to extend the capabilities of your blog, and finding and using free WordPress themes to change the look of your blog.

Chapter 9

Media Management: Images, Audio, and Video

· ·

In This Chapter

▶ Adding images and photo galleries to your blog posts

▶ Adding videos to your blog posts

▶ Uploading audio files

▶ Exploring the WordPress Media Library

· ·

*A*dding images and photos to your posts can really dress up the content. By using images and photos, you give your content a dimension that you can't express in plain text. Through visual imagery, you can call attention to your post and add depth to it.

The same goes for adding video and audio files to your posts and blog. Video lets you provide entertainment through moving, talking (or singing!) streaming video. Audio files let you talk to your visitors and add a personal touch. Many bloggers use video and audio to report news and to broadcast Internet radio and television shows. The possibilities are endless!

In Chapter 8, I discuss the mechanics of composing and publishing a post to your blog. In this chapter, you discover how to add some special touches to your blog posts by adding images, video, and audio to your blog posts, and even find out how to run a full-fledged photo gallery on your site, all through the WordPress.org software and its integrated Media Library. This chapter is pertinent to the WordPress.org platform only.

If you're using the hosted WordPress.com version, check out Chapter 4 for information on adding images, video and audio to your blog.

You add these extras to your blog posts in the Add Media area of the Write Post page. You can add them as you're writing your post, or come back and add them later. The choice is yours!

Inserting Images into Your Blog Posts

Adding images to a post is pretty easy with the WordPress image uploader. Jump right in and give it a go by clicking the Upload an Image icon on the Add New Post page. The Add an Image window lets you choose images from your hard drive or from a location on the Web (see Figure 9-1).

Add an Image   ✕

From Computer   From URL   Gallery (0)   Media Library

Add media files from your computer

Choose files to upload   **Select Files**

You are using the Flash uploader. Problems? Try the Browser uploader instead.

After a file has been uploaded, you can add titles and descriptions.

Figure 9-1:
The
WordPress
Add an
Image
window.

The interface that WordPress uses for file uploads is based on Adobe Flash. Flash is a specific set of multimedia technologies programmed to handle media files on the Web. Some browsers and operating systems are not configured to handle Flash-based applications. If you experience difficulties with the image uploader, WordPress gives you an easy alternative. Click the Browser Uploader link in the image uploader and you can use a non-Flash based uploader to transfer your files.

To add an image from the Web after you click the Add an Image icon, follow these steps:

1. **Click the From URL tab in the Add an Image window.**

   The Add Media File from URL window opens.

2. **Type the URL (Internet address) of the image in the Image URL text box.**

   Type the full URL, including the http and www portion of the address. You can easily find the URL of any image on the Web by right-clicking (PC) or Control-clicking (Mac) and selecting Properties from the menu.

3. **Type a title for the image in the Image Title text box.**

4. **(Optional) Type the caption of the image in the Image Caption text box.**

   The words you type here display underneath the image on your blog as a caption.

5. **Choose an alignment option by selecting the None, Left, Center, or Right radio button.**

6. **Type the URL you want the image linked to.**

   Whatever option you choose determines where your readers go when they click the image you've uploaded:

   - *None:* You don't want the image to be clickable.

   - *Link to Image:* Readers can click through to the direct image itself.

7. **Click the Insert into Post button.**

To add an image from your own hard drive after you click the Add an Image icon, follow these steps:

1. **Click the From Computer tab and then click the Select Files button.**

   A dialog box opens from which you can select an image (or multiple images) from your hard drive.

2. **Select your image(s); then click Open.**

   The image is uploaded from your computer to your Web server. WordPress displays a progress bar on the upload and displays an image options box when the upload is finished.

3. **Edit the details for the image(s) by clicking the Show link that appears to the right of the image thumbnail.**

Clicking Show drops down a box (see Figure 9-2) that contains several image options:

- *Title:* Type a title for the image.

- *Caption:* Type a caption for the image (such as **This is a flower from my garden**).

- *Description:* Type a description of the image.

- *Link URL:* Type the URL you want the image linked to. Whatever option you choose determines where your readers go when they click the image you've uploaded:

  None: You don't want the image to be clickable.

  File URL: Readers can click through to the direct image itself.

  Post URL: Readers can click through to the post that the image appears in. You can type your own URL in the Link URL text box.

- *Alignment:* Choose None, Left, Center, or Right. (See Table 9-1, in the following section, for styling information regarding image alignment.)

- *Size:* Choose Thumbnail, Medium, Large, or Full Size.

WordPress automatically creates small and medium-size versions of the images you upload through the built-in image uploader. A *thumbnail* is a smaller version of the original file. You can edit the size of the thumbnail by clicking the Settings link and then clicking Miscellaneous. In the Image Sizes section, designate your desired height and width of the small and medium thumbnail images generated by WordPress.

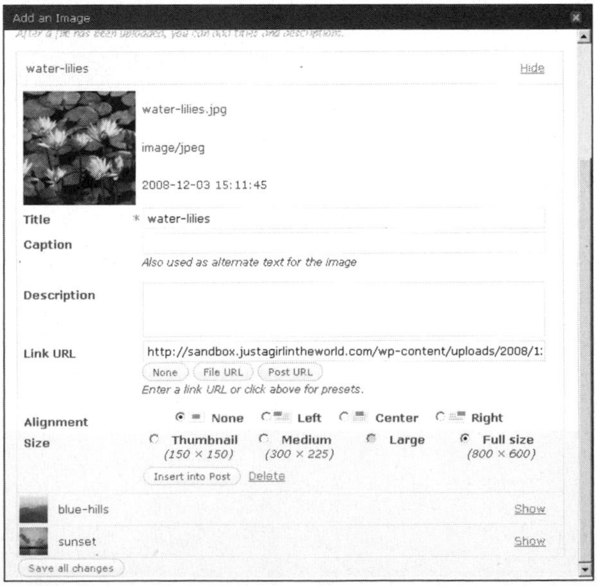

Figure 9-2:
You can
set several
options for
your images
after you
upload
them.

If you're uploading more than one image, skip to the "Inserting a photo gallery" section, later in this chapter.

4. **Click the Edit Image button and edit the appearance of the image.**

5. **Click the Insert into Post button.**

The image uploader window closes, and you return to the Add New Post page (or the Add New Page page, if you're writing a page). WordPress has inserted the HTML to display the image in your post, as shown in Figure 9-3; you can continue editing your post, save it, or publish it.

To see the actual image and not the code, click the Visual tab that's just above the Post text box.

Aligning your images

When you upload your image, you can set the alignment for your image as None, Left, Center, or Right. The WordPress theme you're using, however, may not have these alignment styles accounted for in its stylesheet. If you set the alignment to Left, for example, but the image on your blog doesn't appear to be aligned at all, you may need to add a few styles to your theme's stylesheet.

Figure 9-3: WordPress inserts the correct HTML code for your uploaded image into your post.

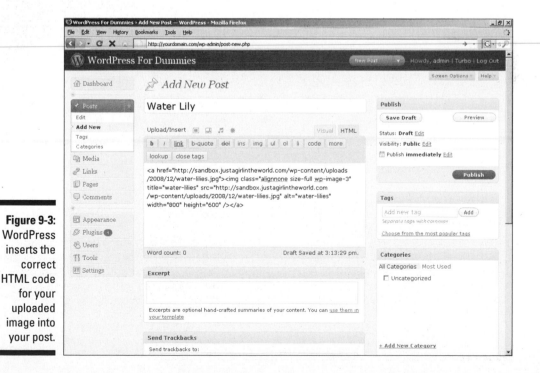

I discuss themes and templates in great detail in Part V. For purposes of making sure that you have the correct image alignment for your newly uploaded images, however, here is a quick-and-dirty method:

1. **Click the Editor link in the Appearance menu.**

   The Edit Themes page opens. All the template files for your active theme are listed on the right side of the page.

2. **Click the Stylesheet template.**

   The Stylesheet (`style.css`) template opens in the text box on the left side of the page.

3. **Add your desired styles to the stylesheet.**

Table 9-1 shows the styles you can add to your stylesheet to make sure that image-alignment styling is present and accounted for in your theme.

Table 9-1	Styling Techniques for Image Alignment
Image Alignment	*Add This to Your Stylesheet (style.css)*
None	`img.alignnone {float:none; margin: 5px 0 5px 0;}`
Left	`img.alignleft {float:left; margin: 5px 10px 5px 0px;}`
Center	`img.aligncenter {display:block; float:none; margin: 5px auto;}`
Right	`img.alignright {float:right; margin: 5px 0 5px 10px;}`

These styles are just examples of what you can do. Get creative with your own styling. You find more information about using CSS (Cascading Style Sheets) to add style to your theme(s) in Chapter 13.

Inserting a photo gallery

You can also use the WordPress image uploader to insert a full photo gallery into your posts. Upload your images; then, instead of clicking the Insert into Post button, click the Gallery tab at the top of the image uploader window (refer to Figure 9-1). This tab displays thumbnails of all the images you have uploaded for your post. Figure 9-4 shows that I have three images uploaded.

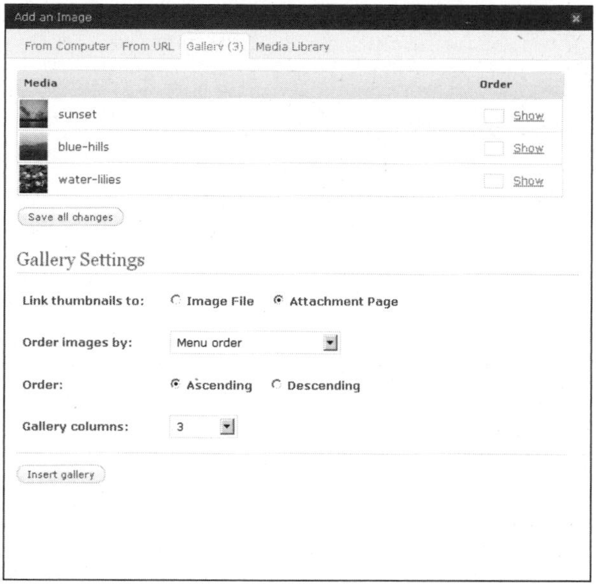

Figure 9-4:
The Gallery
tab of the
image
uploader.

Follow these steps to insert a photo gallery into a blog post:

1. **(Optional) On the Gallery tab, under the Options column, type the order that you want the images to appear in the gallery.**

   Type the number of the sequence in which you want this image displayed. (If you want this image displayed first, for example, type the number 1.)

2. **Set different options for your gallery:**

   • *Link Thumbnails To:* Select Image File or Attachment Page.

   • *Order Images By:* Select Menu Order, Name, or Date/Time.

   • *Order:* Select Ascending or Descending.

   • *Gallery Columns:* Select how many columns of images you'd like to display in your gallery.

3. **Click the Save All Changes button.**

   All the changes you made to each individual image listed in the gallery are saved.

4. **Click the Insert Gallery button.**

   WordPress inserts into your post a piece of short code that looks like this: `[gallery]`.

Table 9-2 shows some gallery short codes that you can use to manually set the display settings for your photo gallery.

5. **(Optional) Change the order of appearance of the images in the gallery, as well as the markup (HTML tags or CSS selectors):**

   - captiontag: Change the markup that surrounds the image caption by altering the gallery short code. Here are some examples: [gallery captiontag="div"] places <div></div> tags around the image caption (the <div> tag is considered a block level element and creates a separate container for the content); to have the gallery appear on a line of its own, the [gallery captiontag="p"] code places <p class="gallery-caption"></p> tags around the image caption. The default markup for the captiontag option is dd.

   - icontag: Defines the HTML markup around each individual thumbnail image in your gallery. Change the markup around the icontag (thumbnail icon) of the image by altering the gallery short code to something like [gallery icontag="p"], which places <p class="gallery-icon"></p> tags around each thumbnail icon. The default markup for icontag is dt.

   - itemtag: Defines the HTML markup around each item in your gallery. Change the markup around the itemtag (each item) in the gallery by altering the gallery short code to something like [gallery itemtag="span"], which places <span class="gallery-item"></span> tags around each item in the gallery. The default markup for the itemtag is dl.

   - captiontag: Define the HTML markup around the image caption for each image in your gallery. Change the markup around the captiontag (caption) for each image by altering the gallery short code to something like [gallery captiontag="p"], which places <p></p> tags around the image caption. The default markup for captiontag is dd.

   - orderby: Defines the order that the images are displayed within your gallery. Change the order used to display the thumbnails in the gallery by altering the gallery short code to something like [gallery orderby="menu_order ASC"], which displays the thumbnails in ascending menu order. Another parameter you can use is ID_order ASC, which displays the thumbnails in ascending order according to their IDs.

Table 9-2	Gallery Short Code Examples
Gallery Short Code	*Output*
`[gallery columns="4" size="medium"]`	A four-column gallery containing medium-size images
`[gallery columns="10" id="215" size="thumbnail"]`	A ten-column gallery containing thumbnail images pulled from the blog post with the ID 215.
`[gallery captiontag="p" icontag="span"]`	A three-column (default) gallery in which each image is surrounded by `<span></span>` tags and the image caption is surrounded by `<p></p>` tags.

6. **Define the style of the `<span>` tags in your CSS stylesheet.**

   The `<span>` tags create an inline element; an element contained within a `<span>` tag stays on the same line as the element before it; there is no line break. You need a little knowledge of CSS to alter the `<span>` tags. Click the Design tab in your WordPress Administration panel, and then click the Theme Editor subtab to edit the stylesheet for your theme. Here's an example of what you can add to the stylesheet (`style.css`) for your current theme:

   ```
   span.gallery-icon img {
   padding: 3px;
   background: white;
   border: 1px solid black;
   margin: 0 5px;
   }
   ```

   Placing this bit of CSS in the stylesheet (`style.css`) of your active theme automatically places a 1-pixel black border around each thumbnail, with 3 pixels of padding and a white background. The left and right margins are 5 pixels wide, creating nice spacing between images in the gallery.

7. **Click the Update File button to save changes to your Stylesheet (style. css) template.**

Figure 9-5 shows my post with my photo gallery displayed, using the preceding steps and CSS example in the default WordPress theme: Kubrick. This code is the gallery short code that I used for the gallery shown in Figure 9-5 — `[gallery icontag="span" size="thumbnail"]`.

Matt Mullenweg, co-founder of the WordPress platform, created a very extensive photo gallery by using the built-in gallery options in WordPress. Check out the fabulous photo gallery at `http://ma.tt/category/gallery/`.

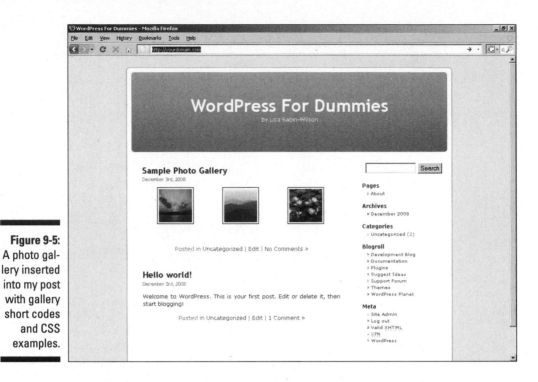

Figure 9-5:
A photo gallery inserted into my post with gallery short codes and CSS examples.

WordPress gallery plugins

Here are a handful of great plugins:

- **NextGEN Gallery by Alex Rabe:** This plugin creates sortable photo galleries, offers display of random and recent thumbnail images in your sidebar through the use of widgets, and more. You can download it at `http://wordpress.org/extend/plugins/nextgen-gallery`.

- **Organizer by Imthiaz:** Use this plugin to organize, rename, resize, and manage files in your image-upload folder. You can download it at `http://wordpress.org/extend/plugins/organizer`.

- **Random Image widget by Marcel Proulx:** This plugin lets you display a random image from your image-upload folder. You can download it at `http://wordpress.org/extend/plugins/random-image-widget`.

- **Mini-Slides by Roland Rust:** This plugin lets you create inline slideshows from your uploaded images. You can download it at `http://wordpress.org/extend/plugins/mini-slides`.

Some great WordPress plugins work in tandem with the WordPress gallery feature. Check out Chapter 10 for information on how to install and use WordPress plugins in your blog.

Inserting Video Files into Your Blog Posts

Whether you're producing your own videos for publication or want to embed other people's videos that you find interesting, placing a video file in a blog post has never been easier with WordPress.

Check out a good example of a video blog at `http://1938media.com`. Loren Feldman and his team produce video for the Web and for mobile devices.

Several video galleries on the Web today allow you to add videos to blog posts; Google's YouTube service (`http://youtube.com`) is a good example of this. To add video from the Web, click the Add Video icon, then click the From URL tab and follow these steps:

1. **Type the URL (Internet address) of the video in the Video URL text box.**

   Type the full URL, including the `http` and www portion of the address. Video providers, such as YouTube, usually list the direct link for the video file on their sites; you can copy and paste it into the Video URL text box.

2. **(Optional) Type the title of the video in the Title text box.**

   Giving a title to the video allows you to provide a bit of a description of the video. It's a good idea to provide a title if you can, so that your readers know what the video is about.

3. **Click the Insert into Post button.**

   A link to the video is inserted into your post. WordPress doesn't embed the actual video in the post; it inserts only a link to the video. Your blog visitors click the link to load another page where the video can be played.

To upload a video file from your own computer and post it to your blog, click the Add Video icon on the Edit Post or Add New Post page, and follow these steps to upload and link a video file in your blog post:

1. **Click the Choose Files to Upload button.**

   An Open dialog box opens.

2. **Select the video file you want to upload, and click Open (or double-click the file).**

   You return to the file uploader window in WordPress, which shows a progress bar while your video uploads. When the upload is complete, a box containing several options drops down.

3. **Type a title for the file in the Title text box.**

4. **Type a caption for the file in the Caption text box.**

5. **Type a description of the file in the Description text box.**

6. **Click the File URL button.**

   It provides a direct link in your post to the video file itself.

7. **Click Insert into Post.**

   A link to the video is inserted into your post. WordPress doesn't embed a video player in the post; it inserts only a link to the video. Your blog visitors click the link to load another page where the video can be played.

Some great WordPress plugins for video handling can enhance the functionality of the file uploader and help you with video display in your blog posts. Check out Chapter 10 for information on how to install and use WordPress plugins in your blog.

WordPress video plugins

Here are a handful of great plugins:

✔ **wordTube by Alex Rabe:** This plugin creates a nice Flash video, YouTube-like player when you insert video files within your posts. No special HTML or programming knowledge is needed. You can download this plugin at `http://wordpress.org/extend/plugins/wordtube`.

✔ **Smart YouTube by Vladimir Prelovac:** This plugin lets you insert YouTube videos into your blog posts, comments, and RSS feeds. You can download it at `http://wordpress.org/extend/plugins/smart-youtube`.

✔ **WP-Vidavee by Vidavee Labs:** This video player/video file management plugin helps you upload, manage, organize, and display the video files that you upload to your blog. You can download this plugin at `http://wordpress.org/extend/plugins/wp-vidavee-film-manager`.

✔ **Video Embedder by Kristoffer Forsgren:** This plugin lets you embed videos from various sources, such as YouTube, MySpace, and Viddler. You can download it at `http://wordpress.org/extend/plugins/video-embedder`.

Inserting Audio Files into Your Blog Posts

Audio files can be music files or a recording of you speaking to your readers; it adds a nice personal touch to your blog, and you can easily share audio files on your blog through the use of the Upload Audio feature in WordPress. After you've inserted an audio file in your blog posts, your readers can listen to it on their computers or download it onto an MP3 player and listen to it on their drives to work, if they want to.

Click the Add Audio icon on the Edit Post or Add New Post page, and follow these steps to upload an audio file to your blog post:

1. **Click the Choose Files to Upload button.**

   An Open dialog box opens.

2. **Choose the file you want to upload, and click Open (or double-click the file).**

   You return to the file uploader window in WordPress, which shows a progress bar while your audio file uploads. When the upload is complete, a box containing several options drops down.

3. **Type a title for the file in the Title text box.**

4. **Type a caption for the file in the Caption text box.**

5. **Type a description of the file in the Description text box.**

6. **Click the File URL button.**

   You can provide a direct link in your post to the video file itself.

7. **Click Insert into Post.**

   A link to the audio file is inserted into your post. WordPress doesn't embed an actual audio player in the post; it only inserts a link to the audio file. Visitors click the link to open another page where the audio file can be played.

Some great WordPress plugins for audio handling can enhance the functionality of the file uploader and help you manage audio files in your blog posts. Check out Chapter 10 for information on how to install and use WordPress plugins in your blog.

WordPress audio plugins

Here are a handful of great plugins:

- **Audio Player by Martin Laine:** This plugin makes it easy to embed a nice Flash MP3 player in your blog posts. No special HTML or programming knowledge is needed. You can download the plugin at `http://wordpress.org/extend/plugins/audio-player`.

- **1 Bit Audio Player by Mark Wheeler:** This easy Flash MP3 player autodetects MP3 files on your site and inserts a stylish player so that your visitors can listen right

from your blog page. You can download it at `http://wordpress.org/extend/plugins/1-bit-audio-player`.

- **Podcasting by Ronald Heft, Jr.:** This plugin supports several media formats and integrates into your WordPress uploading section. Also, it automatically creates a podcast RSS feed that your visitors can easily subscribe to. You can download this plugin at `http://wordpress.org/extend/plugins/podcasting`.

Keeping Media Files Organized

If you've been running your blog for any length of time, you can easily forget what files you've uploaded with the WordPress uploader. I used to have to log in to my Web server via FTP and view the uploads directory to see what I had in there.

Now, the WordPress Media Library makes it very convenient and easy to discover which files are in your uploads folder.

To find an image, video, or audio file that you've already uploaded using the file uploader and use that file in a new post, follow these steps:

1. **Click the Upload Media icon to open the file uploader window.**

2. **Click the Media Library link at the top.**

   You see all the files you've ever uploaded to your blog with the file uploader feature (see Figure 9-6). Files you've uploaded through other methods, like FTP, are not displayed in the Media Library.

3. **Select the file you want to reuse, and click the Show link.**

4. **Set the options for that image: Title, Caption, Description, Link URL, Order, Alignment, and Size.**

5. **Click the Insert into Post button.**

   The correct HTML code is inserted into the Post text box.

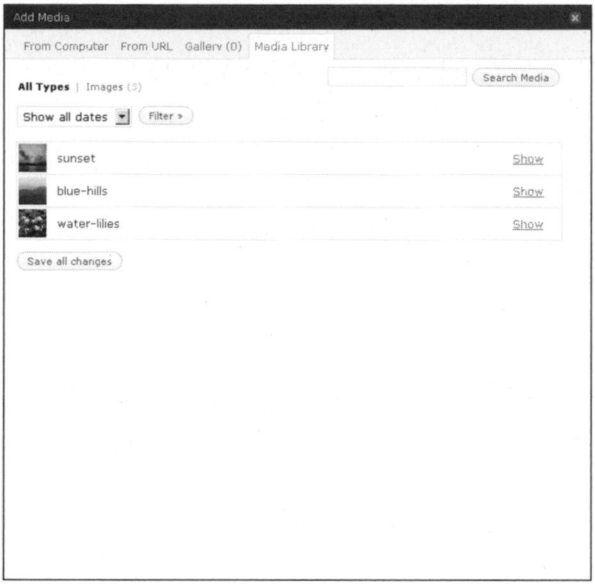

Figure 9-6:
The Media
Library
shows all
the files
you've ever
uploaded to
your blog.

If you only want to view the files you've uploaded and don't need a particular image or file for a new post, click the Edit link in the Media menu, which opens the Media Library page.

The Media Library page lists all the files you've ever uploaded to your WordPress blog. By default, the page displays all types of files, but you can click the Images, Audio, or Video link to specify which file type you want to see (see Figure 9-7).

You can do the following tasks on the Media Library page:

- **Filter media files by date.** If you want to view all media files that were uploaded in October 2008, choose that date from the drop-down menu and click the Filter button; the page reloads and displays only the media files uploaded in the month of October 2008.

- **Search media files using a specific keyword.** If you want to search your Media Library for all files that reference kittens, then you type the word **kittens** in the Search box in the upper right side of the Media Library page. Then click the Search Media button; the page reloads and displays only media files that contain the keyword or tag of kittens.

- **Delete media files.** Click the small white box that appears to the left of every thumbnail on the Manage Media page; then click the Delete button that shows at the top left of the page. The page reloads, and the media file you've just deleted is now gone.

✔ **View media files.** On the Manage Media page, click the thumbnail of the file you'd like to view. The actual file opens in your Web browser. If necessary, you can copy the permalink of the file from your browser's address bar.

Chapter 10

Making the Most of WordPress Plugins

*H*alf the fun of running a WordPress-powered blog is playing with the hundreds of plugins that you can install to extend your blog's functions and options. WordPress plugins are like those really cool custom rims you put on your car: Although they don't come with the car, they're awesome accessories that make your car better than all the rest.

In this chapter, you find out what plugins are, how to find and install them, and how they enhance your blog in a way that makes your blog unique. Using plugins can also greatly improve your readers' experiences by providing them various tools they can use to interact and participate — just the way you want them to!

This chapter assumes that you already have WordPress installed on your Web server. Installing plugins pertains only to the WordPress.org software. If you're skipping around in the book and haven't yet installed WordPress on your Web server, you can find instructions in Chapter 6.

WordPress.com users can't install or configure plugins on their hosted blogs. I don't make the rules, so please don't kill the messenger.

Finding Out What Plugins Are

A *plugin* is a small program that, when added to WordPress, interacts with the software to provide some extensibility to the software. Plugins aren't part of the core software; they aren't software programs either. They typically don't function as stand-alone software. They do require the host program (WordPress, in this case) to function.

Plugin developers are the people who write these gems and share them with the rest of us — usually, for free. Like WordPress, plugins are free to anyone who wants to further tailor and customize his site to his own needs.

Although plugins are written and developed by people who have the set of skills required to do so, I would say that the WordPress user community is also largely responsible for the ongoing development of plugins. Ultimately, the end users are the ones who put those plugins to the true test of the real world in their own blogs. Those same users are also the first to speak up and let the developers know when something isn't working right, helping the developers troubleshoot and fine-tune their plugins. The most popular plugins are created by developers who encourage open communication with the user base. Overall, WordPress is one of those great open source projects in which the relationship between developers and users fosters a creative environment that keeps the project fresh and exciting every step of the way.

Literally thousands of plugins are available for WordPress — certainly way too many for me to list in this chapter alone. I could, but then you'd need heavy machinery to lift this book off the shelf! So here are just a few examples of things that plugins let you add to your WordPress blog:

- ✔ **E-mail notification:** Your biggest fans can sign up to have an e-mail notification sent to them every time you update your blog.

- ✔ **Submit your blog to social networking services:** Allow your readers to submit your blog posts to some of the most popular social networking services, such as Digg, Technorati, and Del.icio.us.

- ✔ **Stats program:** Keep track of where your traffic is coming from; which posts on your blog are the most popular; and how much traffic is coming through your blog on a daily, monthly, and yearly basis.

Chapter 17 gives you a peek at some of the most popular plugins on the scene today. In the meantime, this chapter takes you through the process of finding plugins, installing them in your WordPress blog, and managing and troubleshooting them.

Exploring Manage Plugin page

Before you start installing plugins for your blog, it's important for you to explore the Manage Plugins page in your WordPress Administration panel and understand how to manage the plugins after you install them. Click the Installed link in the Plugins menu to get to the Manage Plugins page (shown in Figure 10-1).

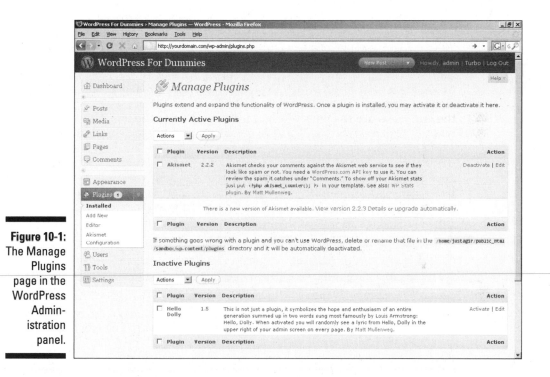

Figure 10-1: The Manage Plugins page in the WordPress Administration panel.

The Manage Plugins page is where you manage all the plugins you install in your WordPress blog. This page is laid out in two sections:

- ✓ **Currently Active Plugins:** These plugins, listed at the top of the Plugin Management page, are currently being used on your site. Figure 10-1 shows that I have one active plugin, Akismet.

- ✓ **Inactive Plugins:** These plugins are not in active use on your blog. These plugins exist in the plugins directory on your Web server, but because you have not activated them, they are listed as available rather than active.

When you don't want to use a plugin anymore, click the Deactivate link to the right of the plugin; the plugin moves to the Inactive Plugins section, indicating that it's installed on your blog but not activated. Likewise, to activate a plugin, click the Activate link to the right of the plugin (the Hello Dolly plugin in Figure 10-1, for example); the plugin then moves to the Currently Active Plugins list, indicating that it's installed and activated.

You can mass manage your plugins on the Manage Plugins page. In the Currently Active Plugins section, you can deactivate all your plugins at once by selecting the box to the left of each plugin name, and then clicking the Deactivate button. Likewise, you can activate or delete the plugins listed in the Active Plugins box by selecting the box to the left of each plugin name, and then clicking the Activate or the Delete button (depending on which action you wish to take). To select all your plugins with one click in either the Currently Active or the Inactive Plugins box, select the box to the left of the Plugin heading.

The Manage Plugins page displays plugins in four columns, which give details for each plugin:

- ✔ **Plugin:** This column lists the plugin name so that you can find it easily when browsing the Plugin Management page. Usually, the name of the plugin is also linked to the plugin author's Web site or a page where you can find additional information and details about the plugin.

- ✔ **Version:** This column lists the version number of the plugin. Sometimes, a plugin author releases an update and changes the version number on the plugin Web site. WordPress alerts you when a new version is available (see "Discovering the one-click plugin upgrade," later in this chapter).

- ✔ **Description:** This column lists a description for the plugin. Sometimes, depending on the plugin, it also gives you some brief instructions on using the plugin.

- ✔ **Action:** This column has two links. If you're looking at an active plugin, the links that appear in the Action column are Deactivate and Edit. You can click the Deactivate link to deactivate the plugin or click the Edit link to edit the plugin file. If you're looking at an available plugin, the links that appear in the Action column are Activate and Edit. You can click the Activate link to activate the plugin or click the Edit link to edit the plugin file.

Discovering the one-click plugin upgrade

For a lot of reasons, mainly security reasons, you really want to make sure that you always use the most up-to-date versions of the plugins in your blog. With everything you have to do every day, how can you possibly keep up with knowing whether the plugins you're using have been updated?

You don't have to. WordPress does it for you.

Figure 10-2 shows an out-of-date version (1.15) of Akismet installed and activated. WordPress displays a message below the plugin description, notifying you that a new plugin is available.

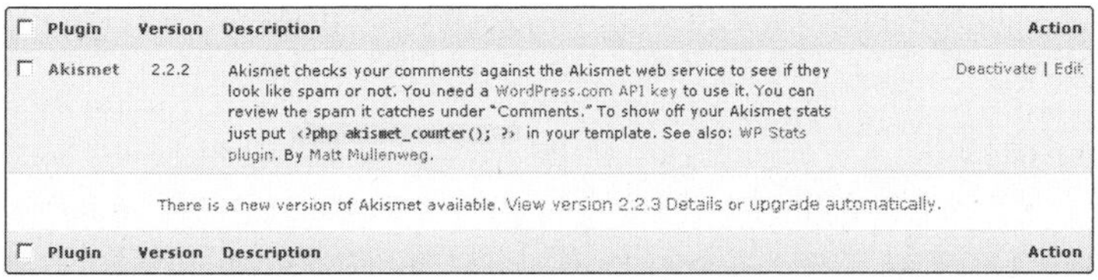

Figure 10-2:
WordPress
tells you
when a
new plugin
version is
available.

	Plugin	Version	Description	Action
☐	Plugin	Version	Description	Action
☐	Akismet	2.2.2	Akismet checks your comments against the Akismet web service to see if they look like spam or not. You need a WordPress.com API key to use it. You can review the spam it catches under "Comments." To show off your Akismet stats just put `<?php akismet_counter(); ?>` in your template. See also: WP Stats plugin. By Matt Mullenweg.	Deactivate | Edit
			There is a new version of Akismet available. View version 2.2.3 Details or upgrade automatically.	
☐	Plugin	Version	Description	Action

WordPress not only gives you a message that a new version of the plugin is available, but also gives you a link to a page where you can download the new version or a link that you can click to upgrade the plugin right there and then — WordPress's one-click plugin upgrade.

Click the Upgrade Automatically link, and WordPress grabs the new files off the WordPress.org server, uploads them to your plugins directory, deletes the old plugin, and activates the new one. Figure 10-3 shows the Upgrade Plugin page that displays while the plugin is being upgraded.

WordPress notifies you of an out-of-date plugin and provides you with the one-click upgrade function *only* for plugins that are in the official WordPress Plugin Directory (http://wordpress.org/extend/plugins). If a plugin you are using is not listed in the directory, then the notification and one-click upgrade function won't be present for that plugin.

Another way that WordPress alerts you that you have out-of-date plugins is in the left navigation menu. When you have an out-of-date plugin, a number appears next to the Plugins menu, indicating that you have a plugin, or plugins, that need to be upgraded. Figure 10-4 shows my Administration panel telling me that I have one plugin that needs to be upgraded. After you upgrade the plugin, the number disappears.

For the automatic plugin upgrade to work, your plugin directory (/wp-content/plugins) must be writable on your Web server, which means that you should have set permissions of 755 or 777 (depending on your Web-server configuration). See Chapter 6 for information about changing file permissions on your Web server, or contact your Web hosting provider for assistance.

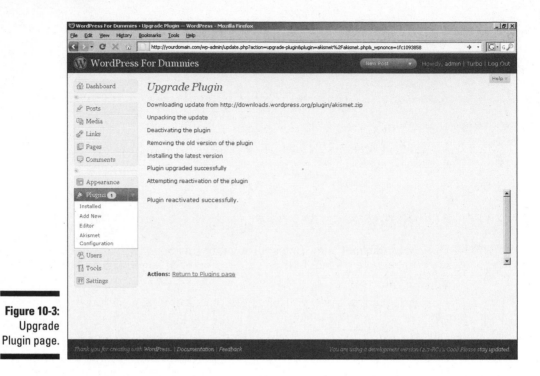

Figure 10-3:
Upgrade
Plugin page.

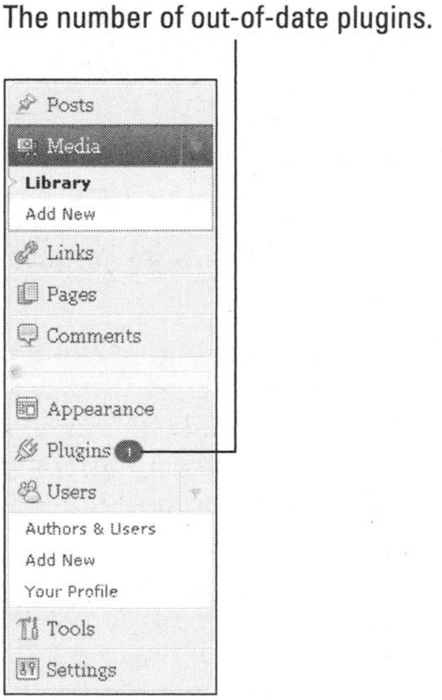

The number of out-of-date plugins.

Figure 10-4:
Bubble
next to the
Plugins
menu alerts
you that
you have
out-of-date
plugins.

Getting the Most out of the Plugins Included with WordPress

At this writing, WordPress packages two plugins with the installation files:

- ✔ **Akismet:** This plugin is essential.
- ✔ **Hello Dolly:** This plugin isn't necessary to make your blog run smoothly, but it adds some extra fun.

Akismet

I touch on Akismet a few times throughout this book. Why so much? It's my humble opinion that Akismet is the mother of all plugins and that no WordPress blog is complete without a fully activated version of Akismet.

Apparently WordPress agrees, because the plugin has been packaged in every WordPress software release since version 2.0. Akismet was created by the folks at Automattic — the same folks who bring you the Sidebar Widgets plugin.

Akismet is the answer to comment and trackback spam. Matt Mullenweg of Automattic says Akismet is a "collaborative effort to make comment and trackback spam a non-issue and restore innocence to blogging, so you never have to worry about spam again" (from the Akismet Web site at `http://akismet.com`).

To use the plugin, follow these steps:

1. **On the Manage Plugins page, click the Activate link to the right of the Akismet plugin name and description.**

   A yellow box appears at the top of the page, saying: "Akismet is almost ready. You must enter your WordPress.com API key for it to work" (see Figure 10-5). An API key is a string of numbers and letters and functions like a unique password given to you by WordPress.com; it's the key that allows your WordPress.org application to communicate with your WordPress.com account.

2. **Click the link in the yellow box to obtain your WordPress.com API key.**

   Clicking this link takes you the WordPress.com Web site. If you have an account already, log in to it. If you don't have an account on WordPress.com, you need to create a WordPress.com account to get an API key. (See Chapter 3 to find out how to create your own WordPress.com account.) Although you have to create a WordPress.com account, you don't need to use it; you just need to get the API key.

3. **Log into your WordPress.com account, click the Users link in the top right corner, and then click the Your Profile subtab to view the Your Profile and Personal Options page.**

   You find your WordPress.com API key at the top of that page, as shown in Figure 10-6. (I have blacked out my own API key because — shhhh — it's a secret, and I'm not supposed to share it!)

4. **When you have your API key, go to the Akismet Configuration page by clicking the Akismet Configuration link in the Plugins menu in your WordPress Administration panel.**

5. **Enter the API key in the WordPress.com API Key box, and click the Update Options button to fully activate the Akismet plugin.**

Akismet catches spam and throws it into a queue, holding the spam for 15 days and then deleting it from your database. It's probably worth your while to check the Akismet Spam page once a week to make sure that the plugin hasn't captured any legitimate comments or trackbacks.

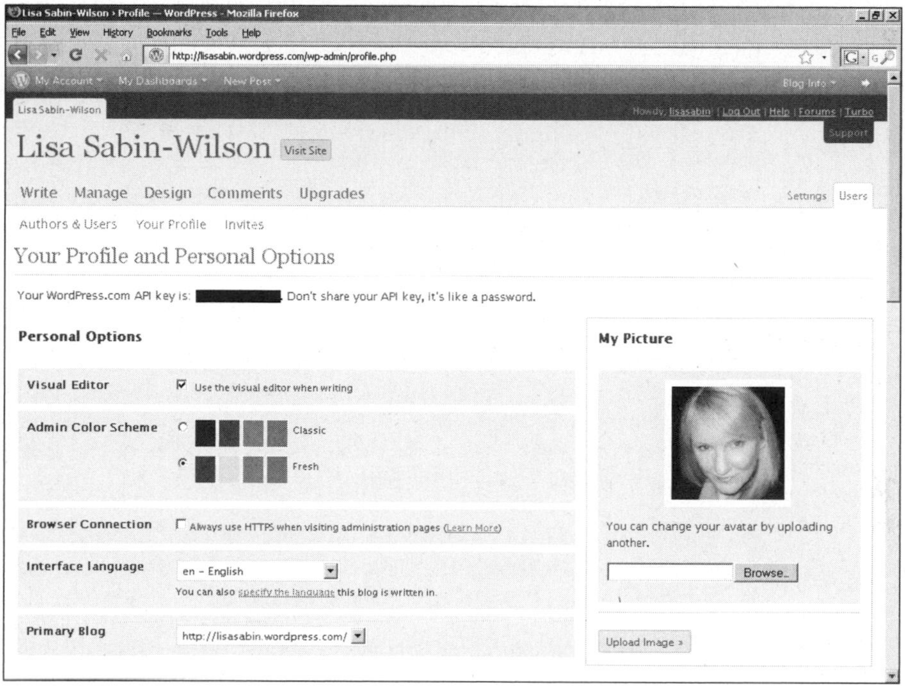

Figure 10-6:
You can
find your
WordPress
API key on
the Your
Profile and
Personal
Options
page in
the Admin-
istration
panel.

You can rescue those nonspam captured comments and trackbacks by doing the following (after you've logged in to your WordPress Administration panel):

1. **Click the Comments menu.**

   The Edit Comments page appears, displaying a list of the most recent comments on your blog.

2. **Click the Spam link.**

   The Edit Comments page now displays all spam comments that the plugin caught.

3. **Browse through the list of spam comments, looking for any comments or trackbacks that are legitimate.**

4. **If you locate one that's legitimate, select the Approve link box directly underneath the entry.**

   The comment is marked as legitimate. In other words, you don't con-sider this comment to be spam. The comment is then approved and published on your blog.

Check your spam filter often. I just found four legitimate comments caught in my spam filter and was able to de-spam them, releasing them from the binds of Akismet and unleashing them upon the world.

The folks at Automattic did a fine thing with Akismet. Since the emergence of Akismet, I've barely had to think about comment or trackback spam, except for the few times a month I check my Akismet spam queue.

Hello Dolly

Matt Mullenweg, co-founder of WordPress, developed the Hello Dolly plugin. Anyone who follows the development of WordPress knows that he is a huge jazz fan. How do we know this? Every single release of WordPress is named after some jazz great. One of the most recent releases of the software, for example, is named Ella — after jazz great Ella Fitzgerald.

So, knowing this, it isn't surprising that Mullenweg developed a plugin named Hello Dolly. Here's the description of it that you see in the Plugin Management page in your Administration panel:

> This is not just a plugin, it symbolizes the hope and enthusiasm of an entire generation summed up in two words sung most famously by Louis Armstrong: Hello, Dolly. When activated you will randomly see a lyric from Hello, Dolly in the upper right of your admin screen on every page.

Is it necessary? No. Is it fun? Sure!

Activate the Hello Dolly plugin on the Manage Plugins page in your WordPress Administration panel. When you've activated it, your WordPress blog greets you with a different lyric from the song "Hello, Dolly!" each time.

If you want to change the lyrics in this plugin, you can edit them by clicking the Edit link to the right of the Hello Dolly plugin on the Manage Plugins page. The Plugin Editor opens and lets you edit the file in a text editor. Make sure that each line of the lyric has its own line in the plugin file.

Using Plugins: Just the Basics

In this section, I show you how to install a plugin in your WordPress blog, using the built-in plugins feature. The auto-installation of plugins from within your WordPress administration panel only works for plugins that are included in the official WordPress Plugin Directory. You can manually install plugins on your WordPress blog, which I cover in the next section.

WordPress makes it super easy to find, install, and then activate plugins for use on your blog. — just follow these simple steps:

1. **Click the Add New link in the Plugins menu.**

   The Install Plugins page opens where you can browse the official WordPress Plugins Directory from your WordPress Administration panel.

2. **Select a plugin to install on your blog:**

   • *Term*: If you want to search for plugins that allow you to add additional features for comments on your site, select Term in the drop-down menu and then enter the word **Comments** in the Search text box on the Install Plugins page. Click the Search button and a list of plugins returns that deal specifically with comments.

   • *Author or Tag:* Select Author or Tag in the drop-down menu and then enter the author or tag name in the Search box and click the Search button.

   You can also search by tag by clicking any of the tag names that appear at the bottom of the Install Plugins page under the Popular Tags heading.

   I want to install of a very popular plugin called Subscribe to Comments (see the next section in this chapter for a description of this plugin). Enter the words **Subscribe to Comments** in the Search text box on the Install Plugins page.

   Figure 10-7 shows the results page for the Subscribe to Comments, which is listed as the sixth plugin.

3. **Click the Install link in the Actions column of the Subscribe to Comments plugin listing.**

   A Plugin Information window opens, giving you information about the Subscribe to Comments plugin, including a description of the plugin, version number, author name, and an Install Now button.

4. **Click the Install Now button.**

   You go to the Install Plugins page in your WordPress Administration panel, where you find a confirmation message that the plugin has been downloaded, unpacked, and successfully installed.

5. **Specify whether to install the plugin or proceed to the Plugins page.**

   Two links are shown under the confirmation message:

   • *Activate Plugin:* Click this link to activate the plugin you just installed on your blog.

   • *Return to Plugins page:* Click this link to go to the Manage Plugins page.

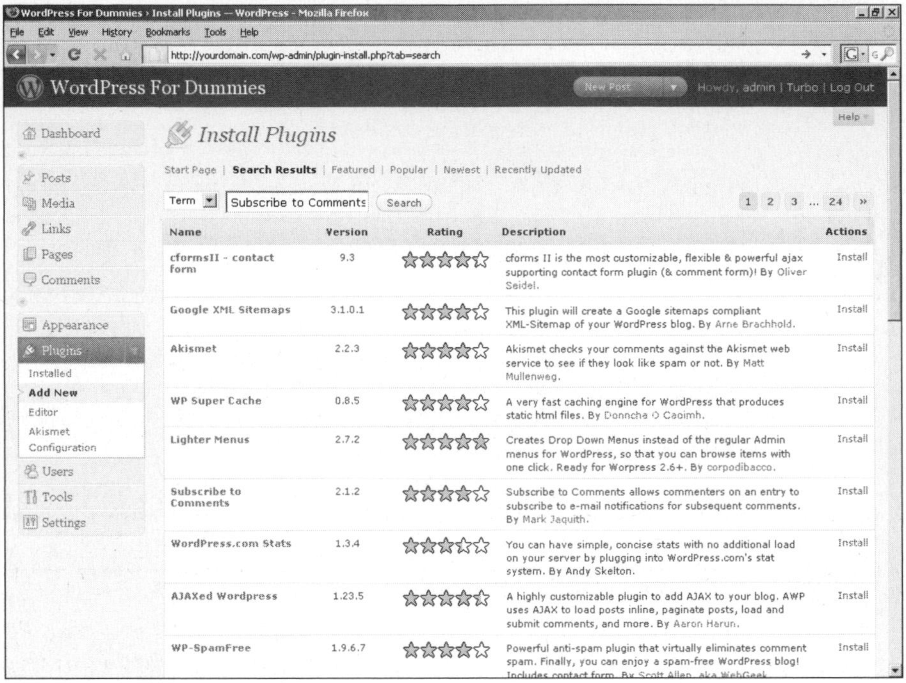

Figure 10-7:
Finding a
plugin to
install using
the built-
in Plugin
Directory
search.

WARNING!

The auto-installation of plugins from your WordPress Administration panel works on most Web-hosting configurations. However, some Web hosting services don't allow the kind of access that the WordPress Plugin Directory needs to complete the auto-installation. If you get any errors, or find that you are unable to use the plugin auto-installation feature, I recommend getting in touch with your Web hosting provider to find out if they can assist you.

Installing Plugins Manually

In the following sections, I show you how to find, upload, and install the very popular Subscribe to Comments plugin, developed by Mark Jaquith. I'm using the Subscribe to Comments plugin as a real-world example to take you through the mechanics involved in downloading, unpacking, uploading, activating, and using a plugin in WordPress.

Subscribe to Comments gives your readers the opportunity to subscribe to individual comment threads on your site so that they receive a notification, via e-mail, when a new comment has been left on the comment thread (or blog post) that they have chosen to subscribe to. This plugin helps keep lively discussions active in your blog.

Installing the Subscribe to Comments plugin takes you through the process, but keep in mind that every plugin is different. Reading the description and installation instructions for each plugin you want to install is very important.

Finding and downloading the files

The first step in using plugins is locating the one you want to install. Table 10-2 outlines the reliable places you can find plugins.

Table 10-2	Where to Find WordPress Plugins	
Resource Name	**Site URL**	**Description**
WordPress Plugin Directory	`http://wordpress. org/extend/plugins`	A centralized repository for WordPress plugins, listed in categories
WP Plugin Database	`http://wp-plugins. net`	A site with a categorized listing of WordPress plug-ins available for download
WordPress Plugin Repository	`http://plugins. trac.wordpress.org/`	Clean, updated, and bug-free plugins

Some rather unscrupulous sites offer WordPress plugins for download, but you may find that you're also downloading some not-so-nice additional files, such as viruses, malware, and spyware. Stick with the tried-and true-sites listed in Table 10-2, and you'll be safe.

To find Mark Jaquith's Subscribe to Comments plugin, follow these steps:

1. **Go to the official WordPress Plugin Directory, located at `http:// wordpress.org/extend/plugins`.**

   The home page opens; see Figure 10-8.

2. **In the search box at the top of the page, enter the keywords** Subscribe to Comments **and then click the Search Plugins button.**

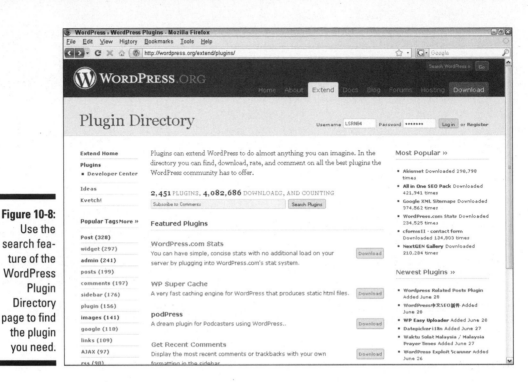

Figure 10-8:
Use the search feature of the WordPress Plugin Directory page to find the plugin you need.

3. **Locate the Subscribe to Comments plugin on the search results page, and click the plugin name.**

   The Subscribe to Comments page opens in the WordPress Plugin Directory, where you find a description of the plugin, as well as other information about the plugin (see Figure 10-9). For example, take note of the important information in the FYI box:

   • *Version:* The number shown in this area is the most recent version of the plugin.

   • *Other Versions:* This link takes you to a page that displays all the previous versions of the plugin. This is helpful if you have to revert to an older version of the plugin if the new version fails on your individual WordPress installation.

   • *Last Updated:* This displays the date that the plugin was last updated by the author.

   • *Requires WordPress Version:* This tells you what version of WordPress you need to successfully use this plugin. For example, Figure 10-9 shows that the Subscribe to Comments plugin requires WordPress version 2.0.6 or higher; that means that this plugin doesn't work with versions lower than 2.0.6. Helpful!

Figure 10-9:
The download page for the Subscribe to Comments plugin.

- *Compatible Up To:* This tells you what version of WordPress this plugin is compatible up to. For example, if this section tells you the plugin is compatible up to version 2.3 — that means you can't use the plugin with versions higher than 2.3. I say usually because the plugin developer may not update the information in this section — especially if there have been no changes to the plugin files themselves. The best way to check is to download the plugin and install it and see if it works! (Figure 10-9 shows that Mark Jaquith's Subscribe to Comments plugin is compatible up to WordPress version 2.3.1 — however, I can verify that it does work in all versions up to the most recent, 2.6.1.)

- *Author Homepage:* This link takes you to the plugin author's main Web site.

- *Plugin Homepage:* This link takes you to the specific Web site for the plugin. Often, this is a page within the plugin author's Web site.

4. **Click the Download button to download the files.**

   If you're using Internet Explorer, click the Download button, and a dialog box opens, asking whether you want to open or save the file. Click Save to save the zip file to your hard drive, and *remember where you saved it.*

If you're using Mozilla Firefox, click the Download button, and a dialog box opens, asking what Firefox should do with the file. Select the Save File radio button and then click OK to save it to your hard drive. Again, *remember where you saved it.*

For other browsers, follow the download instructions in the corresponding dialog box.

5. **Locate the file on your hard drive, and open it with your favorite decompression program.**

   If you're unsure how to use a decompression program, refer to the documentation available with the program.

6. **Unpack the plugin files you downloaded for the Subscribe to Comments plugin.**

Reading the instructions

Frequently, the plugin developer includes a `readme` file inside the zip file. Do what the title of the file says: Read it. Many times, it contains the exact documentation and instructions that you will find on the plugin developer's page.

Make sure that you read the instructions carefully and follow them correctly. Ninety-nine percent of WordPress plugins have great documentation and instructions from the plugin developer. If you don't follow the instructions correctly, at best, the plugin just won't work on your blog. At worst, the plugin creates all sorts of ugly errors, requiring you to start over from step one.

You can open `readme.txt` files in any text-editor program, such as Notepad or WordPad on a PC, or TextEdit on a Mac.

In the case of Mark Jaquith's Subscribe to Comments plugin, the `readme.txt` file contains instructions on how to upload and use the plugin, as well as some answers to frequently asked questions on troubleshooting the installation and use.

Every plugin is different in terms of where the plugin files are uploaded and in terms of the configurations and setup necessary to make the plugin work on your site. Read the installation instructions very carefully and follow those instructions to the letter to install the plugin correctly on your site.

Uploading and Activating Plugins

Now you're ready to upload the plugin files to your Web server. Connect to your Web server via FTP. Locate the plugin files you just unpacked on your hard drive. In the event that the plugin developer didn't include a `readme.txt` file with instructions, check the plugin developer's page for specific instructions on how to install the plugin in your WordPress blog. Specifically, the documentation in the `readme.txt` file and/or on the plugin's Web site should address the following points:

✔ What directory on your Web server you upload the plugin files to.

✔ What to do if you need to change permissions for any of the plugin files after you upload them to your Web server. (See Chapter 6 if you need information on changing file permissions.)

✔ What to do if you need to set specific configurations in the plugin file to make it work.

✔ What to do if you need to modify your theme template files to include the plugin's functions in your blog.

Uploading the files

Mark Jaquith left some nice instructions for you in the plugin zip file. Look for the `readme.txt` file inside the zip files you download from his site.

To install the Subscribe to Comments plugin, follow these easy steps:

1. **Double-click the `subscribe-to-comments` folder in the files you downloaded and unpacked on your computer.**

   A folder opens, containing two files: `subscribe-to-comments.php` and `readme.txt`. (You also see another folder called `extras`. This folder contains the plugin installation instructions in two additional formats: HTML [`readme.html`] and Microsoft PowerPoint [`subscribe-to-comments.pot`].)

   Figure 10-10 shows all the files and folders contained in the Subscribe to Comments plugin.

2. **Close the folder after you've determined that it contains all the necessary files.**

3. **Connect to your Web server via FTP, and open the `/wp-content/ plugins/` folder.**

   This folder contains all the plugins that are currently installed in your WordPress blog.

4. **Upload the entire `subscribe-to-comments` folder into the `/wp-content/plugins/` folder on your Web server.**

   Figure 10-11 shows the plugin files and where they should be located on your Web server. *Note:* The plugins on my Web server may differ from the ones you've chosen to install on yours; however, you can see where I placed the `subscribe-to-comments` folder.

Name	Size	Modified
↑.. Parent Directory		
extras		6/29/2008 3:55 PM
readme.txt	2 KB	2/19/2008 9:03 PM
subscribe-to-comments.php	51 KB	2/19/2008 9:03 PM

C:\subscribe-to-comments

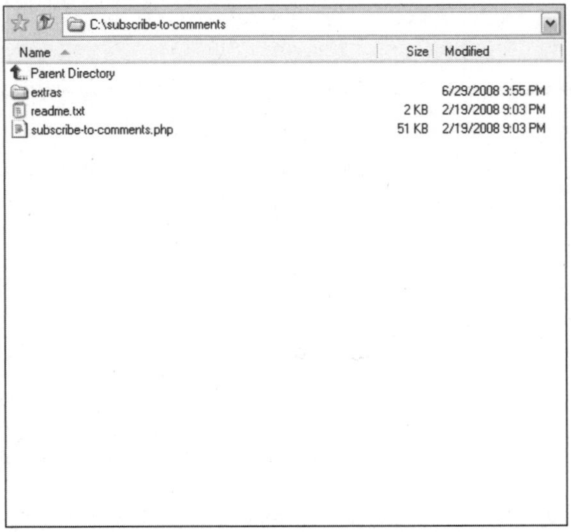

Figure 10-10:
Files and folders in the Subscribe to Comments plugin.

Activating the plugin

When you have the plugin files uploaded to the correct location on your Web server, open your browser, and log in to your WordPress Administration panel. After you log in, head to the Manage Plugins page to activate the Subscribe to Comments plugin:

1. **Click the Installed link on the Plugins menu.**

   The Mange Plugins page opens, listing all the plugins installed in your WordPress blog.

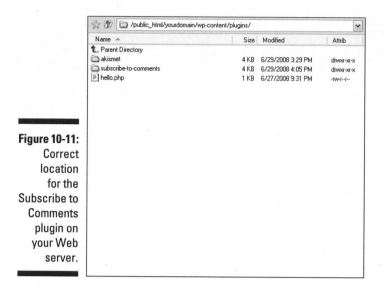

/public_html/yourdomain/wp-content/plugins/

Name ▲	Size	Modified	Attrib
Parent Directory			
akismet	4 KB	6/29/2008 3:29 PM	drwxr-xr-x
subscribe-to-comments	4 KB	6/29/2008 4:05 PM	drwxr-xr-x
hello.php	1 KB	6/27/2008 9:31 PM	-rw-r--r--

Figure 10-11:
Correct
location
for the
Subscribe to
Comments
plugin on
your Web
server.

2. **Locate the Subscribe to Comments plugin.**

   Because you have not activated this plugin, it's located in the Inactive Plugins section at the bottom of the Manage Plugins page.

3. **Click the Activate link to the right of the plugin name.**

   The Manage Plugins page refreshes, and the Subscribe to Comments plugin is now listed in the Currently Active Plugins section at the top of the page.

If you've followed all these steps in your own blog, congratulations — you now have Subscribe to Comments installed. Great job!

Setting Plugin Options

Some, but not all, WordPress plugins provide an administration page where you can set options that are specific to that particular plugin. You can find the plugin administration page in any of these places:

✔ The Settings page (click the Settings menu)

✔ The Tools menu (located in the navigation menu)

✔ The Plugins menu (located in the navigation menu)

You can find the Subscribe to Comments plugin administration page by clicking the Subscribe to Comments link in the Settings menu. The Subscribe to Comments Options page opens (see Figure 10-12).

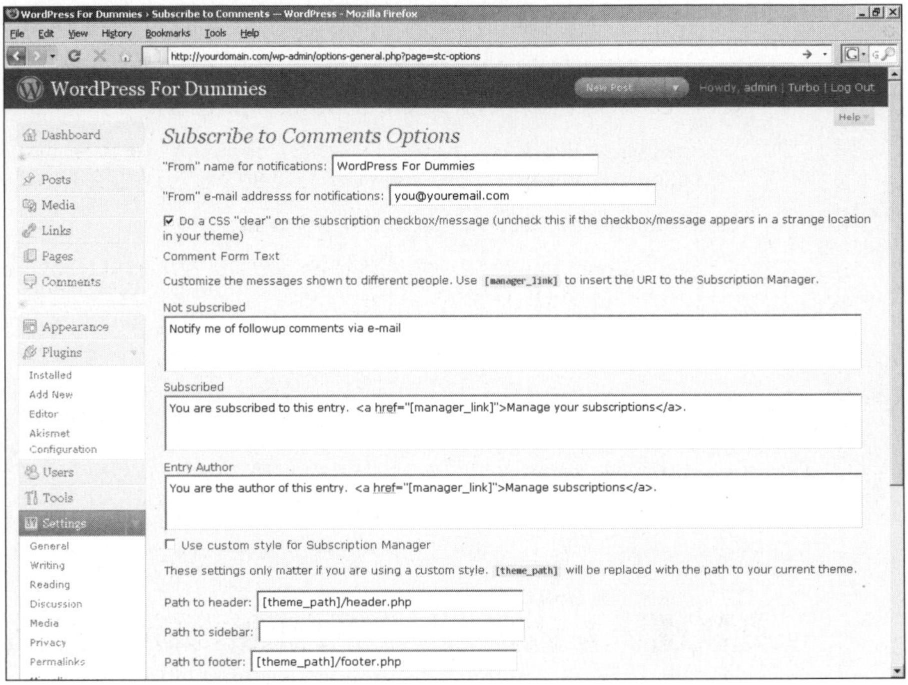

Figure 10-12:
The
Subscribe to
Comments
Options
administra-
tion page.

Uninstalling Plugins

After all this talk about installing and activating plugins, what happens if you install and activate a plugin, and then at some point decide that it just isn't what you want? Don't worry — you aren't stuck forever with a plugin that you don't want. WordPress lets you be fickle and finicky in your plugin choices!

To uninstall a plugin from your WordPress blog:

1. **Click the Installed link on the Plugins menu.**

   The Manage Plugins page opens.

2. **Locate the plugin you want to uninstall.**

3. **Click the Deactivate link to the right of the plugin name and description.**

   The Manage Plugins page refreshes and shows the plugin now in the Inactive Plugins list.

4. Select the plugin.

Place a checkmark in the box to the left of the plugin name.

5. Select Delete and then click the Apply button.

The Delete Plugin(s) page opens and a confirmation message displays asking you if you're sure you want to delete this plugin. (See Figure 10-13.)

6. Click the Yes, Delete These Files button.

The Manage Plugins page refreshes and the plugin you just deleted is gone from the lists of plugins.

Bang! You're done. That's all it takes.

Don't forget to remove any bits of code that you needed to add to your theme templates for that particular plugin; otherwise, they'll cause ugly error messages to display in your blog.

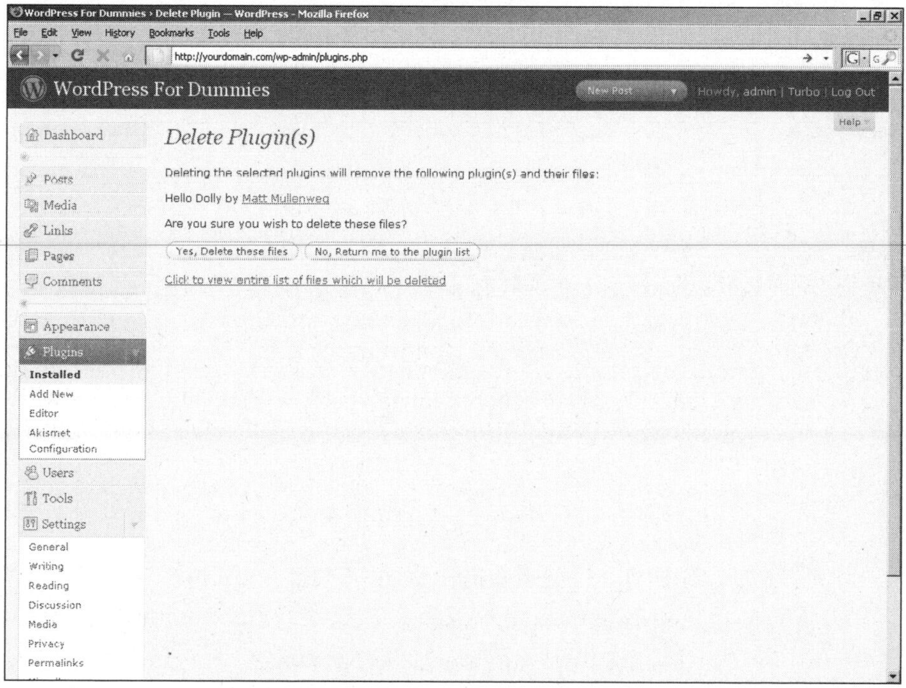

Figure 10-13:
Confirmation
question on
the Delete
Plugin(s)
page.

Understanding the Open Source Environment

The WordPress software was built on an existing platform called b2. Matt Mullenweg, co-founder of WordPress, was using b2 as a blogging platform at the time the developer of that program abandoned it. What did this mean for its users? It meant no more development unless someone somewhere picked up the ball and continued with the platform. Enter Mullenweg and WordPress.

Apply this same concept to plugin development, and you'll understand that plugins sometimes fall by the wayside and drop off the face of the Earth. Unless someone takes over when the original developer loses interest, future development of that plugin ceases. It's important to understand that most plugins are developed in an open source environment, which means a few things for you, the end user:

- ✔ The developers who created your favorite plugin aren't obligated to continue development. If they find a new hobby or simply tire of the work, they can give it up completely. If no one picks up where they left off, you can kiss that plugin goodbye if it doesn't work with the latest WordPress release.

- ✔ Developers of popular plugins generally are extremely good about updating them when new versions of WordPress are released, or when a security bug or flaw is discovered. Keep in mind, however, that no timetable exists for these developers to hold to. Many of these folks have day jobs, classes, or families that can keep them from devoting as much time to the project as you want them to.

- ✔ Beware of the pitfalls of falling in love with any particular WordPress plugin, because in the world of plugin development, it's easy come, easy go. Try not to let your Web site become dependent on a plugin, and don't be surprised if a plugin you love doesn't exist tomorrow. You can use the plugin for as long as it continues to work for you, but when it stops working (such as with a new WordPress release or a security exploit that makes it unusable), you have a rough decision to make. You can

    - • Stop using the plugin, and try to find a suitable alternative.

    - • Hope that another developer takes over the project when the original developer discontinues his involvement.

    - • Try to find someone to provide a fix for you (in which case, you'll more than likely have to pay that someone for her time).

I don't want to make the world of WordPress plugins sound like gloom and doom, but I do think it's very important for you to understand the dynamics in play. Consider this section food for thought.

Finding plugin resources

You can find more information here:

- Chapter 17 highlights ten popular plugins available for WordPress and tells you where to find them. Be sure to check out that chapter to find some useful plugins.

- Lorelle VanFossen maintains a popular blog at `http://lorelle.word press.com`. In this blog, she writes about WordPress tips, tricks, and how-tos. Lorelle dedicated an entire month to WordPress plugins. The entire series, available at `http://lorelle.wordpress.com/tag/wordpress-plugins`, is a great resource.

- Weblog Tools Collection keeps track of new WordPress plugin releases and updates. You can always find great information at `http://weblogtoolscollection.com/archives/category/wordpress-plugins`.

Chapter 11

Finding and Installing WordPress Themes

In previous chapters, I cover how to use the WordPress platform to publish your posts and pages. In those chapters, you discover how to categorize your posts, build your link lists, and set the publishing and profile options in the WordPress Administration panel. In this chapter, I focus on the visual look and format of your blog — in other words, how other people see your blog after you start publishing your content.

In Chapter 10, I introduce WordPress plugins and discuss some of the thousands of free plugins you can use to add functionality to your blog. Similarly, thousands of free themes are available for you to download and use. This chapter shows you where to find them and takes you through the processes of downloading, installing, and using them.

Getting Started with Free Themes

WordPress comes packaged with two free themes for you to use. Most bloggers who use WordPress usually don't waste any time at all in finding a theme that they like better than the Default or Classic WordPress theme. Those packaged themes (which you can find on the Design tab in your WordPress Administration panel) are meant to get you started; you're not limited to using just those two themes. Although both themes are functional, they're kind of plain.

Free WordPress themes, such as those I discuss in Chapter 18, are popular because of their appealing designs and their ease of installation and use. They're great tools to use when you launch your new blog, and if you dabble a bit in graphic design and CSS (Cascading Style Sheets), you can customize one of the free WordPress themes to fit your own needs. (See Chapter 13 for some resources and tools for templates and template tags, as well as a few great CSS references.) Also see the nearby sidebar "Are all WordPress themes free?" for information about free versus premium themes.

By using free themes, you can have your blog up and running with a new design — without the help of a professional — pretty fast. And with thousands of themes available, you can change your theme as often as you want. Chapter 15 presents information on hiring blog professionals, if you decide later that you want a more customized theme for your blog.

Finding free themes

Finding the theme that fits you best may take some time, but with thousands available, you'll eventually find one that suits you. Trying out several free themes is like trying on different "outfits" for your blog. You can change outfits as needed until you find just the right theme.

In July 2008, WordPress launched the official WordPress Free Themes Directory at `http://wordpress.org/extend/themes` (see Figure 11-1).

Are all WordPress themes free?

Not all WordPress themes are created equal, and it's important for you, the user, to know the difference between free and premium themes:

✔ **Free:** These themes are free, period. You can download and use them on your Web site at absolutely no cost. It's a courtesy to include a link to the designer in the footer of your blog — but you can even remove that link if you want to.

✔ **Premium:** These themes cost money. You usually find premium themes available for download only after you've paid anywhere from $10 to $500. The designer feels that these themes are a cut above the rest and, therefore, are worth the money you spend for them. Generally, you're not allowed to remove any designer-credit links that appear in these themes, and you're not allowed to redistribute the themes. (**Note:** You *won't* find premium themes in the official WordPress Theme Directory.) I provide information on where to find premium themes at the end of this chapter.

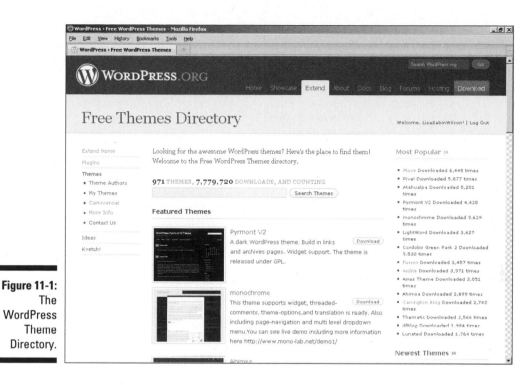

Figure 11-1:
The
WordPress
Theme
Directory.

The WordPress Theme Directory isn't the only place on the Web to find free WordPress themes, but it's the place to find the most functional and *safe* themes available. Safe themes contain clean code and basic WordPress functions that are considered fundamental requirements in a theme to ensure that your WordPress blog functions with the minimum requirements. The WordPress.org Web site lists the basic requirements that theme designers have to meet before their theme is accepted into the themes directory; you can find that listing of requirements at `http://wordpress.org/extend/themes/about`.

Unsafe themes, on the other hand, are developed by people who are looking to take advantage of the blog owners who use them. These particular themes are not allowed in the official WordPress Free Themes Directory. They contain elements such as the following:

✔ **Spam links:** These links usually appear in the footer of the theme and can link to some pretty unsavory places. The designers of these themes hope to benefit from traffic from your site. They count on the idea that most blog owners won't notice the links or know how to remove them.

✔ **Malicious code:** Unscrupulous theme designers can, and do, place code in theme files that inserts hidden malware and/or virus links and spam. Sometimes, you see a line or two of encrypted code that looks like it's just part of the theme code, and unless you have a great deal of knowledge of PHP, you may not know that the theme is infected with dangerous code.

The results of these unsafe theme elements can range from simply annoying to downright dangerous, affecting the integrity and security of your computer and/or hosting account. For this reason, the official WordPress Theme Directory is considered to be a safe place from which to download free themes. WordPress designers develop these themes and upload them to the theme directory, and each theme gets vetted by the folks behind the WordPress platform. In the official directory, themes that contain unsafe elements are simply not allowed to play.

My strong recommendation for finding free themes is to stick with the official WordPress Theme Directory. That way, you know you're getting a clean, quality theme for your blog. You can rest assured that themes from the official directory are safe, and free of spam and malicious code.

Previewing themes

While you're visiting the WordPress Theme Directory, you can easily browse the various themes by using the following features:

✔ **Search:** Type a keyword in the Search box at the top of the page (refer to Figure 11-1) and then click the Search Themes button. A new page opens, displaying themes related to the keyword you searched for.

✔ **Featured Themes:** These themes are listed in the center of the themes directory, randomly. WordPress changes the featured themes listing regularly.

✔ **Most Popular:** These themes have been downloaded most often.

✔ **Newest Themes:** These themes are the latest to be added to the directory.

✔ **Recently Updated:** These themes have been updated most recently by their designers.

When you find a theme in the directory that you want to take a closer look at, click its name to open a page that describes that theme (see Figure 11-2):

✔ **Download:** Click this button to download the theme to your computer.

✔ **Preview:** Click this button to open a new window that shows what the theme looks like in a live blog.

Downloading themes

To download the theme you want, follow these steps:

1. **Click the Download button on the theme page (refer to Figure 11-2).**

   The theme files are compressed in a `.zip` file.

2. **Use your favorite decompression program to unpack the files to your own computer.**

3. **Connect to your Web server via FTP, and upload the entire theme folder to the `/wp-content/themes/` directory of your Web server.**

   The left side of Figure 11-3 shows that I saved the xMark theme files on my computer. The right side of Figure 11-3 shows that I uploaded the xMark theme folder to the `/wp-content/themes/` directory of my Web server.

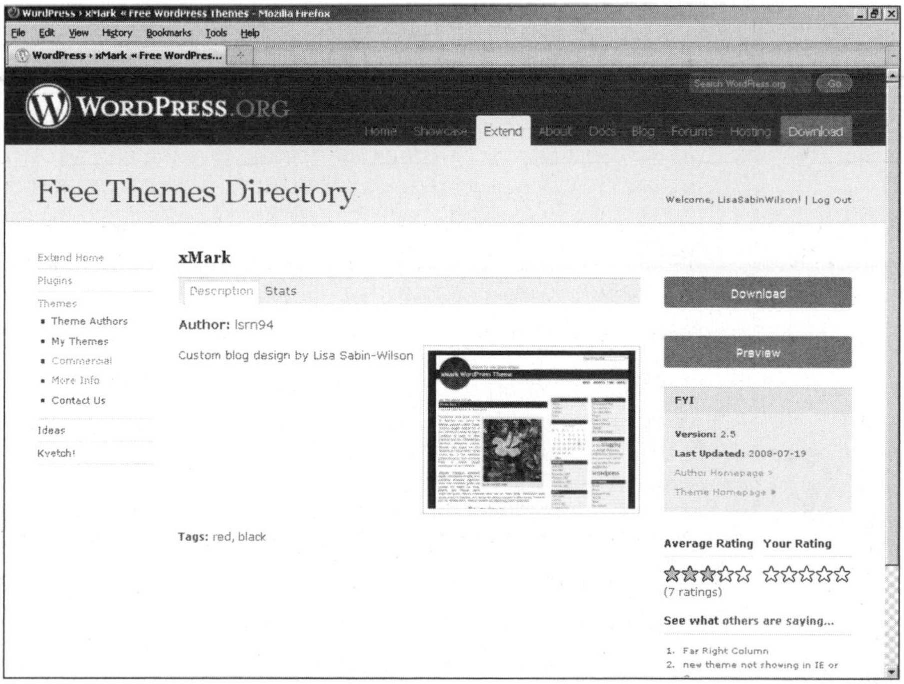

Figure 11-2: Download or preview a particular theme from the Free Themes Directory.

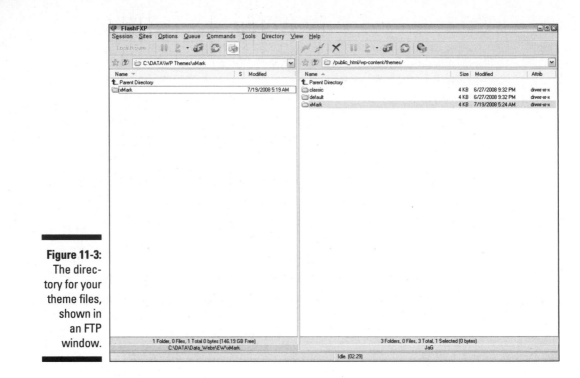

Figure 11-3:
The direc-
tory for your
theme files,
shown in
an FTP
window.

Activating a New Theme

When you have the theme uploaded to your Web server, you can activate it
by logging in to your WordPress Administration panel and following these
simple steps:

1. **Click the Appearance menu.**

   The Manage Themes page opens, listing all the themes currently
   installed in your themes directory. The active theme is shown in the
   Current Theme section at the top of the page. All available themes you
   may have uploaded to your Web server are shown in the Available
   Themes section (see Figure 11-4).

   Available themes appear on the Design tab in alphabetical order. If you
   have a lot of themes in your themes directory, they're displayed ten on
   a page, with Next and Previous links to help you navigate all the themes
   available for your blog.

2. **Click the name or thumbnail image of the theme you want to use.**

   A preview window opens, showing you what your blog will look like with
   this new theme applied (see Figure 11-5).

   Click the X in the top-left corner of the preview window to close the
   theme without activating it.

3. **Click the Activate Theme link.**

   This link, located in the top-right corner of the preview window, is labeled with the theme name. Figure 11-5 shows an Activate WordPress Default link, because that's the name of the theme I want to use.

   WordPress applies the theme you chose to your blog.

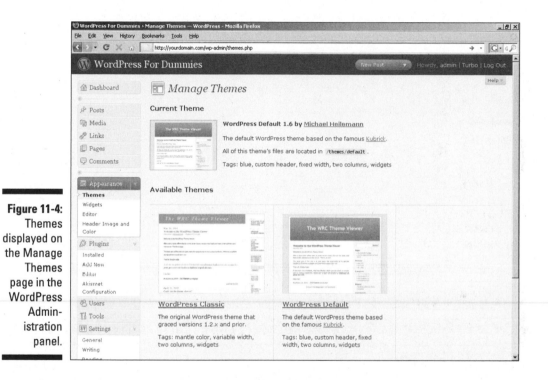

Figure 11-4: Themes displayed on the Manage Themes page in the WordPress Administration panel.

Using sidebar widgets

Most free WordPress themes come with built-in code that lets you take advantage of sidebar widgets for your blog. WordPress widgets are wonderful! (Say *that* ten times fast, why don't you?) Widgets are so wonderful because they let you arrange the display of content in your blog sidebar, such as your blogroll(s), recent posts, and monthly and category archive listings. With widgets, you can accomplish this arranging without needing to know a single bit of code.

In Chapter 5, I cover how to use sidebar widgets. Although that chapter pertains to the hosted WordPress.com platform, WordPress.org users can follow the same steps.

One difference for WordPress.org users is the use of plugins (see Chapter 10). Some plugins have a built-in feature that enables you to include that plugin's functions in your sidebar through the use of a widget. (WordPress.com doesn't have this feature because it doesn't allow uploading and activating various plugins.)

Click to activate theme.

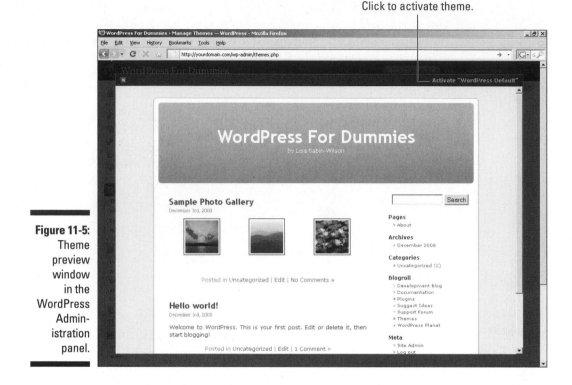

Figure 11-5:
Theme
preview
window
in the
WordPress
Admin-
istration
panel.

Browsing and Installing Themes from the Dashboard

Earlier in this chapter, I covered how to find and install a new theme on your WordPress blog by downloading them from the WordPress Free Themes Directory, uploading them to your Web server via FTP and activating the theme within your WordPress Dashboard. The WordPress platform does give you a much easier way to browse the Free Themes Directory to find, preview, and install themes on your site without ever leaving the comfort of the WordPress administration panel. The following steps show you how to do it:

1. **Click the Add New Themes in the Appearances menu in your WordPress Dashboard.**

   This opens the Install Themes page, where you can find a new theme by browsing the Free WordPress Themes Directory directly from your WordPress administration panel.

2. Search for a new theme.

On the Install Themes page you can search for a new theme by keyword, author or tag. You can also further filter the results by using the Feature Filter check boxes that allow you to filter theme results by color, columns, width, features, and subjects. The Install Themes page is shown in Figure 11-6.

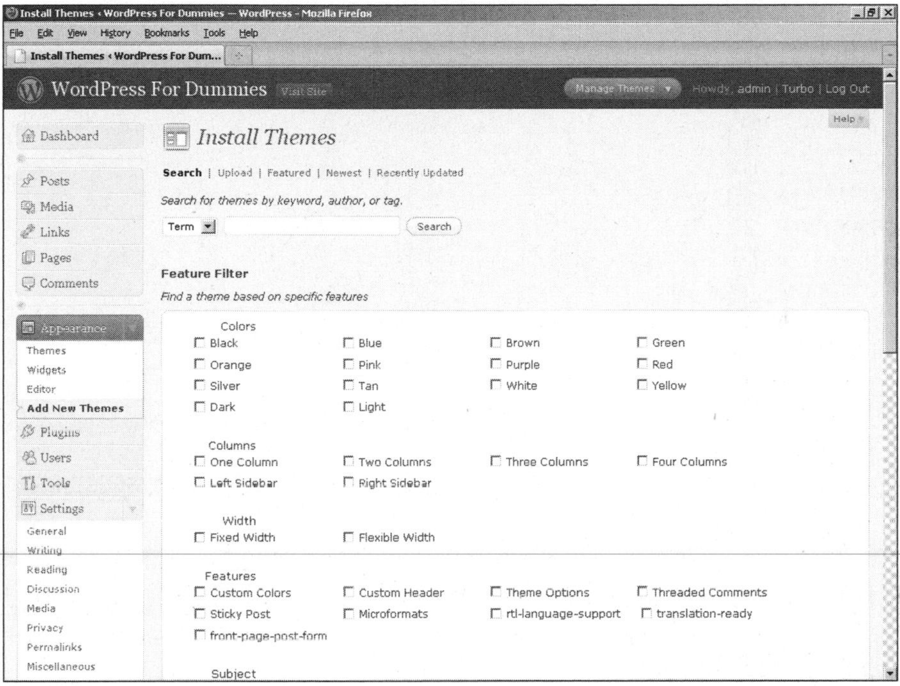

Figure 11-6:
Find new themes on the Install Themes page in your WordPress admin panel.

3. Preview a new theme.

After searching for a new theme, the search results page displays a list of themes for you to choose from. Click the Preview link underneath the theme of your choice to view a sample of how the theme looks. Figure 11-7 shows a preview of a theme called Orange Techno, which I found by searching for the keyword *Tech* on the Install Themes page.

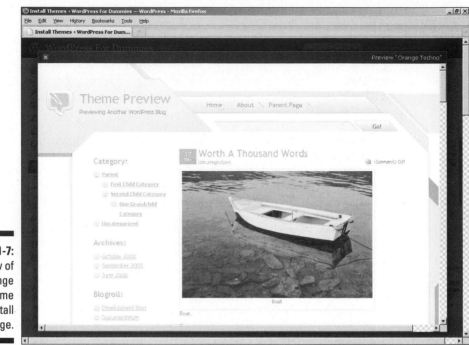

Figure 11-7:
A preview of
the Orange
Techno theme
on the Install
Themes page.

4. **Install a new theme on your blog.**

   After you've found a theme you like, click the Install link underneath the theme name to install the theme on your blog. This pops open a new window with a button labeled Install New @@md click that button to complete the installation.

5. **Activate the new theme.**

   After you click the Install New button, the pop-up window closes and the Installing theme page appears in your WordPress admin panel. Click the Activate link shown on the Installing Theme page to activate and display the new theme on your site.

At the beginning of this chapter, I mentioned that the only themes found in the official WordPress Free Themes Directory are free and have been vetted by the WordPress folks, so are sure to be free of any virus or malicious code. The same holds true for the themes you find by using the Add New Themes feature in your WordPress administration panel. This feature hooks into the official WordPress Free Themes directory, so you are sure to find only those themes that are free and safe.

Deciding to Use Premium Themes

As WordPress becomes more and more popular, I've seen many different business models crop up around the Web that focus on providing WordPress users with premium services and support, such as custom design, consulting, and development, for example. (See Chapter 15 for information on hiring professional services for your blog.)

Premium WordPress themes have become a very popular way for talented designers to provide a service they are very passionate about (designing themes) while making a little money for their efforts, at the same time. There are many schools of thought as to what makes a theme *premium* as opposed to a free theme. Actually, the topic of what is considered premium and what is not, in regards to WordPress themes, is guaranteed to spark passionate debate among designers and theme users, alike. Almost everyone agrees there are indicators of premium themes, however:

✔ Very high quality graphic design and CSS development.

✔ A theme structure with functions that make it very easy for the user to customize and adjust the theme to suit their own needs. This includes, but is not limited to, altering the header graphic/logo and color scheme and changing images and icons.

✔ Comprehensive documentation, providing the user with extensive instructions on how to use the theme, especially if the theme has multiple features and customization options.

✔ Premium themes are fully supported by the designer who created them. Typically, when you buy a premium theme, you should expect full support on the use of that theme for as long as you're using it.

✔ Premium themes are not free. I've seen pricing on premium themes in the range of $10 to $500.

This is not to say that some free themes don't have some, or all, the features I just listed — it's just that, for the most part, they don't. Keep in mind that just because a designer calls a theme premium doesn't mean that the theme has passed through any kind of official quality review. One designer's view of what constitutes a premium theme can, and will, differ from the next.

Fully investigate any theme before you put money down on it. Some things to check out before you pay:

- ✔ E-mail the designer who is selling the premium theme and ask about a support policy.

- ✔ Find people who have purchased the theme and contact them to find out their experiences with the theme and the designer.

- ✔ Carefully read any terms that the designer has published on his site to find out any restrictions that exist with licensing.

- ✔ If the premium theme designer has a support forum, ask whether you can browse through the forum to find out how actively the designer answers questions and provides support. Are users waiting weeks to get their questions answered? Or does the designer seem to be on top of support requests?

- ✔ Do a search in Google for the theme and the designer. Often, users of premium themes post about their experiences with the theme and the designer. You can find out a lot of positive, and potentially, negative information about the theme and the designer before you buy it.

While premium themes are cropping up all over the Web, a handful really stand out with quality products and services. The following three premium themes are tried and true, with a very stable and successful following of clients who use them.

- ✔ **Thesis:** Chris Pearson is the designer of the Thesis, which is a premium theme available in the price range of $87 to $164. The features within the Thesis theme give you full control of your theme functions without having to possess one single bit of coding ability. The Thesis theme can be found at `http://diythemes.com`.

- ✔ **WP Remix:** Designed by R.Bhavesh, WP Remix is a premium WordPress theme that offers all the standard features of a premium theme, plus additional features like WYSIWYG (What You See Is What You Get) page template editing, seven different color schemes, and compatibility with several popular WordPress plugins. The WP Remix theme, priced between $75 and $197, can be found at `http://wpremix.com`.

- ✔ **iThemes:** Cory Miller provides a total of 30 premium themes available for purchase, with prices ranging from $79.95 to $199.95 each. You can also purchase an all-in-one package that includes all 14 themes for a price of $499.95. The iThemes premium themes can be found at `http://ithemes.com`.

You are not able to find, preview, or install Premium Themes using the Add New Themes feature found in your WordPress administration panel (covered in the previous section of this chapter). You can only find, purchase, and download Premium themes at their official Web site and will need to install them via the FTP method I covered in the "Downloading themes" section in this chapter.

Part V
Customizing WordPress

The 5th Wave   By Rich Tennant

DENISE AND JERRY LEVIN — AUTHORS OF "LOST IN THE MALL PARKING LOT," "THE MISPLACED GALLERY INVITATION," AND "THE BAD HAIRCUT—WHY ME?"

Truthfully? If it weren't for WordPress, many of our adventures would have remained untold.

In this part . . .

This part of the book is about digging into WordPress themes and templates, discovering how to tweak template code so you can change the appearance of your blog. A walk-through on essential WordPress template tags and functions, basic HTML, and CSS helps you put together a nice theme to suit your individual style and flair.

Chapter 12

Understanding Themes and Templates

*T*here are those who like to get their hands dirty (present company included!). If you're one of them, you need to read this chapter. WordPress users who create their own themes do so in the interest of:

✔ **Individuality:** Having a theme that no one else has. (If you use one of the free themes, you can pretty much count on the fact that at *least* a dozen other WordPress blogs will have the same look as yours.)

✔ **Creativity:** Displaying your own personal flair and style.

✔ **Control:** Having full control of how the blog looks, acts, and delivers your content.

Many of you aren't at all interested in creating your own templates for your WordPress blog, however. Sometimes, it's just easier to leave matters to the professionals and to hire an experienced WordPress designer (check out Chapter 15) or to use one of the thousands of free themes provided by WordPress designers (see Chapter 11). Chapter 18 also tells you where you can get ten free WordPress themes.

Creating themes does require you to step into the code of the templates, which can be a scary place sometimes — especially if you don't really know what you're looking at. A good place to start is understanding the structure of a WordPress blog. Separately, the parts won't do you any good. But when you put them together, the real magic begins! This chapter covers the basics of doing just that, and near the end of the chapter, you find specific steps to put your own theme together.

You don't need to know HTML to use WordPress. If you plan to create and design WordPress themes, however, you need some basic knowledge of HTML and Cascading Style Sheets (CSS). For assistance with HTML, check out *HTML 4 For Dummies,* 5th Edition, by Ed Tittel and Mary Burmeister, or *HTML, XML, and CSS Bible,* 3rd Edition, by Bryan Pfaffenberger, Steven M. Schafer, Chuck White, and Bill Karow (both published by Wiley).

Using WordPress Themes: The Basics

A WordPress theme is a collection of WordPress templates made up of WordPress template tags. When I refer to a WordPress *theme,* I'm talking about the group of templates that makes up the theme. When I talk about a WordPress *template,* I'm referring to only one of the template files that contain WordPress template tags. WordPress template tags make all the templates work together as a theme (more about this topic later in the chapter).

Understanding theme structure

The rest of this chapter provides important information about the steps to take when building a WordPress theme, but here is a brief overview of the templates that make up a WordPress theme and where you find them, both on your server and within your WordPress Administration panel. Follow these steps:

1. **Connect to your Web server via FTP, and have a look at the existing WordPress themes on your server.**

   The correct location is `/wp-content/themes/` (see Figure 12-1). When you open this folder, you find two default theme folders: Default and Classic.

   If a theme is uploaded to any folder other than `/wp-content/themes`, it won't work.

2. **Open the folder for the default theme (`/wp-content/themes/ default`), and look at the template files inside.**

   At minimum, you find these five templates in the default theme:

   - *Stylesheet* (`style.css`)
   - *Header template* (`header.php`)
   - *Main Index* (`index.php`)

- *Sidebar template* (sidebar.php)

- *Footer template* (footer.php)

These filenames are the same in every WordPress theme. See the "Contemplating the Structure of a WordPress Blog" section later in this chapter, for more information about these template files.

3. **Click the Editor link on the Appearance menu to look at the template files within a theme.**

   This page lists the various templates available within the active theme. (Figure 12-2 shows the templates in the default Kubrick theme.) A text box on the left side of the screen displays the contents of each template, and this box is also where you can edit the template file(s). To view and edit a template file, click its name in the list on the right side of the page.

The Edit Themes page also shows the template tags within the template file. These tags make all the magic happen in your blog; they connect all the templates to form a theme. The next section of this chapter discusses these template tags in detail, showing you what they mean and how they function. A later section provides steps for putting them all together to create your own theme (or edit an existing theme).

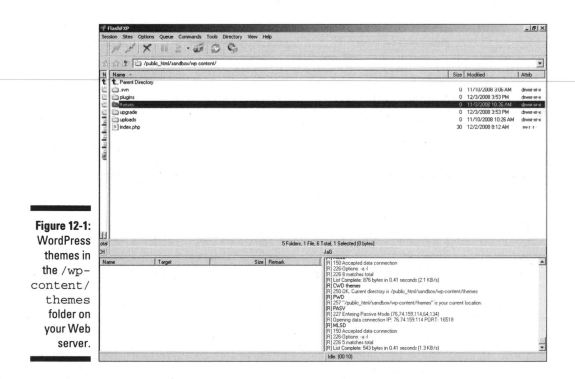

Figure 12-1:
WordPress themes in the /wp-content/ themes folder on your Web server.

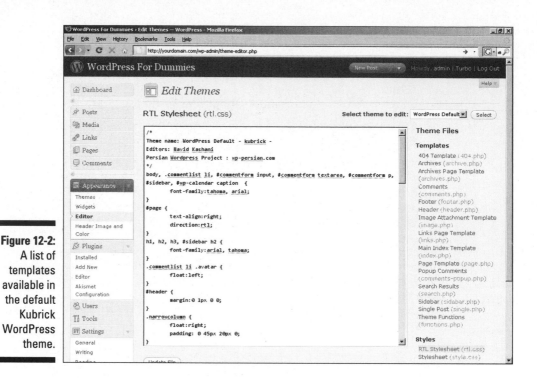

Figure 12-2:
A list of templates available in the default Kubrick WordPress theme.

Connecting templates

The template files don't work alone; for the theme to function, the files need one another. To tie these files together as one working entity, you use template tags to pull the information from each template — Header, Sidebar, and Footer — into the Main Index. I refer to this procedure as *calling* one template into another. (You can find more information in the "Getting Familiar with the Four Main Templates," section, later in this chapter.)

Contemplating the Structure of a WordPress Blog

A WordPress blog, in its very basic form, has four main areas (labeled in Figure 12-3).

Header

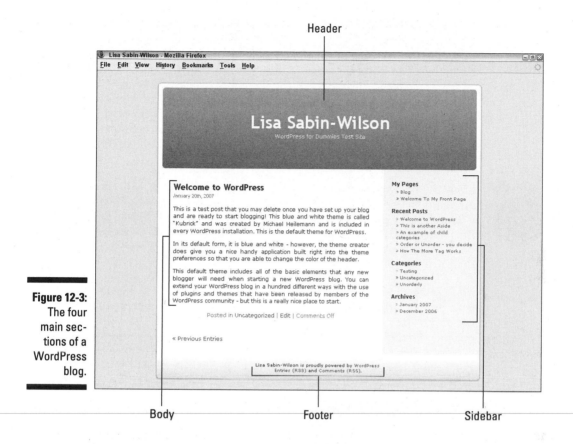

Figure 12-3:
The four
main sec-
tions of a
WordPress
blog.

Body   Footer   Sidebar

These four main areas appear in the default theme that comes in every version of WordPress:

- ✔ **Header:** This area usually contains the name of the site along with the site tagline or slogan. Sometimes, the header also contains a graphic or image.

- ✔ **Body:** This area is where your blog posts appear in chronological order.

- ✔ **Sidebar:** This area is where you find lists of blog-related elements, such as the blogroll, the archives, and a list of recent posts.

- ✔ **Footer:** This area, at the bottom of the page, often contains links to further information about the blog, such as who designed it, which company provides hosting for the blog, and copyright information.

These four areas are the absolute bare bones of a basic WordPress blog template. You can extend these areas and create new sections that carry more information, of course, but for the purpose of this chapter, I'm focusing on the basics.

The default WordPress theme is called Kubrick, and in my opinion, it isn't the best theme to use as an example for people who are brand-new to template creation. It's kind of like teaching your teenager to drive by using a brand-new Lamborghini — just a little too much power under the hood for a beginner. Because this theme is the default theme available in all WordPress installations (including your new blog), however, it makes perfect sense to use something that you can reference while reading this chapter. I don't cover all the tags and templates that the Kubrick theme includes; rather, I touch on the basics to get you on your way to understanding templates and template tags for WordPress.

 Many themes developed for WordPress are free for public use; I strongly recommend finding one that you like and downloading it. Use the free themes as a jumping-off place to get started in theme development. Really, why reinvent the wheel? With the free themes available today, most of the work has already been completed for you, and you may find it easier to use one of these themes than to start a theme from scratch.

Depending on your skill level, you may find a theme that is easier to work with than Kubrick. Each free theme that is available for download is different, depending on what the developer included (such as CSS styling, display options, format, and layout). So experimenting with a few themes is fun and is a great way to learn more about the development of WordPress themes. A great place to find free WordPress themes is the official WordPress Theme Directory at `http://wordpress.org/extend/themes`.

To build a basic WordPress theme that covers the four basic areas of a blog, you need these five templates:

- `header.php`
- `index.php`
- `sidebar.php`
- `footer.php`
- `style.css`

Each WordPress theme comes with a stylesheet (`style.css`), which drives the formatting and layout of your blog template in terms of where the elements are positioned on the page, what the font looks like, what colors your hyperlinks will be, and so on. As you may have already figured out, you don't use CSS to put content on your site; rather, you use CSS to style the content that's already there.

Chapter 13 provides information on tweaking the design of your theme by combining the template tags presented in this chapter with some CSS adjustments in your theme files.

Right now, I'm covering only the basics; at the end of this chapter, however, I provide some ideas on how you can use various templates to further extend your blog functionality — using templates for categories, archives, static pages, multiple sidebars, and so on. After you build the basics, you can spread your wings and step into more advanced themes.

Examining the Anatomy of a Template Tag

Before starting to play around with template tags in your WordPress templates, it's important to understand what makes up a template tag and why.

WordPress is based in PHP (a scripting language for creating Web pages) and uses PHP commands to pull information from the MySQL database. Every tag begins with the function to start PHP and ends with a function to stop PHP. In the middle of those two commands lives the request to the database that tells WordPress to grab the data and display it.

A typical template tag looks like this:

```
<?php get_info(); ?>
```

This entire example tells WordPress to do three things:

- Start PHP (`<?php`).
- Use PHP to get information from the MySQL database and deliver it to your blog (`get_info();`).
- Stop PHP (`?>`).

In this case, `get_info` is the actual tag function, which grabs information from the database to deliver it to your blog. What information is retrieved depends on what tag function appears between the two PHP commands. As you may notice, there's a lot of starting and stopping of PHP throughout the WordPress templates. The process seems as though it would be resource intensive, if not exhaustive — but it really isn't.

For every PHP command you start, you need a stop command. Every time a command begins with `<?php`, somewhere later in the code is the closing `?>` command. PHP commands that aren't structured properly cause really ugly errors on your site, and they've been known to send programmers, developers, and hosting providers into loud screaming fits.

Getting Familiar with the Four Main Templates

In the following sections, I cover some of the template tags that pull in the information you want to include in your blog. To keep this chapter shorter than 1,000 pages, I focus on the four main templates that get you going with creating your own theme or with editing the template tags in the theme you're currently using. Here are those four main templates:

- ✔ Header
- ✔ Main Index
- ✔ Sidebar
- ✔ Footer

The Header template

The Header template for your WordPress themes is the starting point for every WordPress theme, because it tells Web browsers the following:

- ✔ The title of your blog
- ✔ The location of the CSS
- ✔ The RSS feed URL
- ✔ The blog URL
- ✔ The tagline (or description) of the blog

Every page on the Web has to start with a few pieces of code. In every `header. php` file in any WordPress theme, you'll find these bits of code at the top:

- ✔ The `DOCTYPE` (which stands for *document type declaration*) tells the browser which type of XHTML standards you're using.
- ✔ The `<head>` tag tells the browser that the information contained within the tag shouldn't be displayed on the site; rather, it's information about the document.
- ✔ The `<html>` tag (*HTML* stands for *Hypertext Markup Language*) tells the browser which language you're using to write your Web page.

In a WordPress Header template, these bits of code look like the following example, and you should leave them intact:

```
<!DOCTYPE html PUBLIC "-//W3C//DTD XHTML 1.0
        Transitional//EN" "http://www.w3.org/TR/xhtml1/
        DTD/xhtml1-transitional.dtd">
<html xmlns="http://www.w3.org/1999/xhtml" <?php language_
        attributes(); ?>>
<head profile="http://gmpg.org/xfn/11">
```

The <head> tag needs to be closed at the end of the Header template, which looks like this: </head>. You also need to include a fourth tag, the <body> tag, which tells the browser where the information you want to display begins. Both the <body> and <html> tags need to be closed at the end of the template, like this: </body></html>.

Using bloginfo parameters

Interestingly enough, all the information that I just listed about your blog is included in the Header template through the use of a single WordPress tag: bloginfo();.

What differentiates the type of information that a tag pulls in is a *parameter*. Parameters are placed inside the parentheses of the tag, enclosed in single quotes. For the most part, these parameters pull information from the settings in your WordPress Administration panel. The template tag to get your blog title, for example, looks like this:

```
<?php bloginfo('name'); ?>
```

Table 12-1 lists the various parameters you need for the bloginfo(); tag and shows you what the template tag looks like.

Table 12-1	Tag Values for bloginfo(); in the Default Kubrick Template header.php	
Parameter	*Information*	*Tag*
Name	Blog title, set in Settings/General	`<?php bloginfo ('name'); ?>`
Description	Tagline for your blog, set in Settings/General	`<?php bloginfo ('description'); ?>`
url	Your blog's Web address, set in Settings/General	`<?php bloginfo ('url'); ?>`
stylesheet_url	URL of primary CSS file	`<?php bloginfo ('stylesheet url'); ?>`

(continued)

Table 12-1 (continued)

Parameter	Information	Tag
Version	Your version of WordPress, set in /wp-includes/ version.php	<?php bloginfo ('version'); ?>
rss2_url	URL of your RSS 2.0 feed	<?php bloginfo ('rss2_url'); ?>
stylesheet_ directory	URL of your theme's directory	<?php bloginfo ('stylesheet_ directory'); ?>

Creating title tags and popular characters

Here's a useful tip about your blog's `<title>` tag: Search engines pick up the words used in the `<title>` tag as keywords to categorize your site in their search engine directories. The blog `<title>` tag is the code that lives in the Header template between these two tag markers: `<title></title>`. In the default Kubrick theme, this bit of code looks like this:

```
<title><?php if (is_single() || is_page() || is_archive())
       { wp_title('',true); } else { bloginfo('name');
       echo(' &#8212; '); bloginfo('description'); }
       ?></title>
```

It may help for me to put this example into plain English. First, the `<title></title>` tags are HTML tags that tell the browser to display the title of your Web site in the title bar of the browser. Figure 12-4 shows how the title of my personal blog sits in the title bar of the browser window. (The *title bar* is the top bar in your browser. In Figure 12-4, it says Lisa Sabin-Wilson — Designer, Author: WordPress For Dummies.)

Search engines love the title bar; the more you can tweak that title to provide detailed descriptions of your site, the more the search engines will love you. They'll show that love by giving you higher rankings in their results. For more information and tips on search engine optimization (SEO) with WordPress, see Chapter 14.

Here's how to deconstruct the rest of the code between those `<title>` tags:

✔ The first part of this code tells your WordPress blog: If this is a single post, a page, or an archive, display the title of that post, page, or archive first in the title bar:

```
<?php if (is_single() || is_page() || is_archive()) { wp_title('',true); }
```

✔ The second part of the code tells WordPress this: If the page being viewed is anything other than a single post, a page, or an archive, display the site name and description as provided in the WordPress settings:

```
else { bloginfo('name'); echo(' &raquo; '); bloginfo('description'); } ?>
```

If your reader is on a single blog-post page, this tag tells WordPress to display the title of the post followed by the name of your site. This setup is great for search engines, because the name of your post provides some rich keyword content that search engines eat up like candy.

The title bar of the browser window always displays your blog name unless you're on a single post page. In that case, it displays your blog title plus the title of the post on that page.

Within some of the WordPress template tags, such as the `<title>` tag in the earlier example, you may notice some weird characters that look like a foreign language. You may wonder what `&raquo;` is, for example. It isn't part of any PHP function or CSS style. Rather, it's a *character entity* — a kind of code that enables you to display a special character in your blog. The `&raquo;` character entity displays a double right-angle quotation mark. See Table 12-2 for examples of common character entities.

The title bar displays your site name.

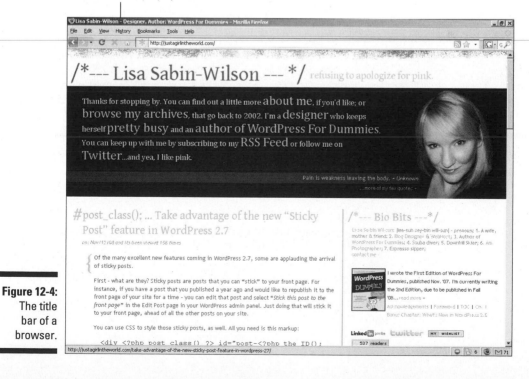

Figure 12-4:
The title bar of a browser.

Table 12-2	Popular Character Entities	
Code	*Description*	*Display*
`&raquo;`	A double right-angle quote	»
`&laquo;`	A double left-angle quote	«
`&bull;`	A bullet	•
`&hearts;`	A black heart	♥
`&diams;`	A black diamond	♦
`&clubs;`	A black shamrock	♣
`&spades;`	A black spade	♠
`&lt;`	A single left arrow	<
`&gt;`	A single right arrow	>

Displaying your blog name and tagline

The default Kubrick theme header displays your blog name and tagline. My blog name and tagline are

- **Blog name:** Lisa-Wilson Sabin
- **Blog tagline:** Designer, Author: WordPress For Dummies

Refer to Figure 12-4 to see these two elements in the header of the site.

You can use the `bloginfo();` tag plus a little HTML code to display your blog name and tagline. Most blogs have a clickable title, which is a site title that takes you back to the main page when it's clicked. No matter where your visitors are on your site, they can always go back home by clicking the title of your site in the header.

To create a clickable title, use the following code:

```
<a href="<?php bloginfo('url'); ?>"><?php
        bloginfo('name'); ?></a>
```

The `bloginfo('url');` tag is your main blog Internet address, and the `bloginfo('name');` tag is the name of your blog (refer to Table 12-1). So the code creates a link that looks something like this:

```
<a href="http://yourdomain.com">Your Blog Name</a>
```

The tagline generally isn't linked back home. You can display it by using the following tag:

```
<?php bloginfo('description'); ?>
```

This tag pulls the tagline directly from the one that you've set up in the Administration panel.

This example shows how WordPress is intuitive and user-friendly; you can do things such as changing the blog name and tagline with a few keystrokes in the Administration panel. Changing your options in the Administration panel creates the change on every page of your site — no coding experience required. Beautiful, isn't it?

In the Kubrick template, these tags are surrounded by tags that look like these: `<h1></h1>` or `<h4></h4>`. These tags are `<header>` tags, which define the look and layout of the blog name and tagline in the CSS of your theme. I cover CSS further in Chapter 13.

The Main Index template

The Main Index template drags your blog posts out of the MySQL database and inserts them into your blog. This template is to your blog what the dance floor is to a nightclub — where all the action happens.

The filename of the Main Index template is `index.php`. You can find it in the `/wp-content/themes/` folder.

The first template tag in the Main Index template calls in the Header template, meaning that it pulls the information from the Header template into the Main Index template, as follows:

```
<?php get_header(); ?>
```

Your theme can work without calling in the Header template, but it'll be missing several essential pieces — the CSS and the blog name and tagline, for starters. Without the call to the Header template, your blog will resemble the image shown in Figure 12-5.

The Loop

I'm not talking about America's second-largest downtown business district, originating at the corner of State and Madison streets in Chicago. I could write about some interesting experiences I've had there . . . but that would be a different book.

The Loop in this case is a function that WordPress uses to display the posts on your blog. The Loop has a starting point and an ending point; anything placed in between is used to display each post, including any HTML, PHP, or CSS tags and codes.

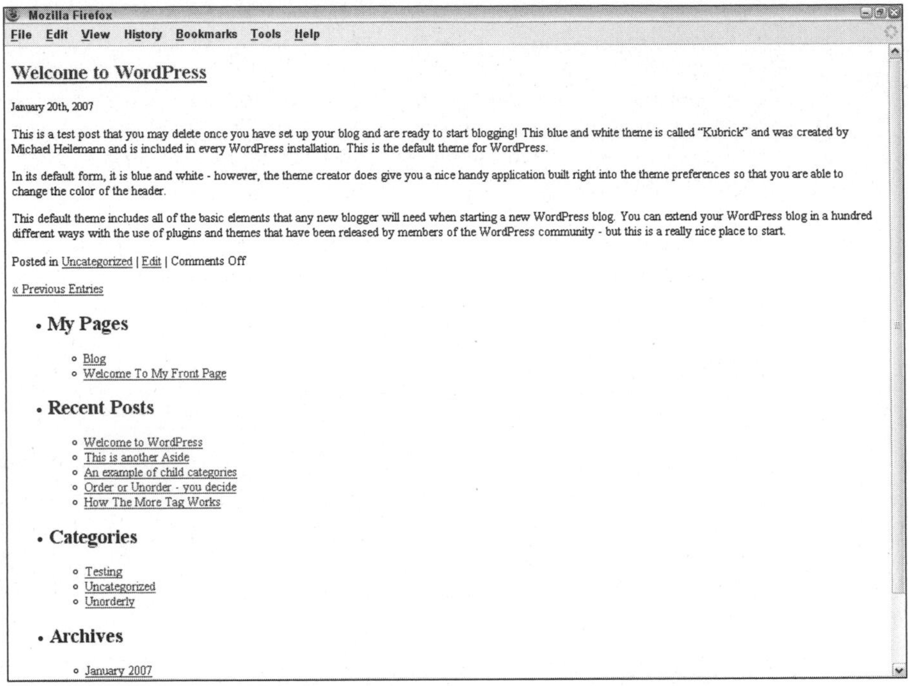

Figure 12-5:
WordPress
blog missing
the call to
the header.
It's naked!

In your travels as a WordPress user, you may run across plugins or scripts with instructions that say something like this: "This must be placed within The Loop." That's The Loop that I discuss in this section, so pay particular attention. Understanding The Loop arms you with the knowledge you need for tackling and understanding your WordPress themes.

Quite a few variations of the WordPress Loop are available, but I cover the most common use in this section. When you understand the common use, you can begin to push the envelope a bit further and use variations to suit your needs. This common use displays your posts in chronological order, starting with your most recent post and followed by less recent posts, ordered by date.

The Loop starts with this code (which is inside the Main Index template of the default Kubrick theme):

```
<?php while (have_posts()) : the_post(); ?>
```

Several lines later is the code that ends The Loop:

```
<?php endwhile; ?>
```

The Loop is no different from any other template tag; it must begin with a function to start PHP, and it must end with a function to stop PHP. The Loop begins with PHP and then makes a request: "While there are posts in my blog, display them on this page." This PHP function tells WordPress to grab the blog post information from the database and return it to the blog page. The end of The Loop is like a traffic cop with a big red stop sign telling WordPress to stop the function completely.

You can set the number of posts displayed per page in the Administration panel. The Loop abides by this rule and displays only the number of posts per page that you've set.

The big if

PHP functions in a pretty simple, logical manner. It functions by doing what you and I do on a daily basis — making decisions based on questions and answers. PHP deals with three basic variables:

- ✔ if
- ✔ then
- ✔ else

The basic idea is this: IF this, THEN that, or ELSE this.

The code directly above the start of The Loop looks like this:

```php
<?php if (have_posts()) : ?>
```

This `if` statement asks the question, "Does this blog have posts?"

If the answer is yes, WordPress proceeds with The Loop, starting with the piece of code that looks like this:

```php
<?php while (have_posts()) : the_post(); ?>
```

This code tells WordPress to grab the posts from the MySQL database and display them on your blog page.

Then The Loop closes with this tag:

```php
<?php endwhile; ?>
```

If the answer to the `if` question ("Does this blog have posts?") is no, WordPress skips The Loop and displays a message that no posts exist. It accomplishes this task through the `else` statement, directly below the end of The Loop:

```
<?php else : ?>
<h2 class="center">Not Found</h2>
<p class="center">Sorry, but you are looking for something
          that isn't here.</p>
<?php include (TEMPLATEPATH . "/searchform.php"); ?>
```

With the PHP, WordPress displays the title *Not Found,* followed by the statement *Sorry, but you are looking for something that isn't here,* followed by the template tag to include a search box that lets users search your blog for more information.

Every good PHP function has to come to an end. The `if` statement ends in the next line of code:

```
<?php endif; ?>
```

Following the `if`, `then`, `else` logic, Table 12-3 breaks down the logic of The Loop. In the "Customizing Your Blog Posts with Template Tags," section later in this chapter, I get into the fun part of providing all the different template tags that you can include within The Loop.

Table 12-3	**Deconstructing The Loop**
Code	**What It Means**
`<?php if (have_posts()) : ?>`	Poses the question "Does this blog have posts?"
`<?php while (have_posts()) : the_post(); ?>`	If the answer is yes, this piece of code tells WordPress to retrieve the blog posts from the database and display them on the page.
`<?php endwhile; ?>`	Ends the display of blog posts, ending the loop.

`<?php else : ?>`
 	
`<h2 class="center">Not Found</h2>`
 	
`<p class="center">Sorry, but you are looking for something that isn't here.</p>`
 	
`<?php include (TEMPLATEPATH . "/searchform.php"); ?>`
	If the answer is no, the blog doesn't have posts. WordPress displays the title *Not Found,* followed by the statement *Sorry, but you are looking for something that isn't here,* followed by the template tag to include a search box that lets users search your blog for more information.

`<?php endif; ?>`	Ends the `if` question.

If, then, and else

In our daily lives, we deal with if, then, else situations every day, as in these examples:

✔ **IF** I have a dollar, **THEN** I'll buy coffee, or **ELSE** I'll drink water.

✔ **IF** it's warm outside, **THEN** I'll take a walk, or **ELSE** I'll stay in.

✔ **IF** I understand this code, **THEN** I'll be happy, or **ELSE** I'll rip my hair out.

The Sidebar template

The filename of the Sidebar template is `sidebar.php`. Typically, the sidebar is displayed on the right or left side of your WordPress template. In the default Kubrick theme, the sidebar is displayed on the right side of the template (refer to Figure 12-3).

Similarly to the Header template, the Sidebar template is called into the Main Index template with this function:

```
<?php get_sidebar(): ?>
```

This code calls the Sidebar template and all the information it contains into your blog page. Chapter 14 addresses some additional ways you can call in the Sidebar template, including having multiple Sidebar templates and using an `include` statement to pull them into the Main Index template.

In the "Using Tags with Parameters for Sidebars," section later in this chapter, you find information on template tags to use in the sidebar to display the usual sidebar elements, such as a list of the most recent posts or a list of categories.

The Footer template

The filename of the Footer template is `footer.php`. Usually, the footer sits at the bottom of the page (refer to Figure 12-3) and contains brief information about the site, such as copyright statements, credits to the theme designer or hosting company, or even a list of links to other pages within the site.

The default Kubrick theme shows site ownership information and RSS feed links for the blog. You can use the footer to include all sorts of information about your site, however; you don't have to restrict it to small bits of information. In this chapter, I cover the typical footer that you see in the default Kubrick theme.

Similarly to the Header and Sidebar templates, the Footer template gets called into the Main Index template through this bit of code:

```
<?php get_footer(); ?>
```

This code calls the Footer and all the information it contains into your blog page.

Other templates

Other templates are in the default Kubrick theme, and I don't cover them in depth in this chapter, but having at least a basic understanding of them is a good idea. The ones I list in this section give you that good, solid kick in the pants you need to get started with understanding WordPress templates. When you have that task licked, you can move on to learning the rest.

These other (optional) templates include

- **Comments template (`comments.php`):** Table 12-10, later in this chapter, lists some useful template tags for WordPress. The Comments template is required if you plan to host comments on your blog; it provides all the template tags you need to display those comments. The template tag used to call the comments into the template is `<?php comments_template(); ?>`.

- **Single Post template (`single.php`):** When your visitors click the title or permalink of a post you've published to your blog, they're taken to that post's individual page. There, they can read the entire post, and if you have comments enabled, they see the comments form and can leave comments (see Figure 12-6).

- **Page template (`page.php`):** You can use a Page template for static pages in your WordPress site.

- **Search Results (`search.php`):** You can use this template to create a custom display of search results on your blog. When someone uses the search feature to search your site for specific keywords, this template formats the return of those results.

- **404 template (`404.php`):** Use this template to create a custom 404 page, which is the page visitors get when the browser can't find the page requested and returns that ugly 404 Page Cannot Be Found error.

The templates in the preceding list are optional. If these templates don't exist in your WordPress `themes` folder, nothing breaks. The Main Index template handles the display of these items (the single post page, the search results page, and so on). The only exception is the Comments template. If you want to display comments on your site, you must have that template.

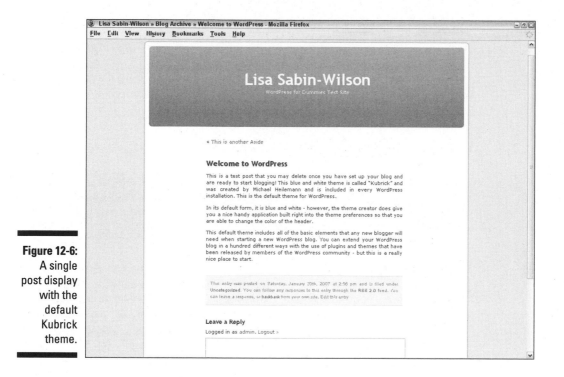

Figure 12-6:
A single
post display
with the
default
Kubrick
theme.

Customizing Your Blog Posts with Template Tags

This section covers the template tags that you use to display the body of each blog post you publish. The body of a blog post includes information such as the post date and time, title, author name, category, and content. Table 12-4 lists the common template tags you can use for posts, available in the default Kubrick theme. The tags in Table 12-4 work only if you place them within The Loop (covered earlier in this chapter).

Table 12-4	Template Tags for Blog Posts
Tag	*Function*
`<?php the_date(); ?>`	Displays the date of the post.
`<?php the_time(); ?>`	Displays the time of the post.
`<?php the_title(); ?>`	Displays the title of the post.

(continued)

Table 12-4 *(continued)*

Tag	Function
`<?php the_permalink(); ?>`	Displays the permalink (URL) of the post.
`<?php the_author(); ?>`	Displays the post author's name.
`<?php the_author_link(); ?>`	Displays the URL of the post author's site.
`<?php the_content('Read More...'); ?>`	Displays the content of the post. (If you use an excerpt [below], the words *Read More* appear and are linked to the individual post page.)
`<?php the_excerpt(); ?>`	Displays an excerpt (snippet) of the post.
`<?php the_category(','); ?>`	Displays the category (or categories) assigned to the post. If the post is assigned to multiple categories, they'll be separated by commas.
`<?php comments_popup_link('No Comments', 'Comment (1)', 'Comments(%)'); ?>`	Displays a link to the comments, along with the comment count for the post in parentheses. (If no comments exist, it displays a *No Comments* message.)
`<?php next_posts_link('&laquo; Previous Entries') ?>`	Displays the words *Previous Entries* linked to the previous page of blog entries.*
`<?php previous_posts_link('Next Entries &raquo;') ?>`	Displays the words *Next Entries* linked to the next page of blog entries.*

* These two tags aren't like the others. You don't place these tags in The Loop; instead, you insert them after The Loop but before the `if` statement ends. Here's an example:

```
<?php endwhile; ?>
<?php next_posts_link('&laquo; Previous Entries') ?>
<?php previous_posts_link('Next Entries &raquo;') ?>
<?php endif; ?>
```

Putting a Theme Together

In this section, you put together the guts of a Main Index template by using the information on templates and tags I've provided so far in this chapter. You create a new WordPress theme, using some of the basic templates included in the default Kubrick theme. The first steps in pulling everything together are as follows:

1. **Connect to your Web server via FTP, click the `wp-content` folder, and then click the `themes` folder.**

   This folder contains the themes that are currently installed in your WordPress blog. (See Chapter 6 if you need more information on FTP.)

2. **Create a new folder, and call it `mytheme`.**

   In most FTP programs, you can right-click and choose New Folder. (If you aren't sure how to create a folder, refer to your FTP program's help files.)

3. **Upload the following files from the default Kubrick theme:**

   - `sidebar.php`
   - `footer.php`
   - `header.php`
   - `style.css`
   - `comments.php`
   - The `images` folder

   You find the default Kubrick theme files in the original WordPress files that you downloaded from the WordPress Web site. Do not upload the `index.php` file, as you are about to create your own `index.php` file in the next section.

Using the tags provided in Table 12-4, along with the information on The Loop and the calls to the Header, Sidebar, and Footer templates provided in earlier sections, you can follow the next steps for a bare-bones example of what the Main Index template looks like when you put the tags together.

When typing templates, be sure to use a text editor such as Notepad or TextEdit. Using a word processing program such as Microsoft Word opens a whole slew of problems in your code. Word processing programs insert hidden characters and format quotation marks in a way that WordPress can't read.

To create a Main Index template to work with the other templates in your WordPress theme, open a new window in a text editor program and then follow these steps. (Type the text in each of these steps on its own line. Press the Enter key after typing each line so that each tag starts on a new line.)

1. **Type** `<?php get_header(); ?>`.

   This template tag pulls the information in the Header template of your WordPress theme.

2. **Type** `<?php if (have_posts()) : ?>`.

   This template tag is an `if` statement that asks, "Does this blog have posts?" If the answer is yes, it grabs the post content information from your MySQL database and displays the posts in your blog.

3. **Type** `<?php while (have_posts()) : the_post(); ?>`.

   This template tag starts The Loop.

4. **Type** `<a href="<?php the_permalink(); ?>"><?php the_ title(); ?></a>`.

   This tag tells your blog to display the title of a post that's clickable (linked) to the URL of the post.

5. **Type** `Posted on <?php the_date(); ?> at <?php the_ time(); ?>`.

   This template tag displays the date and time when the post was made. With these template tags, the date and time format are determined by the format you set in the Administration panel.

6. **Type** `Posted in <?php the_category(','); ?>`.

   This template tag displays a comma-separated list of the categories to which you've assigned the post — *Posted in: category 1, category 2,* for example.

7. **Type** `<?php the_content('Read More..'); ?>`.

   This template tag displays the actual content of the blog post. The `'Read More..'` portion of this tag tells WordPress to display the words *Read More,* which are clickable (hyperlinked) to the post's perma-link, where the reader can read the rest of the post in its entirety. This tag applies when you're displaying a post excerpt, as determined by the actual post configuration in the Administration panel.

8. **Type** `Posted by: <?php the_author(); ?>`.

   This template tag displays the author of the post in this manner: *Posted by: Lisa Sabin-Wilson.*

9. **Type** `<?php comments_popup_link('No Comments', '1 Comment', '% Comments'); ?>`.

   This template tag displays the link to the comments for this post, along with the number of comments.

10. **Type** `<?php comments_template(); ?>`.

    This template tag calls in the Comments template (`comments.php`). All code and information in the Comments template is pulled into the Main Index template at this point. The Comments template is displayed only on the single post page, however, not on the front page of your blog site.

11. **Type** `<?php endwhile; ?>`.

    This template tag ends The Loop and tells WordPress to stop displaying blog posts here. WordPress knows exactly how many times The Loop needs to work, based on the setting in the WordPress Administration panel. That's exactly how many times WordPress will execute The Loop.

12. **Type** `<?php next_posts_link('&laquo; Previous Entries'); ?>`.

    This template tag displays a clickable link to the previous page of blog entries, if any.

13. **Type** `<?php previous posts link('&raquo; Next Entries'); ?>`.

    This template tag displays a clickable link to the next page of blog entries, if any.

14. **Type** `<?php else : ?>`.

    This template tag refers to the `if` question asked in Step 2. If the answer to that question is no, this step provides the `else` statement — IF this blog has posts, THEN list them here (Step 2 and Step 3), or ELSE display the following message.

15. **Type** `Not Found. Sorry, but you are looking for something that isn't here.`

    This is the message followed by the template tag that is displayed after the `else` statement from Step 14. You can reword this statement to have it say whatever you want.

16. **Type** `<?php endif; ?>`.

    This template tag ends the `if` statement from Step 2.

17. **Type** `<?php get_sidebar(); ?>`.

    This template tag calls in the Sidebar template and pulls that information into the Main Index template. (See the "Using Tags with Parameters for Sidebars" section later in this chapter, for further descriptions of tags for this template.)

18. **Type** `<?php get_footer(); ?>`.

    This template tag calls in the Footer template and pulls that information into the Main Index template. *Note:* The code in the `footer.php` template ends the `<body>` and the `<html>` tags that were started in the Header template (`header.php`).

When you're done, the display of the Main Index template code looks like this:

```php
<?php get_header(); ?>
<?php if (have_posts()) : ?>

 <?php while (have_posts()) : the_post(); ?>
<div <?php post_class() ?> id="post-<?php the_ID(); ?>">
 <a href="<?php the_permalink(); ?>"><?php the_title(); ?></a>
 Posted on: <?php the_date(); ?> at <?php the_time(); ?>
 Posted in: <?php the_category(','); ?>

 <?php the_content('Read More..'); ?>

 Posted by: <?php the_author(); ?> | <?php comments_popup_link('No
          Comments', '1 Comment', '% Comments'); ?>
</div>
<?php comments_template(); ?>
 <?php endwhile; ?>
<?php next_posts_link('&laquo; Previous Entries') ?>
<?php previous_posts_link('Next Entries &raquo;') ?>

<?php else : ?>
 Not Found
 Sorry, but you are looking for something that isn't here.

<?php endif; ?>

<?php get_sidebar(); ?>
<?php get_footer(); ?>
```

19. **Save this file as `index.php`, and upload it to the `mythemes` folder.**

    In Notepad, you can save it by choosing File⇨Save As. Type the name of the file in the File Name text box, and click Save.

20. **Activate the theme in the WordPress Administration panel, and view your blog to see your handiwork in action!**

My Main Index template code has one template tag that is explained in Chapter 13: `<div <?php post_class() ?> id="post-<?php the_ID(); ?>">`. This tag helps you create some interesting styles in your template using CSS, so check out Chapter 13 to find out all about it!

Using Tags with Parameters for Sidebars

If you've been following along in this chapter as I've covered the Header and Main Index templates and tags, you have a functional WordPress blog with blog posts and various metadata displayed in each post.

In this section, I give you the template tags for the items commonly placed in the sidebar of a blog. I say "commonly placed" because it's possible to get creative with these template tags and place them in other locations (the Footer template, for example). To keep this introduction to sidebar template tags simple, I stick with the most common use, leaving the creative and uncommon uses to you to try when you're comfortable with building the basics.

This section also introduces *tag parameters,* which are additional options you can include in the tag to control some of its display properties. Not all template tags have parameters. You place tag parameters inside the parentheses of the tag. Many of the parameters discussed in this section were obtained from the WordPress software documentation in the WordPress Codex at `http://codex.wordpress.org`.

Table 12-5 helps you understand the three variations of parameters used by WordPress.

Table 12-5	Three Variations of Template Parameters	
Variation	*Description*	*Example*
Tags without parameters	These tags have no additional options available. Tags without parameters have nothing within the parentheses.	`the_tag();`
Tags with PHP function-style parameters	These tags have a comma-separated list of values placed within the tag parentheses.	`the_tag ('1,2,3');`
Tags with query-string parameters	These types of tags generally have several available parameters. This tag style enables you to change the value for each parameter without being required to provide values for all available parameters for the tag.	`the_tag ('parameter= true);`

You need to know these three types of parameters:

- ✔ **String:** A line of text that can be anything from a single letter to a long list of words. A string is placed between single quotation marks and sets an option for the parameter or is displayed as text.

- ✔ **Integer:** A positive or negative number. Integers are placed within the parentheses and either inside or outside single quotation marks. Either way, they'll be processed correctly.

- ✔ **Boolean:** Sets the parameter options to `true` or `false`. This parameter can be numeric (0=false and 1=true) or textual. Boolean parameters aren't placed within quotation marks.

The WordPress Codex, located at `http://codex.wordpress.org`, has every conceivable template tag and possible parameter known to the WordPress software. The tags and parameters that I share with you in this chapter are the ones used most often.

The Calendar

The `calendar` tag displays a calendar that highlights each day of the week on which you've posted a blog. Those days are also hyperlinked to the original blog post.

Here's the tag to use to display the calendar:

```
<?php get_calendar(); ?>
```

The `calendar` tag has only one parameter, and it's Boolean. Set this parameter to `true`, and it displays the day of the week with one letter (Friday = F, for example.) Set this parameter to `false`, and it displays the day of the week as a three-letter abbreviation (Friday = Fri., for example).

Here are examples of the template tag used to display the calendar on your WordPress blog:

```
<?php get_calendar(true); ?>
<?php get_calendar(false); ?>
```

List pages

The `<?php wp_list_pages(); ?>` tag displays a list of the static pages you can create on your WordPress site (such as About Me or Contact pages). Displaying a link to the static pages makes them available so that readers can click the links and read the content you've provided.

The `<list>` tag parameters use the string style. (Table 12-6 lists the most common parameters used for the `wp_list_pages` template tag.)

Table 12-6	Most Common Parameters (Query-String) for wp_list_pages();	
Parameter	*Type*	*Description and Values*
`child_ of`	integer	Displays only the subpages of the page; uses the numeric ID for a page as the value. Defaults to 0 (display all pages).

Parameter	Type	Description and Values
sort_ column	string	Sorts pages with one of the following options: `'post_title'` — Sorts alphabetically by page title (default).
		`'menu_order'` — Sorts by page order (the order in which they appear in the Manage tab and Pages subtab of the Administration panel).
		`'post_date'` — Sorts by the date on which pages were created.
		`'post_modified'` — Sorts by the time when the page was last modified.
		`'post_author'` — Sorts by author, according to the author ID #.
		`'post_name'` — Sorts alphabetically by the post slug.
Exclude	string	Lists the numeric page ID numbers, separated by commas, that you want to exclude from the page list display (for example, `'exclude=10, 20, 30'`). There is no default value.
Depth	integer	Uses a numeric value for how many levels of pages are displayed in the list of pages. Possible options: `0` — Displays all pages, including main and subpages (default).
		`-1` — Shows subpages but doesn't indent them in the list display.
		`1` — Shows only main pages (no subpages).
show_ date	string	Displays the date when the page was created or last modified. Possible options:
		`' '` — Displays no date (default).
		`'modified'` — Displays the date when the page was last modified.
		`'created'` — Displays the date when the page was created.
date_ format	string	Sets the format of the date to be displayed. Defaults to the date format configured in the Options tab and General subtab of the Administration panel.
title_ li	string	Types text for the heading of the page list. Defaults to display the text: `"Pages"`. If value is empty (''), no heading is displayed; for example, `'title_li=My Pages"` displays the heading `My Pages` above the page list.

Identifying some blog-post metadata

Metadata is simply data about data. In WordPress, *metadata* refers to the data about each blog post, including:

✔ The author name

✔ The category or categories to which the post is assigned

✔ The date and time of the post

✔ The comments link and number of comments

Page lists are displayed in an *unordered list* (you may know it by the term *bulleted list)*. Whichever term you use, it's a list with a bullet point in front of every page link.

The following tag and query string displays a list of pages without the text heading `"Pages"`. In other words, it displays no title at the top of the page's link list:

```
<?php wp_list_pages('title_li='); ?>
```

The next tag and query string displays the list of pages sorted by the date when they were created; the date is also displayed along with the page name:

```
<?php wp_list_pages('sort_column=post_date&show_date='created'); ?>
```

Take a look at the way query-string parameters are written:

```
'parameter1=value&parameter2=value&parameter3=value'
```

The entire string is surrounded by single quotation marks, and there is no white space within the query string. Each parameter is joined to its value by the = character. When you use multiple parameters/values, you separate them with the & character. You can think of the string like this: parameter1=value**AND**parameter2=value**AND**parameter3=value. Keep this convention in mind for the remaining template tags and parameters in this chapter.

Bookmarks (blogroll)

In the WordPress Administration panel, you can manage your links from the Blogroll tab. Before I forge ahead and dig into the template tag for the display of the blogroll, I want to clear up a little terminology.

A *blogroll* is a list of links that you add to the Blogroll area in the Administration panel. The specific template tag used to call those links into your template, however, refers to *bookmarks*. So this begs the question "Are they links, or are they bookmarks?" The answer is "Both." For simplicity, and to ensure that you and I are on the same wavelength, I refer to them the same way that half the planet does — as links.

Here is the tag used to display your blogroll:

```
<?php wp_list_bookmarks(); ?>
```

In Chapter 8, I show you how to add links to your blogroll and also discuss the options you can set for each link. The parameters for this tag give you control of how the links are displayed and put some of the options to work. Table 12-7 shows the most common parameters used for the `wp_list_bookmarks` template tag.

In the Possible Values column of Table 12-7, values that appear in bold are the default values set by WordPress. Keep this convention in mind for all the parameter values in the rest of this chapter.

Table 12-7	Most Common Parameters (Query-String) for wp_list_bookmarks();	
Parameter and Type	**Possible Values**	**Example**
`Categorize` (Boolean) Displays links within the assigned category.	**1 (True)** 0 (False)	`<?php wp_list_bookmarks ('categorize=0'); ?>` Returns the list of links not grouped into the categories.
`Category` (string) Displays only the link categories specified; if none is specified, all link categories are shown.	Category ID numbers separated by commas	`<?php wp_list_ bookmarks('category=10, 20, 30'); ?>` Displays the list of links from the categories with ID numbers 10, 20, and 30.

(continued)

Table 12-7 *(continued)*

Parameter and Type	Possible Values	Example
`category_ name` (string) Displays only the link categories specified by name; if none is specified, all link categories are shown.	Text of the cat-egory names separated by commas.	`<?php wp_list_ bookmarks('category_ name=books'); >` Displays only the links from the Books category.
`category_ orderby` (string) Sorts the order in which links are displayed on your site.	**Name** id	`<?php wp_list_ bookmarks('category_ orderby=name'); ?>` Displays the link categories alphabeti-cally by name.
`title_li` (string) Text title appears above the link list.	**bookmarks** If left blank, no title is dis-played.	`<?php wp_list_ bookmarks('title_ li=Links'); ?>` Displays the Links header. `<?php wp_list_ bookmarks('title_li='); ?>` Displays no heading.
`title_before` (string) Formatting to appear before the category title — only if the `'categorize'` parameter is set to 1 (true).	**<h2>**	`<?php wp_list_ bookmarks('title_ before='<strong>'); ?>` Inserts the `<strong>` HTML tag in front of the link category title.
`title_after` (string) Formatting to appear after the category title — only if the `'categorize'` parameter is set to 1 (true).	**</h2>**	`<?php wp_list_ bookmarks('title_ after='</strong>'); ?>` Inserts the `</strong>` HTML tag after the link category title.

Parameter and Type	Possible Values	Example
`Include` (string) Lists link ID numbers, separated by commas, to include in the display.	If no ID numbers are listed, displays all links.	```<?php wp_list_bookmarks ('include="1,2,3'); ?>``` Displays only links with the IDs of 1, 2, and 3.
`Exclude` (string) List of link ID numbers, separated by commas, to exclude from the display.	If no ID numbers are listed, all links are displayed.	```<?php wp_list_bookmarks ('exclude='4,5,6'); ?>``` Displays all links except for the links with IDs of 4, 5, and 6.
`Orderby` (string) Tells WordPress how your link lists will be sorted.	**name** id url target descriptions owner rating updated rel (XFN) notes length rand (random)	```<?php wp_list_bookmarks ('orderby=rand'); >``` Displays the links in random order. ```<?php wp_list_bookmarks ('orderby='id'); ?>``` Displays the links in order by ID number.
`Before` (string) Formatting to appear before each link in the list.	`<li>`	```<?php wp_list_bookmarks ('before=<strong>'); ?>``` Inserts the `<strong>` HTML tag before each link in the list.
`After` (string) Formatting to appear after each link in the list.	`</li>`	```<?php wp_list_bookmarks ('after=</strong'); ?>``` Inserts the `</strong>` HTML tag after each link in the list.

Here are a couple of examples of tags used to set a link list.

The following tag displays a list of links in the category ID of 2 and orders that list by the length of the link name (shortest to longest):

```
<?php wp_list_bookmarks('categorize=1&category=2&orderby=length'); ?>
```

This next tag displays only the list of links in a category (the Espresso category, in this example):

```
<?php wp_list_bookmarks('category_name=Espresso'); ?>
```

Post archives

The `<?php wp_get_archives(); ?>` template tag displays the blog post archives in a number of ways, using the parameters and values shown in Table 12-8. Again, values that appear in bold are the default values set by WordPress. Here are just a few examples of what you can produce with this template tag:

- ✔ Display the titles of the last 15 posts you've made to your blog.

- ✔ Display the titles of the posts you've made in the past ten days.

- ✔ Display a monthly list of archives.

Table 12-8   Most Common Parameters (Query-String) for wp_get_archives();

Parameter and Type	Possible Values	Example
Type (string) Determines the type of archive to display.	**monthly** daily weekly postbypost	`<?php wp_get_ archives('type =postbypost'); ?>` Displays the titles of the most recent blog posts.
format (string) Formats the display of the links in the archive list.	**html** — Surrounds the links with `<li> </li>` tags. option — Places archive list in drop-down menu format. link — Surrounds the links with `<link> </ link>` tags. custom — Use your own HTML tags, using the before and after parameters.	`<?php wp_get_ archives ('format= html'); ?>` Displays the list of archive links where each link is surrounded by the `<li> </li>` HTML tags.
limit (integer) Limits the number of archives to display.	If no value, **all are displayed.**	`<?php wp_get_ archives ('limit=10'); ?>` Displays the last 10 archives in a list.

Parameter and Type	Possible Values	Example
`before` (string) Places text or formatting before the link in the archive list when using the custom parameter.	No default.	`<?php wp_get_ archives ('before= <strong>'); ?>` Inserts the `<strong>` HTML tag before each link in the archive link list.
`after` (string) Inserts text or formatting after the link in the archive list when using the custom parameter.	No default.	`<?php wp_get_ archives ('after=</ strong>'); ?>` Inserts the `</strong>` HTML tag after each link in the archive link list.
`show_post_ count` (Boolean) This value displays the number of posts in the archive. You would use this if you use the `'type'` of `monthly`.	`true` or 1 **`false` or 0**	`<? wp_get_ archives ('show_post_ count=1'); ?>` Displays the number of posts in each archive after each archive link.

Here are a couple of examples of tags used to display blog post archives.

This tag displays a linked list of monthly archives (for example, January 2008, February 2008, and so on).

```
<?php wp_get_archives('type=monthly'); ?>
```

This next tag displays a linked list of the 15 most recent blog posts:

```
<?php wp_get_archives('type=postbypost&limit=15'); ?>
```

Categories

WordPress lets you create categories and assign posts to a specific category (or multiple categories). Categories provide an organized navigation system that helps you and your readers find posts you've made on certain topics.

The `<?php wp_list_categories(); ?>` template tag lets you display a list of your categories by using the available parameters and values. (Table 12-9 shows some of the most popular parameters.) Each category is linked to the appropriate category page that lists all the posts you've assigned to it. The values that appear in bold are the default values set by WordPress.

Table 12-9	Most Common Parameters (Query-String) for wp_list_categories();	
Parameter and Type	*Possible Values*	*Example*
Orderby (string) Determines how the category list will be ordered.	**ID** name	`<?php wp_list_categories ('orderby=name'); ?>` Displays the list of categories by name, alphabetically, as they appear in the Administration panel.
Style (string) Determines the format of the category list display.	**List** none	`<?php wp_list_categories ('style=list'); ?>` Displays the list of category links where each link is surrounded by the `<li> </li>` HTML tags. `<?php wp_list_categories ('style=none'); ?>` Displays the list of category links with a simple line break after each link.
show_count (Boolean) Determines whether to display the post count for each listed category.	true or 1 **false or 0**	`<?php wp_list_categories ('show_count=1'); ?>` Displays the post count, in parentheses, after each category list. Espresso (10), for example, means that there are ten posts in the Espresso category.
hide_empty (Boolean) Determines whether empty categories should be displayed in the list (meaning a category with zero posts assigned to it).	**true or 1** false or 0	`<?php wp_list_categories ('hide_empty=0'); ?>` Displays only those categories that currently have posts assigned to them.
Feed (string) Determines whether the RSS feed should be displayed for each category in the list.	rss **Default is no feeds displayed.**	`<?php wp_list_categories ('feed=rss'); ?>` Displays category titles with an RSS link next to each one.

Parameter and Type	Possible Values	Example
`feed_image` (string) Provides the path/ filename for an image for the feed.	No default.	`<?php wp_list_ categories('feed_image=/ wp-content/images/feed. gif'); ?>` Displays the `feed.gif` image for each category title. This image is linked to the RSS feed for that category.
`hierarchical` (Boolean) Determines whether the child categories should be displayed after each parent category in the category link list.	**true or 1** `false` or `0`	`<?php wp_list_categories ('hierarchical=0'); ?>` Doesn't display the child categories after each parent category in the category list.

Here are a couple of examples of tags used to display a list of your categories.

This example, with its parameters, displays a list of categories sorted by name without showing the number of posts made in each category and displays the RSS feed for each category title:

```
<?php wp_list_categories('orderby=name&show_count=0&feed=RSS'); ?>
```

This example, with its parameters, displays a list of categories sorted by name with the post count showing and shows the subcategories of every parent category:

```
<?php wp_list_categories('orderby=name&show_count=1&hierarchical=1'); '>
```

Checking Out Miscellaneous but Useful Template Tags

In this chapter, I've picked the most common template tags to get you started. You can find all the rest of the template tags in the WordPress Codex at this URL:

```
http://codex.wordpress.org/Template_Tags
```

A few miscellaneous tags aren't included in the preceding sections, but I want to mention here briefly because they're helpful and sometimes fun. Table 12-10 lists some of these tags, their locations in the templates where they're commonly used, and their purposes.

Table 12-10   Some Useful Template Tags for WordPress

Tags Used in the Comments Template (`comments.php`)

Tag	Function
`<?php comment_` `author(); ?>`	Displays the comment author's name.
`<?php comment_` `author_link(); ?>`	Displays the comment author's name, linked to the author's Web site if a URL was provided in the comment form.
`<?php comment_` `text(); ?>`	Displays the text of a comment.
`<?php comment_` `date() ?>`	Displays the date when a comment was published.
`<?php comment_` `time(); ?>`	Displays the time when a comment was published.
`<?php echo get_` `avatar(); ?>`	Displays the Gravatar of the comment author (see Chapter 7).
`<?php previous_` `comments_link() ?>`	Displays navigation links to the previous page of comments, if you're using paged comments (see Chapter 7).
`<?php next_com-` `ments_link() ?>`	Displays navigation links to the next page of comments, if you're using paged comments (see Chapter 7).

Tags Used to Display RSS Feeds

Tag	Function

`<?php bloginfo`
`('rss2_url'); ?>`
	Displays the URL of the RSS feed for your blog. Usually surrounded by the `a href` HTML tag to provide a hyperlink to the RSS feed:
	`<a href=" <?php bloginfo('rss2_url');`
	`?>">RSS Feed</a>`

`<?php bloginfo`
`('comments_rss2_`
`url'); ?>`
	Displays the URL of the RSS feed for your comments. Usually surrounded by the `a href` HTML tag to provide a hyperlink to the comments RSS feed:
	`<a href=" ="<?php bloginfo('comments_`
	`rss2_url'); ?>">Comments RSS</a>`

Tags Used to Display Author Information

Tag	Function
`<?php the_author_` `description(); ?>`	Pulls the information from the author bio located in the About Yourself section of your profile in the Administration panel, and displays that information in the blog.
`<?php the_author_` `email(); ?>`	Pulls the author's e-mail address from the author profile in the Administration panel.

You can find additional hints, tips, and tricks on creative uses of WordPress templates and template tags in Chapters 13 and 14.

Chapter 13

Tweaking WordPress Themes

. . . .

In This Chapter

▶ Exploring basic CSS

▶ Defining CSS properties and values

▶ Setting a new background color

▶ Creating a header

▶ Changing fonts

. . . .

Chapter 11 shows how you can use free WordPress themes in your blog. Many people are quite happy to use these themes without making any adjustments to them at all. I can't tell you, however, how many times people have asked me how they can customize a theme that they've found. They say things like these:

✔ "I like this free theme I found, but I'd really like to change the header image. How do I do that?"

✔ "I found this great theme, but I really need to change the background color from black to pink. Can I do that, or do I need to hire someone?"

✔ "This theme I have is perfect, although I wish I could change the font from Times New Roman to Tahoma. Can you tell me how to do that?"

The practice of changing a few elements of an existing WordPress theme is *tweaking*. Thousands of WordPress blog owners tweak their existing themes on a regular basis. This chapter provides information on some of the most common tweaks you can make to your theme, such as changing the header image, changing the color of the background or the text links, and changing font styles — and these changes are pretty easy to make, too! You'll be tweaking your own theme in no time flat.

Before you go too wild with tweaking templates, make a backup of your theme so that you have the original files, from which you can easily restore if you need to. You can back up your theme files by connecting to your Web server via FTP (see Chapter 6) and downloading your theme folder to your computer. When you have the original theme files safe and secure on your hard drive, feel free to tweak away, comfortable in the knowledge that you have a backup.

Styling with CSS: The Basics

A Cascading Style Sheet (CSS) is in every single WordPress theme you use in your blog. The CSS provides style and design flair to the template tags in your templates. (See Chapter 12 for information about WordPress template tags.) The CSS for your WordPress theme is pulled in through the Header template (`header.php`) and is named `style.css`.

In your Administration panel, click the Editor link on the Appearances menu, and look at the Header template for the Default WordPress theme by clicking the Header link on the Edit Themes page. You find the following line of code, which pulls the CSS (`style.css`) into the page to provide the formatting of the elements of your blog:

```
<link rel="stylesheet" href="<?php bloginfo('stylesheet_
        url'); ?>" type="text/css" media="screen" />
```

Do not tweak the line of code that pulls in the `style.css` file; otherwise, the CSS won't work for your blog.

CSS selectors

With CSS, you can provide style (such as size, color, and placement) to the display of elements on your blog (such as text links, header images, font size and colors, paragraph margins, and line spacing). *CSS selectors* contain names, properties, and values to define which HTML elements in the templates you will style with CSS. Table 13-1 provides some examples of CSS selectors and their use.

Table 13-1		Basic CSS Selectors	
CSS Selector	**Description**	**HTML**	**CSS**
`body`	Sets the style for the overall body of the site, such as background color and default fonts	`<body>`	`body {background-color: white}` The background color on all pages is white.
`p`	Defines how paragraphs are formatted	`<p>This is a paragraph</p>`	`p {color: black}` The color of the fonts used in all paragraphs is black.

CSS Selector	Description	HTML	CSS
h1, h3, h3, h4	Provide bold headers for different sections of your site	`<h1>This is a site title </h1>`	`h1 {font- weight: bold;}` The fonts surrounded by the `<h1>..</h1>` HTML tags will be bold.
a	Defines how text links display in your site	`<a href= "http://wiley. com">Wiley Publishing</a>`	`a {color: red}` All text links appear in red.

Classes and IDs

Look at the stylesheet for the Default WordPress theme (see Figure 13-1). Everything in it may look foreign to you right now, but I want to bring your attention to two items:

- **#page:** One type of CSS selector. The hash mark (#) indicates that it's a CSS *ID*.

- **.narrowcolumn:** Another type of CSS selector. The period (.) indicates that it's a CSS *class*.

IDs and classes define styling properties for different sections of your WordPress theme. Table 13-2 shows examples of IDs and classes from the `header.php` template in the Default WordPress theme. Armed with this information, you'll know where to look in the stylesheet when you want to change the styling for a particular area of your theme.

Table 13-2	**Connecting HTML with CSS Selectors**	
HTML	**CSS Selector**	**Description**
`<div id="page">`	`#page`	Styles the elements for the `page` ID in your template(s) In this case, the CSS selector name is `page`.
`<div id= "header">`	`#header`	Styles the elements for the `header` ID in your template(s)
`<div id= "headerimg">`	`#header- img`	Styles the elements for the `headerimg` ID in your template(s)
`<div class= "description">`	`.descrip- tion`	Styles the elements for your `description` class in your template(s)

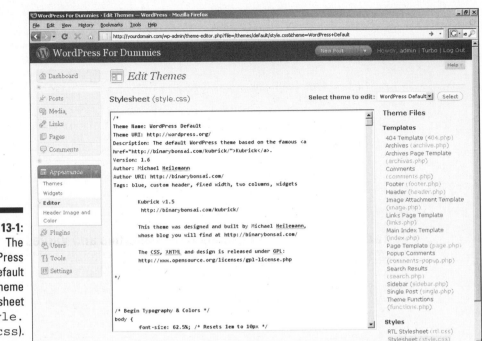

Figure 13-1:
The
WordPress
default
theme
stylesheet
(style.
css).

If you find an element in the template code that says `id` (such as `div id=` or `p id=`), look for the hash symbol in the stylesheet. If you find an element in the template code that says `class` (such as `div class=` or `p class=`), look for the period in the stylesheet followed by the selector name.

CSS properties and values

CSS properties are assigned to the CSS selector name. You also need to provide values for the CSS properties to define the style elements for the particular CSS selector you're working with.

In the Default WordPress theme, for example, the first piece of markup in the Header template (`header.php`) is `<div id="page">`. This ID, with the name `page`, provides styling for the site page.

In the Default WordPress theme stylesheet, the CSS defined for the `page` ID is as follows:

```
#page {
    background-color: white;
    border: 1px solid #959596;
    text-align: left;
    }
```

Every CSS property needs to be followed by a colon (:), and each CSS value needs to be followed by a semicolon (;).

The CSS selector is #page, which has three properties:

✔ The first CSS property is background-color, which has the value white.

✔ The second CSS property is border, which has the value 1px solid #959596 (border thickness, style, and color values, respectively).

✔ The last CSS property is text-align, which has the value left.

Table 13-3 provides some examples of commonly used CSS properties and values.

Table 13-3	Common CSS Properties and Values	
CSS Property	**CSS Value**	**Examples**
back-ground-color	Defines the color of the background (such as red, black, or white)	**Markup:** <div id="page"> **CSS:** #page {background-color: white}
back-ground	Defines a back-ground image	**Markup:** <div id="headerimg"> **CSS:** #headerimg {background: url(images/header.jpg) no-repeat;}
font-family*	Defines the fonts used for the selector	**Markup:** <body> **CSS:** body { font-family: 'Lucida Grande', Verdana, Arial, Sans-Serif;}
color	Defines the color of the text	**Markup:** <h1>Website Title </h1> **CSS:** h1 {color: blue}
font-size**	Defines the size of the text	**Markup:** <h1>Website Title </h1> **CSS:** h1 {font-size: 18px;}
text-align	Defines the align-ment of the text (left, center, right, or justified)	**Markup:** <div id="page"> **CSS:** #page {text-align: left;}

* W3Schools has a good resource on the font-family property here: http://w3schools.com/CSS/pr_font_font-family.asp

** W3Schools has a good resource on the font-size property here: http://w3schools.com/CSS/pr_font_font-size.asp

Changing the Background Color

In Chapter 12, I discuss the Header template (header.php) in detail. In this section, I show you how to tweak the <body> tag in that template. The <body> tag is simple HTML markup. Every theme has this tag, which defines the overall default content for each page of your Web site — the site's *body*.

In the stylesheet (style.css), the body styles are defined like this:

```
body {
font-size: 62.5%; /* Resets 1em to 10px */
font-family: 'Lucida Grande', Verdana, Arial, Sans-Serif;
background: #d5d6d7 url('images/kubrickbgcolor.jpg');
color: #333;
text-align: center;
}
```

The background for the <body> tag uses a color and an image:

✔ **Color:** A hexadecimal (or *hex*) code represents a certain color. Hex codes always start with a hash symbol (#) and have six letters and/or numbers to represent a particular color; in this case, #d5d6d7. Table 13-4 lists some common colors and the corresponding hex codes. (The W3Schools Web site has a great resource on hex codes at http://w3schools.com/HTML/html_colornames.asp.)

✔ **Image:** You can easily use an image as a background for your site by uploading the image to the images folder in your theme directory. That value looks like background: url(images/*yourimage*.jpg). In this case, the image is url('images/kubrickbgcolor.jpg');. (*Note:* The url portion of this code automatically pulls in the URL of your blog, so you don't have to change the url part to your URL.)

You can also use a combination of colors and images in your backgrounds.

Table 13-4	Common Colors and Hex Codes
Color	*Hex Code*
White	#FFFFFF
Black	#000000
Red	#FF0000
Orange	#FFA500
Yellow	#FFFF00

Color	Hex Code
Green	#008000
Blue	#0000FF
Indigo	#4B0082
Violet	#EE82EE

In the case of some basic colors, you don't have to use the hex code. For colors such as white, black, red, blue, and silver, you can just use their names — `background-color: white`, for example.

If you want to change the background color of your theme, follow these steps:

1. **In the WordPress Administration panel, click the Editor link on the Appearance menu.**

   The Edit Themes page opens.

2. **From the Select Theme to Edit drop-down menu, choose the theme you want to change.**

   If you want to change the WordPress default theme, for example, choose it.

3. **Click the Stylesheet template link.**

   The `style.css` template opens in the text editor on the left side of the Theme Editor page (refer to Figure 13-1).

4. **Scroll down in the text editor until you find the CSS selector body.**

   If you're tweaking the default theme, this section is what you're looking for:

   ```
   body {
   font-size: 62.5%; /* Resets 1em to 10px */
   font-family: 'Lucida Grande', Verdana, Arial, Sans-Serif;
   background: #d5d6d7 url('images/kubrickbgcolor.jpg');
   color: #333;
   text-align: center;
   }
   ```

   If you're tweaking a different template, the CSS selector body will look similar.

5. **Edit the `background` property's values.**

   In the default template, you're changing

   ```
   background: #d5d6d7 url('images/kubrickbgcolor.jpg');
   ```

   to black

   ```
   background: black;
   ```

   If you'd like to use a hex code, refer to Table 13-4.

6. **Click the Update File button in the bottom-left corner of the page.**

   Your changes are saved and applied to your theme.

7. **Visit your site in your Web browser.**

   The background color of your theme has changed.

Figure 13-2 shows how I changed the default theme's background color from white to black. The page may not be very pretty, but for the purpose of showing you how you can edit the background color of any theme you're using, it works.

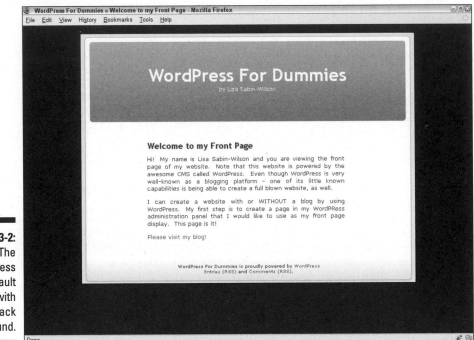

Figure 13-2:
The WordPress default theme with a black background.

Using Your Own Header Image

Most themes have a header image that displays at the top of the page. This image is generated by a graphic defined in the CSS value for the property that represents the header area. In the WordPress default theme, you find the markup for the header image in the Header template (`header.php`), and it looks like this:

```
<div id="header">
<div id="headerimg">
<h1><a href="<?php echo get_option('home'); ?>/"><?php
        bloginfo('name'); ?></a></h1>
<div class="description"><?php bloginfo('description');
        ?></div>
</div>
</div>
```

Several elements are in play within this code:

✔ **<div id="header">:** This line defines the actual image file used for the header of the theme. It corresponds with the #header selector in the stylesheet. To change the image, you change the image-name value in the background property of the #header CSS selector.

✔ **<div id="headerimg">:** This line defines the height and width of the image used for the header. It corresponds with the #headerimg selector in the stylesheet. To change the dimensions of the image, change the height and width values in the background property of the #headerimg CSS selector.

✔ **<h1><a href="<?php echo get_option('home'); ?>/"><?php bloginfo('name'); ?></a></h1>:** This line is the name of your blog, linked to your home page. All this code is wrapped in <h1></h1> HTML tags. (See Chapter 12 for more information on the bloginfo template tags and how they are used in WordPress templates.) The code corresponds to the h1 selector in the theme's stylesheet.

✔ **<div class="description"><?php bloginfo('description'); ?></div>:** This line is the description/tagline of your site, wrapped in <div class="description"></div> HTML tags. It corresponds to the .description selector in the theme's stylesheet.

✔ **</div>:** This line is the div tag that closes the <div id="headerimg"> markup.

✔ **</div>:** This code is the div tag that closes the <div id="header"> markup.

Whenever you open a <div> tag, you have to close it with a </div> tag.

The only element you need to change is the image for the header. When you have the image you want to use to replace the default header image (I recommend using gif, jpg, jpeg, or png formats for this), follow these steps:

1. **Upload your image via FTP to the images folder in the theme directory.**

   If you're changing the default theme, for example, upload your image to /wp-content/themes/default/images/.

  2. In the WordPress Administration panel, click the Design tab and then click the Theme Editor subtab.

    The Theme Editor page opens.

  3. From the Select Theme to Edit drop-down menu, choose the theme you want to change.

    If you want to change the default theme, choose WordPress Default.

  4. Click the Stylesheet template link to open it.

    The `style.css` file opens in the text editor on the left side of the Theme Editor page.

  5. Scroll down in the text editor until you find the CSS selector `#header`.

    If you're changing the default theme, this section is what you're looking for:

```
<div id="header">
<div id="headerimg">
<h1><a href="<?php echo get_option('home'); ?>/"><?php bloginfo('name');
          ?></a></h1>
<div class="description"><?php bloginfo('description'); ?></div>
</div>
</div>
```

    If you're tweaking a different theme, your CSS selector will look similar to this one.

  6. Edit the `background` property's values for the `#header` selector.

    If you want to change the image, you're changing

```
background: #73a0c5 url('images/kubrickheader.jpg') no-repeat bottom
          center;
```

    to this

```
#73a0c5 url('images/newheader.jpg') no-repeat bottom center;
```

    The only thing that changes is the actual image name, from `kubrick header.jpg` to `newheader.jpg`. (Be sure to change `newheader.jpg` to the name of your image file.)

  7. Click the Update File button in the bottom-left corner of the page.

    Your changes are saved and applied to your theme.

Figure 13-3 shows the new header image in my blog.

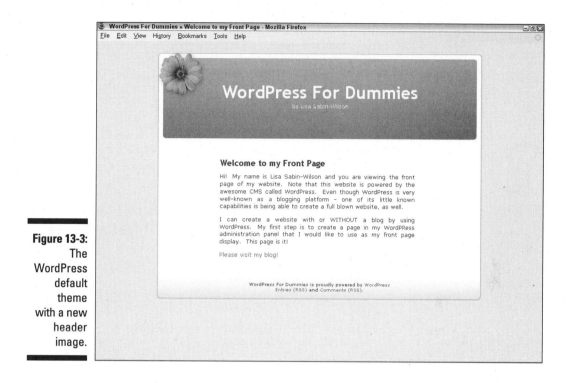

Figure 13-3:
The
WordPress
default
theme
with a new
header
image.

Changing Font Styles, Colors, and Sizes

Fonts come in all shapes and sizes, and you can use CSS to define the font styles that display in your blog. Changing the font can change the look and feel of your blog dramatically, as well as improve your readers' experience by making the text easy on the eyes. Table 13-5 displays some of the most commonly used CSS properties and values for applying font styling to your stylesheet.

Table 13-5	Common Font Styles in CSS
Font Properties	*Sample Value*
font-family	Times New Roman
color	black or #000000
font-size	12px

The Web is actually kind of picky about how it displays fonts, as well as what kind of fonts you can use in the font-family property. Not all fonts display correctly on the Web. To be safe, here are some commonly used font families that display correctly in most browsers:

> ✔ **Serif fonts:** Times New Roman, Georgia, Garamond, Bookman Old Style
>
> ✔ **Sans-serif fonts:** Verdana, Arial, Tahoma, Trebuchet MS

Serif fonts have little tails, or curlicues, at the edges of letters. (This text is in a serif font.) Sans-serif fonts have straight edges and are devoid of any fancy styling. (The heading in Table 13-5 uses a sans-serif font.)

When you want to change a font family in your CSS, open the stylesheet (style.css), search for property: font-family, change the values for that property, and save your changes.

In the default template CSS, the font is defined in the <body> tag like this:

```
font-family: 'Lucida Grande', Verdana, Arial, Sans-Serif
```

You can easily change the color of your font by changing the color property of the CSS selector you want to tweak. You can use hex codes (refer to Table 13-4) to define the colors.

In the default template CSS, the font color is defined in the <body> tag like this:

```
color: #333;
```

To tweak the size of your font, change the font-size property of the CSS selector you want to change. Font sizes generally are determined by units of measurement, as in these examples:

> ✔ **px:** pixel measurement. Increasing or decreasing the number of pixels increases or decreases the font size (12px is larger than 10px).
>
> ✔ **pt:** point measurement. As with pixels, increasing or decreasing the number of points affects the font size accordingly (12pt is larger than 10pt).
>
> ✔ **%:** percentage measurement. Increasing or decreasing the percentage number affects the font size accordingly (50% is the equivalent to 7 pixels; 100% is the equivalent to 17 pixels).

In the default template CSS, the font size is defined in the body tag as a percentage, like this:

```
font-size: 62.5%;
```

Putting all three elements (font-family, color, and font-size) together in the `<body>` tag, they style the font for the overall body of your site. Here's how they work together in the `<body>` tag of the default template CSS:

```
body {
font-size: 62.5%; /* Resets 1em to 10px */
font-family: 'Lucida Grande', Verdana, Arial, Sans-Serif;
color: #333;
}
```

Finding Additional CSS Resources

Table 13-6 lists some excellent CSS resources on the Web that you may find helpful for creating or editing a theme's stylesheet. Or you may want to pick up a copy of *CSS Web Design For Dummies,* by Richard Mansfield (published by Wiley).

Table 13-6	CSS Resources on the Web
Resource	*Location*
Westciv	`http://westciv.com`
mezzoblue's CSS Crib Sheet	`http://mezzoblue.com/css/cribsheet`
WebsiteTips.com's CSS page	`http://websitetips.com/css`
Dave's CSS Guide	`http://davesite.com/webstation/css`
W3Schools' CSS tutorial	`http://w3schools.com/css`

Chapter 14

Beyond Blogging: WordPress As a Content Management System

*I*f you've avoided using WordPress as a solution for building your own Web site because you think it's only a blogging platform, and you don't want to have a blog (not every Web site owner does, after all), it's time to rethink your position. The self-hosted version of WordPress, WordPress.org, is a powerful Content Management System (CMS) that is flexible and extensible enough to run an entire Web site — with no blog at all, if you prefer.

A *Content Management System* (CMS) is a system used to create and maintain your entire site. It includes tools for publishing and editing, as well as for searching and retrieving information and content. A CMS lets you maintain your Web site with little or no knowledge of HTML. You can create, modify, retrieve, and update your content without ever having to touch the code required to perform those tasks.

CMS programs such as WordPress give you the tools and advantages of blog software for managing and maintaining your site. These programs make setting up a Web site much easier than in the past. Before, if you didn't know HTML, you had to hire a Webmaster to maintain your Web site. With WordPress, you can do all that yourself, with or without HTML knowledge. That capability translates into a *huge* cost savings and opens the door to anyone who wants to run a Web site but doesn't have the resources or knowledge to do it. Now you can!

This chapter shows you a few ways that you can use the self-hosted WordPress.org software to power your entire Web site, with or without a blog. It covers different template configurations that you can use to create separate sections of your site. You also discover how to use the front page of your site as a *landing page* (a static page) or *portal* (a page that contains snippets from other sections of your site, with links to those sections), which can include a link to an internal blog page, if you want a blog.

Creating the Front Page of Your Web Site

For the most part, when you visit a blog powered by WordPress, the blog is on the main page. My personal blog at `http://justagirlintheworld.com`, powered by WordPress (of course), shows my latest blog posts on the front page, along with links to the post archives (by month or by category). This setup is typical of a site run by WordPress (see Figure 14-1).

But the front page of my business site at `http://ewebscapes.com`, also powered by WordPress, contains no blog (see Figure 14-2). It doesn't display any blog posts; rather, it displays the contents of a static page I created in the WordPress Administration panel. This static page serves as a portal to my design blog, my portfolio, and other sections of my site. The site includes a blog but also serves as a full-blown business Web site, with all the sections I need to provide my clients the information they want.

Both of my sites are powered by the self-hosted version of WordPress.org, so how can they differ so much in what they display on the front page? The answer lies in the templates in the WordPress Administration panel.

You use static pages in WordPress to create content that you don't want to display as part of your blog but do want to display as part of your overall site (such as a bio page, a page of services, and so on).

Creating a front page is a three-step process: create a static page, designate that static page as the front page of your site, and tweak the page to look like a Web site rather than a blog.

Using this method, you can create unlimited numbers of static pages to build an entire Web site. You don't even need to have a blog on this site unless you want to include one.

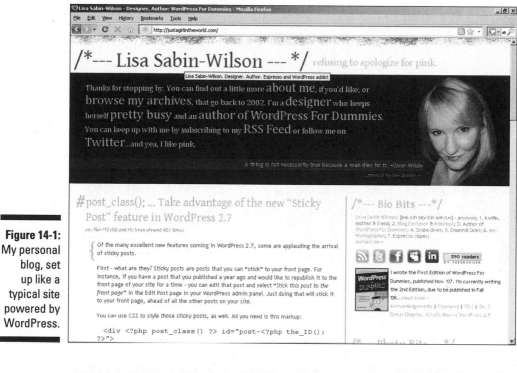

Creating the static page

To have a static page display on the front page of your site, you need to create that page. Follow these steps:

1. **Click the Add New link on the Pages menu.**

   The Add New Page page opens where you can write a new page to your WordPress blog, as shown in Figure 14-3. (Check out Chapter 7 for the difference between a page and a post in WordPress.)

2. **In the Title text box, type a title for the page.**

3. **Type the content of your page in the text box.**

4. **Set the options for this page.**

   I explain all these options in Chapter 7.

5. **Click the Publish button.**

   The page is saved to your database and published to your WordPress site with its own, individual URL (or *permalink*). The URL for the static page consists of your blog URL and the title of the page. For example, if you titled your page "About Me," then the URL of the page is `http://yourdomain.com/about-me`. (See Chapter 8 for more information about permalinks.)

Note that the Page Template option is set to Default Template. This setting tells WordPress that you want to use the default page template (`page.php` in your theme template files) to format the page you're creating. The default template is the default setting for all pages you create; assigning a page to a different template is something I discuss in the "Defining specific templates for static pages" section in this chapter.

Assigning a static page as the front page

Next, you need to tell WordPress that you want the static page to serve as the front page of your site. Follow these steps:

1. **Click the Reading link on the Settings menu to display the Reading Settings page.**

2. **In the Front Page Displays section, select the A Static Page radio button.**

3. **From the Front Page drop-down menu, choose the static page that you want to serve as your front page.**

   In Figure 14-4, I'm choosing to display a static page, and Welcome to My Front Page is the page I want to display.

4. **Click the Save Changes button at the bottom of the Reading Settings page.**

   WordPress displays the page you selected in Step 3 as the front page of your site. Figure 14-5 shows my site displaying the page I created as my front page.

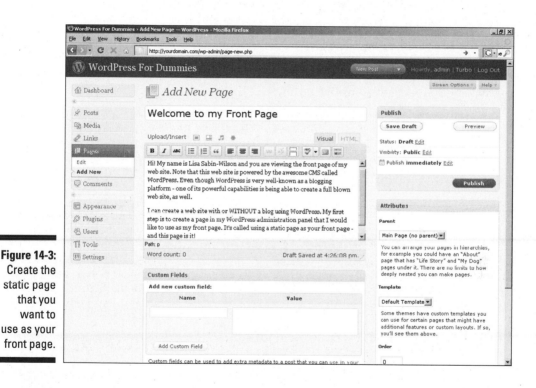

Figure 14-3: Create the static page that you want to use as your front page.

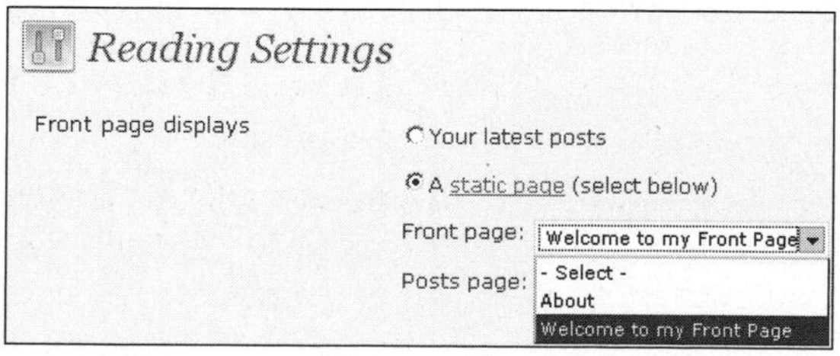

Figure 14-4: Choosing which page to display as the front page.

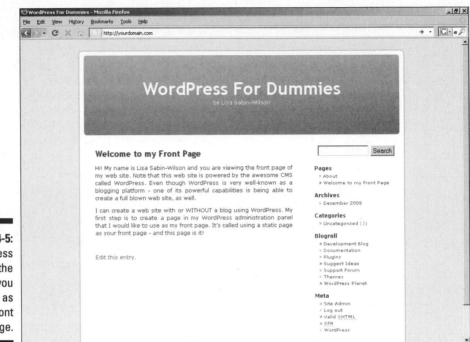

Figure 14-5:
WordPress
displays the
page you
selected as
your front
page.

Tweaking the layout

With a little adjustment of the code in the page.php (Page) template, you can create a front page that doesn't look like a blog at all. Figure 14-6 shows my front page without the usual "bloggy" sidebar containing archive links, blogrolls, meta information, and so on.

Chapter 12 covers template tags and templates that you can use in WordPress, including setting up static-page templates. However, you can use the quick-'n'-dirty method to change your front page from a bloggy-looking page to a nonbloggy-looking page using the WordPress Default Theme. Just follow these simple steps:

1. **Click the Editor link on the Appearances menu.**

   The Edit Themes page opens. All the templates included in the current theme are listed on the right side of the page. By default, the Stylesheet (style.css) is displayed on the left side of the page in the text box.

2. **Click Page Template link on the right side of the page.**

   The Edit Themes page refreshes, with the contents of the page.php template displayed in the text box on the left side of the page.

3. **Locate this code:**

```
<div id="content" class="narrowcolumn">
```

4. **Replace the code in Step 3 with this code:**

```
<div id="content" class="widecolumn">
```

The `widecolumn` class changes the formatting of the page content so that it is wider in width than the `narrowcolumn` class.

5. **Remove the following code, located near the bottom of the `page.php` template:**

```
<?php get_sidebar(); ?>
```

Removing this piece of code removes the sidebar from the static pages on your site. Without this code, the page displays only the content of your page.

6. **Click the Update File button.**

The file is saved, and your site is updated with the changes you just made.

Now visit your front page, and you have something that looks similar to Figure 14-6. When visitors type your URL in the address bar of their browsers, this front page greets them.

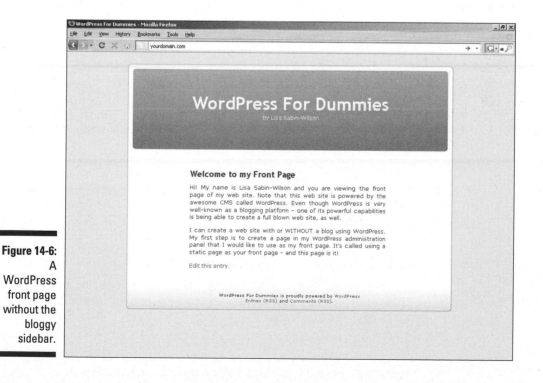

Figure 14-6:
A WordPress front page without the bloggy sidebar.

If you want to add a link to your blog (see the next section), add the following bit of code to the content of the static page you created for your front-page display:

```
<a href="/blog">Please Visit My Blog</a>
```

Adding a Blog to Your Web Site

If you want a blog on your site but don't want to display the blog on the front page, you can add one with the WordPress Administration panel. To create the blog for your site, follow these steps:

1. **Click the Add New link on the Pages menu.**

   The page where you can write a new post to your WordPress blog opens.

2. **Type Blog in the Title text box.**

   Doing this automatically sets the page slug to /blog. (Read more about slugs in Chapter 8.)

3. **Leave the Page Content box blank.**

4. **Click the Publish button.**

   The page is saved to your database and published to your WordPress site.

Now you have a blank page that redirects to http://yourdomain.com/ blog. Next, you need to assign the page you just created as your blog page. To do so, follow these steps:

1. **Click the Reading link on the Settings menu to display the Reading Settings page.**

   The Reading Settings page opens.

2. **From the Posts Page drop-down menu, choose the page you just created, as shown in Figure 14-7.**

   The page is set as your blog page.

3. **In the Blog Pages Show at Most section, type the number of posts you want to displayed in the Posts text box.**

   This setting specifies the number of posts you want to display on that page at any time. If you enter **5**, the blog page shows the last five posts you've made to your blog.

4. Click the Save Changes button.

The options you just set are saved, and your blog is now at `http://`
`yourdomain.com/blog` (where *yourdomain.com* is the actual
domain name).

Now when you navigate to `http://yourdomain.com/blog`, your blog
displays. Figure 14-8 shows my blog page with two posts.

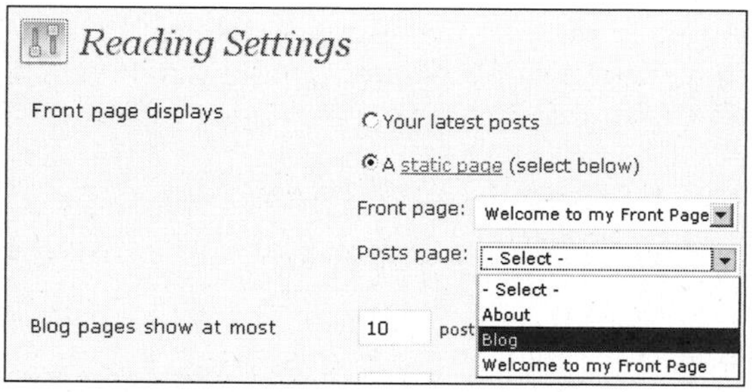

Figure 14-7:
Set these
options
to tell
WordPress
where you
want to
display
your blog.

Figure 14-8:
My blog at
`/blog`
with two
posts dis-
played.

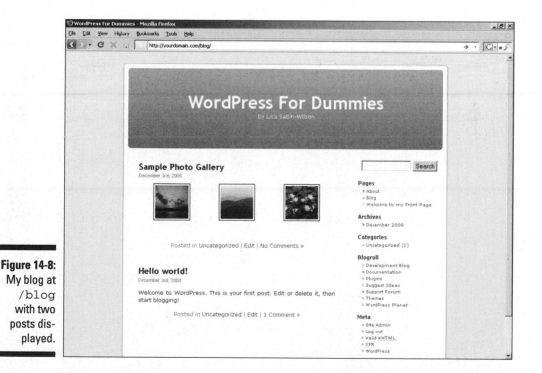

This method of using the /blog page slug works only if you're using custom permalinks with your WordPress installation. (See Chapter 8 if you want more information about permalinks.) If you're using the default permalinks, the URL for your blog page is different; it looks something like `http://yourdomain.com/?p=4` (where 4 is the ID of the page you created for your blog). You can find the URL for a page by clicking the Edit link on the Pages menu. Look for the page you created for your blog display, and click the View link that appears underneath the page title. The page opens in your browser, and you can copy the URL from the address bar in your browser and paste it into the code used in your static page to provide a link to your blog, like this:

```
<a href="http://yourdomain.com/blog">Please Visit My
     Blog</a>
```

Defining Specific Templates for Static Pages

As I explain in "Creating the Front Page of Your Web Site," earlier in this chapter, a *static page* contains content that is not displayed on the blog page, but as a separate page within your site. You can have numerous static pages on your site, and each page can have a different design, which is governed by the template you create. (See Chapter 12 to find out all about choosing and using templates.) You can create several static-page templates and assign them to specific pages within your site by adding code to the top of the static-page templates.

Following is the code that appears at the top of the static-page template I use for my About Us and Our Blog Designers page at `http://ewebscapes.com/about`:

```
<?php
/*
Template Name: About Page
*/
?>
```

Using a template on a static page is a two-step process: Upload the template, and tell WordPress to use the template by tweaking the page's code.

In Chapter 12, I discuss several different template tags you can use in your template. One of those template tags I provide in that chapter is the `wp_list_pages` tag. This tag displays a link to all the static pages you've created on your site so that you can easily display a navigation menu. A navigation menu allows your readers to easily locate and read all the content within your site.

Uploading the template

To use a page template, you have to create one. You can create this file in a text-editor program, such as Notepad. (To see how to create a template, flip to Chapter 12.) To create an About page, for example, you can name your template `about.php`.

When you have your template created, follow these steps to make it part of WordPress:

1. **Upload the template file to your WordPress theme folder.**

   You can find that folder on your Web server in `/wp-content/themes/`. (See Chapter 6 for more information about FTP.)

2. **Log in to your WordPress Administration panel, click the Editor link on the Appearance menu.**

   The Edit Themes page opens.

3. **Click the about.php template link located on the right side of the page.**

4. **Type the Template Name tag directly above the header template tag.**

   The header tag looks like this: `<?php get_header(); ?>`.

   If you're creating an About Page, the code to create the Template Name looks like this:

   ```
   <?php
   /*
   Template Name: About Page
   /*
   ?>
   ```

5. **Click the Update File button.**

   The file is saved and the page refreshes. If you created an About Page template, the `about.php` template is now called About Page in the template list on the right side of the page.

Figure 14-9 shows the Page template, and displays the code needed to define a specific name for the template.

Assigning the template to a static page

When you have the template created and named the way you want it, you assign that template to a page by following these steps:

1. **Click the Add New link on the Pages menu.**

   The Add New Page page opens, where you can write a new post to your WordPress blog.

2. **Type the title in the Title text box and the page content in the text box.**

3. **Choose the page template from the Page Template drop-down menu.**

   The Page Template drop-down menu in the Attributes module by default is shown on the right side of the page. You can reposition the modules on this page; see Chapter 7 for more information.

4. **Click the Publish button to save and publish the page to your site.**

Figure 14-10 shows the layout of my home page on my business site at `http://ewebscapes.com` and the information it contains, whereas Figure 14-11 shows the layout and information provided on the FAQ page at `http://ewebscapes.com/faq` (using the template named `faq.php`). Both pages are on the same site, in the same WordPress installation, with different static-page templates to provide different looks, layouts, and sets of information.

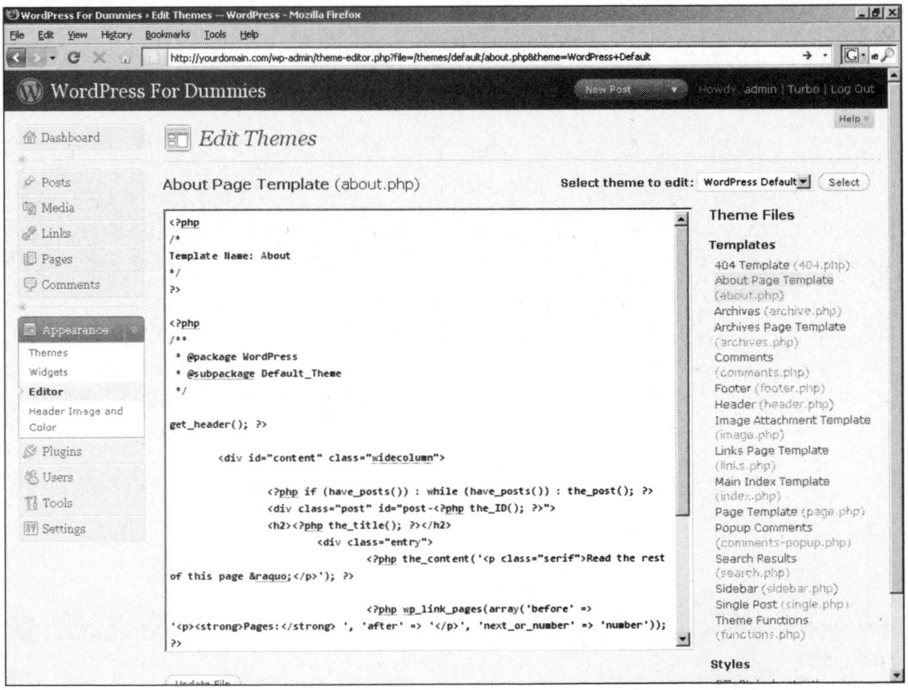

Figure 14-9: Naming a static-page template.

Figure 14-10:
My home
page at
E.Web-
scapes.

Figure 14-11:
The FAQ
page at
E.Web-
scapes.

Creating a Template for Each Post Category

You don't have to limit yourself to creating a static-page template for your site. No, you can completely gorge yourself at the table of WordPress templates and create unique sections for your site, as I did (with an espresso chaser, of course).

Figure 14-12 shows my design portfolio. Design Portfolio is the name of a category that I created in the WordPress Administration panel. Instead of using a static page for the display of my portfolio, I used a category template to handle the display of all posts made to the Design Portfolio category.

You can create category templates for all categories in your blog simply by creating template files with filenames that correspond to the category ID numbers and then uploading those templates to your WordPress `themes` directory (see Chapter 12). The logic to this is as follows:

Figure 14-12: My Design Portfolio page, using a category template file.

✔ A template with the filename `category.php` is a catch-all for the display of categories.

✔ Add a dash and the category ID number to the end of the filename (as shown in Table 14-1) to specify a template for an individual category.

✔ If you don't have a `category.php` or `category-#.php` file, the category display pulls from the Main Index template (`index.php`).

Table 14-1 shows three examples of the category template naming requirements.

Table 14-1   WordPress Category Template Naming Conventions

If the Category ID Is . . .	The Category Template Filename Is . . .
1	category-1.php
2	category-2.php
3	category-3.php

Pulling in Content from a Single Category

WordPress makes it possible to pull in very specific types of content on your Web site through the `<query_posts>` template tag. You place this template tag before The Loop (see Chapter 12), and it lets you specify which category you want to pull information from. If you have a category called WordPress, and you want to display the last three posts from that category on your front page, in your blog sidebar, or somewhere else on your site, you can use this template tag.

The `<query_posts>` template tag has several parameters that let you display different types of content, such as posts in specific categories and content from specific pages/posts or dates in your blog archives. The `<query_posts>` tag lets you pass so many variables and parameters that it's impossible for me to list all the possibilities. Instead, you can visit this page in the WordPress Codex and read about the options available with this tag: `http://codex.wordpress.org/Template_Tags/query_posts`.

First, you have to find the ID number for the category you want to use; then you have to tell WordPress how to display the content with the `<query_posts>` tag.

Finding the category ID number

The unique ID number for a category is not easy to find unless you know where to look. Follow these steps:

1. **Click the Categories link on the Posts menu.**

   The Categories page opens.

2. **Hover your mouse over the name of the category that you need the ID number for.**

3. **Look in the status bar of your browser to view the category ID number.**

   Figure 14-13 shows the category ID in the status bar of Mozilla Firefox. (Internet Explorer and Safari have similar status bars.) The last part of the URL displayed in the status bar is `cat_ID=6`, which means that 40 is the category ID for my WordPress category.

Figure 14-13: Finding the unique category ID number.

Category ID

Adding the <query_post> tag

When you have the category ID number in hand, you're ready to add the `<query_post>` tag to your template.

Here is an example of two parameters you can use with the `<query_posts>` tag:

> ✔ **showposts=X:** This parameter tells WordPress how many posts you want to display. If you want to display only three posts, enter **showposts=3**.

> ✔ **cat=X:** This parameter tells WordPress that you want to pull posts from the category with this specific ID number. If the ID category is 40, enter **cat=40**.

Follow these steps to add the `<query_post>` tag to your template:

1. **Click the Editor link on the Appearance menu.**

   The Edit Themes page opens.

2. **Click the template in which you want to display the content.**

   If you want to display content in a sidebar, for example, choose the Sidebar template: `sidebar.php`.

3. **Locate the ending `</ul>` tag at the bottom of the template for the theme you're using.**

   If you're using the Kubrick theme, the ending `</ul>` tag is the second-to-the-last line.

4. **Type the following code directly above the ending `</ul>` tag:**

```php
<?php query_posts('showposts=3&cat=40'); ?>
<h2>Type Your Desired Title Here</h2>
<?php if (have_posts()) : ?>
<?php while (have_posts()) : the_post(); ?>
<strong><a href="<?php the_permalink() ?>"
        rel="bookmark" title="Permanent Link to <?php
        the_title_attribute(); ?>"><?php the_title();
        ?></a></strong>
<?php the_excerpt(); ?>
<?php endwhile; ?>
<?php endif; ?>
```

In the first line, I indicated the following: `showposts=3&cat=40`. You can change these numbers to suit your specific needs. Just change 3 to whatever number of posts you'd like to display (there is no limit!), and change 40 to the specific category ID number that you want to use.

5. **Click the Update File button.**

The changes you just made are saved to the `sidebar.php` template.

Figure 14-14 shows my blog sidebar with a section called My Latest WordPress Posts, displaying three posts from my WordPress category with titles and post excerpts.

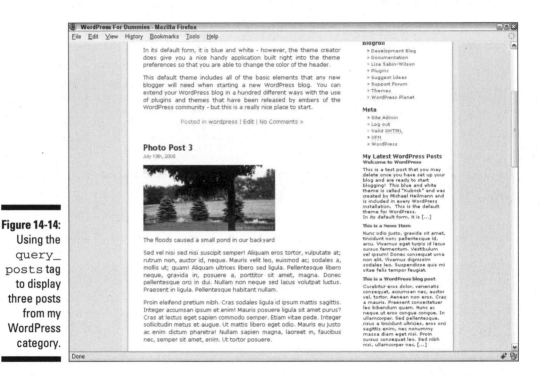

Figure 14-14:
Using the `query_posts` tag to display three posts from my WordPress category.

Using Sidebar Templates

You can create separate sidebar templates for different pages of your site by using a simple `include` statement. When you write an `include` statement, you're simply telling WordPress that you want it to include a specific file on a specific page.

The code that pulls the usual Sidebar template (`sidebar.php`) into all the other templates, such as the Main Index template (`index.php`), looks like this:

```
<?php get_sidebar(); ?>
```

What if you create a page and want to use a sidebar that has different information from what you have in the Sidebar template (`sidebar.php`)? Follow these steps:

1. **Create a new sidebar template in a text editor such as Notepad.**

   See Chapter 12 for information on template tags and themes.

2. **Save the file as `sidebar2.php`.**

   In Notepad, choose File⇨Save. When you're asked to name the file, type **sidebar2.php** and then click Save.

3. **Upload `sidebar2.php` to your `themes` folder on your Web server.**

   See Chapter 6 for FTP information, and review Chapter 12 for information on how to locate the `themes` folder.

   The template is now listed in your theme files on the Edit Themes page (log in to your WordPress Administration panel, click the Editor link on the Appearance menu).

4. **To include the `sidebar2.php` template in one of your page templates, find this code:**

   ```
   <?php get_sidebar(); />
   ```

5. **Replace it with this `include` code:**

   ```
   <?php include (TEMPLATEPATH . '/sidebar2.php'); ?>
   ```

 Using that `include (TEMPLATEPATH` statement, you can include virtually any file in any of your WordPress templates. You can use this method to create footer templates for pages on your site, for example. To do this, first create a new template with the filename `footer2.php`. Then locate the following code in your template:

```
<?php get_footer(); ?>
```

and replace it with this code:

```
<?php include (TEMPLATEPATH . '/footer2.php'); ?>
```

You can do multiple things with WordPress to extend it beyond the blog. This chapter gives you a few practical examples using the default Kubrick theme. The point is to show you how to use WordPress to create a fully functional Web site with a CMS platform — anything from the smallest personal site to a large business site.

Custom Styles for Sticky, Category, and Tag Posts

In Chapter 12, I discussed the method of putting a very basic WordPress theme together, which included a Main Index template using the WordPress Loop. You can use a custom tag to display custom styles for sticky posts, categories, and tags on your blog. That special tag looks like this:

```
<div <?php post_class() ?> id="post-<?php the_ID(); ?>">
```

The part of that template tag that is so cool is the `post_class()` section. This template tag tells WordPress to insert specific HTML markup in your template that allow you to use CSS to make custom styles for sticky posts, categories, and tags.

In Chapter 8, I tell you all about how to publish new posts to your blog, including the different options you can set for your blog posts, such as categories, tags, and publishing settings. One of the settings is the Stick This Post to the Front Page setting. In this chapter, I show you how to custom style those sticky posts — it's not as messy as it sounds!

For example, I have published a post with the following options set for that post:

- ✔ Stick this post to the front page
- ✔ Filed in a category called WordPress
- ✔ Tagged with News

By having the `post_class()` tag in my template, WordPress inserts HTML markup that allows me to use CSS to style sticky posts, or posts assigned to specific tags or categories, differently. WordPress inserted the following HTML markup for my post:

```
<div class="post sticky category-wordpress tag-news">
```

In Chapter 13, I talk about CSS selectors and HTML markup and how they work together to create style and format for your WordPress theme. I can now go to my CSS file and define styles for the following CSS selectors:

- ✔ **.post:** Use this as the generic style for all posts on your blog. The CSS for this tag is

```
.post {background: #ffffff; border: 1px solid silver;
       padding: 10px;}
```

A style is created for all posts that have a white background with a thin silver border and 10 pixels of padding space between the post text and the border of the post.

✔ **.sticky:** The concept of sticking a post to your front page is to call attention to that post, so you might want to use different CSS styling to make it stand out from the rest of the posts on your blog:

```
.sticky {background: #ffffff; border: 4px solid red;
         padding: 10px;}
```

This creates a style for all sticky posts that display with a white background, a thicker red border, and 10 pixels of padding space between the post text and border of the post.

✔ **.category—wordpress:** Because I blog a lot about WordPress, my readers may appreciate it if I gave them a visual cue as to which posts on my blog are about that topic. I can do that through CSS by telling WordPress to display a small WordPress icon on the top right corner of all my posts in the WordPress category:

```
.category-wordpress {background: url(wordpress-icon.
         jpg) top right no-repeat; height: 100px;
         width: 100px;}
```

This code inserts a graphic — `wordpress-icon.jpg` — that is 100 pixels in height and 100 pixels in width at the top right corner of every post I've assigned to the WordPress category on my blog.

✔ **.tag—news:** I can style all posts tagged with News the same way I've styled the categories:

```
.tag-news {background: #f2f2f2; border: 1px solid
         black; padding: 10px;}
```

This CSS styles all posts tagged with News with a light grey background and a thin black border with 10 pixels of padding between the post text and border of the post.

Using the post-class() tag, combined with CSS, to create dynamic styles for the posts on your blog is fun and easy!

Optimizing Your WordPress Blog

Search engine optimization (SEO) is the practice of preparing your site to make it as easy as possible for the major search engines to crawl your site and cache your data in their systems so that your site appears as high as possible in the search returns.

If you visit Google's search engine page at http://google.com and do a search using the keywords *WordPress blog design,* my own site at E.Webscapes is in the top five search results for those keywords (at least, it is as I'm writing this chapter). Those results can change from day to day, so by the time you read this book, someone else may very well have taken over that coveted position. The reality of chasing those high-ranking search engine positions is that they're here today, gone tomorrow.

The goal of search engine optimization is to make sure that *your* site ranks as high as possible for the keywords that you think people will use to find your site. After you attain those high-ranking positions, the next goal is to keep them. Check out *Search Engine Optimization For Dummies,* by Peter Kent (Wiley Publishing) for some valuable information on keeping those high rankings through ongoing optimization of your site.

WordPress is equipped to create an environment that is friendly to search engines, giving them easy navigation through your archives, categories, and pages. This environment is provided by a clean code base, content that is easily updated through the WordPress interface, and a solid navigation structure.

To extend search engine optimization even further, you can tweak five elements of your WordPress posts, pages, and templates:

- ✔ **Custom permalinks:** Use custom permalinks, rather than the default WordPress permalinks, to fill your post and page URLs with valuable keywords. Check out Chapter 8 for information on WordPress permalinks.
- ✔ **Posts and page titles:** Create descriptive titles for your blog posts and pages to provide rich keywords in your site.
- ✔ **Text:** Fill your blog posts and pages with keywords for search engines to find and index. Keeping your site updated with descriptive text and phrases helps the search engines find keywords to associate with your site.
- ✔ **Category names:** Use descriptive names for the categories you create in WordPress to place great keywords right in the URL for those category pages, if you use custom permalinks.
- ✔ **Images and ALT tags:** Place <ALT> tags in your images to further define and describe the images on your site. You can accomplish this task easily by using the description field in the WordPress image uploader.

Planting keywords in your Web site

If you're interested in a higher ranking for your site, I strongly recommend using custom permalinks. By using custom permalinks, you're automatically inserting keywords into the URLs of your posts and pages, letting search engines include those posts and pages in their databases of information on those topics. If your site is hosted by a provider that has the Apache `mod_rewrite` module enabled, you can use the custom permalink structure for your WordPress-powered site.

Keywords are the first step on your journey toward great search engine results. Search engines are dependent on keywords, and people use keywords to look for content.

The default permalink structure in WordPress is pretty ugly. When you're looking at the default permalink for any post, you see a URL something like this:

```
http://yourdomain.com/p?=105
```

This URL contains no keywords of worth. If you change to a custom permalink structure, your post URLs automatically include the titles of your posts to provide keywords, which search engines absolutely love. A custom permalink might appear in this format:

```
http://yourdomain.com/2007/02/01/your-post-title
```

I explain setting up and using custom permalinks in full detail in Chapter 8.

Optimizing your post titles for search engine success

Search engine optimization isn't completely dependent on how you set your site up. It's also dependent on you, the site owner, and how you present your content.

One way to present your content in a way that lets search engines catalog your site easily is to give your blog posts and pages titles that make sense and coordinate with the actual content being presented. If you're doing a post on a certain topic, make sure that the title of the post contains at least one or two keywords about that particular topic. This practice gives the search engines even more ammunition to list your site in searches relevant to the topic of your post.

As your site's presence in the search engines grows, more people will find your site, and your readership will increase as a result.

A blog post with the title A Book I'm Reading isn't going to tell anyone what book it is, making it difficult for people searching for information on that particular book to find the post.

If you give the post the title WordPress For Dummies: My Review, you provide keywords in the title, and (if you're using custom permalinks) WordPress automatically inserts those keywords into the URL, giving the search engines a triple keyword play:

- ✔ Keywords exist in your blog post title.
- ✔ Keywords exist in your blog post URL.
- ✔ Keywords exist in the content of your post.

Writing content with readers in mind

When you write your posts and pages, and want to make sure that your content appears in the first page of search results so that people will find your site, you need to keep those people in mind when you're composing the content.

When search engines visit your site to crawl through your content, they aren't seeing how nicely designed your site is. What they're looking for are words — which they're grabbing to include in their databases. You, the site owner, want to make sure that your posts and pages use the words and phrases that you want to include in search engines.

If your post is about a recipe for fried green tomatoes, for example, you need to add a keyword or phrase that you think people will use when they search for the topic. If you think people would use the phrase *recipe for fried green tomatoes* as a search term, you may want to include that phrase in the content and title of your post.

A title such as A Recipe I Like isn't as effective as a title such as A Recipe for Fried Green Tomatoes, right? Including it in your post or page content gives the search engines a double keyword whammy.

Here's another example: I once wrote a post about a rash that I developed on my finger, under my ring. I wrote that post well over a year ago, not really meaning to attract a bunch of people to that particular post. However, it seems that many women around the world suffer from the same rash, because a year later, that post still gets at least one comment a week. When people do a Google search using the keywords *rash under my wedding ring*, out of a possible 743,000 results returned, my blog post appears in the number-one slot, as shown in Figure 14-15.

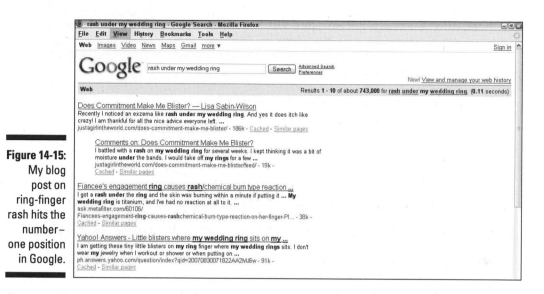

Figure 14-15:
My blog
post on
ring-finger
rash hits the
number–
one position
in Google.

This is how great blogs are! I was actually able to solve my problem with the rash under my finger because one woman from Australia found my blog through Google, visited my blog post, and left a comment with a solution that worked. Who says blogs aren't useful?

Creating categories that attract search engines

One little-known SEO tip for WordPress users: The names you give the categories you've created for your blog provide rich keywords that attract search engines like bees to honey. A few services — Technorati.com being one of the biggest — treat categories in WordPress like tags. These services use those categories to classify recent blog posts on any given topic. The names you give your categories in WordPress can serve as topic tags for Technorati and similar services.

Search engines also see your categories as keywords that are relevant to the content on your site. In this regard, it's important to make sure that you're giving your categories names that are relevant to the content you're providing on your site.

If you sometimes blog about your favorite recipes, you can make it easier for search engines to find your recipes if you create categories specific to the recipes you're blogging about. Instead of having one Favorite Recipes category, you can create multiple category names that correspond to the types of recipes you blog about — Casserole Recipes, Dessert Recipes, Beef Recipes, and Chicken Recipes, for example.

Creating specific category titles not only helps search engines, but also helps your readers.

You can also consider having one category called Favorite Recipes and creating subcategories (also known as *child categories*) that give a few more details on the types of recipes you've written about. (See Chapter 8 for information on creating categories and child categories.)

Categories use the custom permalink structure as well. So links to your WordPress categories also become keyword tools within your site to help the search engines — and ultimately, search engine users — find the content. Using custom permalinks gives you category page URLs that look something like this:

```
http://yourdomain.com/category/Category_Name
```

The `Category_Name` portion of that URL puts the keywords right into the hands of search engines.

Using the <ALT> tag for images

When you use the WordPress image uploader to include an image in your post or page, you're given a Description text box in which you can enter a description of the image. (I cover using the WordPress image uploader in detail in Chapter 9.) This text automatically becomes what is referred to as the <ALT> tag.

The <ALT> tag's real purpose is to provide a description of the image for people who, for some reason or another, can't actually see the image. In a text-based browser that doesn't display images, for example, visitors see the description, or <ALT> text, telling them what image would be there if they could see it. Also, the tag helps people with impaired vision who rely on screen-reading technology, because the screen reader reads the <ALT> text from the image. You can read more about Web site accessibility for people with disabilities at www.w3.org/WAI/References/Browsing.

An extra benefit of `<ALT>` tags is that search engines gather data from them to further classify the content of your site. The following is the code for inserting an image, with the `<ALT>` tag of the code in bold to demonstrate what I'm talking about:

```
<img src="http://yourdomain.com/image.jpg" alt="This is an
ALT tag within an image" />
```

Search engines harvest those `<ALT>` tags as keywords. The WordPress image uploader gives you an easy way to include those `<ALT>` tags without having to worry about inserting them into the image code yourself. Just fill out the Description text box before you upload and add the image to your post. Figure 14-16 shows the Description text box that accompanies the WordPress image uploader.

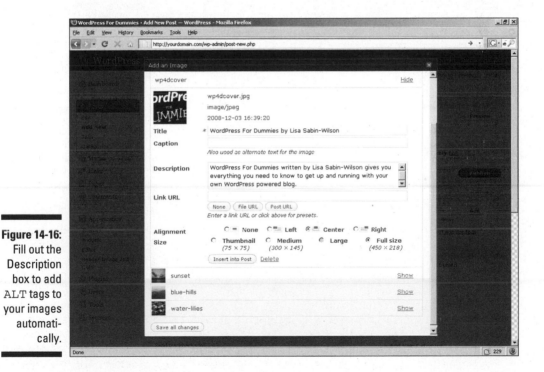

Figure 14-16: Fill out the Description box to add ALT tags to your images automatically.

Finding CMS Resources

Several resources in the WordPress Codex can help you understand some advanced techniques for developing WordPress sites (see Table 14-2).

Table 14-2	Resources from the WordPress Codex	
Title	*Location*	*Description*

Creating a Static Front Page	`http://codex.`
	`wordpress.org/`
	`Creating_a_`
	`Static_Front_`
	`Page`
		You don't want your blog to be on the front page of your site? That's possible with a static front page.

Category Templates	`http://codex.`
	`wordpress.`
	`org/Category_`
	`Templates`
		WordPress lets you create a unique page for each category in the blog.

Template Tags / Query Posts	`http://codex.`
	`wordpress.org/`
	`Template_Tags/`
	`query_posts`
		Use the `query_posts` tag to create dynamic content.

Using Custom Fields	`http://codex.`
	`wordpress.org/`
	`Using_Custom_`
	`Fields`
		WordPress lets post authors assign custom fields to a post.

Chapter 15

Deciding to Bring in the Pros

For some people, hiring a professional is a solution — and sometimes, the only viable solution — for creating a blog that's different from all the rest. Let's face it — some folks would rather chew on nails than try to figure out all the template tags, Cascading Style Sheets (CSS) rules, and graphic design techniques it takes to create a custom-made WordPress template. I hear it from WordPress users (and other blogging-platform users) all the time: "I want a unique look, but I don't know how to do it. I just want to blog."

The question for you to answer is whether you'll be completely satisfied by using a free theme available for all WordPress users, or whether you prefer to hire a professional to provide you a custom theme. Chapter 11 shows you how to find and install free themes that are available to all users of the WordPress.org platform, and Chapter 13 gives you details on how to tweak a free theme. If all this theme information is something you'd rather avoid, however, this chapter gives you information on hiring a professional to help you with the design details. The chapter also covers other types of blog professionals, such as developers and consultants.

Checking Out the Types of Blog Professionals

You have big plans for your blog, and your time is valuable. Hiring a professional to handle the back-end design and maintenance of your blog enables you to spend your time creating the content and building your readership on the front end.

Many bloggers who decide to go the custom route by hiring a design professional do it for another reason: They want the designs/themes of their blogs to be unique. Free themes are nice, but you do run the risk that your blog will look just like hundreds of other blogs out there.

Branding, a term often used in advertising and marketing, refers to the recognizable identity of a product — in this case, of your blog. Having a unique brand or design for your site sets yours apart from the rest. If your blog has a custom look, people will begin to associate that look with you. You can accomplish branding with a single logo or an entire layout and color scheme of your choosing.

Many consultants and design professionals put themselves up for hire. Who are these people? I get to that topic in just a second. First, you want to understand what services they offer, which can help you decide whether hiring a professional is the solution for you.

Take a look at some of the many services available:

- ✓ Custom graphic design and CSS styling for your blog
- ✓ Custom templates
- ✓ WordPress plugin installation and integration
- ✓ Custom WordPress plugins
- ✓ WordPress software installation on your Web server
- ✓ Upgrades of the WordPress software
- ✓ Web hosting and domain registration services
- ✓ Search engine optimization and site marketing

Some bloggers take advantage of the full array of services provided, whereas others use only a handful. The important thing to remember is that you aren't alone. Help is available for you and your blog.

In Table 15-1, I pair the three types of blog experts — designers, developers, and consultants — with the services they typically offer.

Many of these folks are freelancers with self-imposed titles, but I've matched titles to duties as best I can. Keep in mind that some of these professionals wear all these hats and are jacks (or jills)-of-all-trades, whereas others specialize in one area.

Table 15-1	Types of WordPress Professionals
Title	**Services**
Designers	These folks excel in graphic design, CSS, and the development of custom templates.
Developers	These guys and gals are code monkeys. Some of them don't know a stitch about design; however, they can provide you custom code to make your blog do things you never thought possible. Usually, you'll find these people releasing plugins in their spare time for the WordPress community to use for free.
Consultants	If you're blogging for a business, these folks can provide you a marketing plan for your blog or a plan for using your blog to reach clients and colleagues in your field. Many of these consultants also provide search engine optimization to help your domain reach high ranks in search engines.

I wish I could tell you what price to expect to pay for any type of consultant. Truth is, there's no real way for me to make an "On average, you can expect to pay" statement because levels of expertise vary so wildly. I have seen these services range anywhere from $5 per hour all the way up to $300 per hour — and all points in between and beyond.

As with any purchase, do your research, and make an informed decision before you buy. That advice is the absolute best I can give.

Listing all the professionals who provide WordPress services is impossible, but I do list some of the most popular ones in Tables 15-2 through 15-4. My goal is to cover a diverse level of services so that you have the knowledge to make an informed decision about which professional to choose.

Designers

Blog designers can take a simple blog and turn it into something dynamic and exciting. These people are experts in the graphic design, CSS styling, and template tagging needed to create your working theme. Most often, blog designers are also skilled in installing and upgrading WordPress software and plugins; sometimes, they're even skilled in creating custom PHP or plugins. These folks are the ones you want to contact when you're looking for someone to create a nice custom design for your blog (see Figure 15-1).

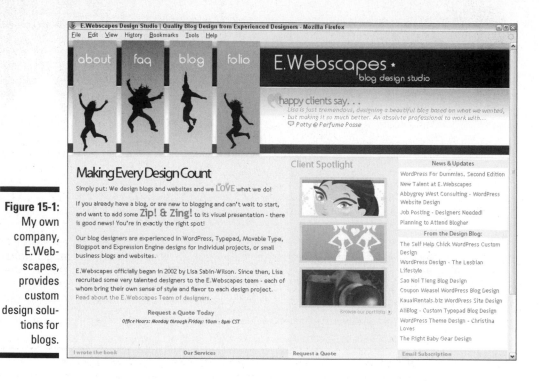

Figure 15-1:
My own
company,
E.Web-
scapes,
provides
custom
design solu-
tions for
blogs.

Some blog designers post their rates on their Web sites because they offer design *packages,* whereas other designers quote projects on a case-by-case basis because every project is unique. When you're searching for a blog designer, if the prices are not displayed on the site, feel free to drop the designer an e-mail and ask for an estimate. Armed with this information, you can do a little comparison-shopping while you search for just the right designer.

The designers and design studios listed in Table 15-2 represent a range of style, pricing, services, and experience. All of them excel in creating custom WordPress blogs and Web sites. This list is by no means exhaustive, but it's a nice starting point.

Table 15-2	Established WordPress Designers
Who They Are	*Where You Can Find Them*
E.Webscapes Design Studio	http://ewebscapes.com
Brian Gardner Media	http://www.briangardner.com
Moxie Design Studios	http://moxiedesignstudios.com
The Blog Studio	http://theblogstudio.com
Hop Studios	http://hopstudios.com

Developers

The WordPress motto sits at the bottom of the WordPress home page:

Code is poetry.

And no one knows this better than the extremely talented blog developers out there today, including the members of the core WordPress development team. A developer can take some of the underlying code, make a little magic happen between PHP and the MySQL database that stores the content of your blog, and create a dynamic display of that content for you. Most likely, you will contact a developer when you want to do something with your blog that is a little out of the ordinary, and you can't find a plugin that does the trick.

If you've gone through all the available WordPress plugins and still can't find the exact function that you want your WordPress blog to perform, get hold of one of these folks. Explain what you need. The developer can tell whether it can be done, whether she is available to do it, and how much it will cost (don't forget that part!). You may recognize some of the names in Table 15-3 as the developers/authors of some popular WordPress plugins.

Table 15-3	Established WordPress Developers
Who They Are	*Where You Can Find Them*
Mark Jaquith	`http://coveredwebservices.com`
Alex King	`http://crowdfavorite.net`
Dougal Campbell	`http://dougal.gunters.org`
Brian Layman	`http://thecodecave.com`
Nich Ohrn	`http://plugin-developer.com`

Consultants

Blog consultants may not be able to do any design or coding work for your blog, but they're probably connected to people who can. Consultants can help you achieve your goals for your blog in terms of online visibility, marketing plans, and search engine optimization. Most of these folks can help you find out how to make money with your blog and connect you with various advertising programs. Quite honestly, you can do what blog consultants do by investing just a little time and research in these areas. As with design and coding, however, figuring everything out and then implementing it takes time. Sometimes, it's easier — and more cost effective — to hire a professional than to do it yourself.

Who hires blog consultants? Typically, a business that wants to incorporate a blog into its existing Web site or a business that already has a blog but wants help in taking it to the next level. Table 15-4 lists some people and organizations that offer this kind of consulting.

Table 15-4	Established Blog Consultants
Who They Are	*Where You Can Find Them*
La Shawn Barber	`http://thelanguageartist.com`
Jim Turner	`http://onebyonemedia.com`
Debbie Weil	`http://debbieweil.com`
Kevin Palmer	`http://socialmediaanswers.com`

Hiring a Professional

With the growing popularity of WordPress, you and I are treated to an ever-expanding market of WordPress consultants, developers, and designers. This situation is an extremely good thing, because the competition keeps them sharp and gives us a wide variety of choices. This section provides information on how to find, hire, and communicate with professionals who make WordPress magic happen.

Finding professionals

Search engines are the most obvious tools to use to look for blog designers, developers, and consultants. By entering the applicable keywords in the search engines, you can find professionals who provide the services you seek. I suggest using keywords like these:

- *Blog consultant*
- *Blog designer*
- *WordPress designer*
- *WordPress developer*
- *Custom WordPress themes*

Aside from search engines, here are some other places you can find blog professionals:

✔ **Other blogs:** Word of mouth is probably the best testimonial when it comes to the services and skills of a group or individual. If you visit blogs on a regular basis, you may notice that bloggers who paid for custom design, development, or marketing services usually display links to the Web sites of the professionals they used and are more than happy to talk about their project details.

When you see a custom blog that you really like, drop the blogger an e-mail and ask about it, or visit the Web site of the professional the blogger used.

✔ **WordPress support forums (http://wordpress.org/support):** You can find many WordPress experts hanging out in these forums, and some of them are available for hire. At the very least, people in the forums can provide great recommendations.

These forums are communities of people from all walks of life, ranging from novices to experts. Check the credentials of anyone you find in the forums, of course, to make sure that he has the experience and knowledge to do what you're asking for.

✔ **WordPress Theme Directory (http://wordpress.org/extend/ themes):** The designers who provide free themes for the WordPress community often hire themselves out for custom projects as well. If you see and like some work by a particular designer on this site, consider dropping that designer an e-mail to find out whether she is available for hire.

✔ **Automattic Web site (http://automattic.com/services/word press-consultants):** The folks at Automattic created Akismet and sidebar widgets, and they're some of the original developers of the WordPress software. They provide a list of qualified WordPress design and development consultants, with each listing linked to that professional's or company's site.

Auditioning your prospects

There are hundreds of designers, consultants, and developers on the Web today, each with his or her own style and skill. There is, literally, something for everyone.

Here are some questions to keep in mind when deciding on the professional you want to work with:

✔ Does he have any experience working with WordPress?

✔ How much experience does she have?

✔ Does his skill encompass just one aspect of what you're looking for, or will you have to hire more than one professional to get the entire job done?

This section helps you evaluate the credentials and skills of various professionals so that you can decide which one to hire for your project.

Blog design practices: What to look for

As a consumer, you should have certain expectations when hiring a professional to design and develop your project. Before paying any amount of money for a professional, make sure that person is as skilled as you need her to be. Keep one very important point in mind: As with anything else in life, you get what you pay for. You wouldn't pay for a Ford and expect a Mercedes, right?

The blog-designing industry has a few standards that you should expect any professional that you hire to meet. If the designer you're considering can't meet these basic standards, I recommend moving on until you find one who can. I'm not trying to criticize anyone here; I've just been on the receiving end of some projects that didn't meet these basic standards. And in keeping with my previous car-buying analogy, if you don't get things right the first time, this lemon will nickel-and-dime you to death — either in money or time investment — for months or even years. Make sure that the person you hire is skilled in the following areas:

- ✔ **XHTML validation:** Web sites are built with programming languages, such as HTML. XHTML validation is kind of like spell-checking or grammar-checking the HTML code against a set of standards put in place by the World Wide Web Consortium (W3C). When your site validates, it's easier for all types of browsers to read and display the underlying code that is the foundation of the design.

   The easiest way to see whether a Web site or blog validates is to use W3C's validation service at `http://validator.w3.org`.

   You can't always gauge a designer's expertise in XHTML validation simply by visiting the sites she has designed. It's very easy for anyone who has administrator access to break the validation (causing the site to have errors in XHTML validation) with just a few simple keystrokes. When a designer hands a project to a client, it's possible for the client to do something, either within the code or within the content of the site, to break XHTML validation.

   You can find a great deal more information about XHTML validation on the W3C Web site at `www.w3.org/QA/Tools`.

- ✔ **CSS-based designs:** The expected standard for Web site and blog design today is making sure that the design is *CSS based,* which means that the format and layout of the site are powered by Cascading Style Sheets. (Other methods include *inline styles,* which are written inside the code rather than pulled in from CSS, and *table-based designs,* which don't render or display as well as CSS-based designs do.) CSS-based sites also have less *code bloat,* meaning that the code contained within the pages is light and the markup lean — something that search engines will love you for!

The easiest way to tell whether a designer used table-based design techniques with inline styling is to look at some of the other sites he's designed. (Usually, you can find examples in the portfolio or gallery section of the designer's site.) View a few sites this person has designed, and then view the HTML source of each site (right-click in the browser window and choose View Source). Designs created with tables and inline styles usually have code that looks something like this:

```
<table width="100%" border="0" cellspacing="0" cellpadding="0"
        background="#ffffff">
```

Instead of using tables and inline styling, a designer can achieve the same results with CSS, which provides a better browsing experience for your visitors.

✔ **Cross-browser rendering:** Multiple browsers are available today, including Internet Explorer, Mozilla Firefox, Opera, Netscape, and Safari. Each browser has its own way of rendering code and CSS. Internet Explorer is especially unique in the way it renders CSS, which creates a bit of a challenge from a design standpoint, because a site needs to look the same in Internet Explorer as it does in all other browsers.

As a blog owner, you want your site to display correctly for all visitors. Every professional designer should be able to accomplish cross-browser rendering, but it is always best to ask and not make any assumptions.

Looking at the pro's virtual résumé

Before you contact a blogging professional to help with your blog, you can find out some pertinent information about who she is, what she does, and what her style is. A little planning and research can go a long way in helping ensure that you're finding a good fit for your project.

Usually, you can find a portfolio for the professional you're considering on his Web site. When you get to the professional's site, look for links labeled something like *Portfolio, Gallery,* or *Clients.*

You can get a good feel for the blogging professional's style and design abilities by browsing through her portfolio of projects. If looking at the portfolio causes you to run screaming from the computer monitor, it's a good bet that this particular professional isn't the one for you. Keep browsing until you find one who's done some design work that you really admire.

Browsing through a blogging professional's portfolio should give you an idea about whether that person has experience working with the WordPress software. If that seems to be the case, keep reading; you'll likely find a wealth of information about the services he offers by looking a bit deeper on the site.

When you're looking at a blogging professional's Web site, determine what standards are most important to that person by trying to find out whether she does the following:

✔ Develops XTHML-valid code and provides nice graphic design.

✔ Ensures that the product provided renders properly in all browser systems. (If you see excuses about why the product renders in only one browser, move on.)

✔ Provides the services you need. (Can all your project needs — domain registration, Web hosting, design work, and software setup and upgrades — be met under one roof?)

While you're on the blogging professional's Web site, make a note of some client URLs, and then visit those sites. Get in contact with these clients, and find out what kind of experiences they had with the professional you're considering. You may want to contact multiple clients to get a good sampling of client satisfaction. Don't have a lot of time for this task? Professional blogging designers, developers, and consultants often post client testimonials right on their Web sites for you to read, although solely relying on published testimonials gives you only one side of the story. Make sure that you contact other clients to get further information on the professional's client relations.

Another way to find more information is to do a Google search on the individual or company name. Type the name in Google's search engine to find out what people are saying on their sites about the professional you're looking to do business with. Usually, bloggers write about their experiences, good or bad, with vendors they've worked with.

Making contact

When you've narrowed your list of candidates, drop them all e-mails with your questions. Be as specific as possible about your needs. Designers and developers can do a lot of things, but I have yet to meet one who can read minds.

Sending an e-mail that says, for example, "I need my blog designed. How much would you charge?" is less effective than something like this:

> "I'm looking for a professional who can create a custom design for my blog.
>
> You can find my blog at www.yourdomain.com *[enter your URL].*
>
> I'm looking for a new template with a three-column layout done in shades of dark and light blue.
>
> The new design must accommodate all my current content and advertising.
>
> In addition to my current content, I have an image that I'd like to include on my blog (which I can send to you when needed). I also need recommendations on plugins."

An e-mail structured like this gives the professional a much better idea of what you're seeking.

In return, e-mails from the person you're thinking about hiring should tell you what to expect in terms of price and when you can expect the project to be completed, and he should answer any questions you've posed.

These professionals all have their own ways of getting from point A to point B in terms of communication. Some communicate via e-mail, some via phone, and some via online help desks. Whichever method a professional uses, open communication is the key. You fully expect your professional to communicate with you; do her the return favor of giving her your ideas and identifying the aspects of your blog that you think are vital and important. A relationship with a good professional can be one that lasts a lifetime — or, at the very least, for the lifetime of your blog.

Agreeing on the contract

When you have chosen the professional you want to work with, the next step is a contract — the agreement between you and the professional — that states what you can expect from each other.

A professional may fax a paper contract to you to sign. Some professionals, however, use virtual agreements, in which all the details of the project are agreed on either through e-mail or through an online form that you fill out. The decision is yours as to which format you are more comfortable with.

At the very least, the contract (or agreement) should contain the following information:

- ✔ **Price and payment schedule:** The price that you and the professional have agreed on, and when and how payments will be made.

- ✔ **Completion date:** The date when you and the professional expect the project to be finished.

- ✔ **Project delivery:** The method that the professional will use to deliver the completed project to you. Delivery may be in the form of electronic transfer via e-mail, project materials published to your Web site, or project materials provided on CD-ROM or DVD.

- ✔ **Project details:** The specifics of the services you can expect the professional to provide. If the project is a design project, the details usually include specifications of the design work. If you're hiring someone to handle marketing services, the professional should detail the services to be performed, such as developing a marketing plan, advertising, and search engine submission.

I'm not a lawyer. The information I've provided here is very general, focusing on the key elements that any contract or agreement should include. Be sure to consult an attorney for specific legal advice concerning contracts.

Part VI
The Part of Tens

The 5th Wave   By Rich Tennant

@RICHTENNANT

In this part . . .

Welcome to The Part of Tens! In this part, I tell you about ten fabulous WordPress themes and ten great plugins that you can use to enhance your WordPress blogging. I also present ten WordPress–powered sites that effectively use WordPress as a CMS (Content Management System).

Chapter 16

Ten WordPress Web Sites Used As a CMS

In This Chapter

▶ Seeing examples of how WordPress powers Web sites

▶ Discovering sites that use WordPress for more than just blogging

S o many blogs, so little time! This chapter focuses on ten successful blogs that use the WordPress software in effective, innovative, and inspiring ways. These blogs go beyond what the WordPress software has to offer out of the box, extending WordPress to present a unique experience for visitors.

I'm not talking just about design in this case. A tremendous number of well-designed WordPress blogs are floating around the blogosphere; picking only ten of them would be a near-impossible task for me. No, what I'm talking about here is how each individual site is set up. Sometimes, you can look at a Web site and not even know that it's a blog or a site built with blog software. This is why people refer to WordPress as a CMS (Content Management System), rather than merely a blogging platform. You can do much more with it than just blog; you can also build fully functional Web sites with it.

The sites in this chapter employ techniques that could be considered "advanced WordPress hackery." These techniques aren't necessarily the kinds that you can perform straight out of the starting gate. Chapters 11, 12, and 13 deal with WordPress themes, templates and template tags, introducing the basic techniques to get you started.

New Music Nation

http://newmusicnation.com

At first glance, many visitors to New Music Nation comment that if it weren't for the credit link at the bottom of the site pages, they wouldn't think that the site was built with the WordPress blogging platform.

New Music Nation is an up-and-coming music review site owned and operated by Dave Powers, the former producer of MTV2's "Subterranean," "120 Minutes," "Hip Hop's Toughest Rhymes," and "Playlistism," to name just a few accomplishments of this music blogger. Dave really did his research before starting New Music Nation.

I was fortunate to have the opportunity to work with Dave on rebuilding his static HTML site from the ground up with the use of WordPress. He came to me with his idea to add a fairly intensive category navigation system throughout his site. New Music Nation has roughly 1,800 categories (and growing), which was a challenging problem when it came to creating a workable navigation system for his readers.

What type of category navigation does the site provide for its visitors?

- ✔ **A search of one particular category by month:** This feature, which isn't a default feature of WordPress, required some custom PHP coding and queries to the MySQL database. This navigation method isn't recommended if you're not a code monkey, but I highlight it here as an example of what is possible due to the extensive nature of WordPress.

- ✔ **A search by keyword and category:** The search feature is part of the basic WordPress installation and is available in most WordPress templates. New Music Nation's search feature adds a twist, however: You can type a keyword and then choose a category from a drop-down menu to search for that keyword within posts in a particular category. This search capability is necessary because the site has approximately 1,800 categories. Dave pared down his choices and decided that he wanted only a few select parent categories to appear in the drop-down menu to let readers search within 5 or 6 of the 1,800 categories.

- ✔ **A subcategory search:** The big challenge was creating an alphabetical navigation system to let readers browse Dave's 1,800 categories. His structure is something like this:

  - Parent category
  - - roughly 850 subcategories

  You can view, for example, the Artists directory. Artists is a parent category, with 850-plus subcategories that single out specific artists. We created a subcategory navigation system to let readers navigate the artists in alphabetical order, by their first names. Click the letter *A* to find artists whose names start with that letter, and so on.

In terms of content, you don't see the typical chronological listing of posts on this site. Instead, you see Dave's most recent posts in each of his parent categories: Reviews, College Radio Buzz, Top 20 Albums Standing, and News Notes. Other features include

✔ **E-mail subscriptions:** Visitors can enter their e-mail addresses to receive e-mail notifications regarding site updates and new posts to the blog.

✔ **Contributors:** If you're interested in blogging about college radio, for example, you can sign up to contribute to the site. Find the handy registration form in the College Radio Buzz category.

Overall, New Music Nation is definitely not an out-of-the-box WordPress blog from a guy who is not so out of the box himself.

AlexKing.org

http://alexking.org

You may recognize the name of this site. After all, it's one of the links in your blog's default blogroll when you first install WordPress. Alex King is one of the original developers of WordPress. Though he is not involved in WordPress development any longer, he remains an invaluable asset to the overall community through his ongoing plugin development and consulting practice.

I had the opportunity to interview Alex about his recent site design. Something he said during our interview struck me as being one of the best testimonials to the extensibility of WordPress:

> *I enjoy bending WordPress to my will — not the other way around.*

And bending, he does. Contorting is more like it. His front page is actually not a blog at all, but a portal that leverages all the content he has available throughout his site without making it look cluttered. Alex includes these features in his front page:

✔ A clean, clearly marked navigational menu to the various hot spots on his site.

✔ Helpful information about and links to the projects featured on the site. Alex is a busy consultant and developer, and he makes great use of this space to spotlight his projects.

✔ Links, with excerpts, to the most recent posts Alex has made to his News category via the RSS category feed.

✔ A column that starts with some pertinent information about Alex himself, including his mug shot.

✔ The most recent post he made to his blog.

✔ A search feature to help readers find what they're looking for (and to give some space to advertisers).

What is noticeably absent from this WordPress-powered site is a chronological listing of blog posts on the front page. The portal works extremely well, considering the vast amount of information and content that Alex has up for public consumption on his site. You can find the traditional blog layout, however, by clicking the Blog link in the navigation menu at the top.

Mosaic Consulting, Inc.

`http://mosaic-consulting.com/`

Mosaic Consulting is a small legal IT consulting company whose work spans the globe. Mosaic chose WordPress as a CMS because of the software's flexibility and extensibility.

The company doesn't run a blog on its site. Instead, it offers an unlimited number of static pages on the site — pages that someone created without ever having to touch a piece of the underlying code in the theme. The site also uses WordPress categories and subcategories in a nice dynamic navigation menu that takes visitors through the various sections of the site.

Mosaic Consulting is not an Internet-based company; neither does it do business in the virtual world. The company works with Fortune 500 corporations and their internal legal teams to help them form solutions to their everyday legal IT problems. It does use the power of the Internet combined with WordPress, however, to provide an interactive online brochure of sorts.

CSS Collection

`http://csscollection.com`

CSS Collection is a showcase site powered by WordPress. The purpose of the site is to showcase what people can do with Cascading Style Sheets when building Web sites and blogs.

Here are some of the site's features:

- **Thumbnails:** The front page includes thumbnail images of sites that make the cut. Click a thumbnail, and you go to the Web site that is being showcased in that entry. The thumbnailing is accomplished through the image handler in WordPress, along with some custom coding done with the Custom Fields tool.

✔ **Interactive ratings:** Click any Web site's title, and you go to a single page where you can comment on the entry, saying why you think that site is really great — or not so great. Through the use of a plugin called Rate My Stuff (`http://deadcantrant.com/projects/rate/`), the folks at CSS Collection let readers rate each site with a star-rating system.

CSS Collection also makes good use of the typical blog layout and functions that you are used to seeing with WordPress, but the blog is not the primary part of the site. Rather, the site keeps a news section active with announcements and updates, using the old-fashioned blog layout that we've come to expect with WordPress. Here are two ways they accomplish this:

✔ **RSS feeds:** CSS Collection pulls a few of the most recent news updates onto its front page to make it easy for visitors to stay up to date with the newest information posted in the news section.

✔ **Categories:** Through the WordPress category system, CSS Collection categorizes the selected sites in a logical, organized fashion, giving you an easy way to navigate the sites reviewed in the CSS showcase.

b5media

`http://b5media.com`

If you're new to blogs and the blogosphere, you may not know about b5media, but I feel confident that you will soon. Eventually, everyone runs into b5media. b5media is the largest blog network on the Internet today, with more than 350 blogs in its network. The people behind the madness are always more than happy to brag about the fact that their network is run entirely with WordPress.

When I started digging around at the company's site, I assumed that b5media was taking full advantage of the technologies provided with the WordPress MU (Multi-User) software. They were quick to correct me. "We are not using WordPress MU at all," they said, "although in many ways, we have duplicated what MU does by using different technologies and scripting techniques that we've developed throughout the process."

RSS is a huge portion of the strategy in place at b5media, which has built a network of niche blogs, including various channels that work with several topics of interest. Although individual blogs are really the target audience at b5, each channel also serves as a "place of discovery," with something for everyone.

The front page of b5media showcases these channels through RSS feed technology and WordPress's built-in Magpie technology. Every time you load the b5media front page, you're treated to a random channel listing with different posts listed there, brought in by the channel feed.

b5media does have a blog on its site, but the blog isn't up front and center. b5 didn't want the blog to be the site's focus; the company wanted to deemphasize the blog and spotlight individual b5 blogs and channels instead. You can find the b5media blog by clicking the Our Blog link in the site's top navigation menu. Snippets of blog content are also pulled into the front page under the b5 Headlines header.

All the blogs that make up the b5media empire are connected through a blogroll. Each site has the b5media blogroll displayed prominently, making it easy for visitors to navigate from one b5 blog to the next. Who needs the rest of the Internet when you have b5? I'm sure that the b5 folks would say the same.

Hot Air

http://hotair.com

Hot Air burst onto the scene in 2006 as the first independently owned, conservative Internet broadcast network, featuring an original daily video newscast. Yes, we're talking politics here. Hot Air was founded by famous media personality Michelle Malkin.

The Hot Air motto is "Exposing new viewers to the revolutionary world of videoblogging, animation, and Internet broadcasting." All this is brought to you through the WordPress blogging platform, which is the site's CMS of choice.

The designer who helped bring Hot Air to life is Peter Flaschner from The Blog Studio (http://theblogstudio.com). During the course of writing this book, I interviewed Peter about the WordPress technologies hard at work at Hot Air and what techniques he used to make it such a striking example of thinking out of the box when it comes to blog development.

Regarding the use of WordPress, Peter had this to say: "WordPress was the chosen platform for this project because of its proven ability for it to withstand a lot of traffic and protection from malicious attacks from their detractors. The owners of the site are all familiar with the use of WordPress, through other projects they've been involved with prior to the launch of Hot Air, so that made the choice an easy one."

The videos are created with a Sony HVR-A1U Digital HDV Handycam and edited with Avid Xpress DV and Adobe After Effects. To get those videos into the blog, Hot Air uses the WP-FLV plugin, created by Roel Meurders, at `http://roel.meurders.nl/wordpress-plugins/wp-flv-video-player-plugin/`. The Hot Air folks insert the Adobe Flash videos directly and seamlessly into the blog posts. The nice design treatment that Peter gave the video display pulls together an extremely dynamic-looking video blog.

As far as the overall format of the blog goes, it doesn't feature the typical chronological blog postings, one after the other. Instead, visitors are treated to video hits that encompass the entire sensory package: information, music, voice commentary, and images.

MommyCast

`http://mommycast.com`

MommyCast lives in the genre of *mommy blogs* — blogs owned and maintained by mothers. But MommyCast takes that concept quite a bit further through its radio program. MommyCast.com is a unique online audio company by and for women who are immersed in the fullness of motherhood and life; the site's motto is "Holding the world together, one child at a time." MommyCast offers interviews with people on topics that encompass all things having to do with motherhood.

I had the chance to speak with Joelle Reeder of Moxie Design Studios (`http://moxiedesignstudios.com`), the design brain behind the MommyCast brand. Joelle had this to say about the decision to use WordPress as the CMS for the project: "The MommyCast show has sponsors who use WordPress, so it was a natural choice for them to go in the same direction. The people behind the project also have used WordPress in the past and were very familiar with the platform."

The people at MommyCast record each radio show and then make it available for download on the site. You can listen to a show straight off the site or download the audio file and listen to the show later.

Through the creative use of WordPress's Custom Fields feature, Joelle lets the MommyCast women insert a cute, eye-catching "Listen Now!" graphic into every post. The post authors don't have to edit any code or even be aware of the underlying code that makes everything happen.

Joelle also implemented a really neat way to bring some visual vitality to each post through image thumbnailing, combined with Custom Fields, that lets them insert small images into each post that calls attention not only to the post but to the post topic. These Custom Fields are called *Call Outs* and they draw the eye in and make you pay attention.

Jane Wilson-Marquis

http://janewilsonmarquis.com/

The Jane Wilson-Marquis Web site is one of two sites in this chapter that are powered completely by WordPress, yet you don't find a blog on the site. That's right — no blog. That's why the site is a perfect fit for this chapter as a showcase of what WordPress is capable of doing beyond the blog!

Jane is a couture bridal- and evening-gown designer, and her site is an extension of her design studio in New York City. The site includes several photos of her dresses and fashion shows in which her work has been exhibited.

The site relies heavily on the following WordPress features:

- Category structure
- Category page templates
- PHP code that allowed several different sidebar templates into different sections of the site
- Static page templates
- WP PageNavi, a plugin (http://lesterchan.net/wordpress/readme/wp-pagenavi.html) that is used for the gallery pages to let readers navigate the dress designs easily

The site has been showcased in several design seminars and conferences, and people usually are very surprised to find that WordPress is the system behind the site. Their first question is usually "Well, where's the blog?" The simple answer: "There is no blog."

Weblogs at Harvard Law School

http://blogs.law.harvard.edu/

For this particular entry, I feel that I need to be collegiate and academic, and get into the Ivy League state of mind. This site is at Harvard, after all, and these folks are *smart*. But I figure that if Reese Witherspoon could do it in *Legally Blonde,* I certainly can hold my own with these Harvard types in this chapter.

Weblogs at Harvard Law School uses the WordPress MU software as a multi-user solution for the large network of law blogs within the community. The application is set up to let anyone with a harvard.edu, radcliffe.edu, or hbs.edu e-mail address host a blog on Weblogs.

I include this site in this chapter to show what you can do with the WordPress MU software solution, as well as the type of network you can manage and maintain with it. On the front page of the site, you can sign up for your own blog. Signing up automatically creates a blog with the domain `http://blogs.law.harvard.edu/your-user-name`.

Weblogs at Harvard Law School also makes fine use of RSS technology in two sections of the site:

- ✔ **Updates:** This section lists all the blogs in the system, listed by order of update, so you find the most recently updated blogs at the top of the list. This feature is very useful if you're a fan of the community and want to keep updated.

- ✔ **Digest:** This section tracks daily happenings in all Harvard Law blogs. You can subscribe to the RSS feed for the Harvard Law Blogs Digest to be notified any time a Harvard Law blog updates.

The entire site and its portal are pretty simple, without a whole lot of magic going on. The straightforward interface gives visitors the information they need. The Harvard Law network takes full advantage of the free themes that WordPress designers release throughout the Web, giving members myriad looks to choose among and making Weblogs a network of unique blogs.

E.Webscapes Design Studio

`http://ewebscapes.com`

I have to issue a disclaimer for this listing: I've owned and operated this site since 1998. I include it in this chapter not so much to self-promote (although that is a bonus!) but as a way to illustrate some great things that you can do with just one installation of the WordPress software. I often refer people to my site when I explain how WordPress not only powers a great blog, but also is the foundation of a fully functional business Web site.

E.Webscapes has several sections:

- ✔ **The front page:** This page contains an introductory message to visitors, some examples of my work, links to news and updates, and the latest article headlines from my Design Blog in the right sidebar. Along the bottom, you find information about book purchases; you also can search the site, find client testimonials and links to my services and terms, and input your e-mail address to subscribe to updates.

- ✔ **The Design Blog:** I update this blog regularly with information about the design projects that my designers and I have completed for our clients.

- ✔ **FAQ:** This page lists frequently asked questions, along with their answers, to help clients and potential clients make informed decisions about my services.

- ✔ **Folio:** This section is the design portfolio that spotlights all the projects that my designers and I have done in the past.

As you can see in navigating the site, all the pages, posts, and categories display a little differently, depending on the purpose of each page. This site was created with a single installation of WordPress; the format and layout were accomplished through the creation of a custom theme.

Chapter 17

Ten Popular WordPress Plugins

In This Chapter

▶ Finding popular WordPress plugins

▶ Using plugins to enhance your blog

*I*n this chapter, I list ten of the most popular plugins available for your WordPress blog. This list isn't exhaustive by any means; hundreds of excellent WordPress plugins can, and do, provide multiple ways to extend the functionality of your blog. And if these ten plugins aren't enough for you, you can find many more at the official WordPress Plugin Directory (http://wordpress.org/extend/plugins).

The greatest plugin of all is Akismet, which I describe in Chapter 10. Akismet is the answer to comment and trackback spam; it kills spam dead. I don't cover it in this chapter because Akismet stands alone as an absolute must for any WordPress blog and comes installed with WordPress.

Chapter 10 contains information on how to locate, download, unpack, install, activate, and manage plugins in your WordPress blog.

WP Print

Developer: Lester Chan

http://lesterchan.net/portfolio/programming/php/#wp-print

WP Print is one of several WordPress plugins developed by Lester Chan. This easy-to-use plugin provides a clean, printable version of your blog posts and/or pages.

Unless your blog theme has a specialized stylesheet for printing, posts and pages print rather messily. WP Print strips most of the style from your theme design (images and formatting, for example) and outputs a clean print of your article with black text on a white background.

You can configure these options:

- **Print Text Link for Post:** This option configures the text of the link you want to show on your blog posts to prompt your visitors to print your article. (The default setting is Print This Post.)

- **Print Text Link for Page:** This option configures the text of the link you want to show on your blog pages to prompt your visitors to print your page. (The default setting is Print This Page.)

- **Print Icon:** Choose between two icons: `print.gif` and `printer_fam fam fam.gif`. The icon you choose appears on your site.

- **Print Text Style Link:** This drop-down menu presents settings for displaying the print link on your site:

  - Print Icon with Text Link

  - Print Icon Only

  - Text Link Only

  - Custom (lets you design your own text link)

- **Print Comments?:** Choose Yes to print comments on your blog post or page.

- **Print Links?:** Choose Yes to print links that appear in your blog post or page.

- **Print Images?:** Choose Yes to print images that appear in your blog post or page.

- **Disclaimer/Copyright Text?:** Type your desired copyright and/or disclaimer statement in the text box. This text appears on the printed copy of your blog post or page.

WP Print doesn't automatically appear on your blog; you need to add a small snippet of code to your blog template in the area where you want the print link to appear. That small snippet of code is this:

```
<?php if(function_exists('wp_print')) { print_link(); } ?>
```

Place the code within The Loop. (See Chapter 12 for information about The Loop.)

While you're at Lester's site, check out all the other plugins he has available. His plugins are well known and very popular among WordPress users.

Subscribe to Comments

Developer: Mark Jaquith

`http://txfx.net/code/wordpress/subscribe-to-comments`

The Subscribe to Comments plugin adds a very nice feature to your blog by letting your visitors subscribe to individual posts you've made to your blog. When they do this, they receive notification via e-mail whenever someone leaves a new comment on the post. This feature goes a long way toward keeping your readers informed and making the discussions lively and active!

The plugin includes a full-featured subscription manager that your commenters can use to unsubscribe to certain posts, block all notifications, or even change their notification e-mail address.

ShareThis

Developer: Alex King

`http://sharethis.com/wordpress`

Every social bookmarking service has its own icon. People put these icons on their blogs as a way to let their visitors know that they could share their content with each social bookmarking service. This was a good concept when only a handful of services existed; then these services started popping up everywhere. Pretty soon, people were putting a dozen — sometimes even two dozen — bookmarking icons on their sites to encourage visitors to submit their content to all those different services.

ShareThis is a plugin that combines an "e-mail this" plugin and social bookmarking service, allowing visitors to share content through e-mail and popular social bookmarking services such as Technorati, del.icio.us, and Digg.

When you've installed the plugin, go to the Options page for ShareThis, and set these options:

✔ **Enter the Widget Code:** Obtain the code from the ShareThis Web site; then copy the code into the text box.

✔ **Display the Link Only on Certain Pages of Your Blog:** By default, the ShareThis link is added at the very end of your blog post and page. You can turn this default option off. Choose No from the Automatically Add ShareThis to Your Posts and the Automatically Add ShareThis to Your Pages drop-down menus that appear on the ShareThis Options page. Then add the ShareThis template tag to your template wherever you want it to display in your blog:

```
<?php if (function_exists('sharethis_button')) { sharethis_button(); } ?>
```

This plugin requires the `wp-footer()` call in the footer (`footer.php`) of your template. If your theme doesn't include a `wp_footer()` call, you can add it easily by opening the `footer.php` template and adding this bit of code:

```
<?php wp_footer(); ?>
```

All in One SEO Pak

Developer: Michael Torbert

`http://wordpress.org/extend/plugins/all-in-one-seo-pack/`

Almost everyone is concerned about Search Engine Optimization (SEO) in blogs. Good SEO practices help the major search engines (such as Google, Yahoo!, and MSN) easily find and cache your blog content in their search databases so that when people search for keywords, they can find your blog in the search results.

All in One SEO Pak helps you fine-tune your blog to make that happen. It automatically creates optimized titles and generates HTML keywords for your individual posts.

All in One SEO Pak has a nice options page where you can fill in all sorts of information about your blog, including keywords and formatting of the post or page titles within your site to make them easy for search engines to index. Find the All in One SEO Pak Options page by clicking the Settings link at the top right corner of your WordPress Administration panel, and then click the All in One SEO subtab.

WordPress Mobile Edition

Developer: Alex King

http://alexking.org/projects/wordpress

Another great plugin from the talented Alex King is WordPress Mobile Edition, which provides a custom display of your blog for a mobile device. Mobile browsers are detected automatically; no configuration is needed.

As mobile Web browsing becomes more and more popular, you want to make sure that your site renders decently in your readers' mobile browsers. This plugin will do it for you. It's fast, it's easy, and it does the job.

WP-DB-Backup

Developers: filosofo, skippy, Firas, LaughingLizard, MtDewVirus, Podz, and Ringmaster

http://wordpress.org/extend/plugins/wp-db-backup/

Throughout this book, I often remind you to back up your files. In my work outside this book, I'm always encouraging my friends and clients to back up.

WP-DB-Backup is a plugin that provides a very easy method of creating a backup of your MySQL database. Remember, the database stores all the important data for your blog: your posts, pages, links, categories, comments, trackbacks, and settings.

If something happens to your database, and you don't have a backup, you'll be starting over from page one. Do yourself a huge favor: Make regular backups of your database by using this plugin. You wouldn't need to use one of those backup files to restore your blog very often, but when you do need to, a backup can make the difference between a good day and jumping off a cliff!

You can choose to have the backup file sent to an e-mail address of your choosing, downloaded to your computer, or stored on your Web sever in a backup folder inside your wp-content folder.

You can also schedule regular hourly, daily, or weekly backups and have those backup files emailed to you.

WP-DB-Backup is a great way to have some peace of mind. If something cata-strophic happens to your Web server, you have a backup of all your blog content sitting safely on your own computer.

WP Ajax Edit Comments

Developer: Ronald Huereca

http://raproject.com/wordpress/wp-ajax-edit-comments/

Using the WP Ajax Edit Comments plugin is a way for you to do a huge favor for the readers of your site, because this plugin lets readers edit their own comments on your blog. I don't know about you, but I have days when I could be considered the queen of typos and grammatical errors, and when I've made such an error in a comment on someone's blog, I've wished that I could log in to his WordPress Administration panel to edit my comment. Those of you who have this plugin installed on your blogs, please accept my gratitude!

This plugin doesn't require your readers to log in to your WordPress Administration panel to edit their comments; they can do it right on the Comments page of your blog. On the Options page, you can set the amount of time you let your readers edit their comments (for example, within 30 minutes of leaving the comment). The developer provides full instructions, including video guides, on the plugin's home page.

cforms11

Developer: Oliver Seidel

http://wordpress.org/extend/plugins/cforms

cformsII lets you create forms within your pages and posts. You can even have multiple forms on one page. You can use forms to provide a variety of features on your site:

- ✔ **Contact forms:** A visitor fills out a contact form with her name, e-mail address, and message. When the visitor clicks the Submit button, the message gets e-mailed to you.

- ✔ **Questionnaires:** A form with a number of questions for site visitors to answer. The questions are posed by the site owner, followed by text boxes to allow the visitor to answer those questions. When the visitor clicks the Submit button, the site owner receives the questionnaire and the answers in an e-mail.

> ✔ **User submissions:** Readers can send images, audio, or video files to you via e-mail.
>
> ✔ **Sales order forms:** I use this form on my Web site (`http://eweb scapes.com/order`). This sales order form asks clients very specific questions about their Web site designs. When they click the Submit button, I receive their full orders in my e-mails.

When this plugin is activated, click the cformsII tab in the Administration panel to load the Form Settings page. Within the cformsII options, you have several ways to build and style your forms.

The plugin's author has extensive documentation and a cformsII user forum at `http://deliciousdays.com/cforms-forum`.

Google XML Sitemaps

Developer: Arne Brachhold

`http://wordpress.org/extend/plugins/google-sitemap-generator`

This plugin lets you create a Google-compliant site map of your entire blog. Every single time you create a new post or page, the site map is updated and submitted to several major search engines, including Google, Yahoo!, and MSN. This plugin helps the search engines find and catalog new content from your site, so your new content appears in the search engines faster than it would if you didn't have a site map.

WordPress.com Stats

Developer: Andy Skelton and Michael D. Adams

`http://wordpress.org/extend/plugins/stats`

With the rise in popularity of the hosted WordPress.com service came a huge demand for the statistics that WordPress.com provides in its Dashboard pages. Users of the self-hosted WordPress.org software drooled when they saw the stats available to WordPress.com users, and the cry for a similar stats plugin for WordPress.org went out across the blogosphere.

Andy Skelton answered that call with the release of the WordPress.com Stats plugin for WordPress.org users. This plugin, installed on your WordPress.org blog, starts collecting all the important statistics that any blogger would want to know about the activity on his blog, including the number of hits on the site per hour, day, or month; the most popular posts; the sources of the traffic on the blog; and the links people click to leave the site.

The stats are provided for you on one easy-to-view page. This plugin doesn't count your own visits to your blog, so you can be assured that the counts are accurate, not inflated by your own visits.

You need a WordPress.com API key for the stats plugin to work. (See Chapter 10 for information on how to obtain a WordPress.com API key.) To enter the key, click the Plugins link in the Administration panel, click the WordPress.com Stats subtab, and type the API key there.

After you've activated the plugin and inserted your WordPress.com API key, click the Dashboard link in the Administration panel to see the Blog Stats subtab. Click this subtab to view your stats.

Chapter 18

Ten Free WordPress Themes

. . . .

In This Chapter

▶ Finding good WordPress themes

▶ Using popular WordPress themes to style your blog

. . . .

*B*ecause I'm a WordPress theme developer and designer, this chapter was probably the most difficult for me to put together. I know, I know . . . I was thinking the same thing as you: "Ten great WordPress themes — no big deal!" Yet it's a very big deal because the themes available for WordPress number in the thousands, if not hundreds of thousands. Many of these themes are excellent, and picking a mere ten was really tough. The list I present here isn't exhaustive by any means. Chapters 11, 12, and 13 give you a few more resources to find a theme that suits your needs.

I kept these criteria in mind when choosing the following themes:

- ✔ **User-friendly:** The best themes incorporate as much detail as possible to let the theme user just load the theme and start blogging without a whole lot of fuss and muss. You can use these themes directly out of the box, but usually, they have a whole lot more to offer if you want to tinker. The key is that you don't *have* to tinker.

- ✔ **Compatible with widgets:** Themes that are set up to use WordPress sidebar widgets are the most user-friendly. Widgets are wonderful, and they make your blogging life incredibly easy by giving you drag-and-drop functionality and control of the content that appears in your sidebar. (If you don't know what widgets are, flip back to Chapter 5.)

- ✔ **Free price tag:** 2007 saw a boom in popularity of premium themes, which you pay to download. Although I don't have anything against this practice, I want this chapter to present themes that you can easily find and use without having to pay a penny.

✔ **Valid code:** A set of standards for Web design and code called the W3C standards, developed by the World Wide Web Consortium (`http://w3c.org`), serves as a sort of proofreading guide for the code in all Web site designs. Although you may not notice it, valid XHTML code goes a very long way toward ensuring that the theme you're using meets that set of standards, and you can be relatively confident that your blog site isn't causing errors in different browsers.

Designers who pay attention to valid code are the designers to look for when you choose a theme for your site, because they understand validation and your need to make sure that your site is reaching all your visitors, no matter what browsers they're using to view your content.

You can tell whether a designer used valid code on his site by using two validation tools on the W3C Web site: `http://validator.w3.org` for HTML code validation and `http://jigsaw.w3.org/css-validator` for CSS code validation.

With these things in mind, I present the top-ten free WordPress themes available for you to try on your site. The Web sites listed for each of these themes have a demo of the theme, so you can actually see it in action. These themes aren't listed in any particular order; each one is just as good as the next.

Cutline

Theme designer: Chris Pearson

`http://cutline.tubetorial.com`

The highlights of this theme are the following:

✔ It has a very clean, uncluttered two-column layout.

✔ Small details in this theme make the big picture shine: detailed treatment of lists, block and pulled quotes, and comment links, to name just a few.

✔ It supports the WordPress Widgets plugin (which you can find at `http://automattic.com/code/widgets`).

✔ It supports the flickrRSS plugin (available at `http://eightface.com/wordpress/flickrrss`).

✔ It supports the Random Header Images plugin (`http://cutline.tubetorial.com/totally-random-header-images-for-cutline/`), which lets you switch header images easily without even knowing how to manipulate the code.

Cutline (shown in Figure 18-1) makes it to the top of my list because I think it's one of the most functional, versatile, and friendly free themes available.

Figure 18-1:
Cutline
WordPress
theme
by Chris
Pearson.

Tarski

Theme designers: Ben Eastaugh and Chris Sternal-Johnson

http://tarskitheme.com

The highlights of this theme are the following:

- ✔ The admin options menu gives you several options to customize your theme and includes several nicely designed header graphics.
- ✔ Its print stylesheet maximizes the paper output of your site for people who are interested in printing your blog posts.
- ✔ It has a two-column layout.
- ✔ Its sidebar is widget ready.

The Tarski theme designers make it very easy for you to personalize your blog without being required to know a lick of HTML, CSS, or coding that is usually required to accomplish the changes necessary to personalize your blog theme. It comes with a choice of header artwork for you to choose from; to change the header artwork, you just select the artwork in the theme options page. The options page for the Tarski theme also provides you with several options you can select to further personalize the theme to suit your needs.

The theme's Web site has comprehensive information on using the theme and its features.

SandPress

Theme designer: Arpit Jacob

`http://clazh.com/sandpress-free-wordpress-theme`

The SandPress theme was the first-place winner of a recent WordPress theme design competition held in June/July 2007 at `http://sndbx.org`. SandPress provides you with a very clean, three-column layout. The theme designer paid very special attention to the small details of the theme, such as fantastic icons that call colorful attention to various sections of your site (such as comments, page navigation, RSS feeds, and so on).

xMark

Theme designer: Lisa Sabin-Wilson

`http://blogdesignsolutions.com`

The highlights of this theme are the following:

- ✔ It's a fully fluid three-column theme. (*Fluid* means that it expands and contracts to fill your browser page, no matter what size your browser is.)
- ✔ It displays blog content on the left and two widget-ready sidebars on the right.
- ✔ Its admin options menu lets you choose various settings for your theme.
- ✔ The theme supports several popular WordPress plugins. The integration is seamless, meaning that if you have the plugins installed in WordPress, they'll work automatically; if you don't have them installed, you won't even notice the functionality.

After you activate the xMark theme, click the xMark tab in the Administration panel to find a few options that you can set for your blog. These options let you make significant choices for displaying certain features on your blog without having to tinker with the actual code inside the template.

Another important feature is that the theme is optimized for search engines, which gives you an edge in having the popular search engines find and list your site.

Stargaze

Theme designer: Joni Ang

```
http://taintedsong.com/2008/02/20/stargaze-wordpress-theme
```

By the designer's own admission, this particular theme is a bit more "girly" than most. Most free WordPress themes do seem to have a distinct lack of femininity, so I thought I would present a female-oriented one here.

Stargaze is a beautiful two-column theme that is widget ready (meaning that you can use WordPress widgets with this theme without having to do any special adjustments to the theme). The color scheme is a nice combination of blue, yellow, and pink, with a variety of nicely placed icons and design elements drawing attention to specific areas of your content.

Carrington

Theme designer: Alex King; Crowd Favorite

```
http://blog.carringtontheme.com
```

Carrington (see Figure 18-2) is a theme built upon a framework that organizes different WordPress features that can be styled distinctly by the users, based on their own, individual tastes. Inside the admin options of the Carrington theme, users find they have the ability to customize the color of links and header of the theme with an easy-to-use color picker, as well as a customizable header image that allows users to further customize Carrington to suit their tastes. Carrington is a clean, simple, and minimalistic theme and supports WordPress features — such as threaded comments, image galleries, and simplified CSS — to make it as easy as possible for users to customize the CSS styling. (See Chapter 13 for great information on tweaking WordPress themes using CSS.)

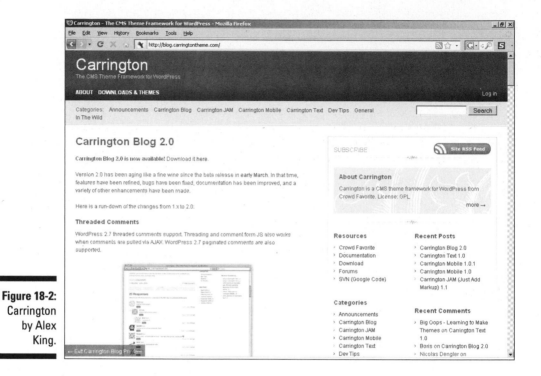

Figure 18-2:
Carrington
by Alex
King.

iTheme

Theme designer: Nick La

```
http://ndesign-studio.com/resources/wp-themes/itheme
```

iTheme is a WordPress theme designed with Macintosh lovers in mind. The theme emulates the design elements and features of the Macintosh operating system, with beautiful blue gradients and Maclike menu headers and icons. This theme has a fully configurable sidebar that allows you to use WordPress widgets, and when they're in your blog, you can drag those widgets around in the sidebar.

Redoable

Theme designer: Dean J. Robinson

```
http://deanjrobinson.com/wordpress/redoable
```

Redoable is the only dark theme that made my list of top tens. The light-text-on-a-dark-background type of theme has gained popularity among designers and theme fans across the blogosphere, but it can make your blog difficult for some visitors to read. I include this theme because of the popularity of this type of look. Aside from readability issues, Redoable is a beautiful theme with a lot of detailed treatment, built on the popular K2 theme.

Redoable has a two-column layout, and its sidebar is widget ready. It supports multiple popular WordPress plugins. (See the theme's Web page for details.) This theme also gives detailed treatment to many design classes, letting you create a unique blog site.

Una

Theme designer: Dino Latoga

```
http://dinolatoga.com/2008/07/04/una-wordpress-theme/
```

Una (shown in Figure 18-3) is a very clean, two-column WordPress theme with a very nice and clean color scheme of tan, brown, and white. Una is widget compatible, so you can begin using WordPress widgets as soon as you activate this theme on your blog.

This theme displays your static page navigation menu at the top of the site, underneath your site title, for easy reader navigation through pages. Una also has a unique front page layout that displays the full text of your most recent post and then displays the last three posts you made prior to that with an excerpt of the post, accompanied by a thumbnail image that helps bring attention by directing your eye to that section of the front page.

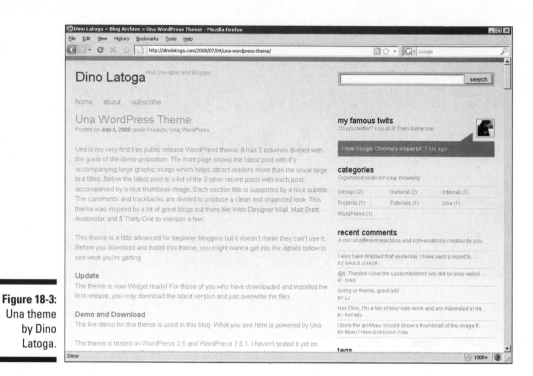

Figure 18-3:
Una theme
by Dino
Latoga.

Gridline Lite

Theme designer: Thad Allender

http://gridline.thadallender.com

Gridline Lite is a minimalist WordPress theme. The theme has clean, simple, light elements, which lets your design focus mainly on content rather than appearance. The theme uses black, white, and gray tones and a two-column layout, with content on the left and sidebar on the right.

Appendix

Migrating Your Existing Blog to WordPress

So you have a blog on a different blogging system and want to move your blog to WordPress? This appendix helps you accomplish just that. WordPress makes it relatively easy to pack up your data and archives from one blog platform and move to a new WordPress blog.

WordPress lets you move your blog from platforms such as Blogspot, TypePad, and Movable Type. It also gives you a nifty way to migrate from any blogging platform via RSS feeds. In this appendix, you discover how to prepare your blog for migration and how to move from the specific platforms for which WordPress provides migration scripts.

Movin' On Up

Bloggers have a variety of reasons to migrate away from one system to WordPress:

- **Simple curiosity:** There is a *lot* of buzz around the use of WordPress and the whole community of WordPress users. People are naturally curious to check out something that all the cool kids are doing.

- **More control of your blog:** This reason applies particularly to those who have a blog on Blogspot, TypePad, or any other hosted service. Hosted programs limit what you can do, create, and mess with. When it comes to plugins, add-ons, and theme creation, hosting a WordPress blog on your own Web server wins hands down. In addition, you have complete control of your data, archives, and backup capability when you host your blog on your own server.

✔ **Ease of use:** Many people find the WordPress interface easier to use, more understandable, and a great deal more user-friendly than many of the other blogging platforms available today.

Both the hosted version of WordPress.com and the self-hosted version of WordPress.org let you migrate your blog to their platforms; however, WordPress.com accepts a few less than WordPress.org does. Table A-1 lists compatible blogging platforms for migration to WordPress.

Table A-1	Compatible Blogging Platforms for Migration	
Blogging Platform	*WordPress.com*	*WordPress.org*
Blogger (Blogspot)	Yes	Yes
Blogware	No	Yes
DotClear	No	Yes
Greymatter	No	Yes
LiveJournal	Yes	Yes
Movable Type	Yes	Yes
RSS import	No	Yes
TypePad	Yes	Yes
Textpattern	No	No
WordPress	Yes	Yes

Preparing for the Big Move

Depending on the size of your blog (that is, how many posts and comments you have), the migration process can take anywhere from 5 to 30 minutes. As with any major change or update you make, no matter where your blog is hosted, the very first thing you need to do is create a backup of your blog. You should back up the following:

✔ **Archives:** Posts, comments, and trackbacks

✔ **Template:** Template files and image files

✔ **Links:** Any links, banners, badges, and elements you have in your current blog

✔ **Images:** Any images you use in your blog

Table A-2 gives you a few tips on creating the export data for your blog in a few major blogging platforms. *Note:* This table assumes that you are logged in to your blog software.

Table A-2	Backing Up Your Blog Data on Major Platforms
Blogging Platform	*Backup Information*
Movable Type	Click the Import/Export button in the menu of your Movable Type Administration panel; then click the Export Entries From link. When the page stops loading, save it on your computer as a .txt file.
TypePad	Click the name of the blog you want to export; then click the Import/Export link in the Overview menu. Click the Export link at the bottom of the Import/Export page. When the page stops loading, save it on your computer as a .txt file.
Blogspot	Back up your template by copying the text of your template to a text editor such as Notepad. Then save it on your computer as a .txt file.
LiveJournal	Browse to http://livejournal.com/export. bml and enter your information; choose XML as the format. Save this file on your computer.
WordPress	Click the Export link on the Tools menu in the Administration panel; the Export page opens. Choose your options on the Export page and then click the Download Export File button, and save this file on your computer. (Chapter 17 lists ten great WordPress plugins, including one that lets you back up your entire database.)
RSS feed	Point your browser to the URL of the RSS feed you want to import. Wait until it loads fully (you may need to set your feed to display all posts). View the source code of the page, copy and paste that source code into a .txt file, and save the file on your computer.

Converting Templates

Every blogging program has a unique way of delivering content and data to your blog. Template tags vary from program to program; no two are the same, and each template file requires conversion if you want to use *your* template with your new WordPress blog. In such a case, two options are available to you:

✔ **Convert the template yourself.** To accomplish this task, you need to know WordPress template tags and HTML. If you have a template that you're using on another blogging platform and want to convert it for use with WordPress, you need to swap out the original platform tags for WordPress tags. Chapters 12 and 13 give you the rundown on basic WordPress template tags; you may find that information useful if you plan to attempt a template conversion yourself.

✔ **Hire an experienced WordPress consultant to do the conversion for you.** See Chapter 15 for a list of WordPress consultants.

To use your own template, make sure that you have saved *all* the template files, the images, and the stylesheet from your previous blog setup. You need them to convert the template(s) for use in WordPress.

Hundreds of free templates are available for use with WordPress, so it may be a lot easier to abandon the template you're currently working with and find a free WordPress template that you like. If you've paid to have a custom design done for your blog, contact the designer of your theme, and hire him to perform the template conversion for you. Also, you can hire several WordPress consultants to perform the conversion for you — including yours truly.

Moving Your Blog

You've packed all your stuff, and you have your new place prepared. Moving day has arrived!

This section takes you through the steps for moving your blog from one blog platform to WordPress. This section assumes that you already have the WordPress software installed and configured on your own Web server (see Chapter 6 for information about installing WordPress.org). You can also apply these steps to moving your blog to a WordPress.com hosted blog (Part II is all about WordPress.com).

Find the import function that you need by following these steps:

1. **In the Administration panel, click the Import link on the Tools menu.**

   The Import page opens, listing blogging platforms from which you can import content (such as Blogger and Movable Type). Figure A-1 shows the Import page for WordPress.com, and Figure A-2 shows this page for WordPress.org.

2. **Click the link for the blogging platform you're working with.**

   WordPress displays a page that lists directions and the information you need to fill in before you begin the import.

The following sections provide import directions for each platform.

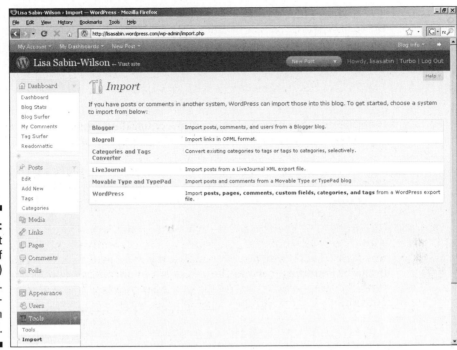

Figure A-1:
The Import
feature of
the (hosted)
WordPress.
com Admin-
istration
panel.

Figure A-2:
The Import
feature of
the (self-
hosted)
WordPress.
org Admin-
istration
panel.

Importing from Blogspot/Blogger

I call it Blogspot; you call it Blogger — a rose by any other name would smell as sweet. The blogging application owned by Google is referenced either way: Blogspot or Blogger. In the end, we're talking about the same application.

To begin the import process, first complete the steps in the "Moving Your Blog" section, earlier in this chapter. Then follow these steps:

1. **Click the Blogger link on the Import page.**

   The Import Blogger page loads and you see a message that says, `Howdy! This importer allows you to import posts and comments from your Blogger account into your WordPress blog.` The message goes on to explain that you need a Google account, and that you need to tell Google you're authorizing your WordPress blog to access your Blogger blog.

2. **Click the Authorize button to tell WordPress to access your account.**

   A page from Google opens with a message that says your WordPress blog is trying to access your Google account (see Figure A-3).

3. **Enter the e-mail address and password you use for Google; then click the Sign In button.**

   The Access Request page in your Google Account opens.

   When you have successfully logged in, you receive a message from Google stating that your blog at WordPress is requesting access to your Blogger account so that it can post entries on your behalf.

4. **Give your permission by clicking the Grant Access button on the Access Request page.**

   If you have many posts and comments in your Blogger blog, the import can take 30 minutes or more.

   After the import script has performed its magic, you're redirected to your WordPress Administration panel, where the name of your Blogger blog is listed.

5. **To complete the import of the data from your Blogger blog, click the Import button (below the Magic Button header).**

   The text on the button changes to *Importing . . .* while the import takes place. When the import is complete, the text on the button changes to *Set Authors* (no wonder it's called the Magic Button!).

6. **Click the Set Authors button to assign the authors to the posts.**

   The Blogger username appears on the left side of the page; a drop-down menu on the right side of the page displays the WordPress login name.

Figure A-3:
Enter your
Google login
information
to authorize
WordPress
to access
your
account.

7. **Assign authors using the drop-down menu.**

   If you have just one author on each blog, the process is especially easy:
   Use the drop-down menu on the right to assign the WordPress login to
   your Blogger username. If you have multiple authors on both blogs, each
   Blogger username is listed on the left side with a drop-down menu to the
   right of each username. Select a WordPress login for each Blogger username to make the author assignments.

8. **Click Save Changes.**

   You're done!

Importing from Blogware

Compared with some of the major players out there today, Blogware is
not a hugely popular blogging platform, and at this writing, the Blogware
import script imports posts only; it doesn't import comments or trackbacks.
Also, the Blogware importer is available only for the self-hosted software at
WordPress.org. WordPress.com currently doesn't provide an import script
for Blogware.

If you use Blogware, follow these steps to migrate your blog to WordPress:

1. **Create an XML file in your Blogware administration interface.**

   Go to the Settings & Security tab in your Blogware Administration panel, scroll down to the bottom of the page, and click the Import/Export link to generate an Export (XML) file.

2. **Save the XML file on your computer as a `.txt` file (for example, `import.txt`).**

3. **Go to the Import page in your WordPress Administration panel.**

   To get to the Import page, follow Steps 1 and 2 in the "Moving Your Blog" section, earlier in this chapter.

4. **Click the Blogware link.**

   The Import Blogware page opens. From this page, you can extract the XML file that you saved in Step 2 into your WordPress blog.

5. **Click the Browse button.**

   A window opens, displaying a list of files.

6. **Double-click the `.txt` file that you saved in Step 2.**

7. **Click the Upload and Import button.**

   Sit back and let the import script do its magic. When the script is done, it reloads the page with a confirmation message that the process is complete.

Importing from DotClear

At this writing, WordPress.com doesn't provide an import option for DotClear–powered blogs. If you're importing a DotClear blog to a WordPress.org blog, follow Steps 1 and 2 in the "Moving Your Blog" section, earlier in this chapter, to go to the Import page. Click the DotClear link, and a page appears that asks for several items of information about your blog (see Figure A-4).

Enter the requested information, including the database user, password, database name, host, table prefix, and originating character set. (If you're not sure where to find the information you need, contact your hosting service provider or DotClear.) Then click the Import Categories button.

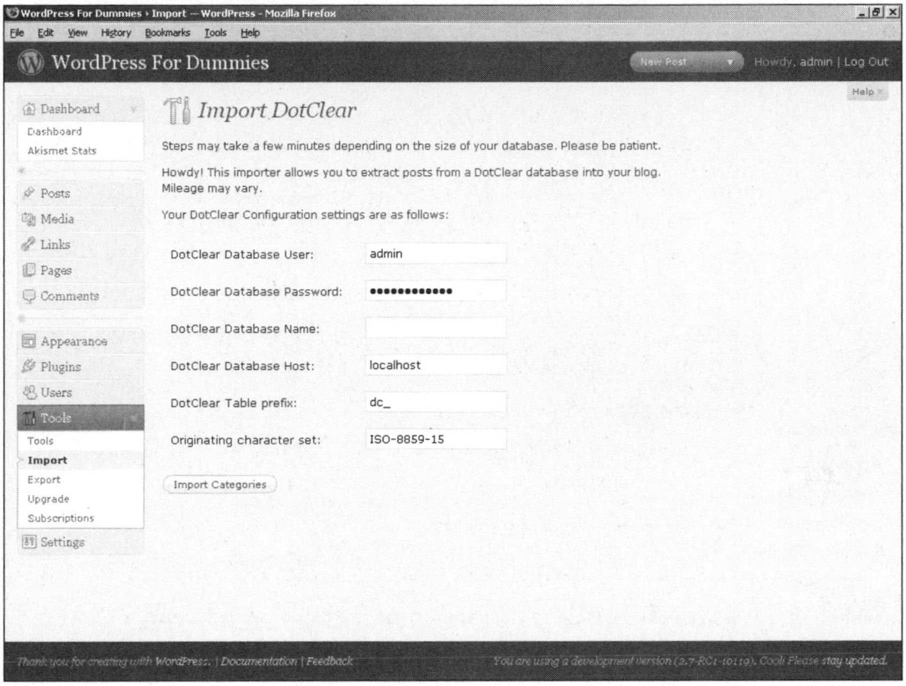

Figure A-4: Import from a DotClear blog to WordPress.

Importing from Greymatter

Greymatter is an old blogging platform that was popular in the early 2000s. Not many bloggers use Greymatter anymore, but for the one or two of you reading this book who may still be using it, WordPress.org does provide an import script for migrating your blog posts, comments, and users. (WordPress.com doesn't offer an import script for a Greymatter blog.)

Go to the Import page (see Steps 1 and 2 in the "Moving Your Blog" section, earlier in this chapter). Then click the Greymatter link and enter the details that the import script asks for, such as the path to your Greymatter files and the last entry number, which you can obtain from your Greymatter control panel. Fill in that information and then click OK to start the import process, as shown in Figure A-5.

If you are unsure where to find the information about your Greymatter files and entries, consult your Web hosting provider or the developer of Greymatter.

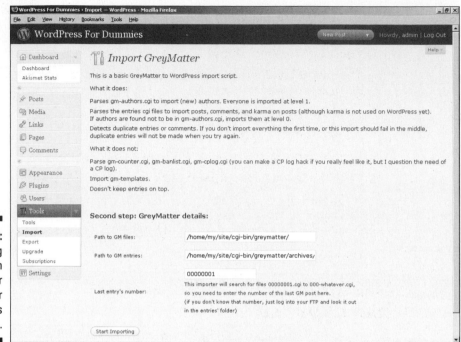

Figure A-5:
Import blog
data from
Greymatter
into your
WordPress
blog.

Importing from LiveJournal

Both WordPress.com and WordPress.org offer an import script for LiveJournal users, and the process of importing from LiveJournal to WordPress is the same for each platform.

To export your blog content from LiveJournal, log in to your LiveJournal blog and then type this URL in your browser's address bar: www.livejournal.com/export.bml.

LiveJournal lets you export the XML files one month at a time, so if you have a blog with several months' worth of posts, be prepared to be at this process for a while. First, you have to export the entries one month at a time, and then you have to import them into WordPress — yep, you guessed it — one month at a time.

To speed the process a little, you can save all the exported XML LiveJournal files in one text document by copying and pasting each month's XML file into one plain-text file (created in a text editor such as Notepad), thereby creating one long XML file with all the posts from your LiveJournal blog. Then you can then save the file as an XML file to prepare it for import into your WordPress blog.

After you export the XML file from LiveJournal, return to the Import page in your WordPress Administration panel, and follow these steps:

1. **Click the LiveJournal link.**

   The Import LiveJournal page opens, from which you can extract the XML file into your WordPress blog.

2. **Click the Browse button.**

   A window opens, listing files on your computer.

3. **Double-click the name of the XML file you saved earlier.**

4. **Click the Upload and Import button.**

   When the import script finishes, it reloads the page with a confirmation message that the process is complete. Then WordPress runs the import script and brings over all your posts from your LiveJournal blog.

Importing from Movable Type and TypePad

Movable Type and TypePad were created by the same company, Six Apart. These two blogging platforms run on essentially the same code base, so the import/export procedure is basically the same for both. Refer to Table A-2, earlier in this chapter, for details on how to run the export process in both Movable Type and TypePad. This import script moves all your blog posts, comments, and trackbacks to your WordPress blog.

Go to the Import page in your WordPress Administration panel by following Steps 1 and 2 in the "Moving Your Blog" section, earlier in this chapter. Then follow these steps:

1. **Click the Movable Type and TypePad link.**

   You see instructions for importing the data you exported from your Movable Type or TypePad blog.

2. **Click the Browse button.**

   A window opens, listing your files.

3. **Double-click the name of the export file you saved from your Movable Type or TypePad blog.**

4. **Click the Upload File and Import button.**

   Sit back and let the import script do its magic. When it's done, it reloads the page with a confirmation message that the process is complete.

This import script allows for a maximum file size of 2MB. If you get an "out of memory" error, try dividing the import file into pieces and uploading them separately. The import script is smart enough to ignore duplicate entries, so if you need to run the script a few times to get it to take everything, you can do so without worrying about duplicating your content.

When the import script is done, you can assign users to the posts, matching the Movable Type or TypePad usernames with WordPress usernames. If you have just one author on each blog, this process is easy; you simply assign your WordPress login to the Movable Type or Typepad username using the drop-down menu. If you have multiple authors on both blogs, match the Movable Type or TypePad usernames with the correct WordPress login names and then click Save Changes. You're done!

Importing from Textpattern

If you're importing a blog from Textpattern to WordPress.org, go to the Import page in your WordPress Administration panel by following Steps 1 and 2 in the "Moving Your Blog" section, earlier in this chapter. (WordPress.com currently doesn't offer an import option for Textpattern.) Click the Textpattern link to display a page that asks for specific information about your blog.

In addition to warning you that the import process "may take a few minutes depending on the size of your database," WordPress warns that it imports from Textpattern 4.0.2+ only. If you have an earlier version, you need to upgrade your Textpattern version before importing. WordPress even warns you that this import script has not been tested on earlier versions of Textpattern, so it's probably a grand idea to upgrade your Textpattern blog before attempting to run this import.

Enter the requested information — the Textpattern database user, password, name, host, and table prefix — and then click the Import Categories button to begin the import process.

Importing from WordPress

With this WordPress import script, you can import one WordPress blog into another, and this is true for both the hosted and self-hosted versions of WordPress. WordPress imports all your posts, comments, custom fields, and categories into your blog. Refer to Table A-2, earlier in this chapter, to find out how to use the export feature to obtain your blog data.

Only files 2MB or smaller can upload via the Import page of the WordPress. com Administration panel. If you have a file that is larger than 2MB in size, you can break it into smaller files and import them as separate files.

When you complete the exporting, follow these steps:

1. **Click the WordPress link on the Import page.**

   To get to the Import page, follow Steps 1 and 2 of the "Moving Your Blog" section, earlier in this chapter.

2. **Click the Browse button.**

   A window opens, listing the files on your computer.

3. **Double-click the export file you saved earlier from your WordPress blog.**

4. **Click the Upload File and Import button.**

   The import script gets to work, and when it's done, it reloads the page with a confirmation message that the process is complete.

Importing from an RSS feed

If all else fails, or if WordPress doesn't provide an Import script that you need for your current blog platform, you can import your blog data via the RSS feed for the blog you want to import. With the RSS import method, you can import posts only; you can't use this method to import comments, track-backs, categories, or users. WordPress.com currently does not allow you to import blog data via an RSS feed; this function works only with the self-hosted WordPress.org platform.

Refer to Table A-2, earlier in this chapter, for the steps required to create the file you need to import via RSS. Then follow these steps:

1. **On the Import page in the WordPress Administration panel, click the RSS link.**

   You find the instructions to import your RSS file, as shown in Figure A-6.

2. **Click the Browse button on the Import RSS page.**

   A window opens, listing the files on your computer.

3. **Double-click the export file you saved earlier from your RSS feed.**

4. **Click the Upload File and Import button.**

   The import script does its magic and then reloads the page with a confirmation message that the process is complete.

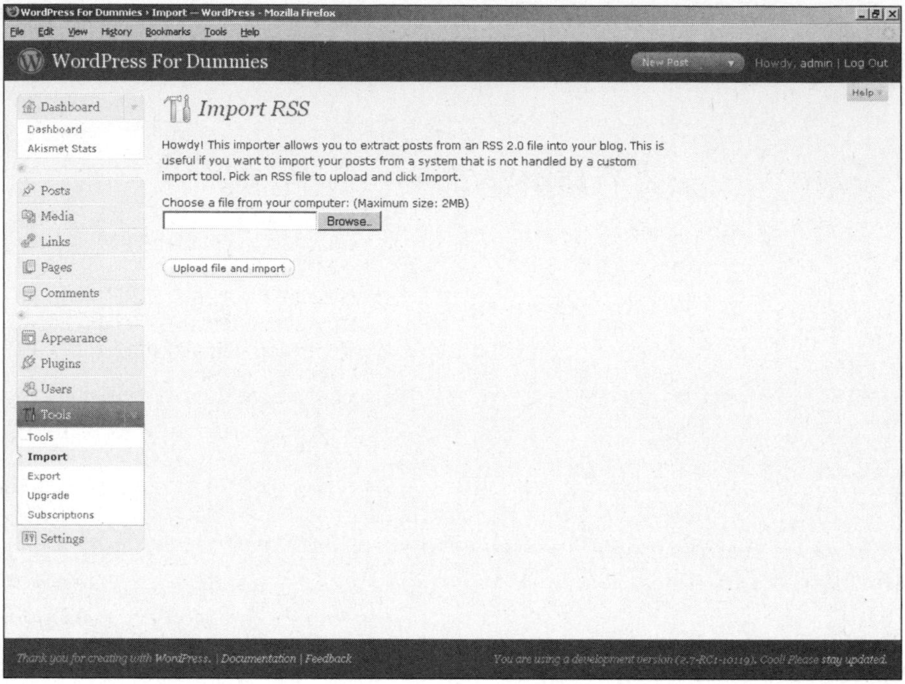

Figure A-6:
Import your
blog into
WordPress
via RSS.

Finding Other Import Resources

The WordPress Codex has a long list of other available scripts, plugins, work-arounds, and outright hacks for importing from other blog platforms. You can find that information at `http://codex.wordpress.org/Importing_Content`.

Note, however, that the WordPress Codex is run by a group of volunteers. When you refer to the Codex, be aware that not everything listed in it is necessarily up to date or accurate, including import information (or any other information about running your WordPress blog).

Index